Foundational Films

The publisher and the University of California Press Foundation gratefully acknowledge the generous support of the Robert and Meryl Selig Endowment Fund in Film Studies, established in memory of Robert W. Selig.

Foundational Films

*Early Cinema and Modernity
in Brazil*

Maite Conde

UNIVERSITY OF CALIFORNIA PRESS

University of California Press, one of the most distinguished university presses in the United States, enriches lives around the world by advancing scholarship in the humanities, social sciences, and natural sciences. Its activities are supported by the UC Press Foundation and by philanthropic contributions from individuals and institutions. For more information, visit www.ucpress.edu.

University of California Press
Oakland, California

© 2018 by The Regents of the University of California

Library of Congress Cataloging-in-Publication Data

Names: Conde, Maite, 1971- author.
Title: Foundational films : early cinema and modernity in Brazil /
    Maite Conde.
Description: Oakland, California : University of California Press, [2018] |
    Includes filmography, bibliographical references, and index. |
Identifiers: LCCN 2018010665 (print) | LCCN 2018012427 (ebook) |
    ISBN 9780520964884 (Epub) | ISBN 9780520290983 (cloth : alk. paper) |
    ISBN 9780520290990 (pbk. : alk. paper)
Subjects: LCSH: Motion pictures—Brazil—History—20th century. |
    Motion pictures—Brazil—History—19th century. | Silent films—Brazil. |
    Brazil—In motion pictures.
Classification: LCC pn1993.5.b6 (ebook) | LCC PN1993.5.b6 c66 2018 (print) |
    DDC 791.4309810904—dc23
LC record available at https://lccn.loc.gov/2018010665

27   26   25   24   23   22   21   20   19   18
10   9   8   7   6   5   4   3   2   1

For Tariq Jazeel.

CONTENTS

ILLUSTRATIONS

This book has evolved over a number of years, in various places and stages, and is therefore indebted to many institutions, colleagues, and friends. The idea took root when I was a graduate student at the University of California, Los Angeles, where I benefited from the supervision of Randal Johnson. His wide-ranging knowledge of Brazilian cinema and his respect for the country's cultural and intellectual output continue to be a source of inspiration. I would like to express my gratitude to Ana M. López and Lúcia Sá for their careful readings and support of the project. Thanks also to my editor Bradley Depew at the University of California Press for his hard work and enthusiasm, to Emilia Thiuri, who helped in the production of the book, and to the wonderful copyeditor Elisabeth Magnus for her careful work and attention to detail.

Throughout the research and the writing of this book, my colleagues at Columbia University New York, King's College London, and the University of Cambridge have been incredibly supportive. Graciela Montaldo and Carlos Alonso encouraged the project when it was still in its very early days, helping to nourish my research. Anthony Pereira read chapters of the manuscript and provided astute feedback. Brad Epps supported a request for extra research leave, and Joanna Page and John David Rhodes have allowed me to teach aspects of my research at Cambridge. Equally indispensable have been the wonderful graduate student communities with whom I have discussed distinct aspects of the book in various seminars.

Many people listened to parts of this project, offered suggestions, posed questions, and provided encouragement. People at the Department of Spanish and Portuguese at Northwestern University were hugely generous in their hospitality and critical energies, as were audiences at the Institute for Germanic and Romance

Languages at the University of London; the Department of Spanish, Portuguese, and Latin American Studies at University College London; the Brazil Institute at King's College, London; and the Department of Cinema and Video at the Universidade Federal Fluminense. Luiz Rebaza Soraluz invited me to participate in a fascinating workshop in visual culture at King's College London, which gave me the opportunity to discuss early visual culture in Latin America with experts in the field. Maria Chiara d'Argenio provided me with the chance to explore Mário Peixoto's work at University College London. The Center for Latin American Studies at Cambridge supported a workshop on early cinema in Latin America, which led to animated discussions with colleagues, including Ana Laura Lusnich. Christopher Bush and other members of the Global Avant-Garde and Modernist Studies Group at Northwestern University provided me with the chance to share parts of chapter 9 with an incredible audience of international scholars and researchers. I was also fortunate to participate in weekend gatherings of scholars interested in Brazilian silent cinema at the Cinemateca Brasileira in São Paulo, among them Luciana Araújo, Samuel Paiva, Sheila Schvarzman, Carlos Roberto de Sousa, and Eduardo Morettin. Thanks to them all for allowing me to gate-crash their gatherings. João Luiz Vieira and everyone in the Department of Cinema and Video at the Universidade Federal Fluminense offered important feedback and encouragement. Audiences at the Brazilian Studies Association (BRASA), Latin American Studies (LASA), and Modern Language Association (MLA) conferences challenged and inspired me as I developed the project.

Many institutions in Brazil, the United States, and the United Kingdom made this work possible and often more pleasant. Special thanks to the Arquivo Geral da Cidade do Rio de Janeiro, particularly Rachel Torres; the Arquivo Mário Peixoto, specifically Saulo and Ayla de Mello and Filippi Fernandes, for providing visual and written documentation for chapter 9, sharing fascinating stories about Mário Peixoto, engaging in endless conversations about early cinema, and making me cups of tea; the Biblioteca Nacional, especially Andrea Barbosa; the Cinemateca Brasileira in São Paulo, particularly Caio Brito, Karina Diniz, Giselle Dias, and Alexandre Miyazato; Hernani Hefner at the Cinemateca do MAM in Rio de Janeiro, who first introduced me to *Cinearte* magazine; the Instituto Moreira Salles in Rio de Janeiro, particularly Joanna Barbosa Balaram; Rodrigo Piquet, for facilitating my work at the Museu do Índio; and the UCLA Young Research Library, particularly Jon Edmundson and Christopher Brennan for making key visual material available to me; and to Philip Stickler at the University of Cambridge's Cartography Unit in the Department of Geography for producing the map for chapter 6.

The book has benefited from a number of grants and scholarships. A Santander Fellowship from 2009 to 2013 allowed me to formulate a clearer vision of the project. An Arts and Humanities Research Council research grant in 2013 enabled me to undertake research in Brazil and expand the project's depth and scope, and a Cambridge Humanities Research Grant in 2015 gave me additional support for further archival research. Jesus College Cambridge has also provided important financial assistance over the years, which has made researching and disseminating the work possible.

Some of Part I of the book was published in "Screening Rio: Cinema and the Desire for the City in Turn of the Century Brazil," *Portuguese Studies* 22, no. 2 (2006): 188–208, and in "Early Cinema and the Reproduction of Rio," in *Visualizing the City*, edited by Alan Marcus and Dietrich Neumann (Routledge, 2007), 31–51. Parts of chapter 4 were published in "Negotiating Visions of Modernity: Female Stars, the *Melindrosa* and Desires for a Brazilian Film Industry," *Studies in Hispanic Cinemas* 10, no. 1 (2013): 23–43, and in "Consuming Visions: Female Stars, the *Melindrosa* and Desires for a Brazilian Film Industry," in *Stars and Stardom in Brazilian Cinema*, edited by Tim Bergfelder, Lisa Shaw, and João Luiz Vieira (Oxford: Berghahn, 2018). I am grateful to the editors for permission to reprint this material here. All translations from the Portuguese are mine, unless otherwise indicated.

Conceived in Los Angeles and written in New York, London, and Cambridge, this book has been supported by the encouragement, enthusiasm, and good cheer of an international group of friends. Cesar Braga-Pinto and Lisa Shaw read parts of the manuscript and provided important feedback, support, accommodation, and friendship. It is impossible to put into words how much they and their help mean to me. Thanks to Dominic Keown, Bryan Cameron, and Rory O'Bryen, whose intellectual vibrancy, solidarity, and laughter have meant more to me than I can say. Additional thanks to Rory and Bryan, who read chapters and offered detailed commentary, critical insights, and invaluable support. Cristian Borges helped with important contacts in São Paulo while I was the United Kingdom, provided friendship, and very crucially introduced me to the *caipirinhas* at Dona Onça, for which I will always be grateful. Jaqueline Armit, Wallace Best, Stef Connor, Ben Crowe, John Ellis-Guardiola, Rogério Ferraraz, Jeff Garmany, Tom Greaves, Helio Guimaraes, Richard Phillips, Preti Taneja, and Michael Vermy have kept my spirits up while researching and writing. Thanks to Matthew Huffman and Jim Williams, and to Eliane and Paulo, for their friendship and for allowing me to stay in their lovely homes in Rio. Finally, most of all, thanks to Tariq Jazeel, who has read every single word here. Without him this book and so much else would not have been possible. With much love and the awareness of impossible reparation, I dedicate this book to you. Obrigada, Rik.

Introduction

The Modern Foundations of Brazilian Cinema

In 1909, Brazilian writer João do Rio documented his impressions of a medium that was still new to his country—film. The apparatus, he declared, "is extremely modern and up to date. This is its principal characteristic." The author added that the medium "is of a new age. The outcome of modern scientific development, it is extra modern."[1] João do Rio was not the only commentator in Brazil to stress film's modernity. Immediately after the first screening in Rio de Janeiro in 1896, journalists began to emphasize the cinema's modern status. One writer for the *Jornal do Brasil,* for instance, commented on the movies' "roots in modern progress," and another for *A Notícia* asserted the technology as proof of the "enormous modern progress that has taken place during the last few years."[2] Domestic exhibitors echoed these descriptions, promoting and celebrating the cinematograph as "the most marvelous of all modern inventions."[3]

These reports appear to support "the premise that the cinema was the fullest expression and combination of modernity's attributes" in Brazil, with the medium participating in what film scholars Leo Charney and Vanessa Schwartz have called "the invention of modern life."[4] Yet film's relationship to modernity in Brazil, as in Spanish America, was far from straightforward or symbiotic. Rather than emerging from and developing in synchronicity with the scientific and technological inventions and revolutions that produced modernity in Europe and the United States, the cinema appeared fully formed on Latin American soil as a foreign import, on board the same ships that brought other manufactured goods from abroad into the country. Consequently, as Ana M. López writes, "In reference to Latin America, it is difficult to speak of cinema and modernity as points of reflection and convergence, as is the presumption in U.S. and European early cinema scholarship. Rather, the development of cinema in the region was not directly linked to the wide scale transformations of the daily experience resulting from industrialization, rationality, and the technological changes of modern life." López states that these transformations were not taking place in early twentieth-century Latin America, where modernity was "still a fantasy and a profound desire."[5]

While it was not the expression of socioeconomic transformations, modernity, I argue, was more than a mere fantasy or desire in turn-of-the-century Brazil. It was, to use Néstor García Canclini's word, a project.[6] This project constituted part of what Angel Rama has called the "second birth of modern Latin America," a continent-wide recolonizing process that involved purging the country of its colonial past and updating its identity, bringing it in line with European civilization.[7] In Brazil this civilizing project was foundational to the politics of the First Republic (1889–1930), which initiated what Jeffrey Needell refers to as "a new era" in the country's history.[8] In 1888 slavery was abolished in Brazil, followed a year later by the ousting of the imperial Portuguese family and the declaration of the Republic. Once in power, the Republican government set out to reinvent the country's identity: the marginal status of Portugal's former colony was to be a thing of the past, and, incorporating European liberal discourses that promoted universal values of civilization and progress, Brazil's social and political elite turned their backs on the country's rural, slaveholding past to rewrite Brazil's identity as a modern nation-state, a nation of order and progress, equal to any other in the Western world.

The configuration of Brazil's new identity cannot be separated from broader changes taking place internationally, wrought by the dramatic expansion of capitalism. By the start of the twentieth century, the economies of European countries and North America was stepping up a gear. Seeking out new markets for their surplus goods, they turned to peripheral nations, like Brazil, which increased their exchange of raw materials for manufactured goods. This economic integration into the global market was accompanied by ideological configurations in which universal discourses of civilization and progress sold a narrative of global citizenship. The Republican elite identified with this narrative and sought to project themselves and the Brazilian nation into the modern world at large.

Brazil's new identity was thus influenced by international changes, as the elites embarked on a civilizing mission to remap the colonial contours of the country by adopting foreign models. In this context the social and political upper classes became receptive to a belief in progress, as it sought to extirpate barbaric elements of the past, which included social life and culture associated with the remnants and memories of slavery. This new attitude was manifested in state policies and ideas. It was also expressed in early twentieth-century urban reforms and immigration policy that aimed at recruiting Europeans, particularly North Europeans, to carry out agricultural labor and to work in new industries. At the level of ideas, European positivism with its emphasis on science and authoritarian social engineering provided a rationale for progress without popular participation or change in the country's traditional sociopolitical structure. This exclusion of the popular was central to transformations in the country's key cities. At the start of the 1900s, the topography of Rio, São Paulo, Recife, and other urban centers was dramatically altered. With inspiration taken from Paris, colonial buildings were razed and replaced with grandiose beaux arts structures, streets were widened, and parks were constructed, all of which provided Brazilian cities with a new, modern identity that reflected the French capital. These urban changes went hand in hand with the removal of the cities' poorer inhabitants—former slaves and working migrants and immigrants—whose popular cultural practices were also outlawed. Music, dances, and rituals like *capoeira, candomblé,* and *umbanda,* with their roots in slaves' African past, were viewed as an attack on progress and were consequently banned and their practitioners imprisoned.[9] Brazil's new identity thus articulated the elite's view that modernization, as a project from above, would forge the country's new era, and their progressive reforms consequently upheld structural relations of marginality and exclusion, as well as traditional hierarchies.

This history encapsulates what Needell illustrates as the contradictions of the elite-led project of modernization during Brazil's First Republic. While the elite was fully receptive to foreign ideas of progress, "imposing them with a steady desire," traditional social relations inherited from the colony and empire prevailed, and there was no attempt to institute a democratic, inclusive mode of national development.[10] Indeed, the new regime continued to favor a land-owning oligarchy at the expense of an emergent industrializing middle class. This process entailed abandoning the path of independent economic development and accepting neocolonialism, whereby Brazil embraced economic liberalism and exchanged its primary goods for imported manufactured items.

This paradox, the intersection of old structures with progressive beliefs, encapsulates what Roberto Schwarz has theorized as Brazilian modernity's out-of-placed-ness, in which foreign ideals and symbolic representations are adopted in a country whose material base does not correspond to them.[11] The classic example Schwarz provides is the nineteenth-century elite's endorsement of European liberal ideologies, even though the Brazilian economy and society were based on the incompatible practice of slavery. This radical disjunction and dissonance between Brazil's socioeconomic reality and its forms of ideological sustenance reveals how foreign philosophies were adopted without any modification of the social order. In this context, modern ideologemes of development were not lived as expressions of the country's material reality but ornamentally and spectacularly.

Brazil's imported or out-of-place modernity thus did not substitute for tradition and traditional identity as in Marx's "All that is solid melts into air." Instead, it evidenced contradictions, or what Canclini emphasizes as a hybridity, a multitemporal heterogeneity, in which modern beliefs coexisted with older configurations and structures.[12] What Canclini stresses in Latin America's hybrid modernity, more than the superficial transplantation of ideological beliefs that did not fit with social reality, is the re-elaboration and reorganization of external models, as local and global combinations express the combining of the modern with residues from the past, a mixture of social structures and sentiments that constitutes what Jesús Martín Barbero analyzes as complex mediations.[13] These complex mediations were evinced in Brazil's First Republic as the traditional social and political elite embraced impulses from abroad in its particular project to invent a modern Brazil.

The cinema was intimately linked to and developed from the hybrid configurations of this particular embrace. The first screening of what was initially called the *omniograph* took place in 1896, only seven years after the start of the First Republic, and the new medium was soon implicated in the period's foreign-inflected modernizing drive. For Brito Broca, the years of the First Republic were characterized by what he calls a *mundanismo,* a worldliness, in which the social and political elite were attuned to and attracted by everything foreign. In this context the upper classes enthusiastically accepted everything from abroad, foods, clothes, and of course ideologies.[14] They also embraced the imported technology of the moving pictures.

The foreign cinematic apparatus soon became part of the elite's worldly utopianism, which producers and entrepreneurs spectacularly relayed to viewers. As testimonies of the initial reception of the new medium reveal, the very presence of the technological media seemed to feed a national self-confidence that modernity was in progress. Imported sights of foreign civilized cities and peoples reinforced this sentiment, allowing Brazilian spectators to envisage themselves as part of the wider modern world. The production of domestic films buttressed this new visual imaginary. Early movies made in Brazil replicated the relationship between cinema and modernity in Europe and the United States, while at the same time creating spectacles of local modern attractions. One of the first films to be screened in Brazil was August and Louis Lumière's *L'arrivée d'un train à La Ciotat* (1895). The impact of this early actuality gave rise to Brazilian versions, *Chegada de um trem em Cadouços* (1894) by Aurélio da Paz and *Chegada de um trem em Petrópolis* (1897) by Vittório di Maio, both of which documented the country's developing railroad as an adequate equivalent of the modern sight screened in the French original. Such local "copies" became common, with a number of filmmakers in Brazil producing counterparts of foreign *vues*. French actualities like *Un boulevard,* which displayed fashionable Parisians promenading, for instance, inspired movies such as *Avenida Central da capital federal* (Avenida Central in the federal capital; n.dir., 1906) and *O corso de Botafogo* (Promenade in Botafogo; n.dir., 1909). which showed civilized Cariocans strolling along Rio's elegant avenues. Seeking out local sights that resonated with foreign vistas, early producers in Brazil adopted international film language to recast the former colony's image as a modern nation, similar to any other in the Western world. It was not just filmmakers that copied foreign vistas. Spectators too emulated the modern visions, refashioning their own local identities to fit in with models from abroad.

From the very start, therefore, film in Brazil spectacularly articulated and projected the desires underlining the Republic's modernizing mission. Inaugurating new techniques for seeing the nation, the cinema helped to make people see and believe in its new, civilized contours. It is this projection that this book charts, looking at how cinema was implicated in the progressive foundations of Brazil's First Republic and its particular invention of modern life. In doing so I show that although film formed a crucible for ideas, techniques, and representations present in other places, its reception and development were intimately entwined with the Republic's national discourse of modernity and its elite-led process of modernization.

ELITE PROJECTIONS OF BRAZIL'S NATIONAL IMAGINARY

Filmmakers in Brazil immediately adopted the imported cinematic medium to screen the country as a modern nation. The very apparatus of film, as well as filmic codes, genres, and cultures consolidated abroad, thus forged what Miriam Hansen calls a "vernacular modernism" by addressing local needs and impulses—historical, social, and political.[15] Movies and their reception and consumption articulated and mediated the desires and experiences of the changes impelled by the Republic's upper class as it sought to update the country's identity.

Brazilian cinema's ties to an elite-led project of modernity complicated the potential of its manifestations of vernacular modernism to function as what Hansen terms "an alternative public sphere," even as it embraced worldliness.[16] Foregrounding the privileged relationship of working people—including migrants and immigrants—to the moving pictures, Hansen and others have elaborated on film's ability to furnish an intersubjective context in which marginalized inhabitants could recognize fragments of their own experience. In Brazil, this ability was contained and constrained by the medium's close links to the country's upper classes. In fact, in Brazil, unlike Europe and the United States, early productions included few so-called factory gate films, in which workers were filmed as they departed from their factory or workplace, in a bid to attract them to shows in order to see themselves on screen.[17] While new industries were featured in Brazilian movies like *A uzina Estrellina* (The Estrellina factory; n. dir., 1930), these tended to abstract workers' bodies from the scenes depicted, with the chief focus being on the factories' modern technologies.[18] If laborers did appear, it was to express and convey the modern workplace's discipline and order. Early cinematic images thus carefully screened Brazil to emphasize the country's civilized modernity.

Indeed, if early accounts of cinema's reception in Brazil stressed its modernity, they also foregrounded the medium's relationship to the country's upper classes.

On June 17, 1898, for instance, a writer for the *Jornal do Brasil* listed viewers present at a screening held at the Super Lumière Cinema in Rio the night before, highlighting "the president of the Republic, Prudente de Moraes, and his family; naval minister Almirante Alves Barbosa; minister of the Supreme Federal Court Dr. André Cavalcanti; Baron Pereira Franco; Attorney General Dr. João Pedro M. Correia de Melo; Captain Marques da Rocha; Colonel Carlos Soares, police commander; General Luís Mendes de Morais; Military Chief Dr. Capistrano do Amaral; secretaries of the Ministry of the Interior Irineu Machado and Érico Coelho e Valadares; Major Zoroastro, head of the fire brigade; and many judges, doctors, lawyers, and notable businessmen."[19] Similarly on February 3, 1903, the *Gazeta de Notícias* referred to the presence of "deputies, senators, and businessmen in suits" at a film show that week.[20]

Such reports provide a glimpse into the constitution of early audiences in Brazil, foregrounding the elite's immediate embrace of the medium. This embrace shaped the content of early movies made in the country. In his overview of Brazil's silent cinema, Paulo Emílio Salles Gomes identifies a key theme of the country's actualities that he refers to as "the ritual of power."[21] The ritual of power, he states, crystallized around the documentation of notable individuals from Brazilian society, including the country's presidents. "From the first civil president to the last military president of the First Republic (1889–1930), Brazilian cinema has not excluded a single leader: Prudente de Moraes, Rodrigues Alves, Campos Salles, Afonso Pena, Nilo Peçanha, Hermes da Fonseca were all filmed governing, visiting regions, receiving dignitaries, inaugurating events, and, eventually, being buried."[22] The subjects of these actualities extended to official events such as military parades, visits of foreign dignitaries, and the inauguration of national monuments. Films like *Inauguração da estátua do Doutor João Mendes* (Inauguration of the statue of Dr. João Mendes; dir. Antonio Campos, 1913), *Viagem presidencial a Campos* (Presidential visit to Campos; n. dir., 1916), and *A posse do novo governo do estado* (Inauguration of the new municipal government; dir. Gilberto Rossi, 1920) fostered identification with Brazil's official politics and politicians, eliciting what Jens Andermann calls "statist ways of seeing."[23]

Exploring cinema's role in disseminating these ways of seeing, this book examines how spectatorship was aligned with existing power structures and how the appeal of early films was that of seeing not ordinary citizens but socially and politically prominent ones—metaphorical stand-ins for the nation. Yet, as I show, the cinema-nation symbiosis was not restricted to these more overtly political films. It was also present in what Gomes calls early actualities' "splendid cradle," which refers to the celebration of Brazil's natural wonders.[24] Filmmakers immediately contributed to this celebration. In 1898, Affonso Segreto filmed Rio's Guanabara Bay from the ship *Brésil* on a return journey from Europe, and José Roberto Cunha de Salles also captured Rio's seascape that same year. Rio's natural wonders, like Sugarloaf Mountain, Corcovado, and the forest of Tijuca, became a popular subject for early actualities. Other films recorded natural sites beyond the then capital, such as Icaraí, Paquetá, and Petrópolis, displaying their waterfalls and landscapes. Late feature films, like *Visita ao Brasil* (Voyage to Brazil; n. dir, 1907), *Nos sertões do Brasil* (In the Brazilian backlands; n. dir, 1927), *O Brasil pitoresco* (Picturesque Brazil; dir. Cornélio Pires, 1925), *O Brasil desconhecido* (Unknown Brazil; dir. Paulino Botelho, 1926), *O Brasil maravilhoso* (Marvelous Brazil; dir. Alfredo dos Anjos, 1928), and *O Brasil grandioso* (Magnificent Brazil; dir. Alberto Botelho, 1923), documented the Paulo Afonso and the Amazon regions. For Gomes, this focus on the country's tropical exuberance was "part of a collective psychological mechanism that compensated for Brazil's underdevelopment."[25] Here, as Jean-Claude Bernardet points out, nature functioned as a response to industrialization, which was not fully in place.[26] The fetishistic gaze at grand natural landscapes, untouched by industry, thus made up for the country's lack of modernity. Yet it also revealed Brazil's potential for future progress by showing untapped virgin territories rich in natural or raw promise. Indeed, cinematographers often recorded the cultivation, harvest, preparation, and shipment of natural products like coffee or wood, with cameras charting every step of the development of nature into international commodity. *Brota do café* (Coffee harvest; n. dir., 1925), *Fazenda Santa Catarina* (Santa Catarina Farm; n. dir, 1927), and *A uzina Estrellina* (The Estrellina factory; n. dir., 1930) all charted the process of transforming primary materials into products for export.

Such documentaries proudly registered the country's participation in the world as a producer of raw materials. This participation was evident in the cinematic recordings of Brazil's International Exposition in 1922, which displayed the country's modern image to the international community. As Eduardo Morettin has shown, the exposition incorporated screenings of Brazilian films within its various expositions, with the state purposely commissioning a number of movies for the international occasion.[27] Visual records of manufacturing and industry, as well as scientific and technological developments, symbolically produced and reproduced a progressive Brazil and placed it in the interconnected space of the International Exposition. Cinema's inclusion in the exposition shows that while films were linked to the politics of the Republic, they were not nationally self-enclosed; they were mediated by another's valuation.

This mediated gaze was seen as fostering a national pride. Commentators often praised the medium's modern sights as means of instilling patriotism and claimed that cinematic visions of the country's progress would be of great service to the nation. Newspaper commentators also stressed the medium's ability to forge a sense of belonging. In a 1928 review of *Voyage to Brazil*, a writer for the *Estado de São Paulo* stated, "All Brazilians are obliged to know their nation! Brazil is one of the largest countries in the world, yet it is unfamiliar to many inhabitants."[28] Such reviews point to the pedagogical role and importance of these films, which would teach spectators about Brazil and inculcate a national culture. Cinematic spectatorship was tantamount to a visual pedagogy and could help to forge what Benedict Anderson has famously called the imagined community of the nation.[29]

For Anderson, the development of print culture created a shared experience and commonality, a horizontal comradeship that helped consolidate the imaginary contours of the nation and create modern subjects and citizens. Following Anderson's argument, Doris Sommer emphasizes the importance of writing in forging Latin American national identity.[30] She focuses specifically on nineteenth-century novels, or romances, many of which appeared as newspaper *folhetins* before being novelized. Written shortly after independence, these foundational fictions helped legitimize new nations and also construct them. Nineteenth-century Latin American literature thus had the capacity to intervene in national history and to create it. The region's writers fulfilled the paradigms of what Angel Rama terms the lettered city, wielding the power of written discourse to help form Latin American societies. In doing so, Sommer notes, they carried out an important pedagogical function: "Novels could teach people about their history, about their barely formulated customs."[31] Constituting forms of civic education, the romances symbolically inculcated readers into the space of the nation.

Literature's role in forging the foundations of the Brazilian nation was taken over and superseded by the mass media, not least given the high rates of illiteracy in the country.[32] If literature had previously designated the place where a national imaginary was articulated, by the start of the Republic it had become clear that the modern and imported medium of film could occupy an increasingly important place in the redefinition of Brazilian society as part of a wider modern landscape. Far from fostering a collective or horizontal consciousness, however, films tethered spectators to the hegemonic and hierarchical visions of the elite. These early films overlapped with the desires of the modernizing few and aimed to inscribe spectators into their official projections, reconciling their progressive spectacles with the traditional bases upon which their hegemony depended. This reconciliation did not hinge solely on the libidinal and erotic dimensions that Sommer notes were crucial to novelistic foundational fictions.[33] In the positivist spirit of the Republic, the rhetoric of love was matched and even overtaken by a rhetoric of science and technology. Stories of star-crossed lovers were no longer the dominant ground for constituting political and patriotic passion. With their masterful ability to rationally order the old world, scientific and technological infrastructures laid the foundations for Brazil's new modernizing period and became key protagonists in its cinematic productions. Indeed, even sentimental melodramas that involved conjugal tales, like Humberto Mauro's *Tesouro perdido* (Lost treasure, 1927), delighted in presenting technical advances, with stunt sequences involving new modes of transportation. As a product of "modern scientific developments," to cite João do Rio, the cinema seemed perfectly suited not just to registering but also to forging the new era. It is in this recognition of the cinema's productive force that I delineate what I call foundational films, films that conceived of a national cinema and of the nation itself. If Sommer has shown us that the national, configured through its narration, cannot be taken as a fixed entity and always comes into being as a system of cultural signification, I demonstrate how by the turn of the century cinema articulated new foundations for composing Brazil by projecting its image as modern. As this book charts film's implantation and development in Brazil, then, it pays close attention to how the country's foundational films became involved in establishing the progressive contours of the Brazilian nation.

BRAZILIAN CINEMA'S ALTERNATIVE MODERNITIES

The symbiotic relationship between cinema and the elite does not mean that film and filmmaking practices were completely and unproblematically complicit with hegemonic visions of modernity. This book shows that as the medium developed commercially, many filmmakers in Brazil sought out alternative spectators in cinematic forms and stories that often countered the progressive ideology of the Republic. In spite of its out-of-placedness, the Republican project of modernity did provoke dislocations in Brazil, including changes in race and gender relations, with the emergence of new social groups and the liberation of women from the traditional enclave of the home. At a more popular level, these transformations included new cultural manifestations of mass-produced and mass-mediated products and a variety of everyday discourses that both articulated and responded to the elite project—newspapers, magazines, fashion, advertisements, all of which changed the fabric of everyday life, promoting new forms of experience, interaction, and public life. The cinema was not closed off from these everyday articulations of modernity. Indeed, I show how filmmakers and exhibitors, seeking to profit from the development of the medium as a mass product, catered to women, migrants, and immigrants in narratives that recognized their particular experiences of modern life. Here films intersected, dialogued with, and borrowed from other cultural forms and practices—vaudeville theater, crime stories, magazines, shopping, maps, and press reports—producing an "impure cinema," to use André Bazin's term, which did not dovetail with official modernity.[34] These movies provided alternative visions of the Republic's project, allowing spectators to mediate their own passage into modernity from their everyday cultural landscape.

This centrifugal pull away from centripetal narratives was evident in popular movies made at the start of the Republic; it was also manifested in late 1920s avant-garde cinematic texts, both written and visual. These cinematic experimentations articulated what Esther Gabara calls a "critical nationalism," which questioned the dominant ideology of progress and development.[35] This critical nationalism was central to writers belonging to the avant-garde movement, *modernismo*, who adopted the language of the moving pictures in their revolt against the progressive version of the elite-led modernization and its adoption of foreign models. So, as this book maps the official foundations of cinema and modernity in Brazil's Republic, it also charts ambivalences within and contestations to its hegemonic lexicon, in both vernacular and avant-garde manifestations.

In its combined explorations of both popular everyday and artistic articulations of the cinematic, the book departs from dominant examinations of cultural modernity in Brazil, which have been largely limited to debates that took place exclusively among intellectuals and within artistic institutions. Scholarly discussions of cultural modernity in Brazil have focused almost entirely on *modernismo,* whose iconoclasm has been theorized as a break with past cultural forms, evidenced most notably in its 1922 Week of Modern Art.[36] This book seeks to challenge the limited range of this conventional focus by exploring how film manifested the politics of modernity more broadly throughout Brazilian society and culture. I place *modernismo's* challenge to the official rhetoric of progress in dialogue with and as part of vernacular articulations of the Republic's progressive project evidenced in cinematic production. In doing so I seek to relocate the very notion of an aesthetic of modernity, as one that pertains not solely to artistic institutions but also to everyday culture. As I show, the cinema, as a product and symbol of Republican modernity, did more than represent and embody official development; it also exemplified the restructuring of everyday society, which started to visualize the possibility and promise of what Dilip Gaonkar calls "alternative modernities".[37]

Like Canclini and Schwarz, Gaonkar and other scholars have worked to dislodge the genealogy of modernity by delineating developments beyond the Euro-American world, which vary according to their social and geopolitical locations but are nevertheless configured along the axis of global capitalism and postcoloniality.[38] In addition to opening "the modern" up to the wider world, such scholarship has foregrounded how the adversary culture associated with high modernism was articulated in different cultural practices around the world, from artistic experimentations to vernacular forms. In Brazil too, high and popular cultural practices registered, responded to, and reflected upon the process of change under way in the country. In doing so they often questioned the Republic's project and revealed other narratives of modernity. These alternative modernities remind us that the spectacular mediations of foreign ideologies in Brazil did not cohere into a homogeneous totality but revealed different domestic configurations, confounding, in the process, any simple bifurcation of the local and the global. Brazil's early cinematic landscape demonstrated this varied articulation of modernity as it displayed sights that reflected alternative experiences and interpretations of hegemonic visions of progress.

"EARLY CINEMA" IN BRAZIL

In its historiographic focus on the implementation and development of cinema in Brazil, this book draws on and intersects with recent Euro-American scholarship on the symbiotic relationship between film and modernity, which has been central to what is now referred to as the field of early cinema. This field of study has revised the traditional bias toward narrative economy and the tendency to mark the initial years of cinema as primitive. More than a period term, *early cinema* functions as a critical category, one that has been accorded more significance and attention ever since the 1978 annual conference of the International Federation of Film Archives (FIAF) held in Brighton in 1978. It refers primarily to films and also media intertexts, industry and market, between 1895 and 1917, after which classical narrative cinema and the industrial mode came to be received and perceived as the dominant mode of filmmaking. In early cinema studies, then, 1917 is seen as marking a definitive break from previous distinctive aesthetic forms, which were predicated not on storytelling but on "presenting and representing the world and lived experience."[39] As Jennifer M. Bean and Diane Negra note, however, this period marker and its uncritical adoption can "limit rather than expand new film historical discourse," and they caution against the universal adoption of early cinema's historical demarcation. Indeed, for these scholars, the paucity of documents from the silent period "must obviate attempts to specify the date and time of an allegedly wholesale shift to a systematic application of classically defined formal means." They argue that "the absence of textual evidence demands that we remain agnostic about the efficacy of rigidified period breaks."[40]

This particular study of the development of film in Brazil troubles the period break between early cinema and cinematic classicism, questioning its historical (and universal) demarcation to reveal an alternative history of early cinema. It does so by taking seriously Alison Butler's caveat that revisionist historiographies must engage in a "politics of location." As she puts it, "History takes *place*."[41] In the Brazilian context, though the first film was allegedly made in 1898, attempts at forging a Brazilian film industry took place only in the 1930s. The time lag between early European and American cinema and early Brazilian cinema certainly speaks to the underdevelopment of Brazilian modernity, specifically with regard to belated technological transfer and implementation. The enjoyment of cinema, however, soon became an integral part of the everyday landscape of Republican Brazil, especially in major cities, as films presented and projected the nation's modern image. Brazil's civilized makeover was thus a key cinematic attraction and point of identification throughout the years of the Republic. Indeed, even narrative films made in the 1920s were careful to showcase the modern images of their stars or to include scenes and techniques (chases with rapid pans and tracking shots) that emphasized the modern technology of filmmaking itself. The broader film culture of stardom, fanzines, and discourses also stressed the medium's modernity.

This book, therefore, explores early cinema in Brazil not as a rigidly defined aesthetic or cinematic period but as a force integral to the invention of modernity. As Charney and Schwartz have shown us, film's connection to modernity was also key to its development in the United States and Europe. This study thus expands the horizon of cinematic modernity, revealing the vibrancy of early cinema's international lexicon. Indeed, while early cinema studies have included rigorous inquiry into the relations between film and the broader culture of modernity, this inquiry has largely focused on European and American experiences, with few scholars examining how cinema was part of the invention of modernity beyond the United States and Europe. In its focus on Brazil, this study endeavors to address this absence. In doing so it seeks to question the bedrock assumption of early cinema studies: that the emergence of film should be examined in relation to industrialization. Situating Brazil's early film and film culture within the span from the arrival of cinema in the country to the end of the First Republic in 1930, I provide a different genealogy for the emergence and development of the cinema, one that examines how its development was governed not by industrial changes but by a political project. By looking at how film interacted in specific ways with the local exigencies of Brazil's history and politics, the book illuminates an alternative history of the relationship between cinema and modernity, exploring its foundations in a different national and cultural site.

In its focus on the early years of film in Brazil, this examination joins a new wave of scholarship that is emerging from Latin America. Key here is the work of a research group that beginning in 2002 has met monthly at the Cinemateca Brasileira in São Paulo to view and discuss Brazilian films from the institute's rich archives, focusing particularly on the country's silent movies. Led by film scholar Carlos Roberto de Souza, their gatherings have generated a new interest in and knowledge of Brazil's silent cinematic productions, which have given rise to developments like the annual Jornada Brasileira de Cinema Silencioso (held at the Cinemateca), seminars and conferences, and courses dealing with the earlier history of cinema in Brazil. These new undertakings have in turn produced a number of publications that examine the development of cinematic production in Brazil from varied perspectives. Notable studies include José Inácio de Melo Souza's exploration of early film in Rio and São Paulo, Eduardo Morettin's work on early actualities, and the group's own edited collection *Viagem ao cinema silencioso do Brasil*.[42]

These Brazilian studies form part of a new trend of attending to earlier years of cinema in Latin America more generally. In the last few years, conferences such as the Congreso de la Associación Argentina sobre Estudios de Cinema y Audiovisual, the Coloquio Interdisciplinario de Estudios de Cine y Audiovisual Latinoamericano in Montevideo, and the Encuentro Internacional de Investigación sobre Cine Chileno y Latinoamericano have increasingly featured panels dealing with Latin America's earlier film history, something that is the sole focus of the Coloquio Internacional de Cine Mudo en Iberoamérica, held annually in Mexico City. This increased critical attention has led to the publication of *Vivomatógrafia*, the first journal dedicated exclusively to silent film in Latin America.

These new scholarly endeavors are making small steps to fill in what López refers to as the virtual absence of scholarly work on silent cinema in Latin America. As López notes, the early years of film in Latin America are the least discussed in the country's media history.[43] In Brazil, this cinematic period has largely been overshadowed by later cinematic events, its significance, in particular, eclipsed by the emergence of the avant-garde film movement of the 1950s and '60s, Cinema Novo. Study of the period has additionally been made difficult by the lack of textual material available—most of the films produced then have disappeared, victims of the ravages of time and fires and the official neglect of preservation. Examinations of these years of cinema have therefore been limited to a small number of extant movies or have focused on unearthing overlooked archival information in order to piece together a more comprehensive prehistory for the advent of national film production in the 1950s, something I elaborate on in chapter 1 of this book. In fact, until the emergence of the recent studies noted above, most of the work dealing with the earlier history of film in Brazil was part of and integrated into broader historical accounts of the country's cinematic production, with subsequent scholarly concerns often informing the viewpoint and method of analysis. Recent work in Brazil by Morettin and others has thus sought to correct these tendencies. This book contributes to that endeavor by examining the implantation and development of film in Brazil before 1930. While other recent studies of early Brazilian film have zoomed in on particular geographical areas or genres, my study zooms out to track film's relationship to a broader topos, locating film's initial years in Brazil within the context of its arrival and elaboration, that is, within the transformative period of the First Republic. In doing so it looks specifically at how the medium's development was caught up in dominant sociopolitical discourses, debates, and concerns that aimed to transform the country into a modern nation. In this era and its discussions, I argue, the foundations of a Brazilian cinema are to be located.

The historical narrative of the book starts with the arrival of the cinema in Rio de Janeiro during the late nineteenth century and explores how its development in the city was closely tied to a makeover of what was then Brazil's capital city, which intended to transform it into a tropical version of Paris. Progressing through chapters that analyze ethnographic films made in the Amazon in the 1910s, part of a wider campaign to map and to civilize Brazil's hinterlands and its indigenous peoples, and the impact of Hollywood on Brazilian film and film culture in the 1920s, the study ends in the late 1920s with the production of experimental films by iconoclastic filmmakers who were attuned to and strongly influenced by European avant-garde movements. Their translation of international experiments with film form into a Brazilian setting illuminates the key aspect of the cinema's invention of modernity in Brazil: from the start it was a global, intertextual experience, addressing models from abroad according to local codes of reception. Key here was the negotiation of cinema's modernity with traditional structures and privileges, especially with regard to questions of race, gender, and class. This process of translation, hybridization, and reconfiguration of foreign (and not just American) as well as indigenous discourses on modernity lies at the heart of *Foundational Films* and its examination of early Brazilian cinema and cinematic practices and cultures. Cumulatively, the book draws on archival work and close reading to chart distinct ways in which the cinema created new imaginaries, cinematic and national, for Brazil and Brazilians and to explore the tensions that often arose from this. One theme of the book is to take seriously the context of reception, notably looking at intellectual and journalistic discussions regarding film and stressing how the extratextual and paratextual illuminate ways in which cinema produced and negotiated the invention of modernity in Brazil. This approach supports Andrew Higson's recommendation that the parameters of national cinema should be drawn at the site of reception as well as production.[44] Taking up his call for a more expansive definition of national cinema, this book focuses on production and also exhibition practices and fan culture.

THE STRUCTURE OF THE BOOK

This book thus examines the historically specific culture of early cinema in Brazil as it intersected with and at times diverged from the social and political context of the modernizing First Republic and its engagement with the world at large. Aiming to illuminate some key aspects of the links between film and Republican modernity, the book, in a cinematographic manner, produces long takes and close-ups on four key topoi in the cinematic landscape of Brazil's Republic. In Part I, "Locating the Belle Epoque of Brazilian Cinema," I examine and revise an era of film production and reception, roughly the years 1906–12, prior to Hollywood's arrival in Brazil and dominance of the domestic market. Brazilian film critics and historiographers have theorized these years as a golden age of Brazilian cinema, a brief period when domestic production was unhampered by what Ana López has called the pressure to face up to Hollywood.[45] In chapter 1 I examine the utopian dimensions of these theoretical approaches and elaborate a topoanalytical approach to the belle epoque's cinematic history, drawing on and contributing to discussions concerning the homologous relationship between early cinema and urban space. Chapter 2 maps out how the introduction and development of film were part of a project of urban transformation that took place in the country's then capital, Rio de Janeiro, at the start of the twentieth century, and aimed to transform the city into a modern global capital modeled on Haussmann's Paris. Analyzing early actuality films and patterns of spectatorship, the chapter examines how the foreign medium's arrival was inscribed and implicated in the city's transformation, helping to chart and project an ideal modern image. In chapter 3, I unearth different aspects of cinema's links to Rio's re-formation. Looking at how films and film culture keyed into popular cultural forms, I outline ways in which some early movies problematized the contours of the new city in cinematic narratives that countered Rio's official map of modernity. Together, the three chapters in this opening part of the book thus chart a new cultural and geographical topography of the early development of the cinema and its intimate relations with Rio, one that, given the absence of extant texts, I trace through intercultural, intertextual, and intermedial connections, looking at films' connections with vaudeville theater, political-satirical magazines, maps, music, carnival, and the illustrated press.

Part II, "Hollywood Revisions," focuses on the consolidation of North American cinema in Brazil, exploring ways in which magazines aided its hegemonic presence in the country. Key here was Brazil's first magazine dedicated exclusively to film, *Cinearte,* which proudly declared itself the natural intermediary between Brazilian spectators and Hollywood producers. At the same time, however, the publication was fiercely patriotic, ardently defending and promoting national film production. In chapter 4, I examine ways in which *Cinearte* disseminated American films and fan culture, which addressed Brazilian audiences, largely conceived of as female, as part of a modern audience of consumers. The magazine's writers became important interlocutors between the US film industry and the domestic consumer, at once providing instruction in the practices of fandom and offering a connection to Hollywood from a Brazilian perspective. I show how *Cinearte*'s writers mobilized female desires through fandom and channeled them to promote domestic movies, as part of a project to forge a national cinema. At the same time the writers downplayed modern depictions of sex roles, especially of women, in order to cater to traditional patriarchal structures still present in Brazil. In chapter 5, I show how this modulation of modernity fed its way into Humberto Mauro's 1927 film *Tesouro perdido* (Lost treasure), an adaptation of Henry King's 1921 movie *Tol'able David.* My close analysis illuminates differences between the Brazilian film and its North American model, especially in terms of race, which, I argue, reveal an allegiance to Brazilian society's patriarchal contours.

The close bonds between cinema and the positivist discourse of order and progress are explicitly brought to light in Part III, "The Rondon Commission: Producing New Visions of the Amazon," which examines the visual archive of what was known as the Rondon Commission. Beginning in 1907, the military officer Cândido Mariano da Silva Rondon was charged with a massive undertaking: the building of telegraph lines connecting the Amazon region and its indigenous peoples with coastal cities. This task of stringing the nation together by telegraph was aimed at forging a unified community of "Brazilians" in the new Republic. Photography and film were part of this political endeavor, for visual technology was used to consolidate and expand the state's order and progress in the tropical backlands. In chapter 6 I examine the Rondon Commission's visual archive, looking at how film and photography together articulated and responded to the Republic's "techno-politics," defined by Timothy Mitchell as an operation of political rule via the technological workings of infrastructures.[46] While noting how photography and film were part of the same techno-material as the telegraph, in chapter 7 I go on to explore how the commission, and in particular its filmmaker Luiz Thomaz Reis, exploited the specific lexicon of film, its moving images, in particular ways, in its endeavor to chart unknown lands and peoples. In doing so I foreground how film's distinctive syntax reveals what Todd Diacon calls the discursive fragility of the commission and its campaign to consolidate a national territory.[47]

Part IV of the book, "Modernism and the Movies," delves into the discursive fragilities in the Republic's progressive narrative by examining avant-garde adoptions of the medium. Key here are new debates regarding film language that developed in postwar France, which rethought the nature and function of the movies away from Hollywood's dominant narrative model and began to seriously consider its formal systems. In this part of the book I look at how these discussions played a decisive role in reconfiguring the medium and its use in Brazil and laid foundations for avant-garde experimentations with film. Chapter 8 explores how, influenced by foreign discussions regarding film form, avant-garde writers belonging to the Brazilian modernist movement deployed cinematic techniques, like montage and simultaneism, in their literary works. This cinematic deployment, I argue, became part of the movement's critical nationalism, which saw *modernista* writers question the hegemonic narrative of modernity imported from Europe to produce what Fernando Rosenberg calls a new geopolitics.[48] This departure from the progressive model of modernity is explored in chapter 9, which analyzes the "cine-poetry" of Mário Peixoto's experimental film *Limite* (1930). In its filmic lyricism, *Limite,* I argue, rejects and refuses the projection of a national modernity and instead registers an ontological and epistemological crisis in Brazil's ideology of modernity. If Peixoto's film articulated a refusal of the dominant narrative of progress, I show how this was not universal to the experimental films made in Brazil during this period. Key here is the city-symphony film *São Paulo, A sinfonia da metrópole*, discussed in chapter 10. Made in 1929 by Hungarian immigrants Adalberto Kemeny and Rodolfo Lustig, the São Paulo film draws self-consciously on international avant-garde "city symphony" films like Charles Sheeler and Paul Strand's *Manhattan* (1921), Dziga Vertov's *Man with a Movie Camera* (1929), and Water Ruttmann's *Berlin: Der Sinfonie der Großstadt* (1927), which focus on the power and excitement of cities. In examining the Brazilian film's engagement with and adoption of the experimental genre, I show how it provides a triumphalist image of São Paulo as a progressive industrial center in a project that ultimately coheres with official discourses of modernity, rather than critiquing them.

Together the four parts of the book illuminate some spaces in which the cinema was introduced and developed in Brazil, looking at how film was bound up with discourses and debates on the Republic's project of modernity and how it sought to articulate its own definitions of the country's modernity. This is by no means a complete map of early Brazilian cinema, and the book does not provide an exhaustive panorama of the country's filmmaking and film culture before the 1930s. Rather, it focuses on some of the roots of cinema's inception and growth in Brazil. Exploring what João do Rio in 1909 referred to as film's embodiment of the modern age, I reveal how the medium was framed by and contributed to the formation of new national and nationalistic concerns. It is in the intersection of the cinema and the national politics of modernity that I explore early cinema in Brazil. Let us now begin this cinematic cartography of Brazil's foundational films.

PART ONE

Locating the Belle Epoque of Brazilian Cinema

1

Early Cinema and National Identity in Brazil

Mapping Out a Space of Analysis

While Brazil's contribution to film history has attracted considerable critical attention since the 1960s, the country's early cinema remains largely obscure in Anglo-American literature. Overlooked by European and North American scholars, the period tends to be disregarded, appearing (if at all) as an embryonic footnote to works focusing on subsequent national developments. The absence of Brazil's film history from Anglo-American studies is symptomatic of the lack of scholarly work dealing with early cinema in the region as a whole. Ana M. López observes that "the early years of the silent cinema in Latin America, roughly 1896–1920, are the least discussed. . . . The period was overshadowed by wars and other cataclysmic political and social events and, subsequently, its significance was eclipsed by the introduction of other media—the Golden Ages of sound cinema and radio in the 1940s and 1950s, television in the 1960s and 1970s."[1] Critical inattention to Latin America's early cinema is far from surprising, since documentation and analysis of the historical era encounter practical difficulties. As López writes, "Studying this period is made . . . daunting by the paucity of available material; most of the films produced in Latin America between 1896 and 1920 have disappeared, victims of the inevitable ravages of time (and fires) and the official neglect of cultural preservation."[2] In the specific case of Brazil, fires at the country's principal archives in 1957, 1969, and 1982, together with a lack of funds for preservation, have had a drastic effect on remnants from this period. Only an extremely small number of shorts and feature films produced before the 1920s have survived destruction and loss, and much of what is available today exists only in fragments. In 2008, the Cinemateca Brasileira generously estimated that only 7 percent of films known to have been made during the silent period exist today, corresponding to merely 210 hours of screening time.[3]

Early Brazilian film production has thus been lost to the historical archive, and the field of Brazil's silent cinema is marked by what Giuliana Bruno describes as an absence "whose texture is larger than the remnance of complete texts." While specific, this loss is similar to that encountered elsewhere in the field of early cinema. Bruno notes that "although the cinema has been in existence for only a century, one faces the prevalence and dissemination of voids, gaps and lacunae" in dealing with the silent period.[4] The lack of Brazilian films made before the 1920s certainly corresponds to this lost landscape of early cinema. In Brazil, however, the absence of extant texts has been met with (and covered up by) an overwhelming presence of historical studies. In fact, though early Brazilian cinema may have received scant attention from European and North American scholars, in Brazil it has been the subject of extensive scholarly documentation.

Documentation of Brazil's early film history began in the 1950s and formed part of the emergence of new intellectual discourses and practices that sought to map a national film history. This endeavor gave rise to what Jean-Claude Bernardet calls Brazil's "classical film historiography." Between the 1950s and 1970s a number of books were published that outlined the history of Brazilian cinema, paying close attention to its initial development. Critics like Alex Viany, Adhemar Gonzaga, and Paulo Emílio Salles Gomes produced historical accounts of the evolution of Brazilian cinema that included chapters dealing with what they called *os primórdios* or "the beginnings."[5] These historical accounts were accompanied by the appearance of studies that focused exclusively on the silent period. The most notable were Vicente de Paula Araújo's *A bela época de cinema brasileiro* (The belle epoque of Brazilian cinema, 1966), Gomes's *Humberto Mauro: Cataguases. Cinearte (1974)*, and Ismail Xavier's *Sétima arte: Um culto moderno* (The seventh art: A modern cult, 1978). These studies examined the contours of Brazil's film production before the 1920s, providing an in-depth examination of the birth of a national film culture. Together the works conspired to put Brazil's silent cinema on the cultural map, and in the process they constructed it as a field of knowledge, to draw from Pierre Bourdieu.

Given the status of early films, however, this field was constructed from a panorama marked by the absence of primary texts. Confronted with this absence, Brazil's film historians adopted an archaeological-forensic approach: they turned to secondary materials—press coverage, advertisements, literary references, memoirs—in order to uncover and piece together evidence of early Brazilian film production. As Bernardet points out, this approach was central to laying the foundations of the country's classical film historiography; it also gave birth to an archive of early Brazilian cinema, housed at the Cinemateca Brasileira, which stored, organized, and systematically classified an extensive collection of secondary materials that became a substitute or prosthesis for the absent body of film texts.

As part of this archiving mission, Brazil's critics brought to life a number of films produced before the 1920s, a treasure trove they dubbed the belle epoque of Brazilian cinema. The cinematic period of the belle epoque (as the histories tell us) roughly spans the years between 1906 and 1912 and constitutes a brief period of intense filmmaking activity in Brazil, when domestic movies were more popular than foreign cinematic products. According to Viany, during these few years "Brazilian movies outdid anything from abroad."[6]

Classical film historiography attributes Brazilian cinema's domination of the domestic market to a vertically integrated system of production, distribution, and exhibition, which allowed filmmakers to produce movies that drew on local events and cultural forms. For Gomes and others, this link with the domestic scene gave rise to "authentically" Brazilian films and the production of national genres. These included the *filmes policiais,* based on real-life crime stories; the *filmes de revista,* musical revues related to Brazil's vaudeville tradition known as the *teatro de revista;* and the *carnavalescos,* documentaries of the carnival celebrations.

The production of these quintessentially Brazilian films ended abruptly in 1912, the year that saw the arrival of Hollywood subsidiaries in Brazil and the development of a strong distribution/exhibition sector geared to imports. These factors precluded national production from prospering commercially in the country and, by blocking local films' access to screens, cut short Brazilian cinema's dialogue with the domestic scene. US dominance of the Brazilian market marginalized homegrown films, alienating spectators from their own cinematic projections and forcing filmmakers to imitate imported productions in an attempt to "face up to Hollywood."[7] The year 1912 thus marks the decline of Brazilian cinema's belle epoque; it also signals the start of Hollywood's ubiquitous hold on the home market, which was organized to fulfill the interests of foreign, mainly US, imports. For Gomes, "The belle epoque ended as Brazilian films were forced off the screens by North American products. It was at that moment that the foreign film became the standard by which Brazilian cinema was to be judged."[8]

Existing prior to Hollywood's ascendancy over the domestic market, the belle epoque has been historically constituted and written as a utopian era, during which national cinema was free from the difficulties that would later plague Brazilian filmmakers as they attempted to compete commercially with Hollywood. If, after 1912, domestic production had to contend with North American cinema's dominant presence in Brazil, classical histories carefully point out that this was not the case in the early years of the twentieth century, which saw the development of "authentic" national films that were untainted by foreign influences. It is because of this uncorrupted and essentially national dimension that historians dubbed the earlier years a belle epoque or "golden age" of Brazilian cinema—for Gomes, "a valid description compared to the following frustrating decades."[9]

The utopian period of the belle epoque has come to occupy a key place in Brazil's classical film historiography, where it enjoys pride of place in accounts of the development of national cinematic practices. The period, moreover, is central to contemporary scholarship. A new generation of Brazilian film scholars, such as Jurandyr Noronha, Roberto Moura, Carlos Roberto de Souza, and Paulo Roberto Ferreira, have reiterated the utopian discourse of the belle epoque, which by the very force of its repetition has assumed the value of a truth. Many of these new scholars were students of the older generation of film historians and were trained at the same institutions, so that the prolongation of discourses concerning Brazil's cinematic past cannot be seen as coincidental. As Michel Foucault shows when speaking of discursive "remanence," it remains in existence by virtue of the support of an apparatus, which includes institutions of knowledge.[10] These reiterations have not been restricted to Brazil. Anglo-American scholars, including Randal Johnson, Robert Stam, Ana M. López, Lisa Shaw, and Stephanie Dennison, have taken part in the same utopian discourse, helping to further spread and cement its veracity. Brazil's classical film historiography has, therefore, not only defined and shaped the field of knowledge of Brazil's early cinema but also set the discursive parameters for the historical criticism of Brazilian film in general.

Nevertheless, while the belle epoque speaks *of* a specific history of Brazilian cinema, it is important to remember that its unearthing and writing is itself situated *in* a particular history. Indeed, the utopianism of the belle epoque bears the hallmarks of the cultural ideologies and politics prevalent in 1950s to 1970s Brazil.[11] During these years, what Antonio Candido calls "a consciousness of underdevelopment" took hold of Brazil.[12] This consciousness was linked to broader national(ist) politics that encompassed an ambitious plan of industrial development, known as developmentalism. Intellectuals turned their attention to what they saw as a continuation of Brazil's colonial relations, which they deemed an impediment to the country's development, understood as an absolute value and an unquestionable end to be achieved. Ideas of national development went hand in hand with notions of liberation and revolution. In this context, nationalism assumed the shape of opposition and resistance to colonialism, and national culture took the dialectics of affirming what was authentic to the nation and repudiating what was alien to the nation as an essential aspect of the broader struggle for autonomy and development. The work produced by the ISEB (Instituto Superior de Estudos Brasileiros; Superior Institute of Brazilian Studies), especially Roland Corbisier's *Formação e problema da cultura brasileira* (The formation and problem of Brazilian culture), took on this pattern, as it argued for an authentic, national critical consciousness to overcome Brazil's underdevelopment and its causes.[13]

Film was inserted into this agenda. Hollywood's ubiquity became a symbol of the legacy of colonialism. Critics of its dominance saw the cinematic apparatus as central in promoting a capitalist ideology and thus in helping to construct Brazilian spectators as Western subjects. Consequently US cinema's normative practices were to be rejected in favor of a national specificity. This rejection marked a stark departure from the imitation of Hollywood's commercial and industrial model that had shaped Brazilian cinema from 1912 onwards. Seeking to gain a foothold in their own market, Brazilian filmmakers established elaborate US-styled filmmaking studios in an attempt to produce international quality movies that could compete with Hollywood.[14]

The Hollywood dream was central to Companhia Vera Cruz, which was established in 1949. Built entirely on the US model, the company went bankrupt in the mid-1950s after producing only eighteen feature films. Vera Cruz's failure was taken as a sign of the impossibility of constructing a First-World cinema in Brazil and contributed to debates concerning the need for an alternative national film industry that was more suitable for the country's social and economic conditions and could help forge a Brazilian identity. These debates were central to the national film bodies and cultural agencies that proliferated during these years. Among them were the Comisão Nacional de Cinema (National Film Commission, 1951); the Grupo de Estudos da Indústria Cinematográfica (Film Industry Study Group, 1956); the Instituto Nacional do Cinema (National Film Institute, 1966); Embrafilme (1966); and the Conselho Nacional de Cinema (National Film Council, 1976).[15] Discussions and conferences held by these state-led agencies led to proposals aimed at promoting a national film industry that would differ from the "antinational" model of Vera Cruz. The proposals encompassed exhibition and distribution laws. They also included ideas for a new kind of cinema, one that was independent and could incorporate a pedagogical function, helping to raise people's consciousness by educating Brazilians against colonialism.

All of this underlay the practices of Cinema Novo, the New Cinema movement, whose "aesthetics of hunger" expressed an aggressive denial of Hollywood's polished production values. Leaving behind industrial dreams and acknowledging Brazil's material disadvantages, Cinema Novo asserted its cultural value and ideological strength by recovering local cultural traditions and seeking to turn scarcity of means into an aesthetic that would make audiences aware of the country's underdevelopment. This rupture with Hollywood's style, typical of modern cinema, was linked to social criticism, and films were part of broader debates regarding politics and aesthetics, articulating the belief that the cinema could participate in developing a new national order.

It was not only filmmakers that sought out alternative avenues of film's development in Brazil. Critics too engaged in debates to define the contours of a "Brazilian cinema."[16] Scholars and historians took on an eminently political function and assumed a key role in shaping official policies regarding filmmaking, highlighting what Bourdieu would call their symbolic power.[17] The various film commissions established during these years counted on the participation of the country's film historians, most notably Viany and Gomes. Their histories were guided by a diagnostic aim of explaining the cinema's difficult or "under-" development in Brazil. Perhaps the best example of this is Gomes's study *Cinema: Trajetória no subdesenvolvimento* (Cinema: A trajectory within underdevelopment), which, as the title suggests, discussed the historical evolution of Brazilian film within a context of underdevelopment, characterized by a tension between colonizers and the colonized.[18] As Bernardet notes, this tension guided Brazil's classical film historiography, which sought to uncover the remnants of a national cinema that had been displaced and obscured by Hollywood. In doing so, it challenged what Xavier refers to as an "amnesia" concerning Brazilian film. That amnesia was linked to the belief that cinema was a foreign medium that had never been successfully implanted in the country, a belief reinforced by the failure of Vera Cruz,[19] and it was exemplified in 1944 when the poet Vinicíus de Moraes, then a film critic for the journal *A Manhã,* emphatically announced that he was not a Brazilian film historian because Brazil had no history of filmmaking. Critics set out to counter these dominant ideas by retrieving a national cinematic past that had been not just physically lost to the historical archive but also erased from memory. Brazil's classical film historiography was therefore part of and contributed to the broader decolonizing struggle for a national cinema. As Gomes put it, "To the extent that the history of our cinema is that of an oppressed culture, the elucidation of its development is transformed into an act of liberation."[20]

These endeavors were, unsurprisingly, well received by the new generation of filmmakers. Director Glauber Rocha, for instance, registered the impact of Viany's work, writing that Brazilian cinema "can be divided into two eras: before and after Alex Viany's book."[21] Carlos Diegues too described the national film histories of these years as "something that made an entire generation aware of its own cinematic tradition, which because of ignorance and prejudice had not been documented."[22] The work of Viany and others therefore encouraged a new generation of filmmakers to become agents in the project of cinematic liberation, and the writing of a film history was linked to the task of making a new Brazilian cinema. While these histories, then, seemed to point to the past, to what Jacques Derrida calls "the memory-economy of the archive," they were also related to the question of Brazilian cinema's present and future development, a factor duly noted by Gomes in his essay "Pequeno cinema antigo": "Ten years ago, only some ten people or so had any interest in our cinematic past. Today, a more reasonable number feel the need to know our cinema. This research obeys the norms of any field of knowledge: to critically engage with Brazil's past in order to serve the present and the future."[23] The work of Gomes and others received broader reception in Brazil. Newspapers and magazines published extracts of their findings, and movie theaters organized retrospectives on national cinema that included the early years, all of which were duly supplemented by symposia and printed catalogs.[24] The accumulation of these activities and their dissemination were guided by a clear pedagogical function: to teach a broader public about the country's cinematic tradition.

The need to critically engage with Brazil's cultural past formed part of a contemporary genealogical concern that, as Bernardet points out, is typical of postcolonial societies: "The search for authentic roots responds to the exterior character of the appearance of these societies. To seek the true birth of a society is an affirmation of authenticity that counters the origins provided by colonizers."[25] Seeking to map the genesis and development of domestic cinema, film histories provided Brazilian filmmakers and the public with a cinematic lineage, laying the foundations for new and future developments. The belle epoque acquired a symbolic role in this genealogy. Documentary evidence and material traces of cinematic activities prior to Hollywood's ascendency amounted to proof of a national cinema and as such pointed to its future promise. The belle epoque in this respect constituted the possible source of a true Brazilian cinema that was free from foreign influences. The idea of a prolific domestic industry existing in harmony with local culture and in the absence of external impacts amounts to what Bernardet calls Brazilian cinema's "foundational myth."[26] According to this myth, national cinema became the victim of outside forces when its dialogue with the domestic scene was violently ended by the arrival of Hollywood in 1912. In Brazil's classic historiography, the mythical golden era of the belle epoque therefore represents not just a utopian age but also an unfinished project that offers the possibility for present and future resumption. The archival collection of secondary texts was backward looking *and* forward looking, since it became a source for a future national cinema.

The belle epoque's afterlife highlights the teleological impetus that underlies classical histories of the cinematic belle epoque whose national configuration will be fulfilled in the future. This echoes and reproduces the teleological impetus of Brazilian cinema narratives in the '60s and '70s. For Xavier teleology was the key organizing principle of Cinema Novo films, which reveal history marching from an initial starting point toward a final *telos,* a narrative that, in keeping with broader political ideologies, reflects the movement of history from colonialism toward national liberation.[27]

Interpretations of Brazil's cinematic belle epoque and the histories that arose from it were therefore intertwined with the cultural politics of the '50s and '60s. Indeed, the early period's delimitation, definition, and meaning emerged from the exclusive paradigms of the period's decolonizing discourses, with the belle epoque defined as a temporal period preceding Hollywood's arrival in Brazil, when production was closed off from the imitative tendencies that would later shape the country's cinematic landscape. Consequently, Brazil's early cinema suffers from what Bernardet highlights as "um recorte" or decontextualization. Shaped by the concerns of subsequent ideas, it has been abstracted from the context of production. The absence of contextual interpretations is evidenced by the fact that histories of "the beginnings" bypass issues of reception and exhibition in favor of an approach that focuses on recovering evidence of a history of filmmaking. Bernardet sees this tendency as part of a historiographic privileging of production, of texts and their content, to the exclusion of the places where cinemagoers engaged with the movies. As he highlights, in dominant formulations of early cinema in Brazil there is little consideration of the conditions of circulation and exhibition that preceded and exceeded films themselves. Consequently, questions of place, society, and ultimately the nation are taken for granted and unproblematized.[28]

By forgoing a consideration of internal determinations, which might have highlighted different methods of production and reception within Brazil, these readings have proposed a system of homogeneous relations between all cinematic phenomena, with the same type of historicity operating in each and every place during the period of the belle epoque. Here differences are reduced to a single national narrative, linking film not just to the myth of a cinematic foundation but also to a future teleology. This teleological narrative idealizes the belle epoque as a paradigmatic "national cinema" in relation to "foreign practices," with the period being seen (or even theorized) as a form of local alterity vis-à-vis Hollywood's dominance.

In his critique of Brazil's classical film historiography, Bernardet stresses the paradox at the heart of the belle epoque, that is, the key role that Hollywood plays in defining this national period of cinema. Despite their sympathies for lost and forgotten films, histories of the belle epoque have been shaped by US cinema and its normative standards. This paradox highlights the political vicissitudes of Brazil's anticolonial theories of the developmentalist years of the '50s and '60s, whose deconstructing of dominant foreign processes gestured toward an unproblematic notion of the nation, defined against the United States. To put it bluntly, Brazilian cinema's nation-ness, configured as an undifferentiated alterity, was elaborated and discovered in the process of reproducing Hollywood as subject, though by registering its inappropriateness for the underdeveloped Brazilian context.

TOWARD A NEW HISTORY OF BRAZIL'S CINEMATIC BELLE EPOQUE

It goes without saying that the context in which Brazil's classical film history was written has radically changed. The official film bodies and institutions it was linked to and impelled by have disappeared, destroyed by a "new" economic climate that has altered the official status of cinema and ended its close relationship to national politics and the state. Likewise, the historical narrative of the '50s and '60s, centered on a belief in the need for development, has ceased to be a marker in the country's consciousness, and the harsh realities of political and economic circumstances have put an end to the revolutionary impulses of Brazilian filmmakers. Writing in 1995, in the midst of this new context, Bernardet highlights the need to review the silent period of Brazilian film and to reassess the history of the cinematic belle epoque beyond the utopian ideas of the past that initially brought it to life.[29] Doing so involves rethinking its national configurations: looking at *whether* and *how* national identity can be considered a force in early Brazilian cinema's history.

Bernardet's emphasis on the need to revise Brazil's cinematic past should not be taken as a call to write a true history or to replace the past history with an updated one. Rather, the critic proposes alternative reading methods and interpretive practices to reformulate Brazilian film historiography. Given the status of films from this period, their loss from the historical archive, Bernardet recognizes that the cinematic past can come into existence only through its presence in secondary referents, adapted or cited. Against the obsession to use these referents to cover up a loss, to fabricate and restore a mythical cinematic past, Bernardet advocates an archaeological method that works on and with fragments and contexts, looking at these remnants not as evidence of a filmic past but as vestiges of an entire cultural field that cinema was part of.[30] This method interrogates secondary texts and the paratexts and intertexts that constitute the surroundings of lost films, exploring the spaces in which they were produced and their interconnections. For Bernardet, this interrogation provides the basis for documenting not just the production of films, now in absentia, but the landscape that the moving pictures were part of and emerged from, revealing a shift from a focus on texts and their content to early cinema and its broader cultural context. This method marks a stark departure from previous narratives as it seeks to free history from the overarching, predetermined nationalist histories of the '50s and '60s and to locate cinematic practices—production *and* exhibition—in their cultural environment, in order to redraw the discourses, cultural forms, and modes they were linked to and engaged with.

Bernardet's proposal parallels broader reevaluations of early film historiography conducted in film studies in general. Since 1978 and the now well-known conference of the International Federation of Film Archives (FIAF) held in Brighton, England, scholars like Tom Gunning, Richard Abel, Charles Musser, and Thomas Elsaesser, among others, have challenged classical views of early film historiography in the Anglo-American field, undermining a teleological model of development whereby the history of cinema is seen as advancing from an embryonic state in the early years toward its maturation in the adulthood of a narrative system by the 1920s. These scholars have put into play a range of methodologies for "doing film history," from examining unused sources to incorporating investigative tools from other disciplines. Such work has helped to redefine the notion of early cinema, which signifies not only a historical period but also and importantly, a critical category that focuses on hitherto neglected areas of investigation. These include exploring film's links with its contemporary cultural practices and sites, like vaudeville theater and shopping arcades. As Jennifer Bean and Diane Negra observe, current usage of the term *early cinema* "emphatically underscores the medium's intimate ties to practices of exhibition, as well as its dependency on media inter-texts and shared cultural mores."[31]

This new film history thus moves away from an emphasis on production and texts to consider distribution and exhibition, looking at wider contexts in which cinema was situated and its relation to the external pressures and influences shaping its development. This contextual and intertextual approach to film study is by no means limited to early cinema. Numerous scholars have argued for the need to challenge the ontology of the film text. Christine Geraghty, for example, writes, "Studying cinema is not just a question of studying films, nor indeed the institutions that produce the films and the economic structures that sustain them. Studying how we watch films—in multiplexes, on video, in theme parks, on television—is an important part of understanding what films mean within a culture and how they fit into the broader range of entertainment activities that might be on offer to audiences."[32] Nevertheless, as Douglas Gomery and Robert Allen note, the study of early cinema frequently requires a cultural approach, since film viewing is often an inappropriate research method given the absence of extant films.[33] This historical focus has opened up new areas of research. It has shown that the study of the sites of exhibition and of media intertexts provides key insights into the development of the medium and the way it was received.

The adoption of a more historical and contextual method for the study of early cinema has fueled an archaeological project that works not to restore a cinematic past, that is, to resuscitate a lost body of film texts, but rather to rethink the medium's cultural significance, especially looking at how film helped to shape new perceptions of time and space central to the onset of capitalist modernity. Leo Charney and Vanessa Schwartz have shown that cinema was from the outset intrinsically part of the cultural developments and historical transformations associated with modernization. Physical changes—the centrality of the city, new forms of production and distribution, and the rise of consumerism, as well as intellectual and aesthetic changes and public interest in representations of real life—were addressed by the medium, which became a key mediator for the constitution of modern forms of culture and subjectivity.

For Charney and Schwartz the cinema was one of the most comprehensive attributes of modernity, and it articulated and responded to the production of new identities that were linked to transformations wrought by the intensification of capitalist modernity. Gunning notes that these modern identities were by no means national. Borrowing a phrase from film historian Michael Raine, Gunning writes that "the cinema was international before it was national," and he claims that in its early days the medium, far from being limited by the borders of an imagined community, refused reified boundaries of place and culture to express a global imaginary.[34] Other scholars have also highlighted early cinema's international configurations. Jonathan Auerbach, for example, states that film "from the start was a market driven phenomenon of global modernity, with films distributed and mimicked across the world map without any clear unilateral direction of influence."[35]

This international identity has significant bearings on the question of "early cinema and the national." Writing with reference to the French context, Richard Abel goes as far as to question whether "national cinema" is a viable epistemological category for dealing with early film.[36] Abel's question touches on the ambiguity of medium specificity: unlike print media, which as Anderson notes provided a key venue for the emergence of a national consciousness, the circulation of moving pictures was never limited to national and linguistic competencies, as cinema was designed to travel around the world. In this sense film expressed a global imaginary; indeed, the frequently stated ability of the moving pictures was "to place the world within your reach." Abel's question, however, also relates to conceptual issues: since American cinema did not assert its hegemony until World War I, it is difficult to argue that Brazil had an early "national" cinema, understood as a sharply monolithic and differentiated category that emerged in opposition to Hollywood's normative practices. If anything, the medium's capacity to circulate beyond national boundaries in its early days would seem to implicate it in processes of globalization, as filmmakers producing silent movies envisioned and catered to international audiences. Mark Shiel and Tony Fitzmaurice have underscored this relationship between cinema and globalization, noting that film "has always operated internationally through the expansionist vision and activities of production companies" and has from the start "been central to . . . processes known as globalization."[37] This suggests that the oppositional paradigms that defined national cinema in the '50s and '60s—in Brazil and beyond—are untenable for dealing with film's early years. Nevertheless, this does not mean that silent film represents an era beyond and above national configurations, that it ignored borders from idealistic motives. If cinema crossed national borders in its first decades, it did so because it followed global pathways opened up by worldwide capitalism and imperialism.[38]

Early film's imperial connections have been foregrounded by Ella Shohat and Robert Stam, who note, "The beginnings of cinema coincided with the giddy heights of the imperial project, with an epoch where Europe held sway over vast tracts and hosts of subjugated peoples." They go on to point out that "the most prolific film-producing countries of the silent period—Britain, France, the US and Germany—also 'happened' to be among the leading imperialists."[39] Early movie shows were part of a new world market in entertainment that included the circulation of movies to imperial outposts. In the 1900s, film companies sent crews to countries across the globe, both to exhibit their own movies and to capture scenes from far-flung places, in a move that resembled the late nineteenth-century "scramble" mentality. For Shohat and Stam these early international views amounted to a form of appropriating a distant place through an image, something that attests to Heidegger's belief that modern man views the world as something that can be appropriated through becoming a picture.

Film's initial global identity therefore exhibited a close historical bond with imperialism, and the medium's international circuits were linked to the political economies that underwrote empire's circulation. Indeed, Gilles Deleuze and Félix Guattari remind us that empire, the projection of political and economic power across space, is a function of international mobility, which cinema was implicated in.[40] This points to a specific context for what Gunning stresses as film's initial global impulse. While the expansion of exploration and trade through the nineteenth century certainly influenced the Enlightenment's concepts of universal rights, the enormous industrial and technological expansion that took place during the nineteenth century converted this ideal into capitalist systems of cooperation and exploitation across the globe. During this so-called second industrial revolution, colonial spheres and peripheral areas were turned into sources of raw material and markets for European and North American manufactured goods, and their cultures received tangible and ideological forms that mapped the pathway from material to commodity as the power that united and made the world go round.

This process did not, though, preclude "the national." Eric Hobsbawm states that while "modern capitalism was and could not but be global, extending its operations to ever more remote parts of the planet and transforming all areas ever more profoundly," it also operated via the "basic building blocks of national economies."[41] Moreover, technological and commercial innovations and transfers set the basis for a permanent traffic in ideas of selfhood and peoplehood, which created imagined communities of modern nationalism throughout the world. To cite Dilip Gaonkar, the expansion of capitalist modernity was "awakened by contact, transported through commerce and administered by empires, bearing colonial inscriptions," but it was also "propelled by nationalism."[42] The international logic of capital in its imperial form did not result in the obliteration of the nation or the local; it operated on the specificity of the national. Indeed, it was during the globalizing nineteenth century that the nation took center stage politically, economically and commercially, consolidating its status as a dominant symbolic unit around the world.

All of this affected early film production. Richard Abel and others have shown that while filmmakers producing silent movies may have envisioned international audiences, they also depended on and expressed national characteristics, as local contexts and companies drove cinema's initial global development. So, although early cinema may have expressed an international imaginary, the nation was still a potent frame of reference for producers and viewers, as well as a key actor in the creation of a worldwide film network. Producers in France, Britain, the United States, and Germany disseminated images of their countries' cultures abroad; they also brought back images of exotic "others" that reinforced their spectators' own sense of national difference.

The cinema's international dimension was thus part of global capitalism, which in turn depended on and helped to produce a notion of nation-ness. This process was not limited to Europe or the United States. In Brazil, the expansion of capitalism went hand in hand with an incipient nationalism, as the internationalization wrought by European imperialism set the foundations for a new national identity. This identity took root at the end of the nineteenth century. In 1888 slavery was abolished, followed a year later by the definitive end of Portugal's imperial presence in the country.[43] These events marked the start of a new regime—the First Republic (1889–1930), which signaled a "new era" for Brazil. Once in power, the Republican regime set out to reinvent the country's identity and transform its peripheral status as a former colony. Incorporating European liberal discourses that promoted international and universal values of civilization and progress, Brazil turned its back on its rural, slaveholding past to rewrite itself as a modern nation-state—a nation of order and progress, as the new flag brazenly announced, that was equal to any other on the global stage.

The Republic thus constituted—to paraphrase Angel Rama—the second birth of Brazil, a nationwide modernizing project that involved purging the country of its colonial past and updating its identity, bringing it in line with European civilization. The contours of this modern identity, however, were far from straightforward. Jeffrey Needell points out that while the Republic represented a "new era" for Brazil, it was also characterized by the continuation of old forces: "The new and changing nation was consolidated and its course continually reaffirmed as colonial, under the concomitant direction of representatives of the country's traditional elites."[44] It was this elite that embraced, or to use Roberto Schwarz's word, "imported," European liberal ideas, in order to update Brazil while at the same time reasserting the social basis of its power.

This amalgamation of old and new, of traditional structures and modernization, highlights what Néstor García Canclini describes as the hybrid nature of modernity in Latin America. Canclini sees Latin American modernization, not as the result of large-scale transformations of industrialization, rationality, and technology, but as a series of renovation projects driven by elite groups. Addressing impulses and models from abroad and creatively adapting them to their local context and sociopolitical needs, Latin America's elites have forged ways of playing with and at modernity, seeking to "elaborate with them their own global project." Consequently, modern Latin American nations are the products of the ambiguous symbiosis of a foreign-inflected modernity and democratic ideologies with enduring oligarchic political structures.[45] The dynamic of cultural hybridity results from the fact that modernity in Latin America does not replace traditional bases of social power—all that is solid melting into air—but often reproduces and rearticulates them.

This hybrid modernity characterized Brazil's Republic, forged on the one hand by the permanence of sociopolitical elites and on the other by dramatic transformations. Indeed, the "new" political regime favored the traditional ruling classes at the expense of an emergent middle class who wanted to create an industrial base and an internal market. This entailed abandoning the path of independent economic development and accepting a form of neocolonialism or imperialism: an economic liberalism in which primary products were exchanged for imported European manufactured goods. While Republicanism signaled a move away from Brazil's Portuguese colonial past, it was annexed into what Mona Domosh has termed Europe's informal imperial dominion, organized not in terms of the direct annexation and control of territory but around the transfer and circulation of goods and the promotion of a modern worldly identity.[46]

Brazil's elites were receptive to European modernity and the belief in progress, and they ardently embraced the new global imaginary. This situation was cemented in 1898 with the administration of President Campos Salles, when the initial revolutionary Republican forces were violently put down. Political stability went hand in hand with an emphasis on European-styled progress, an alliance that marked not just Campos Salles's administration but the historical period of Brazil's belle epoque (1898–1914). During these years, the social and political elite enthusiastically accepted everything from Europe—clothes, foods, language, goods, and political ideas. *Mundanismo* or worldliness, became the order of the day for a select few, shaping their ways of being and thinking. Indeed, Nicolau Sevcenko notes that "the international atmosphere of the belle epoque was such that, on the eve of the First World War, people no longer greeted each other in the Brazilian way, but repeated to each other *Vive la France*."[47]

This worldliness was spectacularly embodied in transformations that took place in the country's then-capital, Rio de Janeiro. Indeed, Sevcenko writes that Rio was "the principal stage for the period's radical processes of change."[48] Although Rio was by no means a provincial town prior to the Republic, during the belle epoque the pace at which it was transformed was phenomenal, so much so that writer Lima Barreto observed that "the city is no longer the same. From one hour to another, the old city disappeared and a new one emerged."[49] Rio's dramatic makeover began in 1902, when its map was radically redrawn and new foundations were put in place for a modern capital. In less than four years, colonial structures were razed and replaced in accordance with a new architectural vision, which was modeled on the 1850s Parisian reforms known as Haussmannization. Impelled by the city's elite, this French-style makeover aimed at expressing the country's modern global identity, one that was profoundly identified with Europe. Grand boulevards were built, lined with luxurious beaux arts department stores that sold the latest European commodities, providing Rio with an aura of opulence and aristocratic majesty that the city's popular classes were not deemed fit to share. As Sevcenko highlights, "People who were not attuned with the European civilized lifestyle were excluded from Rio's worldly identity, its modern contours restricted to the country's traditional elite."[50] If the new city opened itself up to a global imaginary, its modern identity was steeped in exclusions inherited from the past.

The arrival and development of cinema were inextricably linked to Rio's modern makeover. Indeed, the belle epoque of Brazilian cinema cannot be understood as a golden age of *national* filmmaking; rather, it was a cinematic period whose beginnings and development were intimately connected to the changes of the historical period of the belle epoque, which were profoundly seen and felt in Rio. A number of Brazilian film scholars have underscored this link between Brazil's early cinema and the city. Bernardet, for instance, writes that the cinematic belle epoque "is hardly Brazilian; it is above all *Cariocan,* in terms of both production and exhibition," and José Inácio de Melo Souza notes that "cinema contributed to Rio's modernization."[51] Film first made its appearance in Brazil in Rio, and its subsequent development drew on and incorporated the capital's transformations, with an emergent film culture that was based in and contributed to a culturally anchored experience of the city's modern makeover. Far from being national in scope, cinematic practices central to the belle epoque were Cariocan and by the same token decidedly worldly. In fact, the arrival of film, as an imported product, was part of Rio's excitement over international trends, and movies of people and places in modern European cities fed into and helped consolidate the city's new global identity.

The relationship between the cinema and Rio evidences what scholars have highlighted as the homologous relationship between early cinema and the city. James Donald, Giuliana Bruno, Anne Friedberg, and Leo Charney and Vanessa Schwartz, to name but a few, have explored how urbanization and the development of film are inextricably related. These scholars have examined how cinematic representations relied on historical material related to the dramatic growth of cities in Europe and North America in the late nineteenth and early twentieth centuries. They have also analyzed how film was a central experience of the emergence of a modern urban environment, helping to shape people's understanding of the expanding space of the city, and becoming part of their everyday familiarity with growing metropoles. The relationship between the cinema and the city is far from tangential and arbitrary. Donald notes that in its early days film was almost exclusively an urban phenomenon, with movie theaters located in downtown areas and catering to city-based audiences. Consequently, cinematic representations drew on and in turn shaped the city's topography and its residents. Film provided a sense of place to a growing urban population and had a great impact on what Georg Simmel called the mental life of the metropolis, contributing to the emergence of modern urban subjectivities.

This work on the two-way relationship between film and the city has entered larger debates concerning cinema's links to modernity. In providing these discussions with a tangible location, it departs from more ambiguous discussions of modernity, which for Anthony King are rarely "geographically grounded, but float in space."[52] The work thus gives not just cinema but also modernity a particular materialization and location. As Charney and Schwartz write, "Modernity cannot be conceived outside of the city, which provided an arena for the circulation of bodies and goods, the exchange of glances, and the exercise of consumerism."[53]

For Charney and Schwarz modern life seemed urban by definition, yet the socioeconomic transformations wrought by modernity recast the city in the wake of nineteenth-century capitalism. This period brought about a radically new configuration of lived experience created by the increasingly palpable effects of the global expansion of industrial and economic capitalism. Modern life in European and North American cities metamorphosed during these years at unprecedented speeds because of a series of interconnected developments: increased mechanization and electrification of urban life, availability of faster transport, expansion of standardized consumer items of display and for sale, widespread occurrence of mass migrations resulting from depopulation and urban growth, and increasing circulation of cheaper mechanically reproduced images capable of bringing the world home in more intimate ways. Allied to these developments was imperialism. The dramatic changes occurring in European and North American cities at this time were dependent to a large extent on their connections to and domination of foreign markets, a reminder that "imperialism is the very condition for modernity and for the development of the modern city."[54]

Empire's role in forging the modern metropolis is rarely acknowledged by scholars. While Paris, London, Berlin, and other European capitals are often examined as paradigmatic cities, their links to the world outside are hardly recognized. King, for instance, writes that "Benjamin's well-known essay on 'Paris Capital of the Nineteenth Century,' often cited as the classic representation of the modern city, despite its references to the Empire as being at the height of its power and to the world economy, makes no mention of the extensive colonial exploitation intrinsically linked to the commodity production displayed in the arcades."[55] The development and character of modern European cities have instead tended to be interpreted in terms of the evolution of capitalism, urban planning, and social movements, with few scholars examining cross-mappings between empire and European urbanism and looking at how capitals such as London and Paris were shaped by the global history of imperialism. King's work provides a useful corrective to this oversight. His book *Colonial Urban Development* pays particular attention to the important influence of cultural forms of empire on the landscapes of modern European cities, exploring the significance of imperial history for the constitution of metropolitan spaces like London and Paris. Cultural geographers have also looked at the relationship between empire and European urbanism, examining what Felix Driver and David Gilbert dub "imperial cities." Driver and Gilbert, as well as Jane Jacobs, have focused on how imperialism shaped the landscapes and experiences of European cities, highlighting ways in which global processes of imperialism were absorbed and re-presented in the urban context.[56]

This research on imperial cities, however, contrasts with the relative paucity of research that seeks to understand how imperialism conversely shaped the spatial structures of urban imperial outposts, like New Delhi or Cairo, or, for that matter, cities in empires' informal terrain, such as Latin America. If, as King and others have shown, it is impossible to understand the "real development of London or Manchester . . . without reference to India, Africa and Latin America," can the development of Mexico City, Buenos Aires, or Rio also be understood without reference to the former?[57] These oversights are perhaps symptomatic of what Andreas Huyssen calls the "geographies of modernity," which have been determined by metropolitan cities of Europe and the United States, with little examination of the world at large.[58] As Huyssen stresses, cities in Asia, Africa, and Latin America are rarely the focus of attempts to understand the development of the modern city, an omission that is characteristic of work on modernity itself, which has been conceptualized historically in relation to economic, technological, social, and cultural changes occurring in "the West."[59]

Rio's early twentieth-century transformation, in this respect, stages an alternative urban modernity, allowing us to see how the development of the city and of new urban subjectivities was linked to Europe's expansion of capitalism in the world at large. Planned by the Republic's elite, the capital's makeover was very consciously intended to symbolize Brazil's transition from peripheral colony to modern European-styled global nation—a passage that spectacularly illustrated the modernizing ethos of the historical belle epoque and that also depended on the circulation of capital and goods from Europe. The cinema was imbricated in mapping this passage to modernity, and the medium's implantation and initial development revealed profound links with changes taking place, nationally and internationally, that altered the physiognomy of Rio during the years of the belle epoque. Early projections and imported movies helped give life to the new city, providing Cariocan spectators with images of a worldly modernity, and the cinema's introduction in turn depended on new urban infrastructures. Brazil's cinematic belle epoque thus went hand in hand with contemporary processes of change that were concentrated on and condensed in the capital, and film contributed to reconfiguring the city as Brazil's international capital, helping to lay the foundations of a new national identity that was linked to a global imaginary. Far from being an authentic and untainted cinematic period, early Brazilian cinema, or Brazil's cinematic belle epoque, was central to and depended on the Republic's international dimensions as the nation remade itself as a tropical version of the West. It is film's connection to Rio's new worldly urban landscape that the next chapters chart. Moving away from foundational myths, they locate film practices, production, distribution, and exhibition in the transformative period of Rio's belle epoque. In doing so, they show how cinema's global identity took hold in the climate of Rio. What follows is a historically and locally grounded approach that illuminates our understanding of early cinema's international development, reminding us that "to focus on the local is always and at the same time to attend to the global."[60]

2

Cinematic Vistas of Rio de Janeiro's Worldly Modernity

Early twentieth-century Rio de Janeiro: while Italo Calvino's *Invisible Cities* shows us that any attempt to capture "the city" is doomed to failure, this period, more than any other in Brazil's history, witnessed Rio changing in a spectacular manner. What was in play was modernity, not as "a point of reflection and convergence with industrialization, rationality and technological transformations," but as a desire and ultimately a project that changed the material, physical, and social space of Brazil's then capital.[1] These changes were impelled by sociopolitical changes (at the national and international conjuncture): 1888 saw the abolition of slavery in Brazil, followed a year later by a Republican coup that ousted Portugal's colonial presence. Once in power, the new regime began a "domestic civilizing mission" to radically make over the country's identity and bring it into the twentieth century.[2] Incorporating European imperial discourses of civilization, Brazil turned its back on its slaveholding past to reinvent itself as a modern nation, one that would embody and instill the positivistic values of order and progress.

Symbolic icons, like the now famous green and gold flag, were employed to represent this progressive identity; the most important symbol, however, was "the city." This was the historical period when what Beatriz Sarlo calls "the desire for the city" took hold in Brazil, a desire that was intertwined with modernity.[3] A new urban ideal rapidly overtook the previous ideal of a rural utopia and inspired new national cultural forms. Thus José de Alencar's foundational fictions shifted from Amazonian adventures, like *O Guaraní* (1857) and *Iracema* (1865), to urban tales, such as *Senhora* (1875), a spatial trajectory that did not so much mirror as shape the symbolic shift from rural to urban space and from the past to the future.[4]

This literary participation in Brazil's changing spatial paradigms highlights what Angel Rama refers to as "the lettered city"—a nexus between literature, state power, and urban space that has shaped the discursive framework of Latin American modernity. This nexus gave rise to what Rama calls the second birth of Latin America, a project that involved purging the region of its barbaric past and bringing it in line with European civilization. With the inauguration of Brazil's Republic, this project became the cornerstone of intellectual debates as writers embraced the need for the nation to overcome its slave roots and become civilized through adopting European models. Far from being restricted to intellectual debates, the Republic's civilizing project came to provide the material foundations of an urban program, which saw Rio made over into Brazil's "capital of the twentieth century."

The cinema's arrival and early development coincided with and participated in Rio's makeover. As a modern medium, film was seized upon as a vehicle for displaying the capital's new identity, helping to give it life and to make people believe in its present and future manifestations. Films projected the capital's progress laying the foundations of the urban ideal and helping to construct new urban subjects by showing a landscape in which rural identity was a thing of the past. All of this provides a particular case study for what film scholars have highlighted as the relationship between the early development of cinema and the processes of urbanization.[5] The cinema's arrival and initial development in Brazil both depended on and helped to forge a new urban landscape in Rio in both practical and symbolic ways.

This relationship between cinema and the city in Brazil had a very particular starting point: July 8, 1896. On this day, in a small theater in the heart of Rio, the first showing of what was then called the cinematograph took place in Brazil, barely six months after the Lumière brothers had exhibited their invention in Paris. By that time, however, audiences were already accustomed to new media of visual entertainment from Europe. So called pre- or protocinematic forms, like the diorama and the kinetoscope, had become installed in the country's cultural landscape, part of a technological revolution that had begun during the Second Empire (1847–89), impelled by the modernizing monarch Pedro II.[6] Their appearance in Brazil was fostered by regular routes of transatlantic commerce, which brought imported manufactured goods into the country. This traffic rapidly increased with the start of the Republic as the new regime embraced economic liberalism, exchanging its primary products, like coffee, for foreign items. As the new century dawned, more European goods made their way into Brazil, mainly through the principal port of Rio. Between 1889 and 1906, the city's port activity increased threefold, making it the fifteenth-busiest port in the world in terms of commercial imports, surpassed in the Americas only by New York and Buenos Aires.[7] Rio's inhabitants (at least its elite inhabitants) were increasingly able to purchase goods (clothes, foods, household items) from Europe and to experience the latest

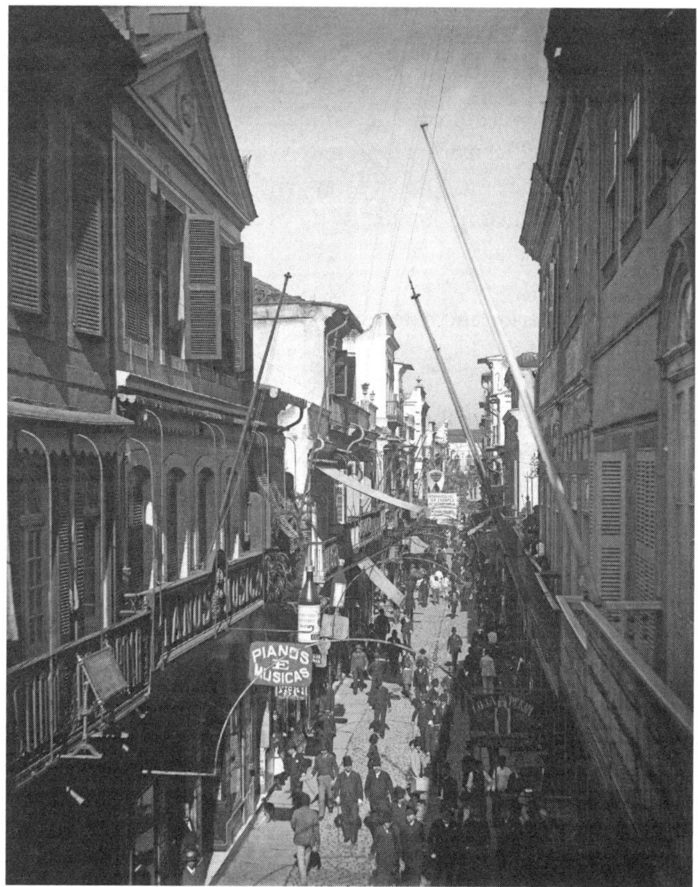

FIGURE 1. Rio's Ouvidor Street, 1890. Marc Ferrez / Gilberto Ferrez
Collection / Instituto Moreira Salles.

imported technologies. As the city received a high number of foreign consumer
goods, what Brito Broca calls a culture of *mundanismo*—worldliness—took
over.[8]

The center of this *mundanismo* was Rio's Ouvidor Street (figure 1). Located
close to the port, the Ouvidor was where French and British merchants settled,
introducing imported luxury goods and commerce into the capital. The Ouvidor
was home to English teahouses, French cafés, bookshops, tailors, milliners and
department stores that sold foreign fashions, and novelty shops that displayed
technological wonders recently arrived from Europe.[9] Journalists praised the street
for the variety of luxurious goods offered there. On July 17, 1890, a journalist for

the *Jornal do Commércio* wrote, "The Ouvidor shines and exalts. Its commerce ranges from the ostentation of luxury to variety goods."[10]

With its seductive display of European luxury goods, the small street in the heart of Rio was a nascent landscape of commerce and consumption, a manifestation of the expansion of the market for foreign commodities in Brazil. As a shrine to commerce, the Ouvidor was Brazil's equivalent to the Parisian arcades analyzed by Walter Benjamin. Benjamin highlights the arcades as a space of extreme cultural and spatial ambivalence, their architectural design—pedestrian streets covered under roofs of iron and glass—upsetting boundaries between light and dark, private and public, interior and exterior. The Ouvidor shared few of the arcades' architectural characteristics—it was an open, not covered, street. Nonetheless, it had its own forms of cultural and spatial ambivalence. With its amalgamation of imported items, the Ouvidor was "a passage" between here and there, between Brazil and the outside world. As Alice Gonzaga puts it, the Ouvidor was "a space in-between" Brazil and the rest of the world.[11]

In its symbolic, iconographic, and commercial density, the Ouvidor can be seen to offer a parallel with the World Fairs that had become popular at the end of the nineteenth century. The fairs gathered together objects from around the world, displaying them for the public gaze. In their scopic value, the objects showcased at the fairs became fetishes: that is, they acquired an ideological value linked with their representation. This representational value was primarily visual and implied a fiction or a fantasy—what I would call a fantasy of worldly belonging. The Ouvidor offered similar fantasies for its visitors. As Needell says, "One went there for *flanerie* and interiorization—that is, a personal identification with the displayed commodities." In this respect, the small street in Rio, "a common space associated with European culture," was "the place for the expression of a fantasy of cultural identification with the rest of the world."[12]

Not all Cariocans, however, shared this fantasy. Needell describes the Ouvidor not as a public space but as a meeting place for the elite.[13] Streetcars connected the street to elite residential districts, with the Ouvidor a mecca for the few. Consequentially, as writer Afrânio Peixoto recalls, the street acquired an intimate, familiar aspect. It was "a narrow street that people would flock to on Saturdays. The entire city squeezed into and rubbed shoulders on this colonial alley. People saw and greeted each other, and not just by clasping hands, they hugged each other like lovers on a couch. In this intimate space, this shared space, the city acquired a familiar aspect; families saw each other, hugged each other, and arranged to do things beyond that space."[14] For Peixoto the Ouvidor was a space where itinerant shoppers would find relatives and friends and even meet loved ones. It was, he says, an extension of the salon society that had dominated colonial Brazil.

It was on the Ouvidor that the movies found their initial home in Brazil. Their appearance there is hardly surprising, given that the medium arrived in the country as another imported product, "on board the same ships that brought other foreign goods into the country."[15] The exhibition of films quickly became tied into the Ouvidor's cultural and social milieu. Films were introduced as part of mixed programs that incorporated other forms of entertainment found on the Ouvidor. Movies were shown in *salões de novidades* (novelty salons) as part of a wider display of foreign novelties, such as x-ray machines; in coffee shops that gave rise to the *café concertos,* recreations of the French *café chantants,* and in German beer halls the *cinemas cervejarias.*

Housed on the Ouvidor, the cinema was thus grounded in a site that displayed international products to cater to the worldly desires of Rio's elite. Yet this global space was not just the site where film was introduced; it also contributed to filmic production. Early films imported into Brazil were marked by what Tom Gunning has identified as a "cinema of attractions."[16] Distinct from what later emerged as the dominant narrative or storytelling forms, which called upon spectators' sustained attention and absorption in a self-contained diegetic world constructed by the film, the cinema of attractions formed a different relationship with audiences based on an aesthetics of astonishment that appealed to viewers' curiosity with the new technology and supplied pleasure through exciting spectacles. Early cinema thus differed from the narrative cinema that began to appear around 1907, as it foregrounded what Gunning calls an "aesthetics of display."[17] For Miriam Hansen these earlier films were presentational rather than representational, with the actual technology constituting the central fascination and object of movies and their reception.[18]

In Rio, too, audiences marveled at the novelty of the cinematograph, its technique constituting an important attraction. A journalist for the *Jornal do Brasil,* for instance, described "150 images rotating one thousand times a second. This film, a plate exposed at an extraordinary speed so as to capture all the movements to be represented, is set in motion by a 20-volt engine."[19] Nevertheless, if writers drew attention to the movies' technology, they also highlighted other ontological and epistemological aspects of the apparatus that complicated its "aesthetics of attraction." As Ana M. López writes, in its early days the cinema in Latin America was "'attractive' in and of itself *and* as an import."[20] Accounts of the early reception of the movies in Brazil highlight the medium's foreign status and cite its worldliness as the key attraction. On July 9, 1896, a journalist for the newspaper *A Cidade do Rio* wrote, "Yesterday we went to the inauguration of one of the most marvelous spectacles that is currently exciting people in the main European capitals." Another for *A Notícia* noted that film was a medium "that has lately provoked much admiration in Paris and all of Europe."[21] More than the technology of film, commentators in Brazil foregrounded the cinema's ability to allow spectators to share and participate in the experience of a new medium that was also exciting audiences elsewhere around the world.[22]

Cinematic images contributed to the cinema's worldly appeal. In the very early days, domestic production was rare and early audiences in Rio were largely fed a diet of foreign films, which depicted street scenes and peoples in sophisticated European capitals. An advertisement for a screening held in Rio's Teatro Lucinda on January 15, 1898, for example, included the movies *O cortejo no casamento do príncipe de Nápoles* (Cortege of the marriage of the prince of Naples), *O cortejo da coroa de Viena d'Austria* (Cortege of the prince of Vienna, Austria), and *Chegada de um trem em Milão* (Arrival of a train in Milan). Writers enthusiastically reported on these shows, praising their ability to provide Brazilian spectators with lifelike views of cities abroad. In 1897 a journalist for the *Jornal do Commércio,* for instance, described the cinema's ability "to parade before our eyes, in its exact dimensions, parts of the Parisian boulevards, with their constant comings and goings of men, women, children, cars, buses, animals, everything." Another writer for the *Gazeta de Notícias* highlighted "the preciseness with which the cinema reproduces scenes and customs in Europe."[23] The cinema was thus perceived as part of a global landscape, as a medium that allowed Brazilian spectators to immediately see and experience the modern lifestyles and practices of cities around the world. As López writes, "With its *vistas* of sophisticated foreign cities and customs (ranging from Lumière's rather sophisticated workers leaving the factory and magnificent locomotives to Edison's scandalous kiss), the imported views could produce the experience of an accessible globality among the urban citizens."[24]

Exhibitors in Brazil played on the appeal of the cinema's worldliness. In March 1898, the Teatro Variedades advertised its *Cinematographo universal,* in which multishot films promised to show viewers "delightful scenes of the world's key marvels."[25] Some incorporated the cinema's internationalism in their forms of exhibition. In 1905 Paschoal Segreto constructed a version of the Hale's Tours that were popular elsewhere in the world (figure 2). Hale's Tours, also known as Scenes of the World, were introduced by entrepreneur George C. Hale at the 1904 St. Louis Exposition in the United States and soon became popular forms of amusement around the world. In the Hale's Tours spectators were placed in the role of passengers, with the exhibition venue replicating a train carriage and the screen showing them images of a passing panorama. The Hale's Tours therefore replicated the illusion of movement in its exhibition, taking audiences on filmic journeys to scenic spots and even foreign lands. These cinematic tours found fertile ground in Rio, where the cinematic experience became linked to a fantasy of global travel. In 1905, Paschoal Segreto exhibited his own versions of the Hale's Tours in his Pavilhão Internacional. Called the *Estrada de ferro mundial* (Global railway), it promised to take spectators on "a voyage around the world in twenty-five minutes."

Segreto's *Global Railway* demonstrates connections between cinema and travel that scholars have highlighted as central to the early experience of film. Jeffrey Ruoff states that a sense of travel dominated the cinema from 1895 to 1905, becoming a

PAVILHÃO INTERNACIONAL

EX-PARIS NO RIO

EMPREZA PASCHOAL SEGRETO

Unico representante na *America do Sul e America Central das fitas da importante fabrica CINES de Roma.*

154, Avenida Central, 154

Ao lado da estação da Companhia Jardim Botanico — TELEPHONE N. 180

Operador *AMADEU SALA*

Sessões diarias, de 1 hóra da tarde á meia noite

Unico cinematographo que apresenta o quadro em tamanho natural

E SEM TREPIDAÇÃO

PROGRAMMA NOVO

1ª PARTE	3ª PARTE
AMOR E PATRIA	**A ORPHANSINHA**
Fita dramatica	Fita dramatica sensacional
2ª PARTE	4ª PARTE
Confissão por telephone	**O DEMANDISTA**
Fita comica	Fita comica

5ª. PARTE

(A pedido)

O piano Irresistivel

a Fita de maior successo cinematographico, verdadeira fabrica de gargalhadas.

ESTRADA DE FERRO MUNDIAL

Viagem á volta do mundo em 25 minutos, de Buenos Ayres ao Japão. Brilhante Panorama que obteve o primeiro premio na exposição Universal de Paris:

Preços: Adultos 1$000 — Creanças $500. — Para as duas diversões: cinematographo e estrada de ferro: adultos 1$500 creanças 1$000.

Illuminação feerica, elegancia, commodidade e conforto

BREVEMENTE GRANDES SURPREZAS

Inauguração de novos apparelhos e fitas de assumptos editados pela *Casa Cines de Roma*

N. B.—A empreza reserva-se o direito de alterar o programma em caso de força maior.

Alugam-se e Vendem-se Fitas

SORVETES ESPECIAES: PRAÇA TIRADENTES, 21

Esquina da Rua do Espirito Santo

E em todas as casas de diversões da Empreza

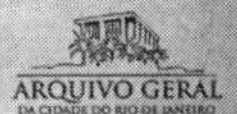

FIGURE 2. Paschoal Segreto's *Global Railway*, 1905. Acervo Arquivo Geral da Cidade do Rio de Janeiro.

common subject for films and an important object for representation.[26] Cinematic technology made images of distant places more readily available to spectators, reorganizing or condensing their experiences of time and space by allowing them to virtually travel to far-flung lands. In Brazil, the cinema's virtual journeys were inherently perceived to be global, and film was immediately highlighted and marketed as a medium that could transport spectators to places around the world. In 1904 Brazilian writer Olavo Bilac emphasized this aspect of the cinema, describing his first moviegoing experience as "a long journey" that in no time at all transported him to distant cities: Paris, London, and New York.[27] Going to the movies was consequently seen as a profoundly international experience, and to step into a movie theater in Rio was to be transported around the globe. This was often reinforced by the names of venues. With titles such as the Pavilhão Internacional and the Parisiense, the city's early exhibition halls reinforced the impression that cinema was a foreign product that could put Brazilians in contact with the world at large.

The cinema thus registered Brazil's insertion into the wider global landscape, epitomized by its ability to quickly and easily transport viewers to the center of modern metropoles. Film's appeal and its early reception in Brazil in this sense articulated and responded to the broader cultural landscape of material goods that placed Brazilians in immediate contact with foreign lifestyles, places, and customs. For Bilac and other Brazilian spectators, travel was not just an "object of representation" or the "most popular and developed subject" of film, it (in)formed the very matrix of a wider material and aesthetic experience, an experience of worldliness that temporarily connected here and there, Brazil and the rest of the world.[28] This passage was empirically linked to the Republic's new era and the worldwide expansion of commerce, as film arrived and developed within a new cultural landscape that was linked to the heights of imperialism in Europe and to the Brazilian belle epoque's worldliness.

NEW URBAN VISTAS

The cinema's sights of civilized European cities fed a fantasy that Brazil's new identity was "in progress," that the new nation was on its way to becoming part of the modern Western world. Indeed, if audiences in Rio were able to immediately see images of Paris and London, the same ones exhibited in these European capitals, then the belief that Brazilians (or at least Cariocans) inhabited a space in the "past" was harder to maintain. Yet as López states, as much as this fantasy was desired it "also created a profound ambivalence and source of anxiety," since "the cinema's complex images of distance and otherness problematized the meaning of locality and self."[29] While early cinematic images with their imported vistas enabled audiences to share in the experience of progress as produced elsewhere, audiences did so only by assuming the position of spectators, becoming voyeurs rather than participants. This produced a self-conscious form of spectatorship, an awareness of the image as image and of the act of looking.

This self-conscious form of spectatorship was produced by and generated a distance between the images of civilization on the screen and the Brazilian reality. As Paulo Emílio Salles Gomes has shown, during its first decade "the cinema vegetated, both as a commercial activity linked to the exhibition of imported films and as the production of local goods."[30] Movie shows were irregular in the city, and the production of domestic films was scarce. After 1906, however, cinematic activities (exhibition *and* production) began to flourish in Rio. Indeed, in 1907 writer João do Rio observed that "in every square there are movie theaters bringing together thousands of people."[31] Gomes attributes this proliferation of cinematic activity to the development of electricity.[32] The year 1906 saw the inauguration of the Riberão das Lajes reservoir on the outskirts of Rio, which provided the capital with electricity for, among other things, entertainment, fostering a vibrant film culture.

The development of electricity was part of a larger program of urban improvements implemented by the Republican regime that were intended to "modernize" the capital. Rio had been subject to minor urban transformations before the beginning of the Republic. With the start of the new regime, however, urban renewal was more urgently proposed as part of an attempt to project a progressive identity for Brazil and also to cater to the city's booming population. Following the start of Republican rule, Rio grew dramatically. From 1890 to 1906, the city's population rose an average of 3.8 percent per year, from 523,000 to 1,158,000. A significant portion of the population was made up of free-floating subjects, including European immigrants, former slaves and freedmen of the city, and recent arrivals from the Northeast, all in search of opportunities in the capital. As a result, many nationalities and languages, as well as many regional identities and cultural practices, filled the streets. The population growth paralleled the chaotic and inadequate expansion of the urban space. The extremely poor population was concentrated in large run-down houses dating from the beginning of the nineteenth century. Known as *cortiços*, these were located in Rio's center around the port. Whole families lived in rented, overcrowded tenements with no plumbing or other infrastructures and in precarious and degrading conditions.

The largely black, *mestiço*, and immigrant populations that inhabited the *cortiços* preserved elements of their past culture and connections to their symbolic roots. For the progressive elite, they represented an obstacle to Brazil's progress. Equally serious were threats to public health posed by the dense cohabitation of people in unsanitary conditions. Rio was the principal commercial port of the country; more than this, it was the capital and, as such, a showcase of the nation. With its pressing needs for capital and immigrant labor, the city was supposed to be an attraction to foreigners. However, it was subject to a series of epidemics

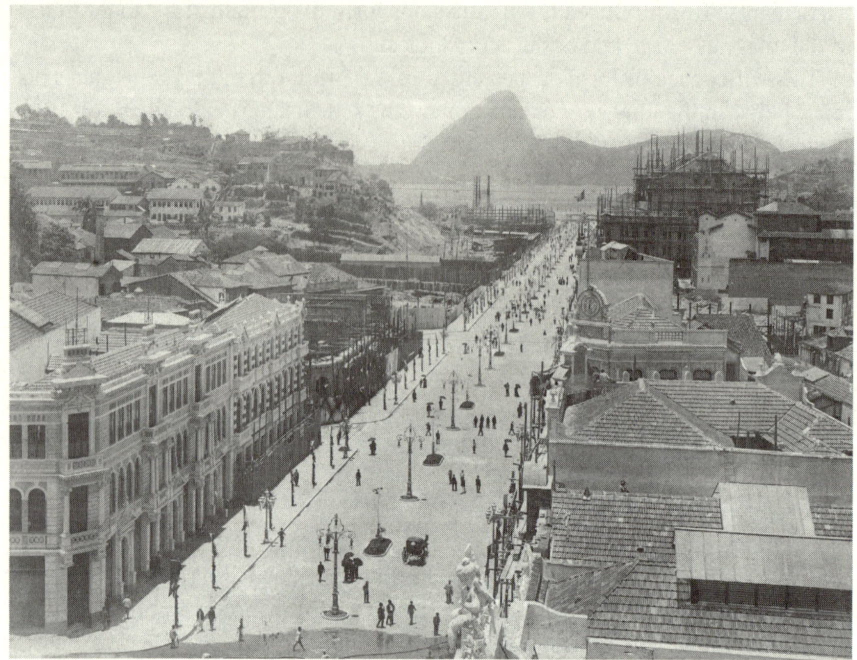

FIGURE 3. Rio's reforms, showing the Avenida Central, ca. 1904. Acervo da Fundação
Biblioteca Nacional—Brasil.

(plague, smallpox, yellow fever) that devastated its population and made it unattractive for foreigners.

Following the start of the Republic, the city map was redrawn and new plans were put in place to modernize Rio. The capital's colonial architecture and older structures were deemed out of date and its streets too narrow for the convenient transfer of imported goods from the port, restricting the expansion of foreign commerce that had become an important aspect of the capital's (and country's) identity.[33] The city center thus became a key target of Rio's reforms. Starting in 1902, the mayor, Francisco Pereira Passos, headed a large-scale effort to reconstruct it and to give Rio a new physiognomy. This involved a radical reconstruction of the city streets and the establishment of a sanitation process, headed by Oswaldo Cruz, to rid the city of epidemics that had made the capital an insalubrious place, especially for foreign visitors. Passos also contracted Lauro Müller as minister of transport and public works to renovate the port, extending and modernizing the dock area and linking it to different parts of the city, thereby facilitating the circulation of foreign goods. By 1904 Rio's new morphology was already visible. Colonial buildings were demolished, old streets were widened, parks were redesigned,

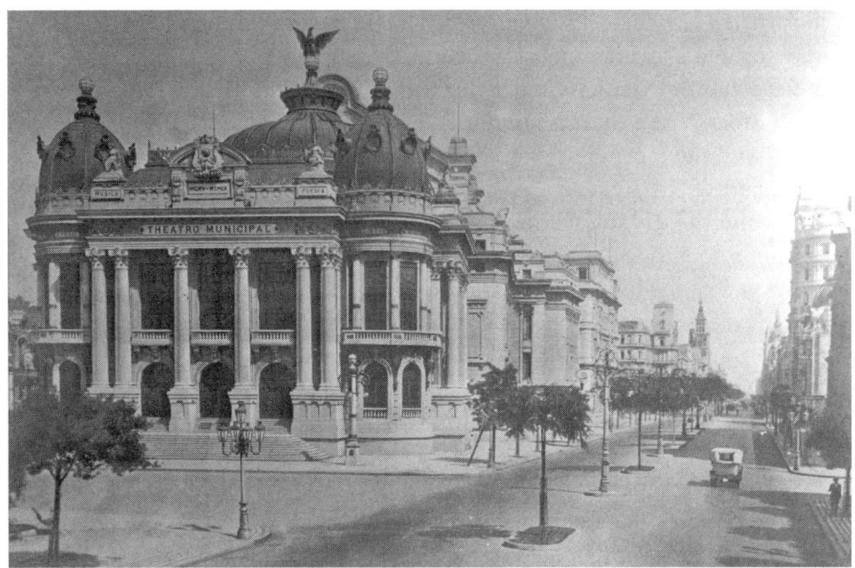

FIGURE 4. Rio de Janeiro's Municipal Theater, 1909. Acervo da Fundação Biblioteca Nacional—Brasil.

and new boulevards were constructed (figure 3). In 1906 the reformed capital was unveiled with much fanfare, in a grand inauguration ceremony that took place on November 15—the anniversary of the proclamation of the Republic. As Needell writes, Rio's reforms were clearly designed as a "monument" to the nation's new modern identity.[34]

The capital's new identity, however, was not born in Brazil. The blueprint for Rio's facelift was the redesign of Paris in the 1850s, known as Haussmannization, which transformed the French capital into what Walter Benjamin called "the capital of the nineteenth century." The Brazilian capital's sweeping boulevards and new gardens were all modeled on Paris.[35] New buildings—like the Palácio Monroe (1906) and the Teatro Municipal (1909)—also incorporated architectural structures and motifs of French Eclecticism, the consecrated expression of the École des Beaux Arts that was featured in Haussmann's Parisian reforms. Indeed, the municipal theater was modeled on Paris's opera house designed by the École's Charles Garnier (figure 4). Rio's patrimony from the French capital even included flora and fauna—with flowers and sparrows imported from Paris.[36]

Contrived by Napoleon III and his prefect Baron Georges-Eugène Haussmann, Paris's midcentury reforms intended to modernize the city's infrastructure. So the French capital became an ideal model for Brazil's new capital. Haussmann's city crystallized not just a modern but also a universal city, one that could be reconstructed anywhere. In Brazil, the transcendence of this urban space was tied to the Republic's broader global designs: the materiality of its built environment expressed the new nation's intent to belong to the modern (Western) world. Indeed, Broca relates the city's imported style to the broader culture of Rio's belle epoque, with the capital's new urban structure reflecting the worldliness that had become part of the city's life.[37]

The centerpiece of this worldly city was Central Avenue (renamed Avenida Rio Branco in 1912). The newly constructed boulevard traversed the capital from east to west, connecting different parts of the city to the port. The major thoroughfare was, as Sevcenko notes, "conceived as a concourse of façades providing the city with beaux arts décor, in ivory and crystal, combined with elegant lamps of modern electric illumination and lights from the windows of fine shops with imported goods."[38] Grand buildings like the Municipal Theater lined the avenue, making it what Needell refers to as Rio's "showcase for civilization."[39]

Needell's description of Rio's new center as a showcase highlights a visual element to its new design. This visuality is (unsurprisingly) similar to accounts of the French model in that, influenced by Benjamin's writings, scholars have stressed the spectacular qualities of Haussmann's Paris.[40] This visuality underpins the account of Rio's changes given by Brazilian sociologist Gilberto Freyre in his study *The Mansions and the Shanties,* where he describes the city's metamorphosis as involving a process of *desasombramento* or unshadowing.[41] Much like Clark's work on Paris, Freyre's study defines this "unshadowing" as inherent in Rio's new physical structures: grand boulevards replaced narrow alleyways, providing the city with a more legible geography and opening the city up to a visual gaze.

Rio's spectacularity was reinforced in a variety of contemporary cultural forms. Developments in the printing press around 1901, specifically the introduction of phototypy, made the reproduction of photographs and illustrations more widely available in Brazil. This led to an obsession with display in the press, which led to the proliferation of illustrated journals like *A Illustração Brasileira* (1900) and *Kosmos* (1904).[42] These magazines published extensive photographs of Rio's reforms, printing images of the capital's reconstruction and its buildings. In 1906 *Kosmos* even dedicated an entire issue to images of the new city, documenting each stage of the capital's reforms and thereby allowing readers to chart its progress. The same period also saw the proliferation of postcards that depicted new sites of the modernized capital (figure 5), as well as official photo albums, with photographs such as those by Augusto Malta and Marc Ferrez (reprinted here) that displayed Rio's new image. Images of the new city were also the prevalent subject of stereopticon slides, cards of twin photographs seen simultaneously through a special viewer to produce a three-dimensional appearance. In these images, the wide-angle views of near-empty spaces largely devoid of people made the new buildings and wide thoroughfares seem like imposing stage scenery. The images reproduced the city

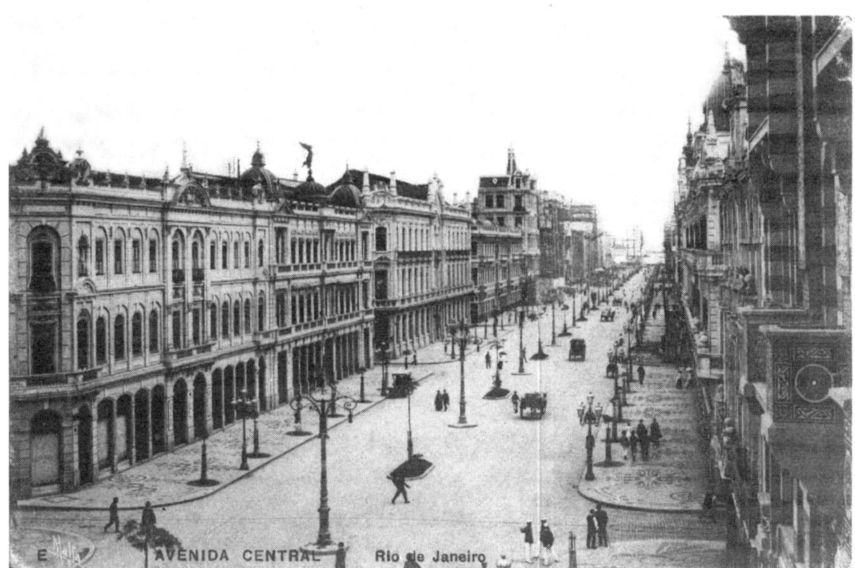

FIGURE 5. Postcard of Rio de Janeiro's new center, 1909. Author's personal collection.

as a set piece, designed to be exploited for visual pleasure. At the same time, the municipal government produced maps that carefully pinpointed the city's new sights, plotting magnificent buildings and monuments along its grand boulevards (figure 6). These visual depictions reinforced Rio's novel geography as a spectacle and a visual attraction—evoking it as an object "to-be-looked-at."

This visuality was not exclusively restricted to Rio's new buildings and avenues. It also focused on the city's population. With the capital's reforms, more people took to the streets to enjoy Rio's new sites and sights. One writer noted Cariocans' increased presence on boulevards, stating that "prior to the city's improvements, Rio was deserted. No one thought of going for walks along the dark and badly paved alleyways that were then called streets. Central Avenue was inaugurated and the streets Carioca, Seventh of September, Assambléia, and Uruguaiana were widened, and the population, which had previously been domestic and home-bound, flocked to these areas. . . . Rio scintillated, and Central Avenue took on the air of a Parisian boulevard, full of light and people."[43]

The press documented these urban adventures. Illustrated magazines published *instantâneos,* showing inhabitants promenading along modernized thoroughfares (figure 7). These photographs were imbued with a pedagogical quality, for they showed readers how to behave in the modern city, displaying the image of an ideal urban inhabitant. Individuals were eager to collaborate in the exhibition of the new life of (and in) the city. Magazines not only carried images of fashionable

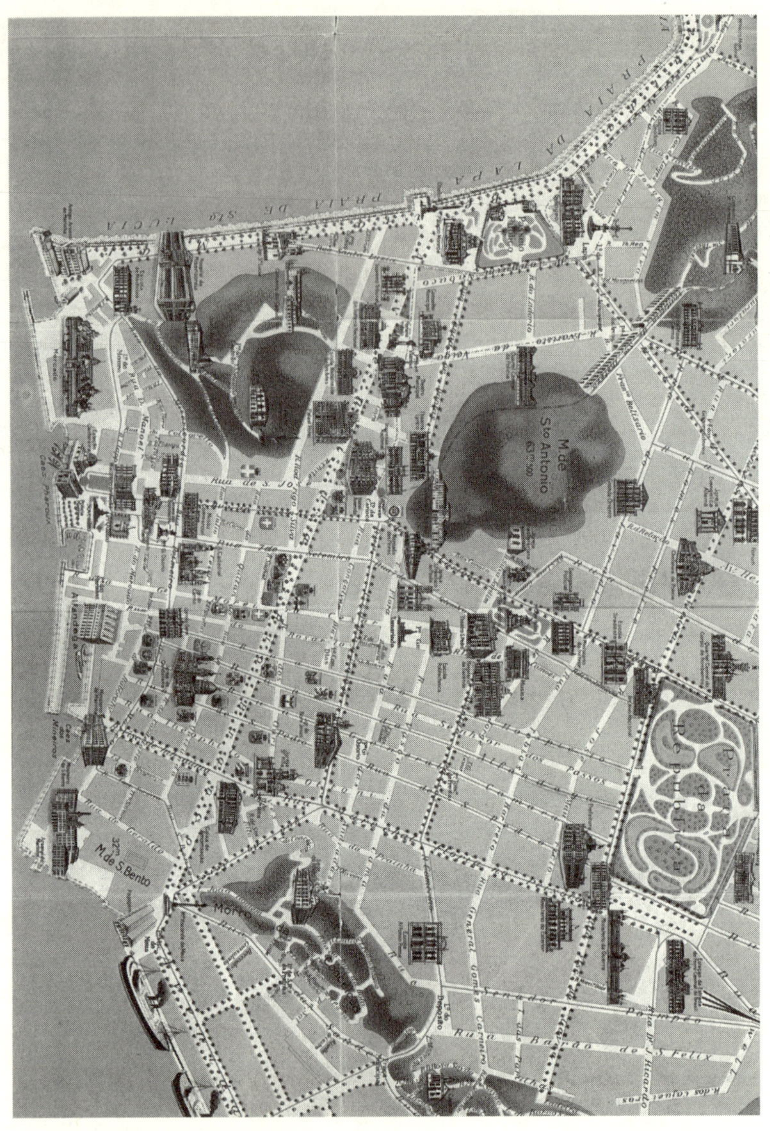

FIGURE 6. Map of Rio de Janeiro's new sites/sights, ca. 1909. British Library, London/ Bridgeman Images

INSTANTANEOS

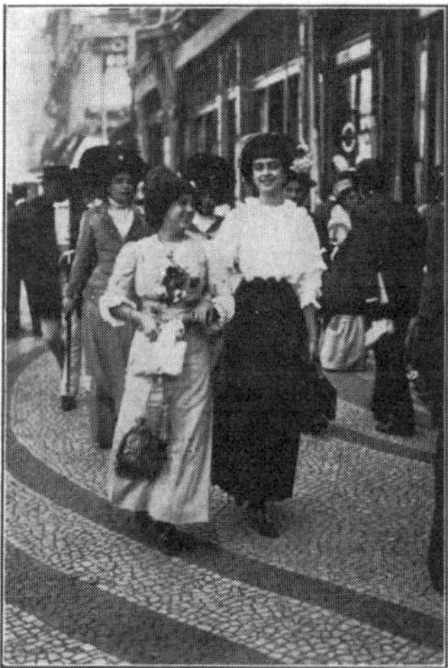

Fazendo Avenida

A REPUBLICA

MENTIRAS E FALSIDADES

O nosso laborioso confrade Ernesto Senna, com aquella positiva actividade a que deve o renascimento de meio bigode e metade da cabelleira, abysmou-se em pesquis historicas e agora, pelas austeras columnas do *Jornal do Commercio* está expondo á curiosidade publica e á colera do Sr. General Quintino Bocayuva, antigos documentos com os quaes pretende lançar luz sobre a individualidade do Marechal Deodoro da Fonseca e a proclamação da Republica.

Desejando auxiliar o illustre consul da Venezuela, que com tanto carinho estuda os pontos controversos da nossa historia, como si da sua fossem, emprehendemos uma série de indagações que nos levam a contestar, de modo formal, a authenticidade dos documentos publicados e a realidade do facto principal a que elles se relacionam.

Segundo a cathegorica affirmação do coronel consul, aos 15 de Novembro de 1889 o Marechal Deodoro da Fonseca proclamou a Republica no Brasil.

Essa affirmação é insustestavel. Não pomos em duvida a existencia, naquelle anno, de um Marechal Deodoro da Fonseca porém negamos que haja praticado a façanha que lhe attribuem.

Consultando os *a pedidos* do *Jornal do Commercio*, as collecções do *Correio da Manhã*, do *Diario de No-*

ticias e as de todos os jornaes que têm circulado no Rio de Janeiro depois de 15 de Novembro de 1889 encontramos a cada passo, estas affirmações :

— a republica é um mytho, a republica é uma falsidade ; a camara dos deputados é uma illusão. Jamais essas affirmações receberam contestação e, consequentemente subsistem, e se ellas subsistem e o orgão da soberania popular é uma illusão e a republica é um mytho — não existe, e não estamos em republica.

Além desses argumentos, que o digno representante da Venezuela não será capaz de destruir, temos os factos recentes : mortes por insolação de arcabuz e congeneres incompativeis com o espirito liberal da ordem republicana.

Ora si a republica não existe, como irrefutavelmente acabamos de demonstrar, não podia ter sido proclamada, como entende o Sr. consul venezuelano, que de forma tão desastrada está emprestando um caracter de realidade historica ás lendas do nosso paiz.

Os nossos creados

— Maria aquelle guarda-civil que você disse-me ser seu noivo, parece que bebe um pouco de mais ; hontem quando sahimos do theatro vimol-o abraçado a um poste. De certo estava na chuva.

— Oh ! patroa, não diga isso. Elle só bebe agua. Elle costuma fazer isso quando pensa em mim.

O Sr. Carlos Porto Carreiro pedio ao Sr. Edmond Rostand para concorrer á Academia Brasileira com as obras que lhe deram entrada na Franceza.

INSTANTANEOS

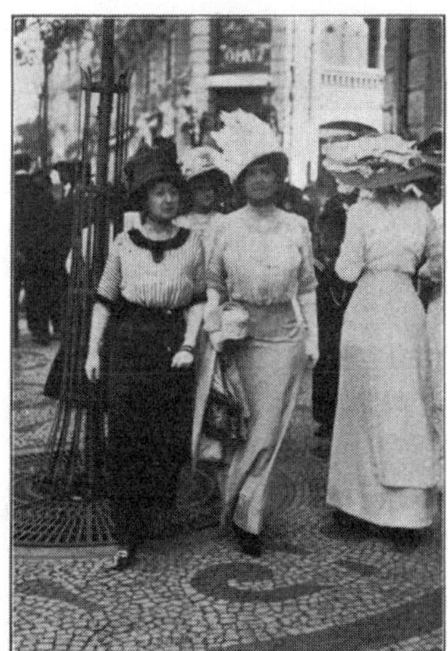

Na Avenida Central

FIGURE 7. *Instantâneos*, 1911. Author's personal collection.

urbanites but also printed announcements telling people to take to specific avenues on a particular day at a particular time in order to be captured "unawares" by their photographers. The *instantâneos* thus took on the Republic's spectacular identity, with individuals themselves simulating scenes of a new civilized urbanity.

Film rapidly became part of this spectacular city in a number of ways. Following its inauguration in 1906, exhibitors migrated from the older Ouvidor Street to Central Avenue, and at least twenty movie theaters opened on the new boulevard in that year, making way for a cinema district later called Cinelândia.[44] The new global center quickly became a cinematic hub, with many of its grand buildings housing specially built movie theaters. These new theaters catered to a new urban public who were out to enjoy the city's attractions. They also spelled an end to the irregular exhibition practices that had previously characterized cinematic activities, and, aided by the development of electricity, they allowed for stable film practices.

Just as the cinema came to be implanted in the renovated city, filmmakers began playing a part in projecting the capital's modern identity. Prior to Rio's reforms, filmmakers in Brazil had focused on what Gomes calls "Brazil's splendid cradle," its "natural splendors, notably those in the capital." They filmed the tropical settings that had commonly been used to iconographically represent the capital—like Sugar Loaf Mountain, Corcovado, and Guanabara Bay.[45] In 1898, for instance, Affonso Segreto filmed Rio's Guanabara Bay in what is credited as the first movie made on Brazilian soil. Following the reconstruction of Rio, however, films rarely focused on such exotic landscapes. Tropical visions gave way to urban locations as filmmakers turned their cameras toward the city's new boulevards. Consequentially, Rio's changes became a popular subject for filmmakers. Films like *Melhoramentos do Rio de Janeiro* (Improvements of Rio; n. dir., 1906) and *Erradicação da febre amarela no Rio de Janeiro* (Eradication of yellow fever in Rio de Janeiro; n. dir., 1909), charted the city's development, while others, like *O corso de Botafogo* (Promenade in Botafogo; n. dir., 1908) and *A Avenida Central* (Avenida Central; n. dir., 1910), displayed Rio's civilized inhabitants, drawing on the scenes of modern urban life popularized by the *instantâneos*.

Gomes suggests that there were practical reasons as to why filmmakers focused on Rio's newer areas: older streets were, he says, "narrow and too dark to be used for filming, which required natural light."[46] It was as if the modern invention of the movie camera was suited only for registering Rio's new identity, at once reinforcing film's affinity with the new space. The movie camera was thus thoroughly aligned with the project to reconstruct Rio as a modern, civilized city. This association of film with the new city had major effects on the content of the cinema in Brazil. Old places and customs were deemed unsuitable for films and were excluded from the modern and civilized identity to be projected to spectators.

This exclusion underlay Rio's urban design, literally and symbolically. The capital's reforms involved the demolition of 590 buildings in the center, whose inhabitants, mainly black people and former slaves as well as immigrant workers, were displaced, fleeing to the *favelas* in the surrounding hills. Reforms also included the destruction of the São Bento and Castelo hills, since these natural features were seen as an obstacles to constructing a modern space. The city's new built space significantly lacked any traces of Brazil's past—particularly its rural and slaveholding past. From the statues ornamenting buildings to the flora and fauna of the city, the capital was devoid of features specific to the country. The new and spectacular city thus canceled out any links with the past, situating itself instead in "a universal empty time." This absence was matched by strict urban policies that, as Sevcenko notes, were based on four strategies: "the condemnation of habits and customs tied to the memory of a traditional society; the negation of each and every element of popular culture that could disrupt the civilized image of dominant society; a rigorous policy of the expulsion of popular groups from the center of the city, which was practically isolated for the exclusive enjoyment of the bourgeoisie; and an aggressive cosmopolitanism that was profoundly identified with Paris."[47] Popular customs and festivities connected to the memory of the past came under attack from the state as part of an attempt to maintain Rio's modern image. *Capoeira, umbanda,* and *candomblé,* practices peculiar to Rio's black community, were banned, and the marginal classes were outlawed from the center, which became reserved exclusively for the use of the elite. Rio's sweeping boulevards were policed for "uncivilized" vagrants so that the city's public space would be limited to those who conformed to its new civilized image. It was at this historical moment that the opposition of civilization versus barbarism became not just "the cornerstone of intellectual debate" but also the very foundations of urban space, giving rise to social and spatial segregation and producing what Zuenir Ventura calls "the divided city."[48]

While Rio's reforms were, as Needell stresses, symbolic, they also had a political intention. The capital's regeneration made what Rama calls "the dream of an ideal ordered city" a reality.[49] Rio was the vision of a modern worldly city, but at the same time it embodied a spatial division and social order that maintained the privileges of the old elite and marginalized the poor. The capital's new civilized space was thus configured in accordance with a vision of an order that reflected an enduring social hierarchy. The new city was the domain of the fashionable bourgeoisie, and the popular classes were banished to the margins and peripheral areas. The cinema participated in this order. With theaters located in the new center, moviegoing became an elite activity and cultural form. Filmmakers visualized and portrayed a spectacular urban space, playing their part in forging the social configurations of the ideal city. If elsewhere the myth or discourse of film's universalism had developed class-specific connotations, the idea that the cinema was the theater of democracy catering to all classes did not take hold in Brazil, where slavery had only recently been abolished and traditional hierarchies and social and spatial divisions were still very much in place.[50]

The political aims of this new ideal city were intertwined with quite practical aims: specifically the attempt to attract overseas (European) credit and commerce as well a new (white) international workforce.[51] In 1904 one writer pointed out the capital's necessary role in impressing European capitalists and immigrants: "The foreigner who disembarks here brings from his brief visit to our impoverished city a sad idea of all of our country. . . . To attempt to turn Rio de Janeiro into a modern comfortable and civilized city, then, is an undeniable and immediate necessity in our economic plight."[52] Rio's spectacular redesign was therefore partly intended to "attract" foreign interest. Here the city's visuality, in its design and its objectification in cultural forms, can be read as an attempt to turn the capital into a material and marketable commodity for foreign interests and ultimately for an external gaze. Indeed, the forms used to depict Rio—maps, postcards, stereoscopes, photo albums, and films—were able and intended to circulate not just nationally but also internationally. This desire to attract European investors threateningly suggested an interest in being recolonized—not by a second-class metropolis, as Portugal was then perceived, but by a first-class European empire, such as France or Great Britain.

As noted, Rio's attraction was not expressed in terms of an exotic otherness, of a prodigious landscape waiting to be exploited, but in terms of a modernity equal to that of any other global metropolis. By subduing its prodigious tropical nature to a more civilized order, Rio was to be converted into a material object, a commodity. This strategy of propaganda was clearly aimed at foreign investors and immigrants who might otherwise shy away from "exoticism" and "tropicalism"— from difference. Despite the ornamental or, to use Roberto Schwarz's words, "out-of-place" qualities of this strategy, it can actually be considered successful. European immigrants arrived and foreign investment soared: Britain's investments in Brazil rose from £37,407,300 between the period 1863 and 1888 to a staggering £112,774,433 between 1889 and 1914. Immigration also increased greatly. In 1890 alone Rio received 106,819 immigrants, whereas immigration into the city in the entire period between 1870 and 1880 had amounted only to 30,000.[53] Needell points out that the "foreign commercial and infrastructural firms" also multiplied in Rio after the reforms and that most of them were significantly located in the new center.[54] This suggests that the urban image projected was actually mirrored by the people and investment it conjured up and not vice versa. It was representation that created the referent, not the other way round. The movie camera was clearly deemed important in this representation—both as a means of narcissistically projecting Rio's new, modern identity to its own urban citizens and of fetishistically displaying it for "others."

Early film practices in Brazil were therefore inextricably linked, materially, symbolically, and politically, to Rio and its dramatic transformation during the Republican period of the belle epoque. The imported medium was from its beginnings part of the city's worldliness, which imported images of far-flung cities only helped to reinforce. This worldliness was more fully concretized in Rio's radical makeover, which projected the Republic's modern global imaginary. Films, like other forms of visual media produced and distributed at the time, registered and projected the capital's new space, helping people to see in and believe in the Republic's urban ideal. The cinema thus played a part in laying the foundations of Brazil's capital of the twentieth century, helping to disseminate its new civilized image for fashionable inhabitants at home and prospective visitors and investors abroad.

3

Alternative Urban Projections in Early Narrative Films

While Rio's reforms projected a new progressive identity, this was far from straight-forward, and the capital's civilized image soon developed ambiguous contours. The belief in progress and the attendant condemnation of the past ironically placed the city's traditional elite in a tenuous position. Furthermore, a new financial and investment culture led to a "get-rich-quick" ethos, and Rio became what Sevcenko calls "a city of upstarts".[1] These upstarts were joined by a new generation of entre-preneurs (including immigrants) who began to forge a new bourgeoisie. Their commercial success depended on maximizing profits, which involved reaching out to a larger public. Previously clear boundaries thus began to blur, and the city's traditional spatial and social divisions were renegotiated. These negotiations fig-ured in the cinema as exhibitors and filmmakers attempted to reap the profits of film as a popular form of entertainment, challenging the medium's exclusive status. While displaying the worldly ambitions of the elite, cinema began to incorporate popular cultural forms, producing an urban film culture that charted ambiguous trajectories between the official and unofficial spaces of the modern urban ideal.

The desire to cater to a broader audience resulted in new exhibition strategies. Adopting practices from the theater, exhibitors began to offer different entrance prices, classified as first- and second-class tickets. Those with first-class tickets were given the best seats in the house, while those with second-class tickets were seated in the nosebleed sections of the movie theater. First-class ticket holders were entitled not only to prime seats within the auditorium but also to pre- and postshow entertainment, which included classical music and refreshments served in elegant *salas de espera,* or waiting rooms. Access to waiting rooms meant that first-class ticket holders avoided standing in line outside the movie theater in the heat and sun with second-class ticket holders. Such ticketing practices led to seg-regation inside and outside the cinema that mirrored the city's own social and spatial divisions. Yet they were crucially a means by which exhibitors could attract a wider audience and reap the economic benefits of cinema's broader appeal. Con-sequently films and film culture started to incorporate the popular tastes of a larger public.

While filmmakers were documenting Rio's modern identity, Brazilian specta-tors were becoming used to new films imported from Europe and the United States, which Gunning refers to as "transitional narratives" to highlight their status in between the cinema of attractions and a more narrative cinema, and had begun to experience a new kind of cinematic identification.[2] North American and Euro-pean filmmakers experimented with storytelling techniques, combining elements of the cinema of attractions with new narrative approaches by mixing real-life scenic elements with well-known stories. In Brazil, filmmakers started to blend urban vistas with well-known popular cultural forms to produce their own transi-tional narratives. The 1909 film *Nas entranhas do morro do castelo* (In the belly of Castelo Hill; dir. Antonio Leal) mixed fact with fiction, detailing the myth of hid-den treasures found during excavations for Rio's reconstruction. Such legends were hugely popular at the time, and in 1905 they formed the basis of a series of *crônicas*, or journalistic essays, written by Lima Barreto, that were published in the newspaper *Correio da Manhã*. The 1908 film *O comprador de ratos* (The rat buyer; dir. Antonio Leal) was also linked to the reconstruction of Rio, specifically to the project to sanitize the city. During the campaign to eradicate yellow fever in Rio, the government announced that it would buy dead rats by the pound. The inhabit-ants of the city's poor neighborhoods found themselves in the midst of a thriving industry, breeding rats to sell to the government. *The Rat Buyer* tells the story of a Niterói native who attempted to sell thousands of rodents until the scam was dis-covered.[3] Writer João do Rio describes this urban con in his collection of essays *A alma encantadora das ruas* (The enchanted soul of the streets); he also mentions how the trick became the subject of a popular song, "The Rat Buyer," that was quite likely featured in the repertoire of the film's screening. These new narrative films, along with the cultural forms they drew upon, incorporated emerging urban or "spatial practices," through which marginalized classes negotiated their own "transition" to the new city.[4]

These transitional narratives are perhaps best exemplified by the development of urban film comedies that began to experiment with more of a narrative line—a diegesis, an event, and character motivation. The 1908 film *Nhô Anastácio chegou de viagem* (Mr. Anastácio has arrived on a trip; dir. Júlio Ferrez), for example, nar-rates the misadventures of a country bumpkin or *matuto*, Mr. Anastácio (played by well-known comedic actor José Leonardo Gonçalves), who is newly arrived in Rio. The film traces his urban adventures, including his first reactions to awe-inspiring sights like the grand buildings that line Central Avenue. Incorporating novel techniques of continuity editing, the film links together disparate locales in fashionable Rio as it follows the *matuto*'s experiences in the capital. In this way *Mr. Anastácio* is tantamount to a travelogue, displaying the city's new attractions in a way that cinematically translates contemporary visual forms such as the postcards, photographs, and monumental maps of such sites. While these other visual representations of Rio were largely devoid of individuals, the urban comedies place a newcomer to the capital at the heart of the film. In fact, the comedy of *Mr. Anastácio* centers on a rural protagonist's experience of the new city, registering the naive and socially backward rustic's unfamiliarity with its worldly space. A symbol of Brazil's rural life, the *matuto* contrasts with more civilized urbanites, the kind that appeared in the fashionable *instantâneos*.

Other urban comedies of the time also focused on the adventures or misadventures of naive rustics in the modern capital. The 1908 film *As aventuras de Zé* (The Adventures of Zé; n. dir., 1908) depicted the activities of an out-of-towner in Rio; and *Paz e amor* (Peace and love; dir. Alberto Botelho), made in 1909, portrayed the urban escapades of a *matuto* called Tibúrcio d'Annunciação. The comedy of these films arises from the tension between the traditional rural customs of the characters and their attempts to decipher the modern spaces and practices of Rio, with its Europeanized ways. This tension reflects the city-countryside dialectic that was a trope in Brazilian culture of the time, in particular the *teatro de revista*.

Brazil's homegrown version of the vaudeville tradition, the *teatro de revista*, took shape in the late 1800s and became particularly popular in the early years of the Republic. The *revistas* relied heavily on circus humor, sociopolitical critique, and especially music, featuring an eclectic array of both imported and homegrown styles, including US fox trots and shimmies, Portuguese *fados*, Argentine tangos, Afro-Brazilian rhythms (*maxixes, lundus*), regional northeastern music, and the light classical work of Carlos Gomes.[5] Thiago Gomes de Melo writes that this heterogeneity made the plays highly polysemic, meaning that they were able to appeal to a wide audience with diverse cultural tastes and backgrounds.[6] At the heart of the play's heterogeneity was Rio. Flora Süssekind observes that the capital was a central protagonist for the plays, which, she suggests, contributed to the "invention" of the new city. It was on the popular stage that Rio's transformations were enacted and celebrated for spectators. Plays showcased the spectacularity of the capital's modernity, making audiences visualize and share in its modern ideal. As Süssekind writes, "The theatrical reviews are concerned, above all, with inventing Rio and exhibiting its details to a hybrid audience, composed of astonished urban inhabitants and amazed spectators. The short and constantly changing scenes and humorous musical numbers allowed audiences to relive the city's radical changes and believe in its utopia."[7] The *revistas* effectively staged and helped make sense of the disorienting changes of Rio's makeover, performing a kind of mediatory pedagogy between the reality of the city and its imaginary place in the individual's mental life. Rio's trans-formations, then, shaped the *revistas'* formal and thematic composition. Initially known as *revistas-do-fim-do-ano,* literally end-of-year revues, the plays condensed the transitions that had taken place in the city during the year, providing audiences with a panoramic overview of the capital's changing landscape.

With their widespread survey, the *revistas* shared a cultural trajectory with the panorama painting, which likewise summed up a city's vast geography. The pano-rama was a 360-degree painting that was illuminated and viewed by audiences in complete darkness in a specially designed circular building. These paintings were hugely successful in Europe throughout the eighteenth and early nineteenth cen-turies. Panoramic paintings found in Brazil favorable conditions for their produc-tion toward the end of the nineteenth century when they were popularized by Víctor Meirelles (1832–1903). During the first years of the Republic, Meirelles exhibited a number of panoramas that offered images of Rio. Many of the paint-ings took events in the city as their subject matter; an example is *Entrada da esquadra legal* (Entrance of the legal squadron), exhibited in Rio on June 23, 1894. In such paintings the depiction of real contemporary events amounted to a visual reenactment of the newspaper, giving sociopolitical events imagistic verisimili-tude. Meirelles's most successful panoramas, however, were aerial views of the capital, depicted, for instance, in *Panorama da cidade do Rio de Janeiro* (Panorama of the city of Rio de Janeiro). This particular painting was a critical success at home and in Europe, where it was shown at the World's Fair in Paris in 1889.[8]

The *teatro de revista,* like Meirelles's work, turned a panoramic gaze on city life and captured the disorienting changes that were occurring in urban space. But while Meirelles's paintings presented a static and panoptic view from a celestial vantage point, the vaudeville plays portrayed an alternative view that was more immediate and intimate. The revues focused on everyday experiences of the city— people and places, customs, fashions, and speech—with a remarkable attention to detail that performed a rhetorical strategy related to what Roland Barthes calls the "effect of the real."[9] They thus made the worldly capital more intelligible and famil-iar, helping to inculcate in spectators the reality of Rio's new configuration.

By 1906, the *revista* plays had virtually disappeared from Rio's theaters. Previ-ously renowned playwrights found it increasingly difficult to stage them; searching for new spaces of reception, they turned to other media, such as newspapers, mag-azines, and film.[10] Historians have highlighted how the new *filmes de revista* drew on a variety culture that they inherited from the stage, relying on a combination of circus gags, saucy humor, musical numbers, and sociopolitical critique.[11] In both the movies and their theatrical intertexts this variety format centered on one sub-ject, the invention of Rio, figured in terms of the dialectic between city and country.

That this city-country dialectic featured in Rio's cultural production is not sur-prising. Between 1890 and 1900 the capital's population had increased by a third, thanks largely to the arrival of rural migrants. In 1900, 25 percent of Rio's population came from rural areas, predominantly in the Northeast. Abolition and a series of droughts led to an enormous wave of migration to Rio during these years (roughly 85,547), as people ventured to the capital in search of work and opportunities.[12] These migrants were crucial to the reception and development of a new urban popular culture, and they became central to an emerging film spectatorship. Filmmakers keen to cater to a broader public began to integrate their experiences narratively and through extratextual practices that became intrinsic to the exhibition of the revue films. Popular stage actors performed live during musical interludes, singing traditional songs from the country's Northeast. Such practices meant that filmgoing was an interactive experience, drawing upon spectators' foreknowledge of narrative conventions and cultural forms, as well as encouraging their participation in musical performances. Audiences were therefore conceived as a productive force of the cinematic *revistas,* crucial to supplying the films with an interpretive dimension. Consequentially, the cinema became an important social space for the city's migrants, providing them with characters, situations, and cultural forms they could identify with and recognize, while also allowing them the vicarious pleasure of laughing at the *matuto*'s out-of-place ways in the new urban context. The *filmes de revista* thus helped individual spectators negotiate their own passage from the country to the city, from their rural past to their urban futures. Offering a new social horizon for their own transitions to the city, they initiated them into the worldly space of Rio, turning them into modern urban subjects.

For López these transitional films rendered through comedy were a function of an attempt "to produce the discursive triumph of positivism" that was prevalent in Republican Brazil and in the foundations of Rio. In them, she says, "The traditional/rural is figured as nostalgically obsolete, a cultural remnant willed into history, while the modernity of the city is presented as natural, inevitable and national."[13] But although these comedies intersect with positivist discourses that underlay the capital's progressive identity, the association is far from straightforward, as the films and their screening provided metaphorical challenges to the new urban ideal. Significantly these "complicit" films counted on audience participation that incorporated "outlawed" cultural forms—particularly songs—offering a nostalgic potpourri of an older folk culture as eclectic as anything in the *teatro de revista.* Comics, clowns, and circus acrobats who were well known from the *circo-teatro* and were extremely popular in the Northeast were also the star-performers of these films and brought with them an irreverent knockabout humor. Indeed, *Mr. Anastácio* and *Peace and Love* exploited the reputation of the famous northeastern clowns José Goncalves Leonardo and Antônio Cataldi, who recreated familiar theatrical gags on and off screen. The cinema in this way allowed for a public recognition of the rural past in the new city at a time when present society emphasized and demanded the opposite. The *filmes de revista* thus forged a complex space of reception and spectatorship that drew on popular experiences and traditional cultural forms as well as the modern space of the city. Spectatorship oscillated between the past and future, between specific memories and new ambitions, between a worldly form of urban subjectivity and a cinema that relied on the shared social space of the theater and cultural legacies. In this respect, it forged what Miriam Hansen calls "an alternative public sphere," one that embraces a position of marginality that is inevitably constructed by dominant forces and emerges not in opposition to them but because of and in spite of them.[14]

The *filmes de revista*, then, catered to audiences who were otherwise excluded from the new city, allowing them to bring their own cultural traditions, needs, and configurations of experience to screenings. The films offered these new urban inhabitants the means by which their older cultural forms could crystallize and respond to the new narrative of progress and could articulate individual dreams and anxieties of the modern city in a communal setting. By virtue of their intertextuality and their dependence on the actual site of exhibition, the *filmes de revista* often contested official discourses of progress and modernity or at least interpreted them in alternative ways. These "alternative" strategies were not new or exclusive to films; indeed, in this regard filmmakers practiced what Antonio Candido calls the dialectic of *malandragem* or trickery, a Brazilian cultural ethos through which the marginalized use dominant discourses and ideologies for their own advantage. In *malandragem,* the marginalized do not just "make do"; they manipulate and divert official discourse, showing what Candido calls the "disorder of order."[15] This subversive tactic was central to the film revues' narrative. In the movies, as in the plays, the *matuto* figured not just as a comic outsider to Rio's modernized city but also as its foil, often showing up the superficiality of its spectacular identity as well as that of its worldly inhabitants. The films *Mr. Anastácio* and *Peace and Love,* for instance, document the *matuto's* encounter with modern Rio and its fashionable inhabitants, particularly its Europeanized social and political elite. In these films the country bumpkin is not simply the subject of humor; his naïveté also exposes the affected nature of the elite's new civilized identity. In contrast to their worldly pretentions, the *matuto* is often invested with integrity and emerges as the protector of a Brazilian moral code and national culture. The city-country dialectic thus crystallizes a conflict between the *matuto's* rural ways and the urban modernity of Rio's upper classes. Excessive performative gestures are part of this conflict. The *matuto* adopts the clothes of a tramp and deploys sharp and irreverent humor and everyday language drawn from the Northeast, contrasting greatly to the Europeanized customs of the civilized elite. The excesses of the *matuto* refuse to be contained within the new order of the Republic's urban ideal and instead highlight its superficialities or out-of-placedness.

The *matuto* is not the only character of the urban films. Far from focusing only on the rural protagonist, these comedies caricatured people familiar to audiences, particularly the political elite involved in implementing and promoting Rio's new identity. By 1906 snapshot caricatures had become a staple of Brazil's illustrated press, in which politicians and other official figures were reduced to comical two-dimensional characters that quickly and visually condensed contemporary political matters for a reading public. The period saw the proliferation of illustrated political satirical publications like *Careta* (figure 8). These magazines featured stories of political developments in Brazil, accompanied by colorful caricatures of politicians. The *filmes de revista* drew on these satirical journals. Many of their writers were involved in contemporary film production. They were early screenwriters who penned narratives for cinematic revues. The publications' caricaturists like Belmonte and J. Carlos were also active in Rio's cinematic world, contributing backdrops to movies, in particular the cinematic *revistas*.[16] Consequently, many of the *filmes de revista* incorporated stories featured in the satirical magazines and included the magazines' well-known caricatures of political figures. The film *Peace and Love,* for instance, explicitly included politicians who had been caricatured in the journal *Careta,* including Brazil's president, Nilo Peçanha. Peçanha was, in fact, crucial to the film's meaning and reception: *Peace and Love* depicted King Olin, a veiled anagram of the president's first name, and the title referred to his inaugural address in which he stated that he would rule with "peace and love." Drawing on the president's caricature in *Careta* as an incompetent leader, the film satirized Peçanha's/Olin's modern nation/kingdom, reducing the Republic to a two-dimensional fantasy space. According to the film's premise, the new regime is a joke, and politicians and their policies are ineffectual.

Brazil's political figures were no strangers to film. Gomes notes the preponderance of movies made during the early period that featured politicians and projected what he terms "a ritual of power" that centered on the figure of the president. He observes, "From Brazil's first civil president to the last military president, Brazilian cinema during the First Republic did not let any of them get away. Prudente de Moraes, Rodrigues Alves, Campos Salles, Afonso Pena, Nilo Peçanha, Hermes da Fonseca; they were all filmed, presiding over and inaugurating events, visiting and welcoming people, and eventually being buried."[17] Movies such as *O Palácio do Catete* (Catete Palace; n. dir, 1900), *Embarque do General Hermes da Fonseca para a Alemanha* (Hermes de Fonseca's departure for Germany; n. dir., 1908) and *Visita do Conselheiro Rui Barbosa à faculdade de direito* (Counselor Rui Barbosa's visit to the law school; n. dir., 1909) captured Brazil's men of power performing their executive duties and projecting what Jens Andermann terms the "optic of the state." The *filmes de revista* drew upon and parodied such portraits. Keying into the satirical press, movies like *Peace and Love* presented alternative visions of the country's political elite, displaying their modern projects as illusory.

The *filmes de revista*'s engagement with politics was thus a dialogue with the satirical press. In fact, the film *Peace and Love* was based on a weekly feature writ-

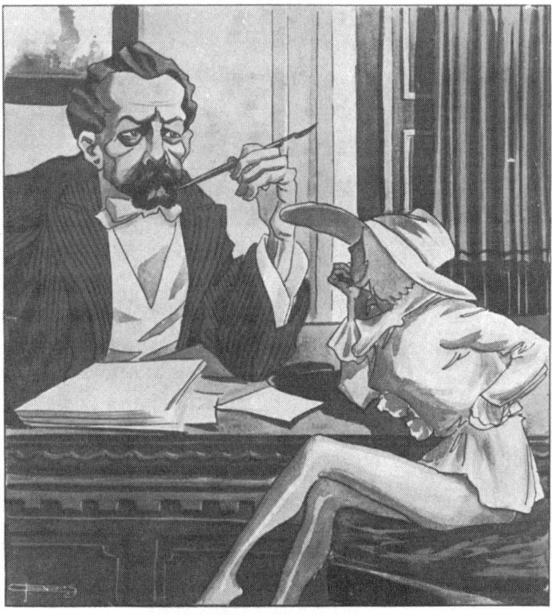

FIGURE 8. Cover of satirical magazine, *Careta*, 1911. Author's personal collection.

ten by José do Patrocínio Filho called "Cartas de um matuto" (Letters from a country bumpkin) that appeared in *Careta* in 1909. The feature is penned by the fictitious Tibúrcio, who writes letters home to his sister in the Northeast, relating his adventures in Rio and detailing his incomprehension with what emerges as a superficial city. Coherence of the film would have depended on audiences' knowledge and familiarity with Tibúrcio, and the movie can be read as an adaptation of these published satires—an offshoot of a cultural practice popular at the time called the *jornal falado,* literally the "spoken press," in which newspaper features were presented live on stage for illiterate or semiliterate audiences in ways that drew upon traditional collective patterns of reception.[18]

With the *filmes de revista,* therefore, the cinema simultaneously projected urban life and drew on past cultural forms, in terms of both production and reception. In doing so, it articulated forms of subjectivity and spaces different from those of the modern ideal spectacularly displayed at the time. Grafting onto older cultural forms for their subject matter, modes of representation, and exhibition, the intertexual *filmes de revista* were an unstable and ambiguous mixture that created conditions for alternative cinema and an alternative modernity in Rio.

OTHER WORLDS, OTHER SPACES: CINEMA AND IMMIGRANT LIFE

The appearance of political satirical magazines like *Careta* testifies to a growing politicization of popular culture at this time. Francisco Foot Hardman relates this to the development of a new urban public, composed not only of rural migrants but also of members of a new international workforce.[19] Immigration to Brazil intensified following the start of the Republic. In 1890 Brazil received 106,819 international migrants compared to the 30,000 who had entered the country from 1870 to 1880.[20] Their arrival was linked to the Republic's modernizing project. Rio's reforms symbolized a broader political transformation that would serve as testimony of the country's transition from an economy based on slave labor to a modern economy based on free labor. This transition provided the practical impetus for an immigration policy that intended to introduce a new European workforce into Brazil. Beginning in the 1880s, Republican leaders emphasized the need to expand the country's working population. This expansion involved more than a quantitative process; it meant bringing in people of "better" quality, Europe's civilized races, who were seen as possessing the modern habits of progress and industry, something that Brazil's former African slaves were not regarded as having. Immigration committees like Rio's Sociedade Central de Imigração (Central Society for Immigration) were founded following the advent of Republicanism. In cooperation with the government they embarked on a program to distribute brochures abroad, advertising steady work and assisted passage for anyone willing to emigrate to Brazil.[21] The country's insertion into the global capitalist market therefore not only stimulated the influx of worldly goods into the country but also fostered the flow of foreigners into Brazil and its cities. Indeed, by 1890, 30 percent of Rio's population had been born in Europe.[22]

Europeans were immediately preferred to an indigenous workforce. Whereas blacks had previously been used for manual labor, following abolition "they were considered unfit to respond to new and modern work practices."[23] Factories and manufacturing industries in particular overwhelmingly employed European immigrants. By 1920 they constituted more than half of the labor force in Brazil's manufacturing industry, with the majority employed in textile companies concentrated in major cities, like Rio, where 82 percent of the city's textile workers were foreign.[24]

This new workforce altered the demographic composition of the capital. It also influenced the cultural landscape. Immigrants played a crucial role in the development of mass cultural forms, including film. Indeed, the overwhelming majority of people involved in film at this time—actors, owners of movie theaters, filmmakers, and distributors—were first-generation immigrants. They had contacts with other filmmakers or distributors in Europe and the United States and were thus able to secure a regular supply of films and equipment, creating filmic channels of communication between Brazil and Europe.[25] Gomes offers historical and social reasons for the preponderance of European immigrants in early Brazilian cinema, noting, "In terms of technical work, Brazilians' inability was prevalent. This situation was a legacy of the past during which manual labor when simple was conducted by slaves and when complex was carried out by foreigners. Such activities were considered undignified for any well-bred person. The cinema was perceived to be complex labor, so all film labor, from laboratory work to projection, was from the start carried out by foreigners."[26]

In the early days films were manufactured rather than produced, with raw stock treated as a commodity sold on the open market like pieces of cloth. So it was entirely appropriate that the business of manufacturing film was in the hands of foreign workers. Taking this analogy between filmmaking and labor practices into consideration, Bernardet suggests that many films made by European immigrants evidenced ties with Brazil's new working-class sites and practices.[27] Early cinema was indeed linked to spaces and labor practices associated with Rio's immigrants. Many of the city's immigrants took up residency in the center, close to the port and to small manufacturing industries in areas like Lapa, Catete, Glória, and Laranjeiras.[28] However, dreams of Brazil as a new land of opportunity quickly dissipated. Jobs were scarce and housing was insufficient to meet the rapid growth in population. For those who did manage to gain employment, working conditions were far from idyllic: a ten-to-eighteen-hour workday without weekend breaks, the legacy of a time when "work had to be made to fill and discipline the day of the slave."[29] The new workers were also subject to xenophobic attacks and were blamed for the city's social ills. International laborers were stigmatized by the city's elite, who viewed them with "a prejudice against manual labor as slave-like."[30] In response to a lack of work, many immigrants took up informal forms of employment. By 1890 approximately one hundred thousand people living in the capital earned a living in the informal sector of the economy as "casual workers, salesmen of their own and/or others' goods, empty bottle buyers, stevedores."[31] Entertainment was another itinerant trade. A number of immigrants who came to Brazil worked as musicians, dancers, and vaudeville performers.[32] They performed in different parts of Rio, ventured to other Brazilian towns, and journeyed to other Latin American countries as part of traveling troupes of entertainers. Cinema became part of this itinerant trade. Jurandyr Noronha writes that after the initial exhibition of the cinematograph in 1896, "the itinerants emerged. That is what projectionists who traveled from city to city, town to town, taking the new medium to their inhabitants, were called." This itinerant movie trade, he adds, was "exclusively composed of Europeans."[33] In the early 1900s, for instance, the Italian Salvatore Lazzaro ran the Cinematógrafo Anunciador Ambulante (the Ambulant Film Announcer), and the Portuguese Artur Machado Lucas operated another nomadic film business, the Rápido Excursionista (the Rapid Excursionist).[34] Other names from the period also highlight the dominance of European immigrants for the medium's initial dissemination: José Cunha Salles, Giacomo Rosário Staffa, Enrique Moya, Vittorio di Maio, German Alves, Paschoal and Affonso Segreto, Aurélio Paz do Reis. Brazil's very first moving-picture entrepreneurs invariably came from Portugal, Spain, and Italy. They organized shows in outdoor parks and rented theaters where they staged variety revues that included plays, music, comedy routines, and movies.[35] Many of these variety shows were free. In 1899, writer Artur Azevedo noted "free shows in public squares in the capital."[36] Instead of entrance prices, exhibitors gained money from the sale of beer and other refreshments or, as in the case of Salles, from gambling activities conducted at the same venues.[37]

Free admission and the diversity of programs were particularly appealing to Brazil's new workers, who would have been drawn to these shows by the inclusion of musical and theatrical performances conducted by troupes from their homelands. German Alves, for instance, regularly included a Spanish *zarzuela* company in his film programs.[38] The locations of these shows also meant that they were accessible to immigrants. Newspapers mention screenings not only in the more "fashionable" movie theaters in central Rio but also on streets in and around Lapa and Catete, precisely the areas immigrants had settled in. Shows were therefore integrated into the daily lives and spaces of Rio's immigrants. They could provide them with a brief respite from work or with a happy diversion from the inhospitable climate they had ventured into. At these shows immigrants could hear music and songs from their native lands and meet other immigrants, apart from kin or neighbors. The screenings thus constituted an important social space for Rio's new inhabitants.

The social dimension of these early shows in many ways replicated and mirrored the function of mutualist associations that Rio's immigrants often belonged to. Stigmatized and barred from access to the dominant culture by reason of language, employment, and customs, immigrants began to depend on each other and soon formed more formal links through clubs or groups. In 1909 there were 438 mutualist associations in Rio alone, with a total of 282,937 members.[39] Among the

Italian associations were the Societá Italiana di Beneficenza e Mutuo Socorro, the Círcolo Italiano Operário, the Associazone Fuscaldense, and the Sociedade Telesio; Spanish groups included El Centro Gallego and El Club Español. As the names suggest, the associations were formed on the basis of national or regional ties.

These associations provided a number of functions, both recreational and practical. Get-togethers featured food, drink, card games, and competitions. The centers staged plays, musical concerts and performances, song recitals, and poetry readings. They also provided important assistance, the kind later offered by the welfare state and insurance companies.[40] The presence of Rio's international workers thus gave rise to new cultural spaces that mediated the loss of their old culture, linguistic environment, and cultural framework and eased the challenges of settling in a new location. Providing a buffer against the pressures of adaptation, the associations were important social spaces that helped immigrants negotiate the often-daunting process of transition from Europe to Brazil.

Advertisements from the period reveal that movie shows were an important part of the mutualist associations' recreational activities. In 1898 the *Gazeta de Notícias* noted that exhibitor Salles had organized "a great festival in honor of the Portuguese Club," which included movies obviously chosen for its particular immigrant audience: *Batalha de flores e desfile das carruagens na cidade do Porto* (Flower competition and the procession of carriages in the city of Porto)*, As grandes touradas em Lisboa* (The great bull runs in Lisbon), and *Banhistas na praia de Belém Portugal* (Bathers at the beach of Belen, Portugal).[41] As noted in chapter 2, early imported vistas offered Brazilian spectators cinematic journeys that transported them around the globe, as befitting Rio's worldliness. For the city's immigrant communities, film also signified the possibility of global voyages, but of a different kind. Far from promoting a modern space devoid of past traditions, memories, and cultures, film offered Rio's immigrants a different spatio-temporal trajectory, taking them back to past times and places.

These alternative cinematic trajectories not only relied on visual depictions of immigrants' native lands but also incorporated extratextual cultural forms, especially music and song. Contemporary newspapers cite the exhibition of films like *La educanda di Sorrento* (The schoolgirl from Sorrento; 1909), *La farfalle* (The butterflies; 1909), *La donna è mobile* (Woman is fickle; 1910), *Vesti la guibba* (Wear the jacket; 1910), *Lucevan le stelle* (The shining stars; 1910), *Questo e quella* (This and that; 1910), *Longe de lei* (Far from you; 1910), *O sole mio* (My sun; 1910), and *Salve aurora* (Hello daybreak; 1910). Film historians have subsequently called these *filmes cantantes* (sung films) because of specific exhibition practices: these were films in which singers would perform standing behind the screen, a practice also adopted in the *filmes de revista*.[42] For Brazilian film critics, the recorded European operas satisfied the cultural pretensions of Rio's elite. However, as the titles indicate, they also catered to immigrant audiences, specifically Italians. Italian singers like Enzo Banino, Amica Peliser, and the duo Santucci and Cataldi were employed to perform the songs live for films. Indeed, in the early days, movies imported from Europe were often accompanied by singers who performed the soundtrack live. This array of extratextual or extravisual practices helped construct affective links to different times and places for immigrant spectators, aiding their transition to a new life in Brazil. The cinema thus provided Rio's foreign workers with what Giuliana Bruno calls "an imaginary binding,"[43] constructed not only in the space of the theater but also, and especially, in the mental geography of reception, the space between the text and spectatorship. In doing so, it bridged a spatial and temporal distance for Rio's foreign workers: it transported and circulated cultural formations, enabling viewers to travel back to their homelands while remaining in Brazil, where they were not yet fully implanted.

In its spatial configuration of combining, in a single location, different places and times, the cinema belongs to the social sites that Michel Foucault has characterized as "heterotopias." In their irreducible heterogeneity, heterotopias are "like counter-sites, a kind of effectively enacted utopia in which the real sites, all the other real sites that can be found within the culture, are simultaneously represented, contested and inverted." Foucault lists the cinema among a number of other sites, like sites of transportation. He discusses it as an example of one particular heterotopia, with the capability of "juxtaposing in a single real place, several spaces, several sites that are in themselves incompatible."[44] The movie theater obviously qualifies as such in the basic premise that it is "a very odd rectangular room, at the end of which, on a two dimensional screen, one sees the projection of a three dimensional space."[45] While this spatial configuration is more or less typical of the cinema throughout its history, Foucault's notion of heterotopia can be taken to describe the specific historical experience of the cinema on behalf of particular social groups—immigrants—for whom the movie theater became a site that helped mediate their transition from their homeland to a new land.

The mediatory function of film for Rio's immigrant communities in many ways mirrored the role of the mutualist associations. It is only to be expected, then, that many films were directly linked to the associations, recording their social, recreational, and also political events. In 1899, for instance, Affonso Segreto filmed the Círcolo Operário Italiano's celebrations of the anniversary of Italy's unification. Segreto and others also documented immigrants' political activities in films such as *Passagem do Círcolo Operário Italiano no largo de São Francisco de Paula* (Procession of the Italian Workers Party in São Francisco de Paula Square; dir. Affonso Segreto, 1900), *Largo de São Francisco por ocasião de um meeting* (São Francisco Square during a meeting; dir. Affonso Segreto, 1899) and *Círcolo Italiano Operário* (Italian Workers Party; dir. João Stamato, 1910).[46] Given immigrants' links to other international filmmakers and distributors, it is possible that these films traveled to other cities and countries, constructing political spaces in and beyond Rio.

Robert Stam notes that many of these early films of political gatherings featured Rio's black population, visually projecting a political community that crossed racial boundaries. He adds that other films that often did so were the *filmes carnavalescos,* which documented Rio's carnival celebrations, such as *O carnaval da Avenida Central* (Avenida Central's carnival; n. dir., 1906) and *Pela vitória dos clubes carnavalescos* (For the victory of the carnival clubs; n. dir., 1909). These movies were also associated with Rio's immigrant communities, particularly Neapolitan groups who celebrated carnival in ways that resulted in complex cultural affiliations. Such mixed social gatherings form the basis of the 1908 film *Os capadócios da cidade nova* (The imposters of the new city; dir. Antonio Leal, 1908), which depicted Praça Onze, a square popular among Africans and Portuguese, Italian, and Spanish immigrants. Nevertheless, while blacks were included in some silent movies, Stam writes that "Afro-Brazilians did not feature prominently in the symbolically white cinema of the first few decades of the century," an omission that reflected a wider attempt to project a civilized nation that would be ultimately seen as white.[47]

One real-life event, however, highlighted a crucial episode dealing with Rio's African population. On November 22, 1910, black corporal João Cândido led a group of soldiers in a revolt against corporal punishment that became known as the *Revolta da chiabata* (The Revolt of the Whip). The abused soldiers, largely black and *mestiço,* commandeered several warships recently acquired from England. Cândido took control of the cruiser *Minas Gerais,* demanding an end to corporal punishment, which carried memories of slavery. The Republican regime was at the mercy of the black soldiers and after they had returned the ships granted them amnesty. The government, however, reneged on its promise, arresting the rebels and murdering many of them. The event generated wide media interest. Magazines closely reported the event, carrying news of the mutiny and extensive photographic documentation. Filmmakers also reconstructed the event in movies like *Revolta da esquadra* (Squadron revolt; n. dir., 1910) and *Revolta no Rio* (Revolt in Rio; n. dir., 1910), and in 1912 the Italian immigrant Carlos Lambertini made *A vida do Cabo João Candido* (The life of Corporal João Candido), dealing with the revolt leader, who had become a popular political hero. The navy ministry confiscated the film in a move that effectively censored the movie.

SCREENING CRIME AND CRIMINALITY

The cinematic reconstruction of real-life events figured in other movies of this period, giving rise to Brazilian versions of the *actualité* films popular in France and elsewhere in Europe. As in France, Brazilian actualities covered a range of subjects, from current events to official ceremonies. Examples include *A festa da Penha no Rio* (Festival in Penha, Rio; n. dir., 1908), *Inundações de ontem em diversas ruas da cidade* (Yesterday's flooding in various streets of the city; dir. Alberto Botelho,

1908), and *Parada militar em 15 de November no Rio* (Military parade on November 15 in Rio; dir. Paulino Botelho, 1909). The most popular, however, were movies that recreated violent crimes, especially those involving the "lower classes." Known as *filmes policiais* (police films), movies like *Os estranguladores* (The stranglers; dir. Antonio Leal, 1908), *A mala sinistra* (The sinister suitcase; dir. Antonio Leal, 1908), *O caso dos caixotes* (Case of the packages; n. dir., 1912), *Noivado de sangue* (Blood courtship; n. dir., 1909), and *O crime da mala* (The suitcase crime; dir. Francisco Serrador, 1912) restaged and shot on location gory crimes that had occurred in Rio.

Leal's film *The Sinister Suitcase,* for instance, recreated events central to the death of Lebanese immigrant businessman Elias Farhat, who was murdered in 1908 by an employee (and rumored lover of his wife), Michel Traad. After decapitating and quartering Farhat, Traad hid his body parts in a suitcase. He then boarded the ship the *Cordillère* and attempted to throw the case containing Farhat's corpse into the sea. Traad was arrested and tried for murder that year. Leal's film of the crime was shown in Rio from October 22 to 24 and was a popular and critical success. The *Gazeta de Notícias* reported that "Ouvidor Street, by São Francisco Square, was at a standstill yesterday because of the people going to the Palace Cinema. The astounding film *The Sinister Suitcase,* which recreates the well-known crime, was being shown there for the first time."[48]

Journalists unanimously praised the movie. A writer for the *Gazeta da Manhã* highlighted its "unique composition . . . . This great tragedy of anger and cynicism is composed of twenty or so scenes, some of them in color, and many taken on location, on the ship and in Rio. Featuring national artists, whose work is impeccable, the film is exciting proof of how much we have progressed in the cinematic art."[49] Reports stressed the technical ingenuity of Leal's film. Lasting thirty-six minutes, it provided Cariocans with one of the country's first feature-length movies. It was composed of twenty-one different scenes, which included the purchase of the suitcase, the strangulation, the ship, the police station, the trial, the widow, and the final remorse. Together these scenes presented spectators with a narrative that charted, in a linear fashion, the progress of Traad's case.

In addition to the film's technical novelty, newspapers drew attention to its accurate recreation of the gruesome murder, which allowed spectators to "relive the well-known crime." A reporter for the *Correio da Manhã,* for instance, told readers that Leal's film would "allow them to see 'live' what had happened in real life, from the murder to the notorious assassin's declarations." This fidelity to actuality was reinforced by production methods. Leal shot many scenes in real locations, at crime scenes as well as in prisons and law courts. *The Stranglers* too was shot in the actual place of the murder; as one reporter noted, "in the house, the bedroom, the bathroom . . . the very same settings."[50]

The films thus provided an indexical link to sites involved in the crimes. These sites were often central to the films' meanings and visual tropes. Advertisements for

The Stranglers, for instance, promised reenactments of violent happenings, and titles for the films' scenes, like "the strangling" and "arrest of the criminal," indicate their link to reality, which was reiterated by filming in the locations where the events had unfolded. Indeed, specific sites are mentioned in the film, like the Avenida Central, where one of the victims, Carluccio, had arranged to meet the robbers; Prainha Pier, where he embarked on his fatal voyage; and the suburb of Jacarepaguá, where Carletto was finally detained by police. The film, like the criminals' trajectory, linked sites in the capital's fashionable center to the margins and remote suburbs. In this this way it underscored the facility with which marginal figures and criminals accessed Rio's elite center, producing fear among the civilized upper classes.

While critics highlighted the realism of the *filmes policiais,* their success was largely due to their prior reporting in the press, which made readers already familiar with the gory events recreated on screen. By the start of the twentieth century, crime stories dominated Rio's newspapers and magazines, giving rise to a new genre of criminal *faits divers* known as *crônicas policiais.*[51] For example, the capital's newspapers dedicated numerous pages to Traad's "astounding crime," informing readers of details from the planning of the murder to the criminal's imprisonment. Other crimes too became notorious in the press. In 1912 *Careta* magazine printed the story of "O caso dos caixotes" (The case of the packages), a robbery and murder conducted by three young Cariocan men; and in 1906 the journal *Kosmos* carried a sensational article under the headline "Um crime empolgante" (A breathtaking crime), describing the massacre of two brothers in Rio (figures 9, 10, and 11). Detailing the ins and outs of gruesome murders, these crime reports marked a radical departure from the press's more fashionable gaze at the capital. With their gory details, they presented an uncanny violation of the otherwise ordered display of the city evidenced at the time.

Films like *The Sinister Suitcase* and *The Stranglers* shared with sensational journalism an interest in exploiting shocking criminal behavior to attract and hold audiences. Nevertheless, the proliferation of these crime stories, in the press and on the screen, also served another function in the redeveloped capital. For Josefina Ludmer, crime stories function as conceptual instruments that play a key role in marking out the boundaries of a civilized city. Such stories are, she says, "one of the instruments most utilized to define and found a civilization: to separate it from the non-civilized and to mark what civilization excludes." Crime in this sense constitutes a "cultural frontier that serves to trace limits, differentiate, and exclude."[52] Ludmer's work highlights the discursive power of crime as a legal category and narrative trope, suggesting its pivotal role in forging a modern city that is based on exclusions. Teresa Caldeira too sees the proliferation of crime narratives in Brazil as constitutive of strategies of exclusion that were central in the formation of the country's modern cities. For Caldeira "talk of crime" plays a part in the organization of Brazil's urban landscape, marking out the boundaries of the civilized city by defining and excluding a criminal other that threatens its order.[53]

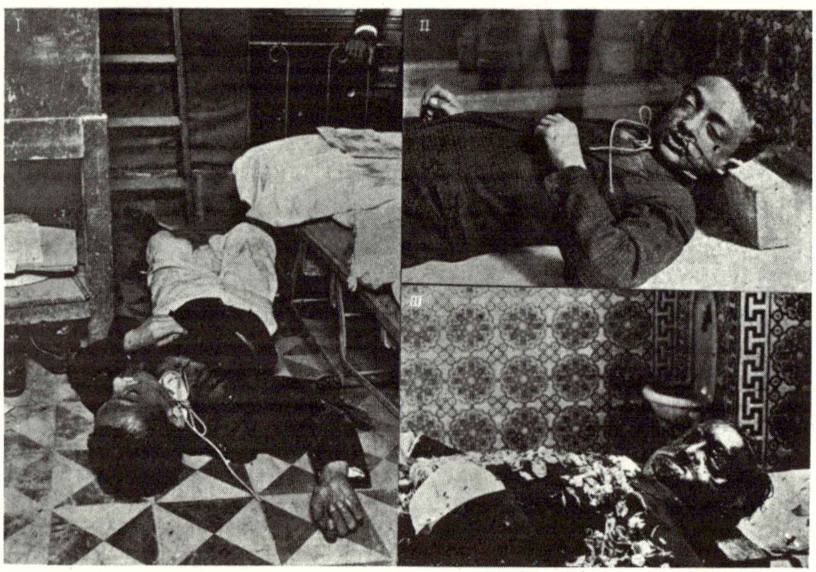

UM CRIME EMPOLGANTE

AS tarifas! A pauta aduaneira! Eis a geratriz maxima do grande crime da rua da Carioca.

A ganancia do Fisco, as exigencias do Fisco, essa voraz e infatigavel ascensão de taxas nos impostos de importação, geraram os contrabandistas. O Fisco sahio ludibriado, e o Crime ganhou proselytos. O contrabando é hoje instituição universal.

Jacob Fuoco poz muitas vezes a corôa da victoria em lides contrabandistas. Ha muitas fórmas de contrabando... Desde que se favorece um commercio contrario ás leis do paiz

De vez em quando a Policia, tambem, ia lá descobrir joias reclamadas pelas victimas de ladrões.

Carlo Fuoco sabia disso. A sua aprendizagem enveredava por esse caminho dos grandes lucros. Ia vendo como se negociava com essa gente; ia habituando a vista no exame do ouro, na avaliação das pedras, e formando o caracter no tracto com os criminosos sombrios. Observava attentamente o exemplo do tio, que lhes falava com autoridade, sem desprezo, e lhes offerecia, summariamente, quantias miseraveis por aquillo que elles tinham pressa de abandonar.

I-COMO FOI ENCONTRADO PAULINO NA RUA DA CARIOCA. II-PAULINO FUOCO NO NECROTERIO. III-CARLO FUOCO NO NECROTERIO

está se contrabandeando. Jacob Fuoco costumava comprar roubos,—como tantos outros vendedores de ouro, aliaz. A generalidade, porém, não descaracteriza o feito. A verdade é que ladrões de mar e ladrões de terra procuravam-lhe a joalheria.

Esses homens eram o caminho da Fortuna. Podiam ser máos, mas a sua maldade não se manifestava ali; era lá para fóra, onde praticavam o crime. Ali apresentavam-se, submissos, trocando o corpo de delicto por moeda circulante, o mais depressa possivel.

FIGURE 9. Press reports of crimes in Rio de Janeiro, *Kosmos* magazine. Author's personal collection.

KOSMOS

Desfilavam successivamente espalmando a mão sobre o *comptoir* pequenos garotos, copeiros e criados de quarto, larapios de todo o genero, bandidos de toda a especie. Ha tantas casas assim! O freguez honesto quando compra a joia não pede certificado da origem...

Carlo Fuoco analysava esse caminho da Fortuna, e aprendia a seguil·o, vendo na Lei, apenas, uma cousa ridicula, na Policia, apenas, uma cousa incommoda.

a passagem dos ladrões cevados na sua joalheria. E, se em tudo isso pensou, a previdencia limitou-se a montar dormitorio lá, onde se quebram as aguas da poetica e formosa Icarahy. O sobrinho que tomasse conta da loja.

Está escripto: *Le cœur de l'homme est là où est son trésor.* Jacob amava muito Carlucio? collocou-o, pois, ao lado dos seus brilhantes e artefactos de ourivesaria.

—

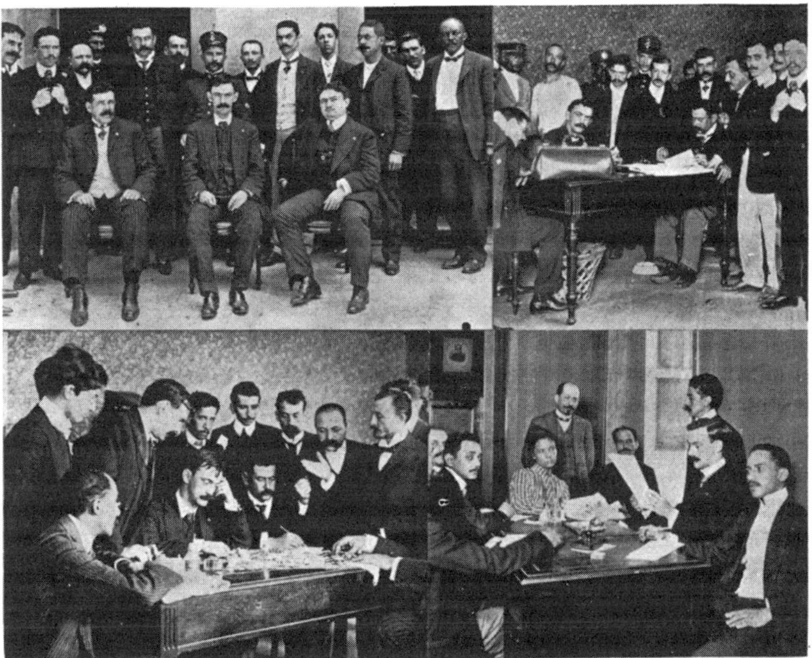

Para Jacob os negocios iam bem. Iriam bem.

Não se lembrava Jacob Fuoco que, não sendo elle o unico a comprar roubos, podiam as suas joias, tambem, ser apetecidas, e levadas sorrateiramente a outro balcão onde se trocassem por moeda corrente. Não lhe occorreu que a mesma Policia que lhe permittia tantas transacções fructuosas podia deixar livre

Os ladrões que tantas massadas tiveram em sua vida para se apoderarem de brilhantes e artefactos de ourivesaria, aqui pulando muros, ali arrombando portas, lá assaltando embarcações, não quizeram expôr-se a perigos para entrar no Estabelecimento da Rua da Carioca. Carlucio tinha as chaves? Pois haveriam as chaves de Carlucio.

Quando?

FIGURE 10. Press reports of crimes in Rio de Janeiro, *Kosmos* magazine. Author's personal collection.

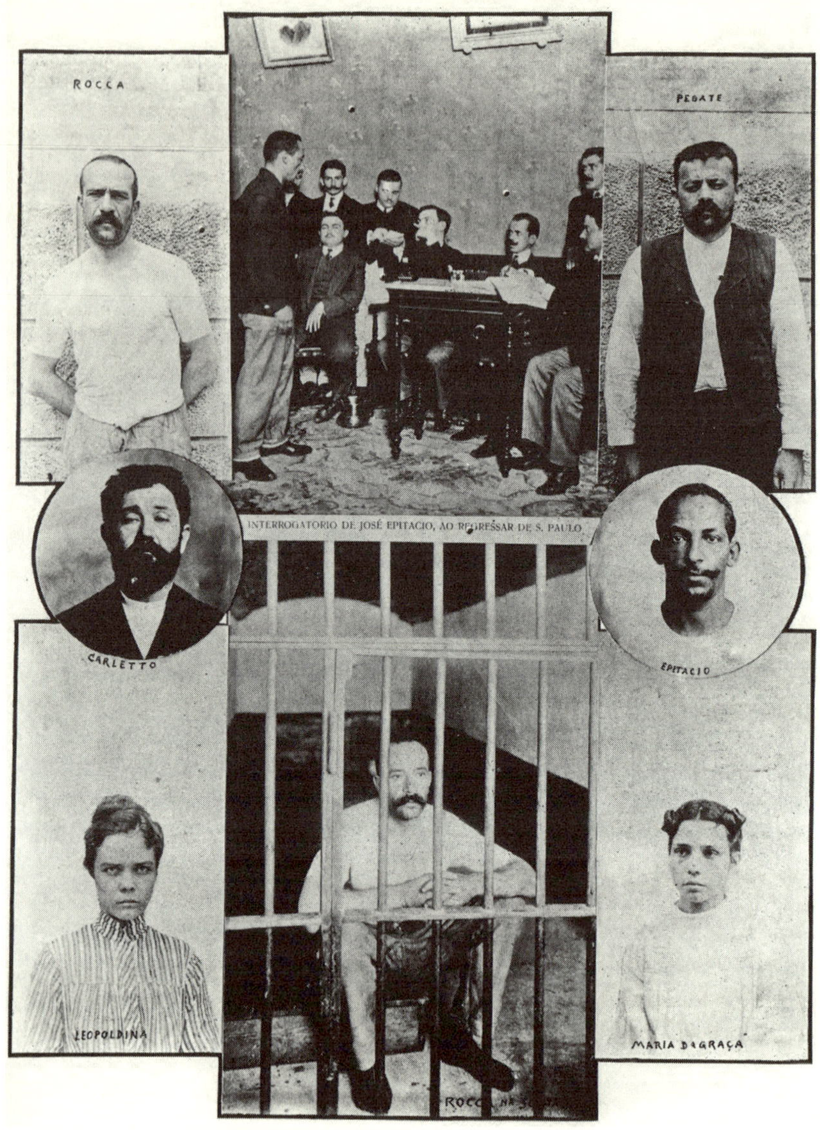

FIGURE 11. Press reports of crimes in Rio de Janeiro, *Kosmos* magazine. Author's personal collection.

"Talk of crime" was prevalent in Rio at the start of the 1900s. Along with the *crônicas policiais,* novels of real-life crimes also proliferated. Examples include Valentim Magalhães's *Flor de sangue* (Flower of blood, 1897), Alfredo Elisário da Silva's *O fruto de um crime* (Fruit of a crime, 1898), Júlio César Leal's *Casamento e mortalha* (Wedding and burial shroud, 1898), and Abílio Soares Pinheiro's *Os estranguladores* (The stranglers, 1906). These novels took inspiration from real-life events in Rio that had been popularized in newspapers and whose familiarity with readers helped make the books best sellers.[54] As Alessandra El Far notes, the popular stories were based on extraordinary and chaotic events that temporarily took readers away from Rio's order. Consequently, "They displaced dominant society's rules and norms, replacing them, even if only momentarily, with complete disorder."[55] The novels thus transformed the city into a dangerous place where criminality and danger could strike at any moment.

The *crônicas policiais* and their cinematic versions participated in this brief journey into a disordered urban world. In doing so they fed the upper class's obsession with threats to order at a time of political and social turmoil. The period witnessed a number of insurrections in Rio.[56] Revolts took place throughout the early 1900s. During these events, those who had been marginalized and forcibly removed from the civilized city returned to the center and laid claim to its elite space, inserting their excluded bodies into the modernized capital. Teresa Meade finds special significance in the fact that rioters tended to target visible signs of Rio's reforms. They "erected barricades to cut off access to the main arteries in the vital business districts . . . and invaded construction sites. . . . The crowds destroyed the Republican capital's newly constructed downtown offices, government buildings and cultural landmarks."[57] The violence directed against the new city suggests a popular consciousness that Rio's Republican-driven modernization was intended to benefit the elites to the exclusion of the broad sectors of the population.

The insurrections of these crowds blatantly challenged the new order of the city and its social divisions and hierarchies. More broadly, they threatened the very fabric of Brazilian society, woven from a system in which individuals were supposed to "know their place." For José Inácio de Melo Sousa, the Traad case was significant in this regard: "This was a subaltern killing his superior. Traad worked for Farhat as a bookkeeper. In a society with profound social differences, urban growth led to a rupture in traditional ties of class interaction. This sociocultural factor cannot be ignored, even though [the murder] took place among first-generation immigrants."[58] It was in this context of a fear of social heterogeneity that the representation of criminality began to organize the cultural landscape just as hierarchies and exclusions were being challenged.

Leal's film, like other *filmes policiais* and the broader culture of crime they formed part of, were thus linked to anxieties regarding threats to Brazil's social order that were occurring in the context of Rio's urbanization. The stories focused on the darker, disordered side of the city, transforming it into a place of danger and fear. An important aspect of this was the crime stories' visual rhetoric. Crime novels and *crônicas* were pervaded by a sadistic voyeurism—the trace of a kind of Grand Guignol in Brazil's cultural life—in which murders, mutilated corpses, and body parts were sensationally described for an eager reading public. This visual morbidity was exaggerated in the *crônicas policiais* that appeared in the press, where written reports of massacres were accompanied by photographs of criminals, their social environment, scenes of their crimes, and even the victims' disfigured bodies splayed out in the city's morgue. It took its most extreme form in cinematic recreations of the gory murders, in films like *The Sinister Suitcase,* where the movie camera responded to and fed the desire to see and delve into the darkest recesses of Rio's criminal underside.

With their focus on cadavers, crime films, like the broader landscape of criminality they belonged to, displayed an anatomical gaze that intersected with a new scientific impulse. Even before the Republic, science had moved from a mere fashion to a discipline.[59] The discipline, however, acquired greater significance in the beginning of the Republican period, when the nation sought to project a progressive image. It was then that the latest scientific theories moved beyond institutes to be more broadly disseminated. Newspapers popularized positivist theories, and naturalist novels, like Aluísio Azevedo's *O cortiço* (The slum, 1890), directed a scientific gaze at Rio, specifically at its "popular" classes. The *filmes policiais* participated in this scientific gaze. In them, however, the popular classes figured as more than an object of scrutiny; they constituted a barbaric threat to the order of civility, one that was visualized not in cultural but in scientific and medical terms. The intersection of film with popularized medical and scientific discourses gave rise to the *filmes policiais,* whose narratives were linked to the city's civilized makeover.

In his "Work of Art" essay, Walter Benjamin associates the medical gaze with the cinema, comparing the movie camera to a surgical operation:

> How does the cameraman compare with the painter? To answer this we take recourse to an analogy with a surgical operation. The surgeon represents the polar opposite of the magician. The magician heals a sick person by the laying on of hands; the surgeon cuts into the patient's body. The magician maintains the natural distance between the patient and himself; though he reduces it ever slightly by the laying on of hands, he greatly increases it by virtue of his authority. The surgeon does exactly the reverse; he greatly diminishes the distance between himself and the patient by penetrating into the patient's body, and increases it but little by the caution with which his hands move among the organs. In short in contrast to the magician—who is still hidden in the medical practitioner—the surgeon at the decisive moment abstains from facing the patient man to man; rather it is through the operation that he penetrates into him. Magician and surgeon compare to painter and cameraman. The painter maintains in his web a natural distance from reality, the cameraman

penetrates deeply into its web. There is a tremendous difference between the pictures they obtain. That of the painter is a total one, that of the cameraman consists of total fragments, which are assembled under a new law.[60]

Benjamin's analogy highlights film as a means of intervention, in which the object scrutinized is fragmented and deconstructed "under a new law." His work points to the enhancement of science by the law, a combination that was central to the Republic and was at the heart of crime novels, *crônicas policiais*, and their cinematic adaptations. Crime stories carefully staged events, laying them out as a linear story beginning with the crime and progressing through to the final resolution—the detection and imprisonment of the criminal by the law. The different scenes of Leal's *The Sinister Suitcase* highlight how the filmmaker adapted this linear narrative to produce a film that traces each stage of Traad's crime, from its planning to its final outcome—imprisonment, ultimately revealing the triumph of justice over crime. The movie ends with a scene or apotheosis entitled "Justice," which contains images of the criminals in prison. Noël Burch notes that early films in Europe and the United States tended to be open ended and lacked the dénouement characteristic of later classical narratives.[61] Brazil's *filmes policiais* would suggest a deviation from this cinematic norm: its final scenes provided a narrative resolution to the crime stories and also a form of ideological closure, revealing the success of the justice system and thereby mitigating the disruptive effect of the violent events.

The *filmes policiais*, then, did more than present real-life crimes. They transformed their details into a narrative of legal resolution, one that was rehearsed over the body of a criminal other. In doing so, their gaze performed a kind of social regulation, in which visuality played a key role in identifying, detecting, and capturing criminals who threatened the order of the civilized city. In this sense the *filmes policiais*, like the *crônicas* they drew on, revealed a dialogue with legal forms of control and policing in Rio. Thomas Holloway notes that only after abolition and with the advent of Republicanism did the police become official enforcers of the law, as social control over workers was transferred from the *patrão* (owner) to civil society.[62] This process led to changes in the policing of Rio, which began to rely on technologically reproduced visual methods of surveillance. In 1907, the city adopted the use of crime scene photography. That year Rio's police department photographed 3,141 suspects.[63] The camera lens was attributed, as Alan Sekula has suggested, with the power to figuratively and literally arrest human subjects.[64] The *filmes policiais* drew on these new forms of policing and their methods as they rehearsed and recreated the visual apprehension of the city's dangerous criminals.

Holloway notes that Rio's new forms of policing were buttressed by the emergence of novel disciplines, especially those related to science and law. In the early 1900s, jurists joined scientists to found Brazil's New School of Penal Law, where legal medicine played a pivotal role in determining and enforcing the standards of acceptable behavior within modern culture and defining society's social ills, especially its criminality. The school's intervention in social life was supported by the theories of Italian criminal anthropologists Cesare Lombroso and Enrico Ferri, whose ideas became particularly influential.[65] Criminologists contended that aspects of individuals' bodily structure that were knowable, measurable, and predictable could be markers of criminal propensities. In seeking to prove their deterministic theories, Lombroso and Ferri analyzed and classified physical characteristics of criminals, using a visual discourse. They especially relied on photography to capture the criminal physiognomy and circulate images among a public audience, a practice that gave rise to "mug shots." Criminology thus entered the domain of mass media, a process that in Brazil also took place in the *crônicas policiais* and their cinematic adaptations.

In Brazil criminology acquired a particular racial dimension in that it was closely tied to debates concerning miscegenation and nationality linked to abolition. Scientists were concerned with the racial question, and photography was placed at the service of creating what Lilia Moritz Schwarcz calls a "spectacle of the races."[66] This spectacle aimed not so much to understand difference as to illustrate it as a form of noncoevalness, which was linked to the past. The production of these illustrations was not restricted to science. Museums located in the city center helped to popularize portraits of *mestiço* types, opening them up to a broader gaze. Magazines too carried ethnographic depictions of a barbaric "other," whose racial "backwardness" helped to define the social and racial subjectivity of a more progressive urban bourgeoisie. This link between race and crime influenced debates regarding policing, as evidenced in Raymundo Nina Rodrigues's 1894 study *Raças humanas e a responsabilidade penal no Brasil* (Human races and penal responsibility in Brazil), which categorized criminal behavior according to race. These theories were instrumental in directing the plans of urban renewal that changed the face of Rio. Ideas from legal medicine, for example, were used to justify the removal of black and *mestiço* populations from the city center because they constituted a threat to public health and social order. Their intrusion into the neighborhoods that had once been theirs was subsequently kept in check by police surveillance that sought to maintain the civilized image of the new center and its citizens. The *filmes policiais* and the cultural landscape it drew on revealed links with the legal and scientific foundations of urban life. By recreating violations of civilization and projecting images of their uncivilized perpetrators, the crime movies played on the fears and anxieties mobilized by the criminal other in stories that visually restaged the superior force of the law and order in the new city.

The *filmes policiais*, like other films from the early period, focused on Rio's urban life, but in ways that provided a contrasting spectacle against which spectatorship and a modern urban subjectivity could be established. Projecting the return of barbarism in their gory tales, they reasserted the need for a civilized society and also justified the exclusion of the lower classes from Rio's new landscape. This exclusion highlighted the traditional limits of the city, established as part of a regimen of order and progress. The *filmes policiais*, however, were far from unproblematic in their visual depiction of a criminal other. By focusing on criminals' lives and the social conditions in which they lived, the movies, like the *crônicas* they drew on, often depicted the supposedly barbaric criminals as unwitting victims in a society rife with unemployment and homelessness, where the rhetoric of progress was far from inclusive.[67] The films often related criminality to illegality at a structural level, linking the marginalized classes to the dire conditions of their existence. What emerged was an ambivalence in popular attitudes toward crime, and the criminal, whose acts of violence were shown to arise from a broader structural violence or from old struggles, often benefited from a wave of sympathy.

The crime films thus contained an implicit critique of Rio's civilized image, something also seen in the *filmes de revista*. These movies not only charted the new visual landscape of the capital and its ideal inhabitants, providing spectators with spectacles of modern life they were to identify with, but also represented alternative narratives that worked against the new ideal of the city space. By doing so, these crime movies show how Brazil's early cinema and its relationship to an emerging public audience became important for imagining alternative spaces inside and outside Rio's enclave of worldliness.

PART TWO

Hollywood Revisions

4

Film and Fandom in
Cinearte Magazine

During the 1910s Brazil's cinematic landscape underwent profound changes. The local and artisanal nature of the initial years became a thing of the past as the medium garnered a wider national audience. This broad reach made the movies a profitable venture for the country's entrepreneurs. Foreign cinema in particular became a lucrative enterprise. With production costs recouped in the domestic market, international film prices undercut local competition. Consequently, more emphasis was placed on the distribution and exhibition of imported movies than on filmmaking, and Brazilians turned their attention to aiding the dissemination of foreign movies. Locally produced films were rapidly displaced from national screens, which were dedicated almost exclusively to showing foreign fare. This situation was exacerbated in the late 1910s and 1920s, which saw the ubiquity of Hollywood in Brazil.

Hollywood became a major presence in the Brazilian market during World War I and was part the United States' broader advance across the globe.[1] Prior to the start of the war in 1914, American cinema's presence in Brazil, and in Latin America generally, had been "largely negligible."[2] This was partly because of perceptions of Latin America as underdeveloped, and hence a difficult region to do business with. The situation left the Brazilian market for imported movies largely to European companies. During the early years French, Italian, and Danish products dominated the country's movie theaters, and US companies failed to gain any substantial place in the Brazilian market. Pathé, Éclair, Gaumont, Pasquali, Roma, Ítala, Ambrosio, Savoia, Celia, and Nordisk films had a particularly strong presence, with agents like Francisco Serrador and Giácomo Staffa operating in Rio and São Paulo on their behalf.[3] By contrast, at the start of the 1900s "Not a single

American firm had a representative in the country."[4] The start of the war radically altered this situation. A lack of raw materials severely curtailed European production, and faltering industries in Europe proved poor competition for the increasingly well-capitalized and technologically sophisticated US industry.[5] America stood poised to triumph in the market as European production declined, and by 1915 it began its advance through Brazil.

Hollywood's entry into Brazil was accompanied by new strategies. Studios set up offices in the country's principal cities in order to directly distribute films to exhibitors, thereby facilitating their control of the market. Fox Film led the way in 1915 when it established a branch in Rio. Other companies followed suit, and by the 1920s most Hollywood studios—Paramount, Universal, Warner Brothers, First National, Columbia—had offices in Rio and branch offices or representatives in major cities or port towns.[6] During these years the importation of US films increased dramatically. Hollywood's fast-paced westerns and melodramas pushed European films off Brazilian screens and further marginalized domestic movies. In 1921 the proportion of American films shown in Brazil reached 71 percent, rising to 86 percent in 1929.[7]

Hollywood's triumph in Brazil involved a concerted effort by American film manufacturers to take advantage of opportunities in Latin America created by the war. In January 1916, *Moving Picture World,* the leading publication for film exhibitors and distributors in the United States, printed numerous articles and editorials that emphasized the financial potential of Latin American countries, including Brazil. A report for Brazil published in the journal in 1917 noted, "The US counts some thirty big moving picture companies [in Brazil] and the Goldwyn organization is cited to prove that much money is to be made in the film game there. The capital of the Goldwyn Company there is said to be $3,000,000 and the director is quoted as saying that these fabulous figures are set to increase."[8] A foreign trade news report in the same journal in December 1918 stated, "South America should prove a fertile field for American film, judging by the success with which our exporters have met in Argentina and Brazil, two markets that acquired a prominent position within the past year."[9] Such reports offered encouragement to film companies and aimed to boost efforts to export movies to Brazil and Spanish America.

This encouragement led to the publication of a Latin American offshoot of *Motion Picture World, Cine-Mundial* (literally Film-World). First published in January 1916, the trade journal declared itself "dedicated to the promotion of cinematographic interests in the United States and Latin American countries."[10] As Laura Isabel Serna observes, however, the publication was more accurately "dedicated to promoting the interests of the US film industry in Latin America."[11] An advertisement for the publication described Latin America "as the most rapidly developing market in the world," noting that "as we go father southward we find fertile markets as Central America, Venezuela, Brazil, Peru, Chile, and Argentina." The same advertisement urged traders, "Surely YOU must be interested in this fastly [*sic*] developing field!!"[12] Such adverts and reports portrayed Latin America as a region with untapped potential that was ripe for studios to explore and exploit. Indeed, an editorial for *Moving Picture World* in December 1916 blatantly announced, "The Yankee invasion of the Latin American market shows unmistakable signs of growing serious. It may before long develop into a rush as to a new Eldorado."[13]

This expansion of film went hand in hand with the promotion of commerce. Victoria de Grazia has shown that Hollywood's push into foreign markets was part of a general increase in US commerce abroad.[14] The American economy had grown hugely since the end of the Civil War, and foreign trade participated in this growth. Between 1900 and 1913, exports increased by 76 percent. The type of exports also shifted, with a decrease in foodstuffs and a rapid rise in manufactured goods, which included film.[15] The war in Europe precipitated this rise, initiating America's reign over what de Grazia calls the "Market Empire" as the country stepped in to fill Europe's diminishing economic role globally.[16] While this advance was material and economic, it was also underlined by ideological discourses. America's consumer goods offered the image of a homogeneous population pursuing the same goals: living a modern life. Indeed, for Mona Donosh, the United States' consumer culture was dominated by a discourse of modernity, and the emergence of what she calls its "commercial geography" was part of a civilizing mission in which America sold itself as the harbinger of a new material civilization.[17] Consumption thus assumed an ideological veil as American products were aligned with a civilizing experience to legitimize their international sales.

Cinema was part of the expansion of the United States' Market Empire, and its visions were intimately bound up with the triumph of American commerce. Film scholars Charles Eckert, Jeane Allen, and Mary Anne Doane have examined the relationship between American cinema and commerce, focusing specifically on Hollywood's role in forging a consumer-oriented culture in the United States. For Eckert, Hollywood's plunge into the American marketplace involved two strategies: the establishment of "tie-ups" with brand-name manufacturers and the showcasing of fashions, furnishings, cosmetics, and other manufactured items. Consequently, the movie screen acted not as a window on the world, as in the Bazinian formulation, but as a specific kind of window—a shop window "occupied by marvelous mannequins and swathed in a fetish-inducing ambience of music and emotion."[18] In these living displays, actors and actresses draped in sumptuous clothes and using new goods served as models that aimed to entice spectators to purchase the items displayed.

Hollywood thus cooperated in selling US items to an expanding consumer market, employing sales methods that were covert and associations that were linked to film's visual regime of desire, its scopic drive. Spectatorship was posited as a form of window-shopping and relied on a narcissistic identification with the world on the screen, in which the spectator was encouraged to desire the possessions of a material environment that was made visually attractive. The display of clothes and furnishings gave rise to what Eckert calls a new cinematic style that revolutionized people's lifestyles and identities.[19] This process was not restricted to the United States. As William Hayes put it in a 1930 radio speech, "The motion picture carries to every American at home and to million of purchasers *abroad,* the visual, vivid perception of American manufactured products."[20] Participating in an export drive, Hollywood movies traveled the globe, introducing international spectators to US films and mobilizing their desires for the American lifestyles and products fetishistically displayed on the screen. As a journalist for the magazine *Collier's* noted, "After the war is won we all know that American trade must be developed enormously. . . . Consider what the American moving picture is doing in other countries. It is familiarizing South America, Africa and Europe with American habits and customs. It is educating them up to the standard of living. It is showing them American clothes, furniture, automobiles and homes, and it is subtly but surely creating a desire for American made articles."[21] Beyond entertainment, US films could function as what one government official at the time termed "silent salesmen," introducing international spectators to products as well as modern and glamorous lifestyles, in a process that effectively turned them into consumers.[22]

This was central to Hollywood's reception in Brazil. Indeed, observers at the time noted the cinema's commercial function, which relied on the aesthetic primacy of visual display and desire linked to consumerism. A 1914 article published in *Careta* magazine entitled "Vida elegante" (Elegant life), for instance, praised "these beautiful live models who, placed in front of the lens, display the latest fashions on the screen" and added, "The cinema does great service to the large fashion houses, bringing these daring clothes to life on the screen with beauty and superiority, which seem less lovely when viewed on mannequins."[23] American trade did indeed follow film in Brazil. By the late 1910s more US-manufactured products and consumer items entered the country, and by the 1920s American exports surpassed those from European countries.[24] This was part of a wider shift away from Europe to the United States, evidenced throughout Latin America.[25] New banking facilities made the United States the region's major creditor, and investments and debts were reallocated from the Old to the New World. For Micol Seigel, this shift went hand in hand with new affiliations that realigned former relations of dependency and colonialism.[26] This realignment was part of the United States' engagement in what has been called informal imperialism, defined by Mark Crinson as a "form of imperialism by which control was established through ostensibly peaceful means of free trade and economic integration."[27] In contrast to the militarism of European imperialism, American hegemony rested on "peaceableness" and promoted engagement with local interests, providing its global expansion with universal applicability.[28] In this economic empire, the "others" that Americans were confronting were considered not political subjects but potential consumers, and the logic of profit depended on an outlook that figured them as similar, with no clear delineation between colony and colonizer.[29] America's informal imperialism thus turned foreigners into consuming subjects and articulated a form of address that was gendered: "Foreign peoples and nations were positioned as consumers and hence as passive feminized subjects, with the United States positioned as the masculine producer."[30]

Brazil, however, was by no means passive in this "empire of consensus."[31] Seigel notes that Brazilians actively sought out America's presence and cooperation.[32] The constriction of transatlantic trade during World War I necessitated a commercial rapprochement with the United States, which became Brazil's key trading partner, overtaking Britain and France. By the 1920s, exports to the United States rose considerably, with Brazil, for instance, supplying two-thirds of the coffee consumed by Americans. The war thus altered trade routes and associations for Brazil, which consciously transferred the axis of its commercial relations away from Europe to the United States. The shift was accompanied by a transfer in foreign policy led by Minister José da Silva Paranhos, Baron of Rio-Branco. Buoyed by coffee's prosperity, Rio Branco adopted an extroverted foreign policy, currying a close relationship with the United States.[33] As Seigel affirms, "All in all Brazil was a warm and active ally of the United States in the early decades of the twentieth century."[34]

This cooperation underlay a Pan-American rhetoric that was rigorously endorsed by the US State Department, which sought to assert its influence in Latin America. Emily Rosenberg observes that culture was central to this effort and was seen as a tool that could be used to achieve diplomatic objectives, including the spread of American civilization. Culture's perceived power guided government policy, within which film played a key role. In fact, President Wilson (1913–21) promoted a vision of cinema as "lending itself importantly to the presentation of America's plans and purposes abroad."[35] Latin Americans, therefore, would benefit not just from the traffic of cinematic goods from the United States but also from the "civilized" values embedded in them. *Cine-Mundial* urged this hemispheric solidarity, asserting that the war had demonstrated the need for the Americas to "live with total economic independence from the influences of the old continent." Pan-American unity was thus posited in terms of a break from Europe, which was cast as dated. For *Cine-Mundial*, film could play a central role in encouraging this break from the past. The publication promoted North American films as "emanating equality," whereas European films reiterated past divisions.[36] The magazine produced a progressive narrative in which all Latin Americans were potential consumers of Hollywood movies and in which all Latin American nations could benefit from and take part in their civilizing visions.

Brazilians participated in this cinematic break from the past. Aware of profits to be made from exhibiting cheaper US movies, film entrepreneurs shifted their attention away from Europe and concentrated on distributing American products. Local distributors were thus at the heart of the readjustment of Brazil's cinematic landscape following World War I, and they played an active role in helping to displace European dominance and replace it with American hegemony over the Brazilian market. Promoting this active cooperation was of course part of North America's imperial strategy, that is, its corporate internationalism; nevertheless, it not only stimulated more trade but also created a local market of new businesses, identities, and pleasures. More than simply oppressive, Hollywood became the site of personal investments, and relations with US film studios were domestically desired.

Brazil's new links with the United States formed part of what Fernando Rosenberg calls a geopolitical shift that occurred in Latin America after the First World War.[37] While European countries had previously been symbols of progress and models to be imitated, the war years set in motion a transformation in South America's cultural and social landscape, such that Latin Americans "no longer voiced a longing to be like Europe."[38] The postwar collapse in France and elsewhere put an end to Brazil's blind faith in European civilization and its universal projection. Social and cultural elites turned to the United States, whose geographical proximity and success in overcoming its colonial past to become an economic powerhouse made it a more fitting model for Brazil. This new geopolitics was intertwined with a redefinition of the location of discourses about modernity, which was no longer seen to emanate from Europe but instead could be developed in the Americas. Far from exerting a simple economic mastery, America offered Brazil a model of liberation from colonialism and suggested that dependency on the old European world was no longer necessary. The country's shift to North America coalesced perfectly with Brazil's desire for a modern identity. Hollywood was part of this new desire. Promoting visions of modernity, US movies encouraged Brazilian spectators to buy into an American way of life and projected the belief that consuming its products could aid in the civilizing process. Hollywood's dominant presence on Brazilian screens was thus part of and helped to foster Brazil's desire for modernity, which in the 1920s was seen as located in the Americas, not Europe.

CINEARTE: HOLLYWOOD'S NATURAL INTERMEDIARY

Hollywood's presence in Brazil was not confined to the country's movie screens. Extrafilmic material spilled out into public space and became a significant part of Brazil's visual culture. By the late 1910s, advertisements for US films circulated widely in the illustrated press. Indeed, Hernani Heffner notes that film became a regular feature in Brazil's popular press only after 1915, when American studios began furnishing magazines with publicity material for their films.[39] News of upcoming movies, films reviews, and photographs of US stars proliferated in colorful weeklies like *Selecta* (1915), *Palcos e Telas* (1918), *Para Todos* (1918), *Cine*

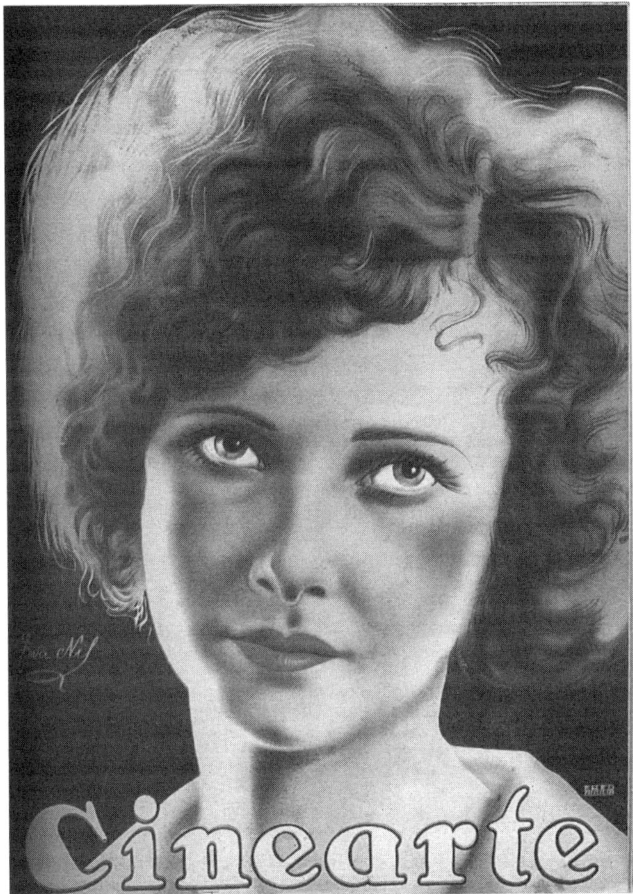

FIGURE 12. *Cinearte,* 1926. Author's personal collection.

Revista (1919), *Scena Muda* (1921), and *Cinearte* (1926). Fostering greater familiarity with Hollywood's products and creating a bond between the distant stars and
domestic spectators, this publicity was a component process of North American
studios' consolidation of the Brazilian market, part of an aggressive strategy that
aimed to make Brazilians "good" spectators of US movies.

An offshoot of the magazine *Para Todos, Cinearte* boasted of its intention to aid
Hollywood's consolidation in the Brazilian market, proudly describing itself as
"the natural intermediary" between the latter and the Hollywood producer (figure
12). Reviews, publicity stills, interviews with stars, and features about Hollywood
actors and directors made the distant world of Hollywood familiar for Brazil's
readers, allowing them to participate in its modern culture. Indeed, for *Cinearte*

the consumption of foreign film culture was an important and desirable national activity that demonstrated Brazil's participation in the wider modern world. This metagoal was clearly evident in the journal's section "The Screen in the Magazine," which enthusiastically documented the latest showings of US movies, claiming that they testified to Brazil's progress and that attending them would be patriotic.

This participation in Hollywood's cinematic world was reinforced through materials in *Cinearte,* which instructed readers in the ways of understanding American movies. The publication fostered the development of a specialized discourse about cinema. In Brazil, covering film and film shows had previously been the province of *cronistas,* whose personalized anecdotes tended to focus on describing films' psychological, social, and cultural effects. Literary and theater critics had also written about film, yet with little knowledge of how to evaluate the medium. The increasing proliferation and popularity of cinema in Brazil's illustrated magazines gave rise to a new generation of film critics, such as Mário Behring, Octavio Mendes, Pedro Lima, and Adhemar Gonzaga, who honed their practice in *Cinearte.* These men saw educating readers about film aesthetics as a key task. Unlike their predecessors, they focused on specifically cinematographic qualities rather than simply recounting movie narratives. Regular sections, such as "The Art of Filmmaking," "Cine-Graphology," and "Some Techniques," introduced aspects of film form and language, like montage, close-ups, mise-en-scène, lighting, and editing, teaching readers how to evaluate cinema's plastic qualities. Through this kind of pedagogy, *Cinearte* helped to increase film's prestige in Brazil and to elevate the popular entertainment to an art form, as expressed by the magazine's title.

Ismail Xavier has argued that the concept of the nation played a key role in *Cinearte*'s conception of the art of film. The magazine denigrated European cinema, dismissing its documentary realism as "uncivilized" and an affront to "commercial good taste." By contrast, writers like Gonzaga and Lima praised American films, which epitomized "a good cinema."[40] The glamorous stars and luxurious sets were celebrated as sophisticated, Hollywood's productions were elevated for epitomizing a modern ideal and were given the rank of what the magazine called "the seventh art." *Cinearte* in this way not only promoted Hollywood but also legitimized its universal language, naturalizing its implantation in Brazil.

Cinearte did more than teach readers how to evaluate films critically. It also instructed them in the practices of fandom, encouraging viewers' intimate investment in US stars. The magazine urged readers to write fan letters to their favorite actors and actresses. Write-in sections like "Ask Me Another Question" published stars' addresses as a means of facilitating this communication. Articles with titles such as "Stars' Letters" and "Actors Answer Letters" informed readers of how American actors dutifully read and responded to fan mail.[41] Such features encouraged Brazilians to engage directly in American film culture. Contests that invited readers to nominate "the most beautiful actress and the most handsome actor," or that challenged them to guess the blurred-out star from a movie scene, also promoted this engagement with Hollywood.[42] Asking readers to demonstrate firsthand knowledge, the contests stimulated fans to keep abreast of developments in US cinema.

Cinearte thus brought Hollywood into the lives, homes, and cultural imagination of Brazilian readers, domesticating its products. This domestication was particularly apparent in stories featuring stars at home. The magazine often depicted Hollywood actors relaxing with families "far from the screen and the studio."[43] In 1929, for instance, *Cinearte* published a spread of "Wallace Beery, his wife Rita Gilman, his car, his home, his dog."[44] Showing the star at home, the feature counters the glamour of Beery's Hollywood lifestyle, its difference, through the ordinariness of the setting. The images in this way aimed to demonstrate that Hollywood's stars are "just like us," something Richard Dyer identifies as a key component of the star persona. Indeed, Hollywood actors and actresses were often Brazilianized in *Cinearte*. The magazine frequently adapted star names. Clara Bow, for instance, was referred to as Clarinha Bowa, underscoring an affectionate adoption of the foreign actress. Interviews with US stars also went out of their way to underscore their similarities to Brazilians. A 1926 interview with Ruth Roland, for example, notes that she and other stars were "simple people with the same virtues as us," adding, "Like us, they like to go to the beach."[45] Images reinforced this connection to the distant world of Hollywood. February and March issues often included photographs of American actresses dressed in attire "for carnival," as if the distant Americans were ready to participate in Brazil's pre-Lenten festivities.

Cinearte's domestication of Hollywood helped to reduce its foreignness, bringing it closer to readers and consumers. In his essay "The Work of Art in the Age of Mechanical Reproduction," Walter Benjamin refers to a possible history of the modes of human perception and to the decay of the aura that characterizes contemporary perception. This decay is associated with the development of mass culture and with consumers' desire to bring things closer spatially and humanly, annihilating the uniqueness of the work of art through its reproduction. *Cinearte* functioned in much this way. Its features and images brought Hollywood and especially its stars closer to readers, projecting them not as distant gods (to use Dyer's wording), but as ordinary, even "Brazilian," and intimately connecting them to the domestic landscape.[46]

Photographs and publicity stills encouraged this intimate engagement. Supplements and full-page photo spreads of actors and actresses, often autographed, could be pulled out and personally collected by readers, thus creating a personal investment in Hollywood's film industry. These images helped bridge the space between readers' homes and Hollywood movies, between the United States and Brazil, allowing consumers to successfully navigate the distance between these two different worlds. This was central to the section "From Hollywood to You," in which *Cinearte*'s Hollywood correspondent, L. S. Marinho, penned articles from Los Angeles, providing readers with firsthand accounts from the movie capital. His articles focused on diverse topics, from the latest screenings to updates about specific productions. Marinho thus provided *Cinearte*'s readers with an insider's take on Hollywood and offering them a personal entry point. This was emphasized by Marinho's stories of his encounters with stars, which allowed him to get up close and personal with these glamorous individuals. Photography was a key component of these reports. Images portrayed Marinho alongside well-known actors and actresses, firmly locating the Brazilian correspondent in the modern world of film.

Marinho's features forged an image of Brazil as being "at home" in Hollywood as a means of making the Brazilian public identify with American film culture. One striking example of this strategy was the proliferation of photographs that depicted stars reading the Brazilian publication. An image published in 1928, for instance, shows Ruth Roland leafing through the pages of the magazine. Mirroring Brazilians' own act of reading the fanzine, *Cinearte* becomes a link to the United States, much like Marinho, an object that creates identification of the modern world of Hollywood and its stars with the everyday space of Brazil and its anonymous readers.

Cinearte thus indisputably helped to consolidate Hollywood's presence in the Brazilian market by mediating its products for readers and reducing its foreignness. The journal's intimacy with US cinema in some senses fostered a narcissistic overidentification with American film culture, and indeed with America, which became an object of admiration and desire. Both Paulo Emílio Salles Gomes and Xavier note that this identification was enacted by the journal itself, which mirrored the format and style of US fanzines like *Photoplay*.[47] For these Brazilian critics, such mirroring was a form of surrender and passive subjection to Hollywood's dream factory that turned on the logic of reification—that is, a mimetic empathy with American cinema and its products.

CINEARTE AND BRAZIL'S NEW WOMAN

Gomes's and Xavier's discussions of *Cinearte* intersect with a wider current of criticism associated with the nationalizing and decolonizing impulse that marked discussions of Brazilian film and culture in the 1960s and '70s and gave rise to the Cinema Novo movement. Intersecting with issues concerning film, modernity, and national identity, their work has highlighted how 1920s Brazilian film culture was shaped by foreign models and paradigms, specifically Hollywood, something that *Cinearte*'s mimicry of *Photoplay* epitomizes. The Brazilian magazine's relationship with American cinema, however, was not purely passive, nor did it completely collapse distinctions between Brazil and the United States. Indeed, the journal's marketing of US movie culture opened up a space for Brazilian film fans to actively project their own modern desires and transform their own identities in spectacular ways.

Central to this was *Cinearte*'s overwhelming appeal to female readers. Noting the preponderance of advertisements for female products in the fanzine, João Luiz Vieira suggests that women constituted the principal audience for *Cinearte,* which visually and textually inscribed them into its address.[48] This gendered address is not surprising. In the 1920s Brazilian exhibitors and filmmakers purposely set out to cultivate a female audience. This appeal to women linked the cinema with the consumer culture that was taking root in Brazilian cities, a culture that, as in other parts of the world, was strongly associated with women.

With the expansion of import-export trade, consumer goods became part of Brazil's urban life, altering everyday lifestyles, especially for women. Department stores, stocked with an array of commodities, began to appear in cities catering to a new market of female shoppers. Brazil's first department store was Parc Royale, which opened in Rio in 1870.[49] Susan Besse notes that Parc Royale initially "sold nothing but expensive imports to an exclusive clientele."[50] This changed in the 1910s, when, with the increase of imported items, it began to lure middle-class shoppers to its establishment. As more people succumbed to the attractions of conspicuous consumption, "new and ever larger department stores experienced a heyday" in Brazil.[51]

The illustrated press promoted new commodities, which were sold as offering a modern form of femininity. Magazines like *Revista da Semana* (1921) were abundantly adorned with advertisements for beauty aids, household appliances, furniture, and clothing, and they carried pictures that accompanied articles on how to dress fashionably and decorate the home. In this way, the magazines emphasized a new role for women. Female readers were targeted as consumers whose desires for foreign items could contribute to the country's modern makeover. Consumerism was thus intimately articulated with a patriotic discourse, and women were woven into the nation's wider refashioning.[52] As Besse argues, commodity fetishism, or the displacement of desire onto material goods, was seen as a powerful stimulus for forging Brazil's modern identity, and female consumers were encouraged to participate in its material progress.[53]

The cinema, a modern commodity, was linked to this world of commerce from the very start. As noted in chapter 2, the medium made its first appearance in the country on Ouvidor Street, Rio's foremost commercial district. In their documentation of Brazilian movie theaters, João Luiz Vieira and Margareth Pereira observe that this connection between film and consumerism continued, and in the 1920s movie theaters were primarily located in shopping areas.[54] Given this location it is hardly surprising that cinematic practices drew on and were part of Brazil's consumer culture. The fashionable lifestyles and clothes depicted in foreign films could be purchased in stores just beyond the threshold of movie theaters. Exhibitors capitalized on this connection. They lined the interiors of cinemas with advertisements for the kinds of products that audiences gazed at on the screen; they also included advertising slides for local stores before and after screenings.[55]

Filmmakers too cashed in on the movies' link with commerce, producing *posados de propaganda,* a genre that mixed fiction and advertising. Movies like *Um roubo na casa Michel* (Robbery at the Michel Department Store; dir. Antonio Campos, 1918) and *24 horas na vida de uma mulher elegante* (Twenty-four hours in the life of an elegant lady; dir. Arturo Carrai, 1920) displayed products sold by the commercial establishments that financed their production.

The cultivation of the connection between cinema and consumer culture was not limited to films. The popular press was an important ally too. In the pages of newspapers, advertisements for imported beauty products and clothes dominated the women's sections, where daily cinema news also appeared. Similar types of advertisements proliferated in illustrated magazines. Cinema-specific magazines in particular promoted consumer goods. In addition to selling American films, *Cine-arte* promoted the consumption of products. Advertisements for a range of goods— toothpaste, face cream, fashion, perfume, makeup, and furniture—featured extensively in the magazine, which became an important and lucrative advertising outlet.

For Marina Maluf and Maria Lúcia Mott, the explosion of advertisements, particularly of fashion-related content, in the Brazilian press contributed to the transformation of visual depictions of femininity, giving rise to a new image of womanhood. The press became fascinated with the emergence of Brazil's new woman, who was intimately linked to the consumer landscape. Illustrated journals published snapshots of fashionable ladies in downtown areas in their *instantâneos.* The photographs were vivid illustrations of women's increasing visibility, testifying to the changing sexual boundaries of public life. The emergence of this new woman was widely discussed and commented on. Journalists observed that the "static woman became the active woman."[56] Writers too noted the demise of "romanticism's tubercular and lyrical woman" and the emergence of "an athletic Eve."[57]

Cartoonist J. Carlos synthesized the contours of this new woman through the cultural construct of the *melindrosa,* which became a mainstay of print media and particularly of magazines. As Beatriz Resende writes, "With her short hair, heart-shaped lips, bangs covering her forehead, light and transparent clothes, short skirts, and long necklines, sometimes wearing a cloche hat, sometimes not, but always seductive, the *melindrosa* is the image of the age of the shimmy. Moreover, the *melindrosa* evokes the space she freely moves through, the vertiginous and cosmopolitan city of the 1920s." Resende adds that "the *melindrosa* emerges from the pages of its illustrated magazines, she walks through the city's streets, crosses its avenues, shops, goes to the movies, meets friends in coffee shops, and uses public space."[58] Donned in the latest foreign fashions and linked to the city and its new venues of entertainment, the *melindrosa* was a visual embodiment of modernity, projecting a radical makeover in the image of female identity, superimposing on traditional values of motherhood and domesticity the appeals of the modern life of the city, its spaces of pleasure and its consumer-oriented culture.

As Resende's description highlights, the *melindrosa* was inextricably linked to Brazil's consumer landscape, her image emerging from the pages of magazines. Publications featured numerous illustrations of Brazil's "It girl" alongside commentaries on her modern lifestyle, self-consciously drawing on discourses regarding changing femininity and the purchasing power of new women. Magazines such as *Revista Feminina* and *A Cigarra* catered to female consumers. These magazines dedicated considerable space to publicizing and applauding women's public lifestyles, and they printed articles written by female authors that focused on and, in turn, catered to the consuming desires of new women. Female readers were crucial largely because the publications depended on revenue from department stores advertising aimed at female shoppers.[59] They featured colorful advertisements that extolled the wonders of technological items and fashions, inciting women's desire to participate in the growing and increasingly profitable consumer market.

The period also saw the publication of dime novels, known as *livros de bolso* (pocket books), whose narratives and characters drew upon and catered to this expanding market of new women. In Madame Chrysanthème's 1922 novel *As enervadas* (The enervated girls), the female narrator Lúcia details her "modern memories" that include "delicious promenades to the movies, in order to hear warm music and the rhythm of tangos."[60] Benjamin Costallat's book *Mademoiselle Cinema* describes the adventures of a *melindrosa,* Rosalina Pontes, that include shopping, reading magazines, and going to the movies. These novels achieved commercial success in Brazil. *Mademoiselle Cinema,* for instance, sold a remarkable 140,000 copies in the 1920s, becoming a best seller. These texts emphasize the profitability of the new cultural scene geared to female consumers. They also testify to cinema's place within it. In Costallat's novel the *melindrosa,* Pontes, is closely associated with the cinema. As the title indicates, her identity emerges from film, which refashions her into a new woman. This identity, however, is not viewed positively. One of the novel's characters condemns the *melindrosa*'s filmic life, telling her, "I finally understand why they call you Mademoiselle Cinema! It's because you are false; like the movies, you are false, artificial, and a lie."[61]

This condemnation in Costallat's novel expresses anxieties regarding the perceived dangers of women's increasing mobility, presence in public space, and freedom from the strict controls of patriarchal familial structures. It also articulates attitudes to mass culture, which as Andreas Huyssen notes, has often been inscribed as female.[62] Linked to this were concerns about the malevolent forces of American mass culture, including film. Perceived as embodying an antinationalist subjectivity that threatened the vision of Brazilian modernity promoted by the Republican elite, the *melindrosa* image clearly challenged the traditionally defined gender roles that many believed were crucial to the country's safe progress.

Hollywood's consolidation within the Brazilian market had a profound impact on Brazilian women. Gaylyn Studlar notes, "In the 1920s the American film industry operated on the assumption that women formed their single most important audience."[63] US movies were explicitly addressed to a female spectator, and American producers and filmmakers openly and aggressively solicited women in narratives that featured heroines as central protagonists. Serial melodramas, such as *The Exploits of Elaine* (1915), *The Perils of Pauline* (1917), and *The Hazards of Helen* (1923), centered on women who embarked on public adventures and engaged in physical stunts. As Ben Singer observes, the narratives of these serials are primarily concerned with displaying the heroine's agility and resourcefulness, and they obviously exclude traditional portrayals of female domesticity and helplessness. Laura Mulvey observes that women's agility was also a key feature of the 1920s flapper films, which delighted in the public mobility of the female protagonists.[64] Dances, parties, and trips to fairgrounds featured in movies like *It* (dir. Clarence Badger, 1927), *Flaming Youth* (dir. John Francis Dillon, 1923), *The Flapper* (dir. Alan Crossland, 1920), and *Our Dancing Daughters* (dir. Harry Beaumont, 1928), providing ample opportunities to focus on women's active bodies. In these films the heroines not only embrace the pursuits of modernity but actually embody them. Modern styles of dress, dancing, drinking, smoking, and especially shopping define the very identity of the films' protagonists. Indeed, shopping is inscribed into the life of the principal character of the film *It*, played by Clara Bow, who works as a salesgirl in a department store.

Such films traveled to Brazil and had a particularly strong influence on female spectators. June Hahner notes that "novel attitudes and images of female behavior arrived in Brazil from the United States in easily assimilated form through the movies. Films portrayed women as independent working girls, modern heroines, and even sexual temptresses."[65] Besse similarly states that in Brazil "female moviegoers gained as role models sexy flappers and independent working girls who stepped out of traditional roles of resignation and modesty."[66] Maria Fernanda Bicalho too writes that in Brazil "the image of woman constructed in [Hollywood] was incorporated into everyday life, conditioning women's experience and the construction of their self-image."[67] Hollywood thus disseminated new models of femininity, something that was often commented on in the Brazilian press. Noting the showcasing of fashion in American films, one particular reporter stated, "The American model is being enthusiastically adopted by Rio's young girls."[68] In 1923 the social commentator Belmonte wrote that American actresses like Joan Crawford were "the models of the fair sex of my country" and observed that Hollywood films were effectively teaching Brazilian women how to behave, act, and dress.[69]

Cinearte's promotion of Hollywood incorporated this pedagogy. Articles paid particular attention to American actresses' behavior and especially their clothes. In an interview with Mary Philbin, for instance, correspondent Marinho carefully describes her modern appearance, noting that she is "dressed in the latest fashions and smoking a cigarette."[70] An article about Lily Damita also foregrounds the actress's style, beginning with a detailed explanation of her dress: "Our star appeared; she arrived in a ball gown, in the latest style, white tulle, adorned with small flowers."[71] In addition to these observations, *Cinearte* also included features that instructed readers in Hollywood stars' fashionable ways. One particular photo spread of Dorothy Sebastian consists of a series of images of the star illustrating how to wear a turban.[72] Another, titled "Lois Wilson Has Decided to Follow the Latest Fashion," depicts the actress getting her hair cut into a bob.[73]

Cinearte thus used Hollywood stars to promote a new image of femininity to readers, one that rested on appearance. In doing so, the publication linked fandom to consumerism. The advertisements for fashion and beauty products that appeared in its pages allowed female readers to make themselves over into new women, just like the American actresses. As if to emphasize this, the magazine routinely included images of female stars modeling fashions. Photographs featured actresses like Norma Shearer, Jean Arthur, and June Collyer in different outfits, ranging from elaborate gowns to bathing suits. Photo spreads with titles like "This Is How They Dress in Hollywood," "Hollywood Dresses," and "Film Fashion" explicitly highlighted clothes worn by various stars. Providing female readers a glimpse of the latest fashions in America, these images offered them the chance to make themselves over into modern women whose identity reflected that of the Hollywood stars.

Cinearte even offered anonymous Brazilian women the chance to become stars. In 1926 Fox sponsored a contest in Brazil in order to find "the next Brazilian thing." The winners were offered a year's contract with the US studio and so the chance of a career in the movies. A clear marketing ploy to stimulate local interest in the studio's films, the competition generated much attention in the pages of *Cinearte*, which exclusively promoted it for Fox. Asking, "Who Wants to Be a Fox Star?" announcements informed readers of this "magnificent opportunity to embrace a film career."[74] The magazine covered the competition extensively, reproducing numerous images of potential stars. Women submitted to *Cinearte* studio portraits of themselves in sleeveless dresses, bobbed hair, and swimsuits. Their dress and pose followed the conventions established by the American studios, and the images mirrored the photographs of Hollywood's fashionable women that appeared in the Brazilian fanzine. Consumerism was inscribed in this reflection. The Brazilian makeup company Mendel advertised its products as part of Fox's competition and even offered the successful participant money to spend on its lipsticks, rouges, and other products.

Fox's competition thus held out the promise that Brazilian hopefuls could make over their identities and occupy the places held by US stars. *Cinearte*'s promotion of the Fox contest in this sense fostered the mimicry that Gomes and Xavier argue was central to the magazine's relationship with Hollywood. The publication encouraged women readers to narcissistically identify with American stars, producing a female subjectivity whose nonfetishistic gaze relied on an intimacy with the fanzine's images. Luring its readers into the role of overinvolved subjects, this reading of *Cinearte* and its female address posits its women fans as deprived of their own subjectivity and transformed into the passive objects of Hollywood's powerful dream factory.

This is of course reminiscent of broader accusations about women's relationship to mass culture and consumerism. As Huyssen reminds us, women have traditionally been interpreted as lured by the "dreams and illusions" of mass culture, which they consume rather than actively produce.[75] The same accusation has been directed at female film fans, who, as Joli Jenson points out, have historically been defined "as a response to the star system" and thereby passive, "brought into enthralled existence by the modern celebrity system."[76] Yet if *Cinearte* and its promotion of Fox's contest encouraged women's mimetic relationship to Hollywood and its stars, it also endowed its female fans with a sense of active involvement, telling them, "What was an impossible dream yesterday is today within your grasp."[77] The magazine offered Brazilian women an opportunity—however remote—to realize their dreams and transform themselves into the images they gazed at in the pages of the magazine and on the screen. By enabling women to ponder and visualize their own transformation, the contest reproduced them not as consumers but as actors, giving them the opportunity to recreate themselves by sending their images into the public domain. In other words, the contest and *Cinearte* revolved around creating desires for a new modern identity in their readers, which enabled them to experiment with ideas of personal revision and to move from being passive readers to engaging actively in their own transformation.

This active participation and agency in film culture was not restricted to Fox's contest. Write-in sections and quizzes to guess the most beautiful star also provided an opportunity for fans to display their cultural capital regarding American cinema. In providing this outlet, *Cinearte* was, of course, in no way subversive; it participated in the strategy of spectatorial identification and intimacy created and fostered by Hollywood. But while the magazine was imbued with the American studios' market-driven ideology, it still offered a practical way for women to become knowingly and actively involved in film culture and in the process to negotiate their own new identities beyond the limited domestic realm traditionally ascribed to them. The magazine thus did not encourage a total investment in illusion but was predicated on the assumption that women could participate in an engagement with film that might include (for want of a better word) fetishistic pleasure, a pleasure that was consumerist in nature. This fetishistic pleasure played with the disparity between an ideal object of desire (Hollywood's modern visions) and an individual lack (Brazilian reality). It also and crucially worked on the premise of attainability: modernity was possible and women could personally embody it.

Cinearte's coverage of Fox's competition continued well after the winners had been announced. The publication reported on the activities of the successful candidates, documenting their movie careers in the section "Brazilians in Hollywood." Central here was the female winner, Lia Torá. The Brazilian magazine included numerous features and interviews that proudly informed readers of Torá's Hollywood movies and her life in America. These included extensive photographs of "our Lia" and publicity stills from her films, in which she very much appears as a glamorous Hollywood star. Torá's success story clearly symbolized the promise of the movies for Brazil's women and foregrounded their ability to transform fans' lives, literally.

In 1929 Fox terminated Torá's contract. The Brazilian actress, however, remained in Hollywood, where she formed her own production company, Brazil Southern Cross Films. Its first project was *Soul of a Peasant,* which was directed by her husband Júlio de Moraes and starred Torá. *Cinearte* reported on Torá's movie in prose and especially in photographs. The images documented the Brazilian star's latest Hollywood makeover, in which she was very much an active agent in the production of her own image. Torá's career allows us to see how Brazil's female fans' engagement with American film culture in *Cinearte* offered them the opportunity to negotiate their own modern identities, turning their attentions from Hollywood to themselves in practical ways. For Brazilian women, the cinema became a path from tradition to modernity, and many, like Torá, embraced it to assert their freedom from the constraints of the past and to fashion identities for themselves as New Women.

CREATING A BRAZILIAN DREAM FACTORY

This opportunity to project and create a new identity through *Cinearte*'s promotion of US film culture was not restricted to women. As noted earlier, the publication offered a specialized discourse about cinema that enabled readers to engage critically with film language. In doing so its writers encouraged audiences to develop their own critical sensitivities concerning Hollywood's movies. The publication in this way opened up a discursive space in which American cinema could be evaluated and at times contested. Indeed, reviews for US films were often quite scathing. The publication, for instance, dismissed *The Canvas Kisser* (1925) as a "puerile film" with "a weak narrative."[78] It observed that *The Perfect Man* "could have been better, much better," and in a review for *The Runway* it stated that Cecil B. De Mille "could have made much more of this; the initial parts of the film could have been extraordinary with better care and treatment. The story has some good parts but lacks direction."[79]

Readers often participated in these critiques and were especially damning of American movies that depicted Brazil negatively. In a letter that appeared in the section "Letters to the Projectionist" in 1928, one fan declared, "We need to eradicate offensive productions from our country; we need to eliminate studios, like

Fox, who use the seventh art to discredit our nation. We must forge our cinematic independence. We must support the development of film in Brazil in order to free ourselves from foreign visions that depict us as barbaric, as a nation where civilization does not exist. Up with Brazilian cinema!"[80] If *Cinearte*'s promotion of Hollywood's films and its stars rested on a discourse that emphasized their similarities to Brazil, American movies' depiction of Brazil as barbaric violently disavowed this narcissistic fantasy of sameness, projecting an image that was distant and alienated from North America. As the reader's reaction illustrates, this alienation opened up the space for a desire for a national cinema that would project a civilized image of Brazil for spectators at home and abroad. *Cinearte* fostered this desire, ardently promoting Brazilian cinema in the pages of its magazine. In fact, *Cinearte* was, perhaps paradoxically, fiercely patriotic. With its slogan "All Brazilian films must be seen," the magazine promoted and defended domestic cinema, hoping to stimulate an interest in national productions.

While Hollywood dominated the Brazilian market during this period, domestic filmmaking did not cease. Bicalho writes that "the 1920s saw a new burst of cinematographic activity, with a significant increase in the quality of movies produced."[81] Between 1921 and 1930, on average 16.7 feature films were produced in Brazil per year, mainly by companies located in regional cities beyond the Rio–São Paulo axis in Recife, Campinas, Porto Alegre, and Cataguases. Alongside reports on US movies, *Cinearte* documented these cinematic ventures, endowing the independent regional projects with a united Brazilian identity. The section "Brazilian Films" documented productions taking place around the country. Adopting a template from Hollywood fanzines, it featured synopses and reviews of domestic movies. It also published photographs of actors and actresses, in poses and clothes so similar to those of their US counterparts that, as Gomes notes, readers had to carefully read the captions to determine their nationality.[82] In this way *Cinearte* created a Brazilian star system, its spectacular movie stars projecting the image of a thriving national film industry. Hollywood's ubiquity and the limited exhibition of domestic films, however, meant that the public had little access to the films the Brazilian stars appeared in, and their consumption of Brazilian cinema was relegated to features in *Cinearte*. Gomes thus writes that the magazine "was concerned with creating a fiction that had the greatest semblance of an appearance of reality but had little basis in it."[83]

Given the fictional qualities of this star system, it is hardly surprising that Gomes highlights the system's mimetic qualities, in keeping with the broader mimeticism he sees articulated by *Cinearte*. Certainly, *Cinearte* included commentary that reinforced this, as the magazine's writers themselves often stressed the Brazilian stars' debt to Hollywood. A feature in the October 9, 1929, issue referred to actress Lelita Rosa as "the national Greta Garbo" and called Lia Jardim "the Brazilian Clara Bow."[84] Consequently, for Xavier, *Cinearte*'s star system exemplifies "the mimicry that articulated an attempt to define a Brazilian cinema based on imported parameters."[85] Reflecting the homogenizing impulses of Hollywood and its domination over markets, *Cinearte*'s star system highlights, consciously or not, the dilemma of dependency that was a marked feature of Brazilian film criticism in the 1960s and '70s.

Yet *Cinearte*'s Hollywood-style stardom had a practical aim; its endeavor was, as the journal stated, to "make names. They will guarantee the success of our new films."[86] The magazine emphasized the importance of North America's publicity-driven strategies. Publicizing movies was deemed "the industry's soul."[87] Stars were fundamental to this process, as they were able to "attract the public to our cinema, without having to count on film itself."[88] Such statements point to an unlimited and unconditional belief in the power of publicity and an overwhelming faith in the agency of magazine readers. Stardom did not merely project a national film industry; it was considered capable of conjuring it into existence, with stars manufacturing a Brazilian dream factory. The display of stars' bodies signified, not a fiction of the cinema's presence in Brazil, but rather the commercial possibilities of an industry that could capitalize on the desires of a growing market of mass consumers, especially female consumers.

Regional filmmakers like Gentil Roiz and Humberto Mauro targeted female audiences, appealing to them on the basis of intertexts and ideological discourses, with particular narratives and especially stars. Indeed, it was not only as consumers that women became crucial to this period of Brazilian cinema. Films created new vocations for women, as well as significant social positions and public images. The production of regional films created a demand for actresses not just to fill the scenes but also to play leading roles. Carmen Santos, Nita Ney, Lia Torá, Eva Nil, Didi Vianna, Eva Schnoor, and Lelita Rosa took on starring parts in movies such as *Retribuição* (Retribution; dir. Gentil Roiz, 1924), *Braza dormida* (Dormant embers; dir. Humberto Mauro, 1928), *Tesouro perdido* (Lost treasure; dir. Humberto Mauro, 1927), *Vício e beleza* (Vice and beauty; dir. Antonio Tibiriçá, 1926), *Mocidade louca* (Crazy youth; dir. Felipe Ricci, 1927), *Morfina* (Morphine; dir. Nino Ponti and Francisco Madrigano, 1928), *A carne* (Flesh; dir. Leo Marten, 1924), *Quando elas querem* (When they love; dir. Eugênio Kerrigan, 1925), and *Sangue mineiro* (Blood of Minas Gerais; dir. Humberto Mauro, 1929). These films created an opportunity for many women to improve their social standing and transform themselves. For example, Carmen Santos, the daughter of poor immigrants, worked as a shopgirl in a department store in Rio until 1919, when she responded to an advertisement for a competition for film actors in the magazine *Para Todos*—a life history that makes obvious the productive link between cinema and the expansion of female consumption.[89]

The appearance of actresses like Carmen Santos in Brazilian films emphasized the public visibility of women, and many narratives reinforced their new place in society by incorporating generational conflicts between traditional and modern ideals of womanhood. Clarinda, for example, the main character in *When They Love*, played by Laura Letti, is caught between her desire for independence and her sense of duty to her family, and she ends the film by flying her own plane to São Paulo in pursuit of her future husband. The film evokes a certain pleasure in Clarinda's physical movement as well as her interaction with technology. This interaction is a marked feature of *Crazy Youth*, whose narrative centers on the adventures and predicaments of Yvonne Teixeira, played by Isa Lins. Early on in the film her car breaks down, leading her to embark on a number of intrepid escapades.

Female characters are at the center of or at least implicated in the dramatic activity of these movies. In *Lost Treasure* and *Retribution* the female stars are caught up in stories involving bandits in search of a treasure map. In *Lost Treasure* the heroine Suzana (played by Lola Lys) is kidnapped by villains who want the map, and in *Retribution* Almery Steves is part of a couple that, in search of treasure, confronts a group of bandits. In other films, the drama evolves from sexual conflicts and love triangles. Directors like Mauro introduced sexual and even conjugal conflicts into their plots. In *Blood of Minas Gerais* Santos plays a millionaire's adoptive daughter who is driven to attempt suicide when the man she loves is unfaithful to her. She wanders into the countryside and tries to drown herself but is rescued by two young men, who are cousins, who then both fall in love with her.

These films incorporated the publicness of Brazil's new woman by depicting female characters engaging in outdoor spaces and activities or dealing openly with sexual conflicts. Santos played up to her role as a new woman in interviews. In the magazine *Palcos e Telas* she stated, "In Mendes [in the state of Rio de Janeiro] I became a horsewoman, launching myself across hills and valleys in mad gallops, falling into precipices, almost dying three or four times. Today I can ride a horse like any fearless cowgirl. In Rio I trained to row. I race around on a motorbike and can drive a car at full speed with such daring that my chauffeur goes around saying I'm crazy."[90] Referring to her horse riding and driving, Santos places herself at a great distance from previous domestic ideals of femininity. In fact such ideals are noticeably missing from most of the films: their narratives are structured by the dissolution of the home, figured by the number of absent fathers and especially mothers, often leaving young female protagonists to articulate and negotiate new kinds of domesticity and femininity. In *Retribution* and *Blood of Minas Gerais*, the heroines are both orphans seeking to make their own place in society. The dissolution of the family is a marked feature of films dramatizing the fate of fallen women, such as *Morphine* and *Vice and Beauty*, where the traditional cult of womanhood and the home is most blatantly challenged. In both of these films, the female characters abandon, or are forced to abandon, domestic duties, and they embark instead on a life of pleasure that consequently destroys their own happiness and stability as

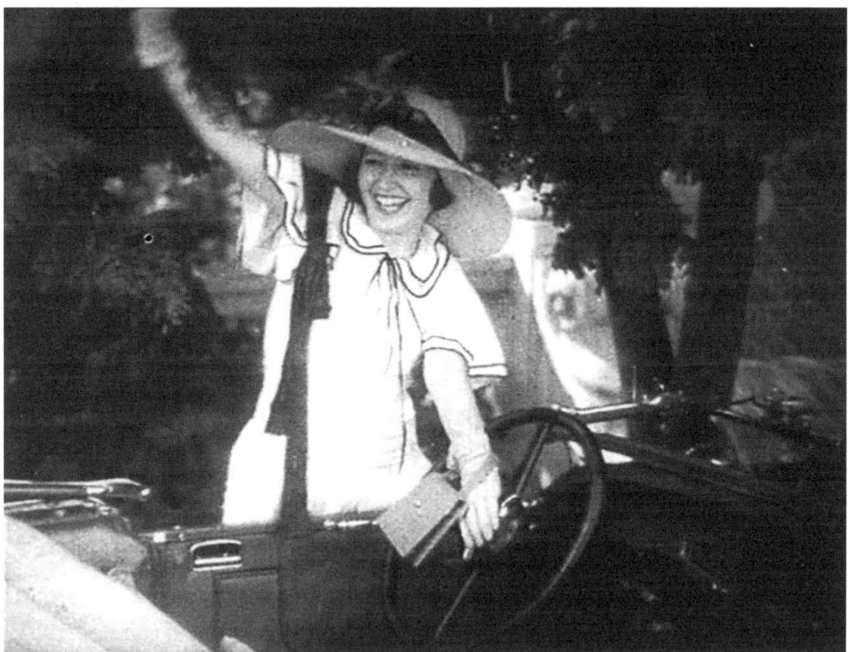

FIGURE 13. Carmen Santos in *Blood of Minas Gerais*, 1929. Acervo Cinemateca Brasileira, Secretaria do Audiovisual do Ministério da Cultura.

well as that of others. *Vice and Beauty,* for instance, stars Lelita Rosa, playing a prostitute who disrupts the blossoming relationship of Antonio and his childhood sweetheart Anita. In *Morphine,* Nita Ney's character is introduced to the eponymous drug by an attractive suitor who then forces her into a life of prostitution. These films convey a moral lesson that young girls who abandon the home and succumb to the temptations of a modern, carefree life will descend into a life of prostitution, making them become figures of pathos. The movies thus displaced the split between tradition and modernity onto young female stars at a time when definitions of femininity and indeed of Brazil as a nation were being radically revised.

The stardom of these actresses was partly derived from their image as champions of a modern lifestyle that involved car driving, sexual dilemmas, and fashionable clothes (figure 13). Indeed, more than their actions, it was their physical appearance that underlined their status as stars. With their slender build, bobbed hair, and pale complexions, the actresses epitomized the new woman. Drawing on women's magazines, filmmakers highlighted stars' modern style, dressing them in the latest fashions and surrounding them with elegant furnishings. Films paid particular attention to the appearance of the actresses, and directors made sure they were attired in modern clothes. Discussing his film *A carne* in 1924, director Leo Marten noted that "the interiors were all filmed in the luxurious rooms of the Hotel Seventh of September, which the prefect kindly lent me. Additionally the furniture is extremely lavish, consisting of old and expensive pieces. . . . The clothes too are the highest quality, chosen under my guidance. Among these, Lenita's dresses are, of course, the best."[91] Movies such as *Dormant Embers* included parties and scenes of dancing, which provided ample opportunities to display sumptuous gowns on their female stars.

This became central to *Cinearte*'s politics of stardom. Photography was key to the journal's construction of Brazilian stardom, and the magazine went out of its way to emphasize its stars' modern image. Ana Pessoa writes that "objects, clothes, props, and makeup are used to create a sensual atmosphere, mixing the dramatic eroticism of the vamp with the ambiguous mystery of the femme fatale. Turbans, furs, tiaras, pearls, crowns of flowers, wonderful materials adorn the actresses' body."[92] Female stars were commonly promoted as spectacles of a conspicuous modernity that enhanced their sexual attractiveness. The emphasis on their attractive bodies, a marker for their sexual independence, became a privileged site of visual pleasure in these movies, providing a relay of desire and identification with a modern world of fashion and consumerism that was linked to the United States and also Brazil. Indeed, the actresses' visibility in these films and their intertexts gave them an emblematic status in the contemporary landscape: they were Brazil's own mannequins of modernity.

The nexus between women, cinema, modernity, and consumption, however, was not universally celebrated. Actresses were denigrated, and the period saw severe reprobation leveled at female stars, whose public visibility was considered synonymous with sexual chaos that was precipitating a social crisis. Families often objected to their daughters entering the movies, and many actresses, like Augusta Guimarães and Davina Fraga, had to defy family and societal prejudice in order to embrace screen life.[93] Recalling her years as a film actress, Didi Viana emphasized the stigma attached to women working in the movies, observing, "There is something that saddens me greatly. It is seeing how the problem of 'being an artist' is regarded in Brazil: the bad name that a girl who works in the movies is given. Believe it or not, I am different now. I think differently. I thought I could flirt like any girl. But then I found out that as a movie artist I couldn't enjoy that right without suffering the effects of terrible criticism."[94] As Viana notes, actresses were disdained and their reputations were subject to harsh moral scrutiny. Newspapers cited the fact that many actresses, such as Antônia Denegri, had worked in cabarets as proof that they were morally suspicious and condemned them as "prostitutes of modernity."[95] Far from demure, the actresses engaged in a self-display that was perceived as tantamount to prostitution in that it was interpreted as an attempt to garner indiscriminate attention.

NEGOTIATING THE RESPECTABILITY OF
BRAZILIAN MOVIES

The threat of female stars led to the development of a particular politics of stardom that aimed to carefully balance the new woman and the visual pleasures she afforded with more traditional qualities. Bicalho notes that the cinematic *melindrosas* that appeared in Brazilian films embodied contrasting types: "the innocent woman" and "the vamp."[96] Cinematic narratives as well offset the modernity of female stars by negotiating their attractive images into more reassuring places, a strategy that no doubt helped films avoid censure. Yet it was in *Cinearte* that such negotiation really came to the fore.

As noted previously, the journal explicitly aimed to elevate film's cultural status. Discussions of the cinema's artistic qualities helped to legitimize the medium, which was promoted as offering modern, yet high-class products. The magazine's star discourse was part of this attempt at cultural legitimization, exploiting and reconfiguring Hollywood's templates. Far from a superficial implant, the very notion of stardom helped to distinguish actresses from the crowd and from everyday working women. While *Cinearte*'s promotion of Hollywood's stars endeavored to present them as ordinary, its depiction of their Brazilian counterparts stressed their "otherworldliness." In one issue, for instance, Lia Torá is described as "a saint with a halo in search of an altar. With divinely feminine eyes that emanate sincerity, beauty, and art."[97] In the same issue Carmen Santos is called "a star descended from heaven and converted to the form of a woman."[98] The magazine also imbued Brazil's female stars with an elusive "It" quality, defined as an innate attractiveness that could not be acquired. Such descriptions countered the idea of stardom as an inherent quality and the belief that anybody can be a star. In *Cinearte*'s politics of stardom, Brazilian stars were born to be stars, their vocation divinely inscribed and predestined.

The Brazilian stars' modern image was key in reinforcing their extraordinariness. Sumptuous dresses worn by actresses in publicity shots and movies emphasized their modernity, placing them in stark contrast to previous models of femininity, yet the expensiveness of the materials (pearls, furs, tiaras) also imbued these clothes with a sense of luxury that associated the actresses, and by extension film, with high society. In this respect these female stars differed significantly from the new working women that figured in 1920s Hollywood cinema, like Clara Bow, Louise Brooks, and Evelyn Brent. Shelley Stamp and Miriam Hansen note that Hollywood movies of the period often featured women eking out a living in the paid labor force, in narratives that assumed a more egalitarian discourse addressed primarily to working women.[99] Hollywood films thus often opened up depictions of female behavior that went beyond the domains of traditional respectability. By contrast, Brazil's movies of the same period featured few if any working female characters, and their stars invariably played the roles of daughters from families linked to the traditional landed gentry, as seen in *Blood of Minas Gerais*, *Dormant Embers*, and *Retribution*. The films associated their modern women with the elite, not the emerging middle or working class, and they did not ground the texts in a modern social reality. Instead, they offset the modern body of their cinematic *melindrosas* by more traditional qualities, with their attractive images and active performances negotiated back into more reassuring places.

Indeed, the ubiquitous happy ending of these films features the defeat of villains and the triumph of marriage, with female characters realizing their true desires for domesticity and coupledom. *Blood of Minas Gerais*, *Lost Treasure*, and *Retribution* all end in marriage, with the young girls finally reestablishing their correct place in the domestic realm. Many of the more risqué "fallen women" films also reassert women's traditional domestic role in their narrative endings. At the end of *Vice and Beauty* Antonio's wayward life is saved by his love for Anita, and in *Morphine* Nita Ney's character overcomes her modern vices and reconciles with her family. In these movies, the destruction of modern female characters is resolved at the narrative level by the restoration of a traditional order. This tension between modernity and tradition often figures in the movies' mise-en-scène: the traditional landscape (a marker of the productions' regionalism and of a Brazilian cinema) features prominently in these films, in panoramic shots that depict idyllic scenes reminiscent of the country's romantic cultural tradition, rather than modern society. The setting contrasts and conflicts (often quite awkwardly) with the female stars' modern image and their activities. In *Retribution*, for instance, Almery Steves's fashionable dress and especially her high heels look out of place in the natural landscape and effectively deter her from catching the bandits, a task left to the men. Acknowledged visually, the new woman's activity is thus circumscribed by the narrative, which ultimately reinforces traditional patriarchal roles.

The new woman in Brazilian films was therefore associated with traditional society, which was reflected and reinforced in *Cinearte*. The magazine carefully balanced the modern style of its female stars with portraits of their respectable backgrounds and portrayed them according to a formula that paid obeisance to past notions of femininity. Interviews with actresses were invariably conducted at home in the presence of husbands, mothers, and fathers, all duly supported by photographs. For instance, an article on Lia Torá published on January 2, 1929, featured images of the star at home with her sister, niece, mother, and grandmother, firmly rooting her in a domestic setting and to past generations of Brazilian women. Portraits were often accompanied by personal revelations. Such features were in keeping with Hollywood's publicity machine, which fed readers information about stars' personal lives. While *Cinearte* employed this strategy, it did so keeping within the limits of a discourse that emphasized family and respectability. Writers reported on stars' home-loving nature, contrasting it to their modern image. Meeting Lia

Jardim, the star of *Morphine*, Lima noted, "When I was introduced to Lia Jardim I immediately saw how photographs deceive. Of medium height, more on the short side, with short hair, she seemed like an inoffensive flapper, very nervous, gentle, attentive, sweet, and docile."[100] Here the journalist remarks on a contradiction between the star's image and her real self. By stressing the reality of Jardim's child-like stature and docility, he downplays her sexual attractiveness and thereby attenuates any potential threat the star's modernity may pose.

Cinearte presented female stardom as the preserve of innocent ladies from respectable families. In an issue published on January 16, 1929, Lima noted that actresses were "people of a certain stature in society, not just anyone from the street. This raises the moral status of film."[101] In another issue he wrote that stars were "distinguished young family girls, society girls," and that this "provide[d] the cinema with a greater seriousness."[102] The rags-to-riches stories of stars' lives that were featured in US fanzines were not present in *Cinearte*. Actresses' humble backgrounds were significantly absent from the magazine; instead journalists penned stories of their decent upbringing, supported by photographs. At a time when the country was undergoing profound changes, its social and economic structures threatened by the forces of modernity, *Cinearte* reinscribed its modern stars within reassuring traditional parameters. Consequentially, the publication manufactured a fiction of Brazil's female stars and, by extension, of the country's cinema as a modern industry that presented little threat to tradition.

All of this can be seen as part of the bid for respectability that was at the heart of *Cinearte*'s campaign for Brazilian cinema. It involved making sure that the cinema was seen as a modern commercial industry that could at the same time meet the expectations of the country's traditional elite. As Xavier suggests, the progressive sectors would be pleased to see the cinema as an industrial venture with clear economic advantages, while the traditional sectors' concerns would be also be appeased.[103] This strategy influenced female stardom, which masked the challenges of modernity by projecting an image that catered to a new female market and also the country's entrenched traditions. Far from being an outright mimicry of Hollywood's dream factory, 1920s Brazilian stardom incorporated and reconfigured foreign models in ways that catered to the promises and challenges of the country's modernity and its cinema.

This negotiation was not limited to film and stardom. In their analysis of Brazilian magazines during this period, Marina Maluf and Maria Lúcia Mott observe that female consumers were also ultimately promoted as wives and mothers.[104] The consumer goods available to women that were so eagerly advertised and promoted by the press—clothes, makeup—while reflecting the emergence of a new woman were also sold as opening up the possibility of marriage. The rewards of stylishness, good grooming, and consumerism were male admiration and love. Technological products too, which released women from the drudgeries of domestic chores, were sold as products that allowed women more time to indulge in making themselves more attractive to men (and hence marriage material) or in tending to their husbands and children. Public forms of mass consumption were in this way translated into private forms of reproduction that occurred within the traditional sphere of family life. Such discussions sought to contain the new woman's consuming desires safely within the home and the family, just as films circumscribed actresses' visibility in the domestic space. The new woman's public appearance was permitted and even encouraged but only if she was to be seen as a wife or mother.

THE COLOR OF STARDOM

While Brazilian stars may therefore have projected modernity, the past lingered on in their star texts. Not only gender but race was bound up with this retention of a traditional order. However liberating their new images may have been, *Cinearte*'s female stars were homogeneously white in the very racially mixed population of Brazil. The respectability of Brazilian stardom was a sign of a traditional modernity, and discourses around their images were achieved through repressions that supported and maintained socioeconomic inequalities and hierarchies. Indeed, the visibility of Brazilian stars in *Cinearte* draws attention to the invisibility of blackness in the magazine and in feature films. From this point of view, the possibility of liberation embodied by the stars allowed Brazilian film and film culture to avoid the social and political discourse of freedom and equality in a country that was still intensely anxious and phobic about race.

Gomes, Xavier, and Robert Stam have underscored the racial discourses implicit in *Cinearte*'s politics of stardom. As Xavier shows, the magazine's ideas of a "good cinema" rested on racist notions that were implicit in its notion of *photogénie*. Developed by French film theorists, like Jean Epstein, to advance the specific potentialities of film as a seventh art, *photogénie* was translated by *Cinearte*'s writers as an epidermic notion of beauty, associated with luxury, hygiene, stars, and whiteness.[105] European and especially Soviet cinema was denigrated. Describing Soviet films, critic Octavio Mendes wrote, "A cinema that preaches revolution, that teaches the weak not to respect the strong, the servant not to respect the master, that shows dirty, bearded, unhygienic faces and sordid events and extreme realism is not cinema."[106] The critic by contrast praised Hollywood films as offering "an adorable photogenic youthfulness."[107]

> Imagine a young man, a young girl, who go to watch a Tom Mix movie, a typical Hollywood film. They will see a clean-faced, shaven hero, with well-combed hair, agile, a gentleman. The girl will be beautiful with a good figure, a gentle face, modern hair-style, photogenic. Then there is a comedic figure and a villain, who are also hygienic and distinct, the only thing distinguishing them is a moustache. Also a modern farm, photogenic, the subordinates submit themselves to their superiors

happily and with great satisfaction, and there is a rhythm, which is the rhythm of life today, light, agile, modern.[108]

As Stam notes, although this passage does not explicitly refer to race, its call for clean and hygienic as opposed to dirty faces suggests a coded reference to the subject.[109] Combining ideas of *photogénie* with a politics of stardom, Mendes's account of cinema offers an aristocratic model of racial perfection and an aesthetic preference for "good appearance" that divides people who have it from those who do not.

These ideas influenced *Cinearte*'s promotion of national films. Reviewing Cornélio Pires's Brazilian documentary *O Brasil pitoresco* (*Picturesque Brazil*, 1925), Mendes, for instance, wrote:

> When will we stop this fad for displaying Indians, mixed races, black people, savages, and other rare creatures of this land? Imagine that these films are seen abroad. Besides, lacking art and technique, they will convince foreigners that we are a country like Angola, the Congo, or even worse. It is unacceptable to ignore our urban boulevards, gardens, squares, works of art, etc., and instead show bandits, a *mestiço* selling alcohol, a group of Negroes bathing in a river and things like that. The future of cinema lies in feature films, which are well directed and well acted and above all look good.[110]

For the magazine's writers, Brazilian cinema clearly meant Hollywood-style feature films in sophisticated settings, with photogenic urban environments and white stars. These films would project an "ideal" image of Brazil as a modern civilized nation for spectators at home and especially abroad, becoming, as one editorial stated, "a powerful tool of propaganda."[111] This propagandistic cinema, the journal announced, "must involve purifying our reality, showing our works of engineering, our beautiful white people, our natural wonders." By contrast, realist films and documentaries were deemed especially unsuitable, since "you cannot control what is shown and undesirable elements can infiltrate them." *Cinearte*'s writers thus advocated for "studio-made films, like the North American model, with well-decorated interiors, featuring agreeable people."[112] Such films were "a work of true patriotism that is linked to the economic future of our country. Our nature may be beautiful, but no one will pay to see it. Our films will be disseminated throughout the world, showing that Brazil is modern."[113]

America's studio-based films were thus put forward as the model for a national cinema that could ensure that foreign audiences would have a "better" conception of Brazil. A Hollywood-styled stardom was part of this. Indeed, *Cinearte* particularly promoted Fox's star search as a patriotic endeavor. While the publication proposed that the contest would provide an appropriate outlet for Brazilians to embark on a cinematic career in Hollywood, it also emphasized the search as an important tool of diplomacy. The winners, "full of beauty and freshness," would improve Brazil's reputation and image abroad, performing important political labor for the nation.[114] This "freshness" and "beauty" were racialized, as those entering the competition were required to have white skin. The Aryan model of white skin was adopted for the female stars promoted in the magazine. Actresses' brightly lit photographs exaggerated their whiteness and provided them with an angelic glow that imbued the surrounding texts with a sense of purity that was clearly mediated by a traditional economy of race.

Film's propagandistic function therefore rested on projecting an ideal image of Brazil as a modern nation, conveniently ignoring the realities of a predominantly mixed-race society. As Stam notes, such attitudes whitewashed Brazilian cinema, which disregarded Afro-Brazilian actors. While black performers were increasingly present in the country's entertainment industries, notably its recording industry, they failed to find a place in its cinema, which until the 1930s was almost exclusively white.[115] The same attitudes also marginalized documentary practices in Brazil's film history. The realism evident in European and Soviet films was dismissed as revealing "unsavory" landscapes and peoples, and in its place *Cinearte* promoted Hollywood feature films as ideal models to be adopted by Brazilian filmmakers. *Cinearte*'s specialized discourse on the cinema, gleaned from Hollywood, thus had a formative influence not just on film consumption but also on film production in Brazil, giving rise to movies that adopted and adapted the Hollywood template and helped to mediate competing cultural discourses on modernity.

5

Beyond Hollywood

Reading Slave Relations in Humberto Mauro's Lost Treasure *(1927)*

Publishing reviews for Hollywood films, articles about US movies, and gossip about their stars, *Cinearte,* Brazil's first film magazine, introduced a specialized discourse that taught readers how to understand American cinema. This discourse also taught Brazilian filmmakers how to make Hollywood-styled movies, and the publication particularly influenced the new generation of regional filmmakers that emerged in the 1920s. Indeed, the magazine not only documented developments in foreign filmmaking endeavors but played a key role in catalyzing film production in Brazil. Its section "Amateur Cinema" was particularly influential in encouraging new talent and in constructing a sense of a national film industry (however precarious) that, like Hollywood, focused on studio production and to which stars were central. *Cinearte* clearly perceived US movies to be universal, and its editors believed that Hollywood's mode and aesthetics could be adopted to forge a national cinema.

The regional films that emerged in 1920s Brazil thus invariably appropriated North America's cinematic language, mimicking its classical form. That *Cinearte* endorsed Hollywood as ideal for domestic production is not surprising given the publication's narcissistic identification with North American cinema. For both Paulo Emílio Salles Gomes and Ismail Xavier this identification was a symptom of the strength of US imperialism and, by extension, of Brazil's dependency on US dominant power, with cinematic mimicry inextricably related to questions of coloniality.

Jean-Claude Bernardet has recently returned to the question of mimeticism in Brazilian cinema. Referring specifically to the 1920s, Bernardet interprets the reproduction of the imported product as an attempt by domestic filmmakers to satisfy Brazilian audiences whose tastes were increasingly being formed by US films.[1] From this point of view, appropriation emerges as an attempt to "face up to Hollywood."[2] As Bernardet points out, this pragmatic approach was not viewed negatively at the time. On the contrary, the ability to assimilate US cinema's modern techniques was praised as spectacular proof of Brazilians' ability to overcome backwardness and become modern.[3]

This path of achieving Brazilian modernity through appropriating foreign models is suggestive of the concept of "out-of-place ideas" elaborated by Roberto Schwarz. The example Schwarz provides is the nineteenth-century elite's adoption of modern European liberal discourses. As Schwarz points out, this adoption took place while the country's economy and society were still based on the incompatible practice of slavery, with liberal ideas therefore being out of place. For Schwarz, this does not mean that modern discourses were inauthentic; in fact, he specifically writes that for the elite the "test of reality and coherence" was of little importance. Rather, functioning as "second-degrees ideologies that do not describe reality, not even falsely," liberal ideas were "adopted with pride as proof of modernity." In other words, they adorned the elite and validated their pretensions of progress, while hiding a reality that remained mired in the illiberal social system of slavery.

The juxtaposition of a modern ideology and a traditional milieu has important consequences for the analysis of Brazil's cultural texts. Indeed, Schwarz notes that the contradictory marriage between liberalism and slavery generated a disjuncture that has been an internal and active element in the country's cultural production. Brazilian culture, he writes, "unceasingly affirms and reaffirms European ideas, yet always improperly."[4] This is reminiscent of Gomes's discussion of Brazilian cinema's mimetic relationship to Hollywood as evidencing a similar disjuncture, which he calls "our creative incapacity for copying," revealing a distance from North American cinema's universal(zing) form.[5] Cinematic mimicry in this sense becomes "an inappropriate signifier" of imperialism and coloniality, and Brazilian cinema's imitation of Hollywood reveals deviations that include Brazil as a partial presence and destabilize the North American model while also copying it.[6]

These departures are reminiscent of what Román de la Campa, referring to a broader Latin American context, describes as *détour*—a reflexive practice in which mimicry is always fraught with inconsistencies and contradictions.[7] Such contradictions point to what Néstor García Canclini refers to as the hybrid nature of Latin American modernity, which consists neither of a homegrown culture nor of straightforward duplication.[8] These contradictions were part of 1920s Brazilian film culture, as argued in the previous chapter with regard to *Cinearte* and its relationship to Hollywood as it negotiated images from abroad with the needs of Brazil's own process of modernization. They were also at play in film production. Although filmmakers during this period reproduced Hollywood's model, they did so improperly, to use Schwarz's wording, revealing a dissonance between the foreign form and the domestic text. A dialectical relationship between here and there,

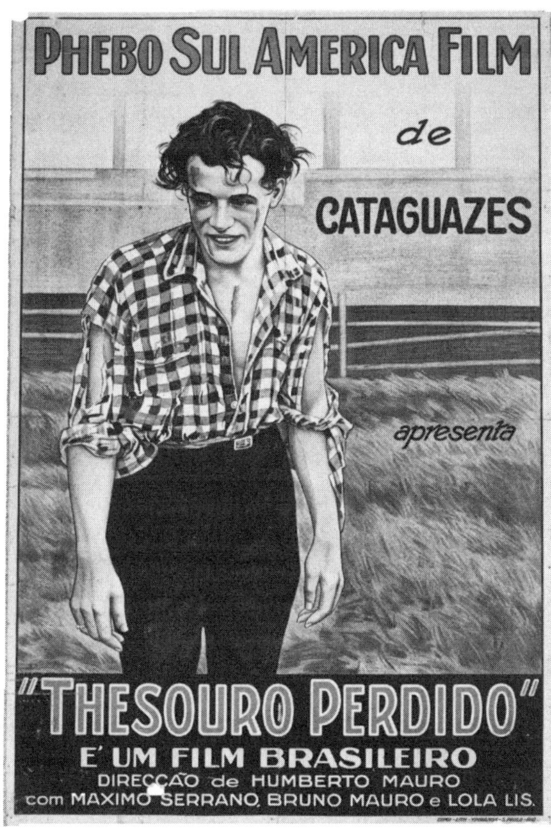

FIGURE 14. Poster for *Lost Treasure*, 1927. Acervo Cinemateca Brasileira, Secretaria do Audiovisual do Ministério da Cultura.

between repetition and difference, structures the period's cinematic mimicry. This dialectic is evident in Humberto Mauro's 1927 film *Tesouro perdido* (Lost treasure) (figure 14).

LOST TREASURE AND *TOL'ABLE DAVID*: IMITATION AND DIVERGENCE

Lost Treasure's US patrimony is extremely specific. Gomes points out that Mauro's film was modeled on Henry King's *Tol'able David* (1921), which was released in Brazil in 1924 and was hugely successful, both commercially and critically. Gomes notes that Mauro "not only saw the film, he also studied it, and watched it again in 1926 under the tutelage of *Cinearte*'s editor Adhemar Gonzaga."[9]

The narrative of King's film revolves around the central protagonist and hero David Kinemon, played by Richard Barthelmess. The son of a West Virginia tenant farmer, David longs to be treated as a man by his family and neighbors, especially Esther Hatburn, the pretty girl who lives with her grandfather on the neighboring farm. He is constantly reminded, however, that he is still a boy, tol'able, but not a man. David eventually gets a chance to prove himself when outlaw Iscah Hatburn and his sons, Luke and Little Buzzard, move into the Hatburn farm against the will of their cousins, Esther and her grandfather. Esther initially tells David not to interfere, saying he is no match for her cousins. The outlaws soon wreak havoc: they kill the Kinemon family's pet dog and cripple David's older brother, Allan, while he is delivering the government mail. David's father sets out to administer vigilante justice but has a heart attack. David is determined to go after the cousins in his father's place, but his mother talks him out of it, arguing that, with his father dead and his brother crippled, the household, including his brother's wife and newborn son, depends on him.

Impoverished by these events, the family is turned out of the farm and forced to live in a small house on the edge of town. David asks for his brother's job but is told he is too young and is given work at the general store instead. When the mail driver loses his job, David finally gets a chance to drive the hack. He loses the mailbag near the Hatburn farm, where it is picked up by Luke. David goes to the farm to demand the bag and confront the criminals. He is shot in the arm by the younger brother but, revived, fights back and shoots Iscah and, after a prolonged fight, also shoots Luke. During the struggle Esther flees to the town and tells everyone that David has been killed. While a crowd prepares to look for the young boy, he arrives in the hack, fulfilling his mission of delivering the mail. Victorious, David is received as a hero, having proved that he is a man. In true Hollywood fashion, the happy ending sees the hero united with the girl he loves and a new family unit formed for the future.

Like *Tol'able David*, *Lost Treasure* takes place on a farm in a rural town—Arraial do Principe in the state of Minas Gerais. Two brothers, Bráulio (played by Bruno Mauro) and Pedrinho (played by Máximo Serrano), live on a *fazenda* or plantation owned by Hilário. Susana's father, Hilário (played by Antonio de Almeida), has looked after the boys since their parents' death. The depiction of the family in Mauro's film is therefore different from that of *Tol'able David*. While King's movie centers on a domestic unit, there is no such focus in *Lost Treasure,* which features an incomplete family.

As noted in the previous chapter, fragmented families, particularly featuring orphans or widowed parents, were a common trait of Brazilian films of the 1920s. In *Lost Treasure* the male protagonists, Bráulio and Pedrinho, are orphans and Hilário is a widower. The family thus stands out by its absence, foregrounding a problem of historical continuation based on filiation. Filiation—the ties that unite parents to children, and past to present—is broken in Mauro's movie, and the codes that order traditional life are undone. *Lost Treasure's* incomplete family in this way touches on the topos of familial crisis crystallized in contemporary moralizing discourses, which were related to the social transformations precipitated by the forces of modernity.[10]

The motif of familial crisis in Mauro's film represents a departure from its US inspiration. In *Tol'able David* the family is from the start omnipresent and complete. Moreover, it is essential to the process of narrative modeling and a fundamental mode organizing the material of the film. The family in crisis in *Lost Treasure* is also significantly different from the family in Brazil's nineteenth-century "foundational fictions," which nurtured and were nurtured by the extended familism of traditional patriarchal society.[11] In these novels the family functions as a metaphor for historical continuity. Such continuity is broken in 1920s *Lost Treasure,* and indeed other Brazilian films of the 1920s, which instead point to a lack of genealogy and to dispossession.

The theme of family crisis was by no means restricted to Brazilian films of this period. It was also evident in literary production. Familial decline features in a number of Brazilian novels from the turn of the century onwards, such as Júlio Ribeiro's *A carne* (Flesh, 1888) and Benjamin Costallat's *Mademoiselle Cinema* (1923). Machado de Assis also portrays the impossibility of filiation and the crisis of patrimony in *Memórias póstumas de Brás Cubas* (Posthumous memoirs of Bras Cubas, 1881) and *Dom Casmurro* (1889). In both novels Machado dismantles familial history as a narrative model that was present in his earlier works, like *A mão e a luva* (The hand and the glove, 1874) and *Helena* (1876). In doing so he brings the uprootedness of the family to the level of speech and discourse, individualizing the voice of the narrators who are cut adrift from the family. The first-person self-conscious prose of these novels thus suggests the truncation of the traditional patriarchal family, as well as historical change.

Lost Treasure, then, is part of a broader trend of problematic genealogical fictions that began to mark Brazilian culture from the end of the nineteenth century, in which traditional patriarchy is either absent or in decline. In Mauro's film, Hilário assumes the absent patriarchal role, becoming Bráulio and Pedrinho's *pãe*—a surrogate father. As a friend of the boys' deceased parents, Hilarío represents a link to the brothers' past. The past reappears more forcefully in the film, however, in the form of a map of lost treasure that Hilário gives to Bráulio on his eighteenth birthday—an inheritance from his late father. The map is thus an object that symbolically connects Bráulio to his forebears and links the present to the past. The film registers this symbolic connection in the crosscutting between the map and a portrait of Bráulio's parents. As an inheritance, the map points to the possibility of reconnecting or recovering a patriarchal authority and filiative order that is lost. This possibility, however, is threatened by the sudden appearance of two outsiders:

the European criminal Raul Litz (played by Alzir Arruda) and the working-class outlaw Manuel Faca (played by Mauro), who set out to steal the map and claim the lost treasure for themselves. In the attempt to usurp Bráulio's inheritance, the strangers kidnap Susana (played by Lola Lys) and hold her ransom, leading to a struggle between the male protagonist and the villains. The happy ending sees the villains defeated, the heroine liberated, and the hero united with the girl.

While *Lost Treasure*'s narrative differs from *Tol'able David* in its treatment of the family, it nevertheless visually echoes its US predecessor. The most obvious echo is the setting. Mauro's visual treatment of the natural environment is strikingly similar to *Tol'able David*'s. Like King's film, *Lost Treasure* includes scenes of the countryside. The initial sequences of both films, for instance, feature static outdoor shots, which visually privilege the rural—fields, rivers, and animals. This gaze at the pastoral in both the Brazilian and US movies establishes the bucolic setting that is soon upset by the criminals.

The visual iconography of Mauro's film is, therefore, remarkably close to its American predecessor. Indeed, the Brazilian movie's depiction of the villains is virtually analogous to that in King's movie, in terms of their actions (in both films the villains mistreat dogs who are part of the families' lives), their appearance (they are bearded and sport moustaches), and ways in which they are filmed (centered close-ups). This recognizable iconography extends to the other cinematic elements. Mauro's film adheres closely to the formula of King's, featuring outsiders who disturb the rural idyll, a conflict between hero and villain that is expressed in the struggle for physical possession of the heroine as well as possession of a prized object (the mailbag and treasure), a chase scene, and a final resolution that sees the villains defeated and the hero and heroine united. But while *Lost Treasure*'s style is fully in keeping with that of *Tol'able David,* its underlying narrative structure departs from that of the American movie, particularly in terms of the familial motif.

For Bernardet, structural deviations from US movies were common in 1920s Brazilian films. "What is imitated in 1920s Brazilian cinema is not the basic dramatic structure but rather the style: gestures, happy endings, chases, etc."[12] He adds that the films' imitation relates to "what we may call epidermal cinematic forms, to differentiate them from basic structural forms."[13] So although the period's filmmakers successfully copied the style of US movies, they improperly reproduced their underlying structure, revealing a dissonance between the Brazilian films' Hollywood style and their narrative organization.

Bernardet interprets this disjuncture between style and structure as the result of Brazil's cinematic incompetence. His reading is reminiscent of Gomes's work and its foregrounding of Brazilian cinema's "creative incapacity for copying." Gomes interprets this incapacity as rooted in the country's underdevelopment, so that Brazil's "incompetent" films reflect society's tradition or backwardness. From this perspective, the structural divergence of 1920s Brazilian cinema from US movies points to ideological incongruities that emerge as the result of importing Hollywood's model to a Brazilian context that embraced modernity without fully dissolving traditional social structures and relations. Although Brazil's elite promoted progress, patrimonial social relations inherited from the colony prevailed during the Republic.

LOST TREASURE'S DIVIDED HEROISM

Brazil's past social structure becomes a determining element in the organization of *Lost Treasure*'s narrative, attaining the status of its formal principle, as the film's plot and characters play out ideological themes and concerns of the period. As previously noted, the past is present in *Lost Treasure,* where it is figured by the treasure map, Bráulio's inheritance. Indeed, though in *Tol'able David* the actions of the hero propel the narrative, in Mauro's film the map motivates the action. The map unleashes desires for the lost treasure in the central protagonist, Bráulio, for whom the promise of riches would make him an appropriate suitor for the landowner's daughter Susana, whom he secretly loves. The film thus links the treasure, as a desired object of possession, to the body of the heroine. Parallel editing emphasizes this connection, interspersing shots of the hero gazing at the map with images of him looking at a photograph of Susana.

The juncture of Susana's body with the map in *Lost Treasure* signals the object's fetishistic character, insofar as it substitutes for Bráulio's erotic attraction for the heroine's body. In this case it stands in for the sexuality that is never depicted in their relationship. It is notable that Bráulio's desiring gaze at Susana in the film is never direct but always mediated by her photograph. Rather than sexual, Bráulio's desire for Susana is strongly figured as fraternal and familial. Sequences depicting him contemplating Susana's picture underscore this, as they visually reiterate shots in which the hero gazes at his parents' portraits, equating Bráulio's affection for the female protagonist with his own familial past.

The hero's desire for his guardian's daughter, then, is not sexually threatening; it is, however, almost incestuous. Raised together, Bráulio and Pedrinho are, we are told, like brothers to Susana. Jobst Welge notes that incest was a key cultural metaphor for family crisis in European nineteenth-century literature.[14] In Eça de Queiroz's *Os Maias* (1888), for instance, the genealogical order of the aristocratic family line is beset by incest. This differs from Latin America's foundational fictions, where, as Doris Sommer has shown, endogamous desire was not taboo and was actually part of the literary project of founding a national family.[15] As she demonstrates, rather than signaling an evolutionary end or future impasse, incest in Latin American novels of the 1800s, like Brazil's *Iracema* (1865) and *O Guaraní* (1857), symbolized the continuation of a traditional familial order, which was projected into the present and future.

In *The Masters and the Slaves,* Gilberto Freyre discusses the conservative function of incest in Brazilian society. "Those marriages, so common in our country since the first century of colonization, of uncle with niece and cousin with cousin, were quite sufficient. These were marriages the obvious purpose of which was to prevent the dispersal of property and to preserve the purity of a blood-stream of noble or illustrious origin."[16] Instead of broadening and widening family relationships and the distribution of wealth and property, incestuous marriages tended to concentrate the latter in the hands of the few and to limit the former. Incest thus functioned to preserve Brazil's traditional patriarchal lineage and restrict its privileges. All of this is relevant to *Lost Treasure*'s narrative. In Mauro's film Bráulio's endogamous love for Susana and their eventual union signal not just narrative resolution but also a solution to familial crisis, as they point to a possible future emerging from an order that is linked to a traditional patrimony and the past.

Bráulio's familial desire is played out in a daydream in which he imagines the life he could have if he finds the lost treasure. In the dream he pictures himself with Susana seated in the plantation house, where they are visited by Pedrinho. The sequence is reminiscent of the fantasy in *Tol'able David* in which the eponymous hero, dressed in an elegant suit rather than his usual rags, drives a sophisticated mail hack, while Esther looks on lovingly. While the dream in Mauro's film is similar to the Hollywood version, the content is significantly different. In Bráulio's projection there is no desire for individual improvement and self-enhancement; instead the Brazilian hero yearns to be part of the established space of the plantation family. Individualism and self-improvement, defining traits of American philosophy and key drivers of Hollywood plots, are absent from Bráulio's dream, and the desire for personal fulfillment becomes a negative trait in the Brazilian movie.

Susana's body and the map are also objects of desire for the outsiders in *Lost Treasure*. In contrast to Bráulio, their desire for Susana is figured sexually, with the villains' lascivious gaze at her body prefigured by their consumption of magazines featuring naked women. Bráulio's repressed desire is projected onto the criminal others, permitting the male hero to pursue purer, more respectable familial goals. The villains' desiring gaze is ultimately intrusive, as they visually survey and then penetrate the farm, kidnapping Susana in order to exchange her body for the map. The heroine is thus turned into a public object of exchange, and the criminals' exogamous desire transforms her into commerce. The criminals' libidinous gaze is clearly transgressive, as it violates physical and spatial boundaries. This transgression is distinctly coded as national and class related. Digressing from the narrative proper, two sequences provide the spectator with knowledge of the criminals' background, revealing Litz's status as a European outlaw and Faca's working-class background. *Lost Treasure*'s narrative thus revolves around an anxiety of penetration by outsiders that is physical and also geographical and social. Litz's and Faca's status as outsiders is iconographically depicted. The villains inhabit a rundown cabin where animals are mistreated and personal desires are acted upon. The dilapidated space is clearly opposed to the clean, calm setting of the traditional farmstead, in which everyone peacefully coexists.

The criminals' transgression is linked to their goal of material enrichment and advancement, that is, their attempt to appropriate Bráulio's inheritance for themselves. Their goal stands as a clear contrast to Bráulio's intentions, and consequently two antithetical forces, the material and the antimaterial, structure the film. This conflict instigates the narrative proper, that is, the need to rescue the stolen object/heroine and save the woman from the dangers of outside intrusion. Positioned as the singular object of desire between the hero and the villains, Susana figures as the symptomatic center of this rescue narrative, which is played out with familiar scenarios from contemporary Hollywood rescue films. The narrative paradigms of these American movies invariably include the hero's investigation and a chase to recover and liberate the abducted woman. Miriam Hansen observes that in US rescue movies the hero's primary urge is to save the woman he loves and to keep her on the path of virtue. She adds that safeguarding women's respectability is the guiding principle of Hollywood's rescue films and their chivalrous plots.[17] This principle is also detected in Mauro's film, where the drama of the outsiders' threat to Susana is enacted through crosscutting and accelerated editing, and close-ups of the criminals' penetrative gaze at the female protagonist's body.

Lost Treasure thus reenacts the familiar scenario of Hollywood rescue films. It also resurrects female and male prototypes: the active hero and the helpless heroine. Yet as Gomes and more recently Luciana Corrêa Araújo point out, heroism is far from straightforward in Mauro's film.[18] The narrative clearly establishes Bráulio as the central protagonist and hero: he possesses the treasure map and has a love interest in Susana. His background and desires are at the heart of the film's plot, which places him at the center of its progress. Point-of-view shots also make him a key point of identification for spectators. The film evidently privileges Bráulio narratively and also visually. Indeed, Gomes observes that Bráulio's status as a hero is signaled, above all, by the film's visual and iconographic register. Bráulio possesses the ingredients of a Hollywood-styled hero, as defined by *Cinearte.* He is "good looking, masculine, strong and essentially photogenic, and is consequently the film's key focus of attention."[19]

Bráulio undoubtedly possesses all the characteristics to defeat the villains and rescue Susana. Surprisingly, however, he never fulfills this chivalrous task. The hero disappears from the film when Hilário's daughter is abducted, leaving his younger brother instead to save the heroine. When Bráulio finally reappears and locates Susana, Pedrinho has already rescued her and killed the villains. The narrative therefore frustrates Bráulio's heroism, and he emerges as an "impotent hero."[20] As Gomes writes, Bráulio "brings nothing decisive to the film's denouement."[21]

Lost Treasure therefore departs from its American model *Tol'able David.* The film's final rescue is realized not by the central protagonist but by a secondary character, and the film's heroism is divided between the leading man and a subsidiary.[22] This division is underscored by the rivalry between the two brothers, who both secretly love Susana. As Araújo points out, divided heroism was evident in other Hollywood-inspired films from this period.[23] *O segredo do corcunda* (The hunchback's secret; dir. Alberto Tavares, 1924), *Retribuição* (Retribution; dir. Gentil Roiz, 1924), and *A filha do advogado* (The lawyer's daughter; dir. Jota Soares, 1926) all feature ineffectual heroes who do not eliminate villainy. This task is instead completed by a secondary male protagonist who struggles against the criminals and rescues the damsel in distress. In *The Hunchback's Secret,* for instance, the leading character João fearlessly confronts the violent overseer of a plantation, who has attacked old Marcos and the landowner's daughter. In spite of João's bravery, it is Marcos who finally defeats the overseer. In Gentil Roiz's *Retribution* a handsome traveler, Arthur, helps Edith look for a treasure chest left to her by her dead father. A criminal gang is also after the hidden money and tries to steal it from her. Attempting to protect Edith, Arthur fights the villains, but he fails to overcome them and they imprison him and the heroine. The captives are rescued when Edith's brother calls the police. Finally, in *The Lawyer's Daughter* Heloísa kills the villain who attempts to rape her. She is arrested and goes to trial without any evidence to prove she acted to defend her honor. Her fiancé, a well-known journalist, investigates the crime in order to clear her name. His investigation, though, is fruitless. The heroine is rescued at the last minute by the family's gardener, Gerôncio, who confesses at the trial that he allowed the villain to enter the girl's bedroom. In this film, the gardener aids the villainous act and also rescues Heloísa to reestablish order and justice, making him what Bernardet calls a "righteous character."[24]

For Bernardet, the righteous character "allows the hero, who remains passive, to benefit from his actions. The righteous character sanctions the hero's passivity and is useful for him: he brings about a virtuous resolution, while allowing the films' heroes to not implicate themselves in any action. The righteous character is important because he allows the beneficiaries of his deeds to not get their hands dirty."[25] As Bernardet observes, regardless of their passivity, the heroes of these films nevertheless benefit from the happy ending brought about by the righteous others. In *The Hunchback's Secret* João marries the landowner's daughter; similarly in *Retribution* Arthur receives the treasure and the girl, and in *The Lawyer's Daughter* the young lawyer marries the exonerated Heloísa. In Mauro's *Lost Treasure* Bráulio too enjoys the outcome of Pedrinho's heroic actions. His brother dies while saving Susana, leaving the leading protagonist to reap the financial and amorous rewards. For Gomes, "There is something profoundly unfair about this situation. The decisive actions were carried out by Pedrinho, who deserves the treasure and Susana. But Pedrinho has been killed and Bráulio receives everything."[26]

NARRATIVE LABOR, SLAVE LABOR

The struggle between the hero and the villains in *Lost Treasure,* as in other films of this time, is thus not depicted as a straightforward confrontation. Araújo writes that "there are very few films made during the 1920s in which the leading protagonist directly confronts the villain or indeed acts to resolve conflicts."[27] In Mauro's film, Bráulio does nothing to solve the central drama. He is fundamentally passive in terms of the narrative. His passivity, however, does not signal a departure from the traditional cinematic alignment of men with activity that marks Hollywood narratives. In spite of his narrative passivity, Bráulio does not assume a feminized status in the film. *Lost Treasure* displays the leading man's physical prowess, carefully portraying his active ability to overpower the criminals. An early flashback, for instance, depicts a struggle between Bráulio and Litz. Bráulio begins the fight after the outsider's inappropriate remarks to Susana, which, we are led to believe, are of a sexual nature. The hero thus initiates the fight in order to defend the heroine's respectability. Easily overpowered by Bráulio, Litz attempts to escape in his car. As he does so, Bráulio grabs the automobile's bumper and literally stops the villain in his tracks. The leading man's physical strength is a visual attraction in this long sequence, and his body is given over to scopophilia. This exhibitionist impulse is not grounded in the hero's sexual objectification. It focuses narcissistically on his physical potency, which rescues him from feminization. That this sequence appears early on in the film is significant. Bráulio's masculine strength is not achieved or earned along the course of the narrative's trajectory, as in Hollywood films, including *To'able David*; it is an essential part of his character and a given from the start.

The showcasing of Bráulio's strength and mastery is an unambiguous gesture that signals his power and ability to overcome villainy. In other words, the film unmistakably tells the spectator that the hero *can* act; he simply *does not* act. The leading man in this sense is not implicated in work: to use Bernardet's words, he does not "get his hands dirty." Narrative labor is instead actively carried out by the complementary and subsidiary male figure, Pedrinho. A "passive/active" division of male labor therefore structures the film's depiction of heroism and drives its narrative resolution. This division is expressive of Brazil's traditional patriarchal social relations, and specifically of the master/slave paradigm formed in colonial plantation society.

As Alexandra Isfahani-Hammond notes, master/slave categories have become profoundly rooted in Brazil's mentality and culture. Joaquim Nabuco predicted the legacy of these categories as early as 1883, before abolition. In his masterpiece *O abolicionismo* (Abolition), Nabuco argued that the slave system in Brazil had so thoroughly saturated thought and behavioral codes that the country might never be freed from its legacy. For the statesman and abolitionist, master/slave relations were completely inculcated into Brazilian society, in every geographical region, so much so that their effects would not easily, or perhaps ever, be eradicated. "Slavery," he wrote, "is an evil that no longer requires new sources to poison our blood, which today can dispense with the relationship between master and slave since it has already injected itself into the national bloodstream. It is not therefore by the simple emancipation of slaves that this infection, for which the national organism acquired such an affinity, will be destroyed."[28] Nabuco suggested that Brazilian culture and society were so deeply saturated in the behavioral and psychological processes of slavery that it would continue to function even when it had been officially, legally, and verbally abolished on paper.

For Nabuco, then, slave relations were deeply ingrained in Brazil and consequentially hard to root out. He contended that the master/slave division would be part of the country's future social relations, evidenced especially in the stigma associated with labor. Nabuco noted that since the masses were the descendants of either slaves or masters they would inherit the combined failings of both groups, which, he added, were really the same, as in general "the slave is simply a man who lacks a slave, and the master is a slave who lacks an owner."[29]

While Nabuco stressed correspondences between the master and slave roles, that is, their endemic participation in the system of slavery, it is worth pointing out the vital labor divisions that structured their intimate relationship. As César Braga Pinto notes, this division is ambiguously present in Freyre's *The Masters and the Slaves*. In his description of plantation society, Freyre writes, "Each white master at the manor had two left hands and each black man two right hands."[30] Stressing the master's dependency on the slave, Freyre acknowledges that the seignorial system exploited the slave's physical labor, making the white man inept at such labor and allowing him to "not get his hands dirty."

The legacy of master/slave relations thus led to an aversion to manual labor, which was "carried out by inferiors."[31] This aversion is at the heart of *Lost Treasure*'s divided heroism in the separation between the passive Bráulio and the active and righteous character Pedrinho. It is significant in this respect that Mauro's film carefully contrasts the two brothers. Pedrinho is portrayed as manually proficient. He makes wooden toys for the local children, and, largely depicted in external shots, he is firmly associated with the plantation's working life. Bráulio by contrast appears to have no manual skills. Mainly portrayed inside the house, seated at desks and perusing paperwork, the older brother is linked to the intellectual and the internal, rather than the external, workings of the traditional farmstead, acquiring a status that is reminiscent of the traditional master's. In this respect, it is unsurprising that the secondary character carries out the hero's work. The advantages of Pedrinho righteous acts are, as Gomes writes, shamelessly enjoyed by the key protagonist/master, who is deserving of them not by his actions but by his very condition.[32] As if to stress the hero's rightful condition, Bráulio burns the treasure map at the end of the film, noting, "I already have my reward. Susana is my treasure." The leading man renounces material desires and personal gain, and his final recompense is the formation of a family with Susana. The closing shot displays the hero and heroine together in the luscious landscape of the rural location, their coupledom asserting the restoration of a traditional order.

The tension between the categories of master/slave, so rooted in Brazilian society, therefore, penetrates and contaminates *Lost Treasure*'s narrative, marking its depiction of heroism and the struggle between the hero and villains, which departs from the dramatic structure of the North American model. This departure relates to the sociopolitical and cultural force field of Brazilian society, its assertion of past social relations, even in the face of radical changes, and, in comparison to US society, the weakness of a new bourgeoisie. While the style projects Hollywood's modern cinema, its narrative is rooted in traditional social systems that continue to permeate Brazil. The film's closure, the formation of a family headed by Bráulio, clearly borrows from Hollywood but nevertheless responds to the Brazilian context. This ending sees the reassertion of the traditional homestead and of patriarchy and the resolution of the familial crisis. This resolution is present in other Brazilian films from this period. *Retribution* and *The Lawyer's Daughter* both have happy endings that feature marriage and the defeat of villains and that ultimately reaffirm patriarchal norms and reestablish "the world as it was."[33] In these movies, the genealogical crisis is resolved at the narrative level, and familial order is (re) established as an ideological confirmation of the continuation of social relations. In *Lost Treasure* this continuation is founded in sexual and sociocultural endogamy that excludes the participation of the other. Indeed, once the heroine is rescued, the outsiders' cabin burns down, so that the fire destroys all traces of the threatening others.

The reassertion of a traditional order in Mauro's film has significant consequences for the depiction of the female protagonist, Susana. Women's empirical presence in 1920s Brazilian movie culture is acknowledged by the heroine's centrality to *Lost Treasure*'s drama. The film lingers on the actress's appearance (her bobbed hair and flapper dress), but female desires are significantly absent. This is underscored in Bráulio's dream in which he envisages an ideal future for himself. As noted, the sequence is reminiscent of David's fantasy in King's *Tol'able David*. In the US movie, the female protagonist, Esther, is significantly present in the hero's fantasy. As David imagines himself as a sophisticated hack driver, he also pictures her gazing adoringly at him. The dream is of course David's projection, but it includes or imagines Esther's desires, foregrounded by her point-of-view shots at the male hero. In Bráulio's dream Susana is not provided with comparable shots. In fact, her gaze is nonexistent throughout the entire film. Female expression is lacking in *Lost Treasure,* and the heroine figures only within the representation of masculine desires and ultimately power. Eschewing the woman's perspective, the film foregrounds and revitalizes masculine and patriarchal presence and potency.

The heroine in *Lost Treasure* thus enforces a male order, and she becomes merely a placeholder for patriarchy in Brazil's modern society. Mauro's film in this sense overlooks changing gender roles, reasserting instead traditional sexual mores. There is, in fact, very little that could be considered transgressive in the film's depiction of femininity. Wearing short yet clean and predominantly white dresses, the heroine visually communicates decency and respectability, making her abduction by Litz and Faca all the more worrying and her rescue all the more urgent. Unlike Esther in *Tol'able David,* Susana does not attempt to escape from her abductors and does not try to flee from their cabin. She is associated very clearly not with action but with sentiment and suffering. Her "sentimentalization" is accentuated by an aura of overexposed bright lighting, which gives Susana an angelic quality. This is matched by the mawkish nature of Lola Lys's acting style, particularly in the abduction scenes, which register her docility.[34] Lys is figured in more traditional ways, and the appearance of Brazil's new women is reflected only in her centrality to the film's plot and in her image or style.

SHOWCASING TRADITIONAL BRAZIL

Lost Treasure's narrative thus reaffirms a familial order, rescuing the traditional patriarchal family for Brazil's modern context. This emphasis on tradition is at play in the movie's depiction of the rural location. Gomes highlights comparisons between *Lost Treasure's* bucolic setting and that of *Tol'able David.*[35] Both films linger on outdoor shots, included narratively as markers of the peaceful idyll that the villainous others disturb. The natural setting is used in both films to support the plot. In *Lost Treasure,* though, shots of the countryside are stretched out in time and not simply concentrated dramatically. Sequences of the picturesque setting are not subordinate to the narrative; their energy extends beyond it. Indeed, even in the dynamic chase scene the plot becomes lost in the display of the rustic location. *Lost Treasure's* gaze at the land thus provides the viewer with moments of pictorial contemplation in a way that is reminiscent of the "cinema of attractions." Mauro's film solicits spectator attention, incites curiosity, and supplies pleasure in exhibiting the natural setting, which becomes of interest in and of itself and as a marker of regional and national specificity.

This showcasing of the national was in keeping with the contemporary emphasis on forging a Brazilian cinema, which *Cinearte* ardently promoted and defended. In its endorsement of *Lost Treasure* the fanzine focused almost entirely on reproducing its landscape shots, rather than displaying its stars, as it did with other movies of the period. In his work on Brazilian cinema's mimicry of foreign film, Bernardet discusses what he refers to as an opposite tendency, which "consists in showing the public precisely what foreign movies cannot display: Brazil. Something that is specifically Brazilian." Bernardet notes, "During the silent period, this tended to be landscape shots." He adds: "This valorization of the virgin Brazilian landscape functions as a response to modernization, which is not Brazilian. Brazil's grand and sumptuous nature, untouched by industrialization, is offered as an opposition to modernity."[36]

Brazilian cinema's natural gaze is then also a gaze at the traditional world. This display was evident in a host of films from this period. Documentaries such as *O Brasil grandioso* (Magnificent Brazil; dir. Alberto Botelho, 1923), *O Brasil desconhecido* (Unknown Brazil; dir. Paulino Botelho, 1926), *O Brasil pitoresco* (Picturesque Brazil; dir. Cornélio Pires, 1925), *Nos sertões do Brasil* (In the Brazilian backlands; dir. Paulino Botelho, 1927), *Viagem ao Brasil* (Journey to Brazil; n. dir., 1927), and *O Brasil maravilhoso* (Marvelous Brazil; dir. Alfredo dos Anjos, 1928) were imbued with a patriotic energy that steered their view away from urban modernity toward nature. These films took Brazilian spectators on journeys around their own country, inculcating a form of national pride. *Lost Treasure*'s landscape shots are linked to this cinematic focus on Brazil's patrimony, and the film's display of nature brings tradition back to the modern context. The film's real location, Minas Gerais, specified at the start of the movie, reinforces this. Well known for its colonial heritage and customs, the state has often been sought out by Brazilian writers, artists, and intellectuals as a repository for traditional culture. In an effort to Brazilianize the country's arts, for instance, modernist writers traveled to Minas Gerais in 1924, seeking to discover the heart of the nation and its past.[37] *Lost Treasure*'s focus on the natural landscape intersects with this search, and the film displays a national scenery, placing Brazil firmly on the cinematic screen.

In its picturesque projection of the nation, *Lost Treasure* is influenced by the country's Romantic painting and iconography. An example is the opening shot of a rural setting. This is followed by a scene in which Susana and Pedrinho, along with farmhands and children, socialize together. The film's opening presents viewers with a romanticizing gaze. The sense of peaceful unity that arises from the depiction of the plantation's idyll harks back to Romanticism's harmonious depiction of the country's nature and people and to what Marilena Chauí calls Brazil's "foundational myth." For Chauí this myth projects an image of the country as populated by a cheerful people and devoid of conflict. Like every *fundatio*, it also assumes an unbroken internal connection to a past that is perennially present.[38] Brazil's foundational myth thus offers up the past for the present and future. In doing so it reasserts traditional patriarchal social relations.

Lost Treasure's landscape thus reinforces and upholds the underlying narrative of the film and its emphasis on the preservation of traditional social structures. The film's narrative stages the anxieties and crisis wrought by the desire for modernity and for social change but resolves these by asserting the presence of the past in the present. In doing so, the film projects a contradictory modernity, revealing the new era's acceptance of traditional mores. *Lost Treasure*'s mimetic relationship of *Tol'able David* and of Hollywood cinema more generally is thus not one of outright imitation. The film adopts features and styles from its modern model that would have been familiar to Brazilian audiences while at the same time reflecting, in its narrative structure and setting, a traditional constellation, providing reassurance that the passage to the future need not be threatening and that the country's foundations can find a place in modern Brazil.

It is worth pointing out the absence of black actors in Mauro's film. Significantly, Bráulio's subservient other is his own brother, so that a white character and actor carries out the leading man's labor. This absence is not surprising. As noted in the previous chapter, Afro-Brazilians were notable for their invisibility in Brazil's silent cinema, and black actors failed to find a place in the country's early films.[39] A notable exception is Soares's *The Lawyer's Daughter,* where the gardener, Gerôncio, is played by black actor Ferreira Castro. In his analysis of Soares's film, Arthur Autran notes that Castro's acting style exaggerates facial gestures and behavior, resulting in a form of zoomorphism.[40] This zoomorphism is present in at the start of *Lost Treasure* in the depiction of the harmonious plantation. A young black child lights a cigarette and begins to smoke, the close-up zooming in on his mouth and eyes. The brief shot is intercut with a close-up of a frog also smoking a cigarette, the intercutting creating equivalence between the Afro-Brazilian child and the animal. The animalization clearly invokes the paradigm of blacks as primitive and inferior on the evolutionary scale and projects the colonialist zeugma yoking native and animal. In doing so, the scene, included as a comic counterpoint, projects the inferiority of Brazil's African population, reinforcing racial hierarchies and invoking well-known racist stereotypes. That the same stereotype is evoked in *The Lawyer's Daughter* suggests that the rare presentation of black figures in Brazil's early films inevitably reiterated racist tropes, portraying Afro-Brazilians' subordinate role. These films, like Brazilian society itself, were clearly unable to face up to sociopolitical debates concerning equality and freedom, and past attitudes to former slaves emerged in the brief presence of black actors on the screen. While mimicking Hollywood, these Brazilian films were clearly attentive to the challenges of Brazilian modernity and helped to project past attitudes, including attitudes toward race, into their narratives and style. Far from over, tradition still had a place in *Lost Treasure* and other Hollywood-inflected films of 1920s Brazil.

PART THREE

The Rondon Commission

Producing New Visions of the Amazon

6

Picturing the Tropics

Forging a National Territory through
Photography and Film

In 1905 Brazilian writer Euclides da Cunha (1866–1909) traveled to the Amazon as part of a joint Brazil-Peru expedition that aimed to determine the borders between the two nations. The trip had a profound impact on Euclides, who became obsessed with the idea of writing a book about the region, entitled *O paraíso perdido* (Lost paradise). This book would do for the Amazon what his celebrated *Os sertões* (1902) did for the northeastern *sertão*: introduce the educated urban population of the South to the backlands they knew nothing about. Euclides, however, never completed his project. Instead he produced a series of essays, most of which he later turned into the first part of the book *À margem da história* (On the margins of history), published posthumously in 1909. As Lúcia Sá argues, the essays hardly provide us with an account of the Amazon in the twentieth century, but they do offer a compelling testimony of Brazil's attitude to the region at the time.[1]

In his essays Euclides describes the "lost paradise" of the Amazon as a fecund but prehistoric and dangerous place. The area is, he says, "the last unfinished page of the Book of Genesis." Its nature is "portentous but at the same time incomplete." Its flora display an "imperfect grandeur," with trees that "return to a much earlier time."[2] This undeveloped Eden breeds disorder. The great rivers "disturb the land" and "uproot entire forests."[3] In this inconstant and primeval land, human life can only be nomadic or worse still, savage, so the region is populated by "frightening tribes who have become the greatest fear for even the most daring of explorers."[4] With its extreme and teeming natural disorder and its inhabitants threatening outsiders, the Amazon is a *terra ignota,* a blank space on the nation's map.

Euclides's writings on the Amazon clearly replay colonial representations of the tropics as excessive, disorderly, and inhabited by barbarians. As Susana Hecht

131

notes, they also echo his epic *Os sertões,* published in 1902.[5] The Amazonian essays contain structural elements that parallel his former book. In the works a detailed description of the landscape is followed by an account of those who inhabit it, with both texts incorporating the panoramic-anatomical impulse that, as Sylvia Molloy notes, permeated Latin American culture in the late nineteenth and early twentieth centuries.[6] Nevertheless, while Euclides's topographical-corporeal description of the Amazon echoes *Os sertões,* there are significant differences between the texts. Documenting the Canudos rebellion against the Republic's civilizing forces, Euclides's portrait of the *sertão* oscillates between deploring the region and its inhabitants as backwards and admiring them for their tenacity in the face of the army's modernizing campaign. Mixing scientific inquiry and observation with romantic prose, *Os sertões* offers an ambivalent account of the area, revealing what Luiz Costa Lima refers to as the aporias of the Republic's civilizing mission.[7]

These aporias are absent in Euclides's writings on the Amazon. While the author represents the region as a domain that breeds disorder, he unequivocally depicts the lost Eden as a place urgently requiring redemption. There is, he writes, "an urgent need for measures to rescue this hidden abandoned culture."[8] The ambivalence toward the Republic's modernizing mission so central to *Os sertões* is nonexistent in Euclides's Amazonian essays, which stress a necessity to subdue the lost paradise's excessive nature and integrate the area and its peoples into the national narrative of order and progress. The "promised land," he claims, "can contribute substantially to our development" and must "be incorporated into our progress."[9] This incorporation, Euclides adds, is to be provided by modern technology, which can civilize the primitive land and people, making both "stable" and "profitable" for the nation.[10]

Euclides was not alone in advocating technological intervention in the Amazon. A few years earlier, in 1901, Luíz Cruls, director of Brazil's National Observatory, also argued that technology might improve the inhospitable environment. "A region's climate does not constitute an element beyond change; it can be modified depending on the nature of intervention."[11] By the start of the Republic, then, it was believed that Brazil's wilderness could be transformed by modern technology. The disordered Amazon and its inhabitants were to be reclaimed by improvements brought about by technological developments. These proposals were fully in keeping with the Republic's positivist blueprint for national development.[12] Following Comtian doctrine, Republican leaders saw technology as a dynamic agent in generating progress and argued that technological inventions could manipulate the dangerous land and peoples in order to bring about Brazil's betterment.

The new centrality of the Amazon as a site for Brazil's progress epitomizes the emergence of a new discourse that reconfigured relations between the coastal metropoles and the tropical backlands. Instead of marginalized places to be ignored, the tropics were to be subjugated and turned into productive territories by technology, which was imbued with an active modernizing agency. This discourse was firmly rooted in the state's positivist belief in the evolutionary idea of mutability and perfectibility, by which the imperfect Amazon could be transformed into a modern terrain. Key to the Republic's modernizing mission, this belief brought the peripheral space more squarely into the country's national imaginary. The remote location was reimagined as a site for Brazil's development in a process that evidenced a rethinking or relocating of modernity. No longer was modernity deemed something foreign or "out of place" that needed to be imported; now it was something that could be nurtured at home. The Amazon's time had come, and with technology the remote region was to be annexed as part of the Republic's drive to be modern. Visual technology, both photography and film, was implicated in this process and was used to consolidate and expand the state's progress in the backlands.

This reimagining of the tropics responded to changes taking place in the Amazon, which were linked to new commercial interests wrought by Brazil's increasing participation in the global capitalist economy. The need for more land to meet overseas demands for the intensification and diversification of crops and primary materials made the Amazon a particularly attractive region for national growth. Crucial here was the region's rubber boom. Between 1900 and 1910, Brazil exported 50 percent of the world's rubber production, so the region was seen as having huge potential for development.[13] In this new commercial landscape, Brazil's map was redrawn, and the isolated region became the focus of attention. This attention gave rise to what Sá and Hecht foreground as internal colonialism, as distant frontier lands and peoples were integrated into the nation-space in a process of state capture. As Jens Andermann notes, key to the Republic was "the material and symbolic expansion into areas that had remained outside the space of colonial rule, or which had been only marginally integrated into colonial or post-independence society."[14] Technology was central to this expansionist logic and its colonizing drive, part of the project to produce a new spatial order.[15] The technological was used to appropriate frontier space, to remove the tropics as a plane of exteriority, and to forge a nation at one with itself.

Euclides's proposals for technological intervention in the Amazon were soon realized. In 1907, army officer Cândido Mariano da Silva Rondon (1865–1958; figure 15) led a group of military engineers in the Commissão de Linhas Telegráficas Estratégicas de Mato Grosso ao Amazonas (Strategic Telegraph Commission of Mato Grosso to Amazonas), commonly referred to as the Rondon Commission. Managed by the Ministry of War and Industry and the Ministry of Public Works, the commission was charged with the massive undertaking of constructing the first telegraph line across the Amazon. The new invention was considered a marvel of modern engineering, and its very presence in the peripheral area was seen as the first step in civilizing Brazil's most distant location and providing it with a new order. As one of the expedition's members put it, people in the interior were "now

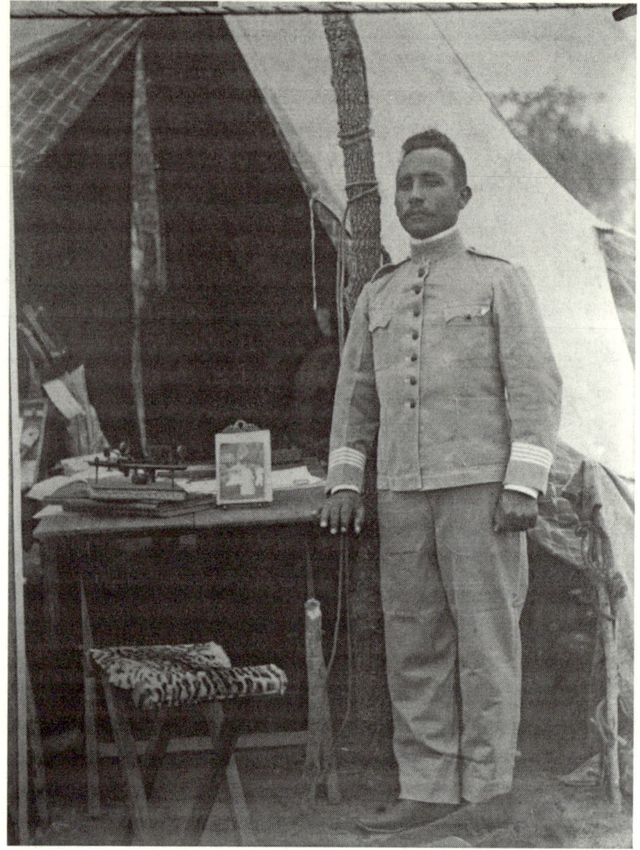

FIGURE 15. Major Cândido Mariano da Silva Rondon, undated.
Acervo do Museu do Índio / FUNAI—Brasil.

experiencing the first civilizing elements of the telegraph—the sound of progress."[16] The new technology was thus endorsed as exposing the primitive region and peoples to civilization and enlightening them to modern ideas and ways of life circulating around the country and, indeed, the world.

One of Europe's great inventions of the late nineteenth century, telegraphy made it possible to transmit human thought across space by means of electricity. For the first time, ideas could traverse vast distances almost instantly, bringing places and people together. The invention of the telegraph therefore broke "the nexus between communication and physical distance," a technological leap that in Brazil could bridge the distance between the Amazon and the coastal cities.[17] The telegraph could thus become an instrument in homogenizing the nation-space.

With its ability to conquer vast distances in no time at all, the technology could link together far-flung populations and places in a new telegraphic assemblage that would annex the disparate territory and its peoples. Telegraphy could create a new national network that would diminish the region's seclusion and help consolidate a centralized political administration over the entire country, something that was desperately needed in the federalist constitution of the Republican state.

The need to bridge this distance assumed urgency with the start of the Republic. When the new regime took over, Brazil was by no means unified. Three of the largest provinces, Mato Grosso, Goiás, and Amazonas, which constituted 40 percent of the national territory, remained "inaccessible to the rest of the country and segregated from national life."[18] It was believed that this isolation impeded the country's progress and undermined the state's integrity, a drawback that had been foregrounded during the Paraguayan War (1865–70). Officials in Rio learned of Paraguay's invasion of Mato Grosso a full six weeks after the fact, as news from the region was slow to reach the capital and mostly incorrect. Indeed, the *Diário do Rio* announced the end of the war a year early. The war highlighted the lack of a national communications system. It additionally foregrounded the precariousness of frontier lands, where state presence was absent. Conflicts between incomers and indigenous groups and territorial disputes with local *caudilhos* and neighboring countries reinforced this precariousness. They also highlighted varying political, social, and cultural allegiances that threatened the country's integrity. Assimilating the regions and their peoples became key for the Republican regime as a way of affirming the state's territorial sovereignty, and frontier expansion became synonymous with an attempt to readjust the power balance between local leaders and a still feeble central authority.

The expansion of the telegraphic network began almost immediately after the start of the Republic. In 1890, the Commissão Construtora de Linhas Telegráficas de Mato Grosso (Commission to Construct Telegraph Lines from Mato Grosso) was founded. Led by Rondon, in just five years the unit built 360 miles of telegraph line connecting the coast to the province of Mato Grosso, linking Cuiabá with the rest of Brazil (figure 16). In 1900, the government appointed Rondon to build a line between Cuiabá and Corumbá, toward the border with Bolivia and Paraguay. Between 1900 and 1906 the commission built sixteen telegraph stations, exploring around 2,500 miles of the territory of Mato Grosso. With the success of Rondon's activities, in 1907 he was charged with extending the telegraph from Mato Grosso to the Amazon. The new line would reach the country's final frontier and traverse lands that had rarely been seen or mapped: that is, it would cross the *terra ignota* that Euclides da Cunha described in his essays. By 1916, the commission had laid down 1,500 kilometers of telegraph lines and "pacified" thirty-five thousand Indians, helping, as Todd Diacon puts it, to "string together the nation." Telegraphic expansion aimed to homogenize Brazil by penetrating and colonizing the remote

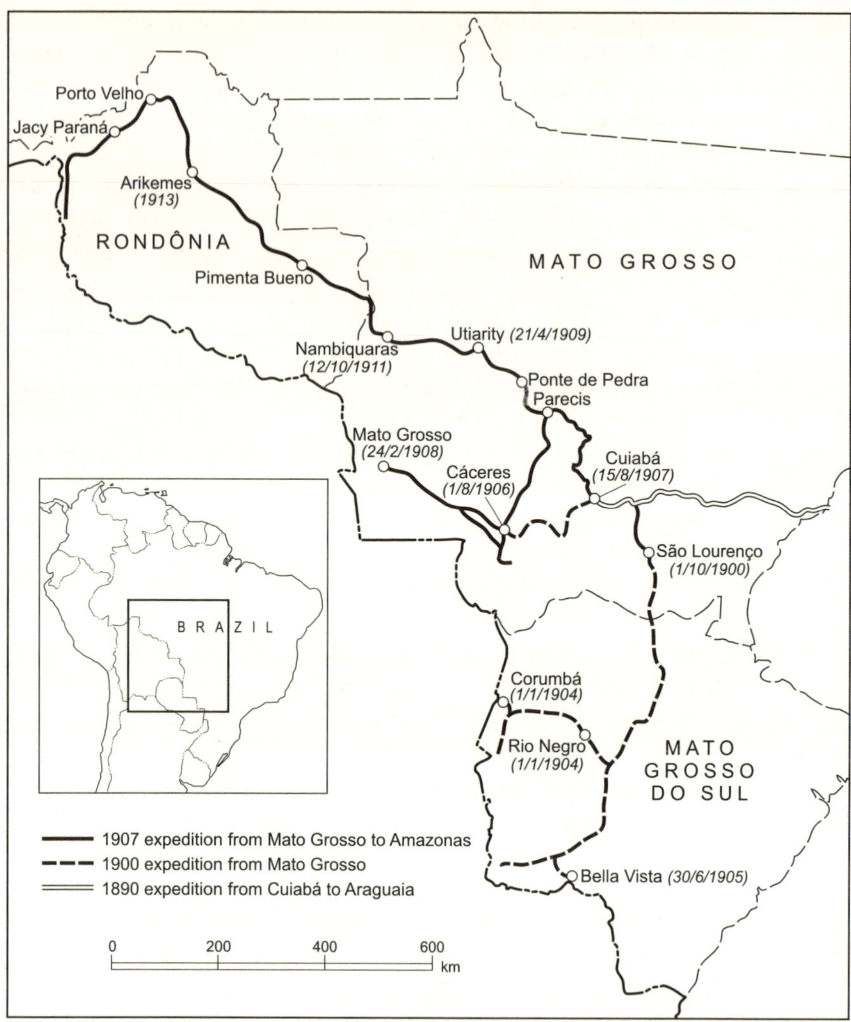

FIGURE 16. Map of the Rondon Commission's expeditions.

area, and the commission's Amazonian activities contributed to a politics of nationalization or Republicanization. Rondon's participation in this was reinforced by his appointment in 1927 as inspector of frontiers, a position that charged him with the task of protecting and policing Brazil's borders.

The purpose of the telegraph, then, was to forge a homogeneous political space. It was also to create a homogeneous economic space that would help open up Brazil to the production and distribution of goods from the tropics. Economic homogeneity depended on the creation of an unimpeded space of circulation, so the telegraphic infrastructure was integral to the organization of the Republic's new market economy. This economy had its roots in the regime's positivist project, which sought to rationally engineer a new country, ordering it according to the free circulation of goods. The extraction of primary resources that underpinned this new order depended on the conquest of space and the annihilation of the distance between the Amazon and the coastal cities. Rondon's telegraph instigated this conquest and opened up the path to subsequent communication infrastructures, such as the building of bridges, railroads, and highways, all of which accelerated the transport of humans and products to and from the frontier and intensified capitalist relations by transforming the region's prodigious nature into a commodity. The capture or accumulation of territory and of capital was therefore central to the Republic's nationalization, and the commission's telegraphic expedition was the initial step in the process that aimed to convert the unruly Amazon into a territory that had an economic value. Commercial concerns firmly underwrote the civilization of the tropics. As Rondon noted, "Wherever the telegraph goes, there people will experience the benefits of civilization, with the establishment of order the development of man and industry will follow, for commerce will connect the societies of the coast and the interior. We will excavate the backlands, make them productive, submit them to our authority, bring them closer to us, and make the most of their savagery and richness."[19] The telegraph promised to expand progress throughout the nation and to promote national unity by symbolically and physically bringing the region into a national network and submitting it to the state's authority.

If this progress was driven by technology, it was also buttressed by science. Geographers, botanists, zoologists, and ethnographers from Brazil's scientific institutions accompanied the commission, providing its activities with an aura of seriousness and credibility. The nation's scientific institutions expanded out into the field, paralleling the national expansion of the telegraph and the state. Science was part of the diffusionist logic of state expansion, and it yielded an unprecedented volume of data from the unknown periphery. Topographers marched alongside military engineers, charting the *terra ignota* for reconnaissance, general information, and subsequent civilization. Ethnographers documented the indigenous populations, collecting data about their languages, customs, and physical characteristics. Men of science published reports and drew up surveys that identified areas suitable for occupation and assessed indigenous peoples' potential for civilization. These exercises depended on a technique and a goal to represent a stable national reality in what were said to be unknown, chaotic lands inhabited by unknown, savage people. Scientific labor sought to fix and give transparent space to the unfamiliar tropics and incorporate them into the nation's power grid as a precondition for settlement or civilization. The production and accumulation of knowledge embodied a will to know the peripheral region and to make its inchoate jungle and nomadic peoples productive. The region would progress through a colonial teleology, from wild space to a civilized and economically productive place.

While this process was technologically and scientifically impelled, it was also represented visually. Rondon made extensive use of photography and film to record the expeditions, producing a vast visual archive of the commission's activities. Focusing on the land and its people, this archive took up the panoramic-anatomical impulse manifested elsewhere in cultural production, visually exploring unknown landscapes and bodies and bringing them into the nation's gaze. Between 1907 and 1930, the commission produced 1,800 photographs and nine films that helped to fix a particular image of the Amazon and its people as ready for development. This production of the image of a modern nation in the making was not isolated. In the Republic's positivist spirit, faith in the documentary power of photography and film gained momentum: pictures and movies of new infrastructures and engineering works—railways, roads, urban improvements—were used to disseminate the possibility of civilization in the tropics, allowing people to see and believe in the Republic's modernizing mission.[20] The images encoded the regime's project of modernity, making it appear real at the subjective level. Photographs and films provided visible proof of the regime's technical expansion, visually substantiating its modern project for viewers. Images of the commission's progress through the unruly jungle thus verified the conquest of the tropics and helped project the success of the Republic's civilizing campaign, justifying the narrative of national progress.

PHOTOGRAPHY, FILM, AND THE TECHNO-POLITICS OF THE RONDON COMMISSION

The Rondon Commission's extensive use of images is perhaps unsurprising. As anthropologist Christopher Pinney has argued, the telegraph, photography, and film are part of the same techno-material regime of modernity. They transport data from remote regions, creating a network that enables them to be known and controlled. In Brazil, the technological regime opened up distant sites and brought them aurally and visually into the purview of the Republic. Along with the telegraph, photographs and films brought people and places together in a new national configuration. The techno-visual assemblage in this sense articulated the wider rationale of integration and of a politics of containment, virtually defining the contours of the state.

The construction of telegraph stations in various outposts reinforced this process of national containment and integration. Manned by military engineers, the bases were physical proof of the Republic's presence and authority in the remote lands. The outposts thus affirmed the state's scope and power, making its territorial presence and possession of the lands patent. This was supplemented by symbolic practices implemented by Rondon. In addition to building telegraph lines and roads, the commission introduced civic rituals into the remote areas. Flag raising was a daily activity in telegraphic garrisons, as were military processions. These rituals were moments when the public display of Republican sovereignty and authority in "the lonely corner of the Amazon" was made manifest.[21] Indeed, the the ceremonies, in their military grandeur, provided the Republic with a model of command over the disparate areas; they also introduced rural peoples to conventions of modern behavior, based on regimented order and obedience. To cite Laura Antunes Maciel, the rituals were "a civil lesson" and a "school of discipline," and the telegraphic outposts became bases from which to mold national subjects.[22]

Such rituals thus served Republican nationalism. So did other practices. The commission purchased a gramophone to play the national anthem twice a day. It acquired a projector to display images of the president and other political leaders, as well as national spaces.[23] These apparatuses projected the sights and sounds of the state to the backlands in technologized ceremonies whose content was both patriotic and progressive. In doing so they operated as auxiliaries, or prostheses, for the state. Technology was clearly perceived as central to conquering the distant province, and it was utilized to bring the Amazon and its peoples into the space of the nation. These media were thus not just about projecting the power of the Republic; they were also about addressing and interpellating the region's population, turning them into modern subjects of the state by exposing them, via the mediation of technology, to the politics of the rest of the country.

Technology, then, participated in what Homi K. Bhabha refers to as "processes of subjectification," creating citizens attuned to the needs of the state.[24] In doing so it constructed a particular kind of state power over the indigenous, which Antonio Carlos de Souza Lima calls "tutelary power."[25] By introducing the fruits of industry, technology would "demonstrate to the savages the power of modernization" and transform or "elevate" them into civilized Brazilians.[26] The politics of inculcation was thus yoked to Darwinian evolutionism and its teleological narrative, and technology was figured as a medium that would make the barbaric Indians modern.

Film and photography participated in the symbolic interpellation of the Amazon and its indigenous populations. Visually capturing the distant lands and peoples, they opened up hidden bodyscapes to the gaze of Brazil's coastal populations, drawing them into national space. Films and photographs then visually bridged the space between the remote region and the coast. This collapse of space was matched by the breaking down of temporalities, as the "unmodern" region was brought into a modern field of vision. The commission's films and photographs thus enacted what Roland Barthes has illuminated as the double temporality and spatiality of modern visual technologies, illogically bringing the "there-then" into the "here-now."[27] This conflation of time and space supported the homogenization of Brazil. The images enabled audiences to see the commission's marvelous undertakings in the field and apprehend the wonders of the national territory, allowing them to visually discover the entire country. Photographs and films visualized and made public the country's new organization of time and space.

This intimacy between the techno-material regime and the needs of the state reveals how Republican rule was virtually enacted through technology, which created a new national terrain and new national subjects. The restructuring of the country through the technological network of telegraphy, film, and photography was intended as a means of political subjection, what Timothy Mitchell has referred to as "techno-politics"—an operation of political rule through the technological workings of infrastructures.[28] Through the telegraph, film, and photography, the Republican regime sought to reorganize lands and peoples via technologized domains far removed from formal political institutions. Key to this social and spatial reordering was a new form of political rationality that gave rise to an apparatus of governmentality, in the Foucauldian sense, which worked not by repression but by assimilation.

This political relationship between technology and national government was brought out in the technologized rituals discussed above. It was also reinforced by other forms of technological cultural production, notably the press. Benedict Anderson has emphasized the vital role that the development of print culture played in forging the "imagined community." Newspapers, he writes, offered readers a mass ceremony that helped integrate them into the nation's homogeneous space-time. In Brazil, the telegraph became inextricably linked to the press. With the expansion of the telegraph, newspapers sent journalists to the disparate corners of the nation to report on events taking place around the country. Columns with titles such as "Via the Telegraph" and "Telegraphic News" proliferated in the press, providing readers with immediate updates from distant places. As Flora Süssekind has demonstrated, technology reshaped experiences of time and space and by doing so altered the perceptions and sensibilities of Brazil's urban populations, helping in this instance to nationalize them.[29] For Maciel, the telegraph and its relationship to the newspaper were crucial in forging a national identity beyond the capital, fostering an "awareness that Brazil was not just Rio."[30]

This consciousness was not just written; it was also visual. Images of the commission's activities circulated widely in cities, helping to publicize its modernizing labors. With this in mind, Rondon founded a Central Office in 1910. Located in Rio, the office was directed by military engineer Amílcar Armando Botelho de Magalhães, who was charged with promoting the commission's work around the country, providing a wide vision of its expansionist drive. Magalhães penned letters to newspapers and composed stories of the expedition for the press. These stories were illustrated with photographs, which provided visual verification of their contents. Images also enlivened scientific reports in geographical and anthropological journals, the photographs providing reliable evidence of discovery and knowledge. Photographic lantern slides and movies of the campaign also became an essential part of Rondon's lectures, which took place in scientific institutions and museums as well as public venues. In his lectures Rondon entertained audiences with tales of danger and examples of the commission's triumphs, all of which were verified by photographs and films. As Diacon states, the lectures were "a multimedia extravaganza that illustrated Rondon's words with an extensive slideshow and the screening of a Commission-made documentary."[31]

The Central Office thus coordinated an extensive expansion of information pertaining to the commission's work in the Amazon, with photography and film key to this. The office in this sense corresponded to what Bruno Latour, in his history of scientific observation, calls a "center of calculation." According to Latour, "centers of calculation" function as pivots in flows of information, coordinating networks of information and diffusing and systemizing data. Latour emphasizes the role of technologies of inscription in these centers—writing, mapping, and visual technologies.[32] Visual technology, photography and film, was indeed fundamental to Rondon's Central Office, as it calculatedly helped to disseminate and standardize information about the commission's explorations, placing its labor in the purview of a wide audience.

Photographs and movies provided images of areas and peoples that urban audiences had never seen before. They projected an image of the entire country and helped create the contours of the imagined community by expanding the boundaries of the nation's cognitive map. Imagistic production thus enabled people to see the commission's undertakings in the field and apprehend the wonders of the nation, allowing them to visually discover Brazil for themselves. Cinema and photography helped chart the Republic's national terrain, by bringing into view its expansion and making the imaginary of a homogeneous space palpable. Visual technology was aligned with the project of state capture, participating in the Republic's techno-politics.

UNPACKING THE TRUTH VALUE OF THE VISUAL SIGN

Rondon immediately contracted artists to accompany the expeditions and produce visual illustrations—engravings and watercolors—of flora, fauna, and indigenous peoples. Such visual labor, however, was soon taken over by photography and then film. These modern technological forms were believed to provide an unmediated and hence more objective record of expeditions, reinforcing their scientific seriousness. This belief rested on the apparatus's technological properties. As Maciel notes, "The mechanical eye registered and captured reality, and there was therefore no possibility of questioning the fidelity of the image. It was seen as a faithful reproducer of life, capable of reproducing reality as it truly existed."[33]

The mechanical reproductive capacity of photography and cinematography imbued these media with what Tom Gunning calls "a truth claim," that is, the belief that they could accurately depict reality.[34] This truth claim relied on what has become identified with Charles Peirce's term *indexicality* and the visual accuracy of photography and film. Indexicality depends on a physical relation between the object photographed and the image created. The chemical connection to what was depicted, the fact that, as Walter Benjamin wrote, mechanical forms of visual reproduction were "seared" with reality, suggested that they might be capable of conveying facts about which there was no question.[35] In this respect they departed radically from the more subjective quality of artistic representations. Photographs and films were seen as bearing the imprint of their subjects and thus conveyed a regime of evidence that led back to the object that created the imprint. With their noninterventionist nature, photography and film provided greater impartiality and replaced the more sensuous encounter of the artist, whose subjective interpretations could deviate from the empirical reality of the object encountered. Mechanical forms of reproduction could then transcend the vagaries of art, or what André Bazin terms "the sin of subjectivity," and photography and film were imbued with a rhetoric of truth and transparency.[36] They offered an emanation of an external reality and fell within the realm of the rational and objective.

Rondon's adoption of photography and film was guided by this idea that technical media were faithful reproducers of an external reality. The commission held "a faith in the truth value of the visual sign" that was in keeping with a positivist belief in technology.[37] The technologies were employed to secure and propagate an accurate account of the commission's expeditions, offering valuable proof of its progress in the field. This was important in the face of growing criticism. The high costs of field-work, along with newer advances in telecommunications (notably radio), threatened the campaign's viability. A 1917 newspaper report dismissed Rondon's expeditions as outdated and announced that the government was wrong to "spend rivers of money building useless telegraph lines when the radio telegraph would have provided an ideal service at a fraction of the cost."[38] Others directly criticized the commission's strategy. According to an article in the *Jornal do Commércio,* the Rondon Commission was trying to do too many things at once. It was part technological service, part geographical mission, part ethnographic inquiry. The final line of the article asserted, "Enough with this clowning around with the monies of the treasury."[39]

"Clowning around" with government funds became an oft-repeated phrase in criticism of the commission's work. The federal government, some felt, had spent untold sums of money on Rondon's project, yet there was little to show for the outlay. Telegraphic traffic remained light after the line's inauguration in 1916. The commission's own figures support this charge. Reports noted traffic, but the majority of telegraphs sent and received along the line originated with the commission. In 1921, only 5,320 private telegrams were sent on the line, compared to 22,774 official messages. The line's revenue also contradicted the idea that its construction was leading to development. The Amazon witnessed little growth in revenues between 1909 and

1914, and revenues even dropped with the decline in rubber trade during the 1910s.[40] Several politicians sought to close down the commission, which in the early 1910s had to contend with budget cuts of close to 60 percent. Visual documentation was thus not impartial or objective; it was carefully constructed to promote and justify Rondon's activities. The "truth value" of photography and cinematography was harnessed as a tool of propaganda, legitimizing Rondon's endeavors and countering objections to his work, and was used to sell a message of the expeditions' success. As Maciel writes, visual documentation and dissemination authorized the commission's activities, playing "a "fundamental role in exhibiting its work" and constituting a powerful regime of evidence about its value.[41]

Photos and movies became an important part of the commission's excursions. Commercial photographers and filmmakers were deployed to record expeditions. Alberto Braud was employed between 1900 and 1906 to visually chart the building of the line in Mato Grosso. Luiz Leduc and Joaquim de Moura Quineau joined the commission in 1907 and 1908 respectively, and José Louro and Affonso Henrique de Magalhães took part in 1910, taking photographs and recording films.[42] These men had the technical skill and chemical knowledge of the visual technologies, but they had to contend with considerable technical and logistical difficulties. The inhospitable climate (extreme temperatures, sunlight, humidity, dense forest, mosquitoes, hostile natives) and the unwieldiness of their gear (they had to carry heavy equipment, chemicals, glass plates, a darkroom tent, and huge cameras) made their efforts difficult and eventually put an end to the commission's use of commercial photographers and filmmakers. In 1912, Rondon established a photography and film section within the Central Office and enlisted military officer Major Luiz Thomaz Reis (figure 17) to take over the production of photos and films. Imagistic production became intertwined with the commission's military support, for photographers and filmmakers, like Reis, were not civilian entrepreneurs but trained military operators, seen as more equipped for working in arduous conditions.

When Reis took over, the commission had already accumulated numerous images, produced by many photographers and filmmakers. Nevertheless, in spite of this variety, the imagistic production was remarkably uniform, revealing an official line of what was to be recorded and how. Photographs and films focused on three themes: the expeditions' progress through the inhospitable lands, including working and living conditions; the land traversed, with charting of flora and fauna; and the bodies and customs of indigenous peoples. Maciel attributes this uniformity to Rondon himself, noting that visual production "was carried out under his direction."[43] Photographers and filmmakers, including Reis, worked under Rondon's orders and in doing so gave vision to the hegemonic project of homogenizing Brazil, visually translating the commission's aims. As Reis noted at the time: "Living in the twentieth century, we have to focus our lenses on the new horizons in Brazil's west that have been opened up to civilization, linking this to the brave

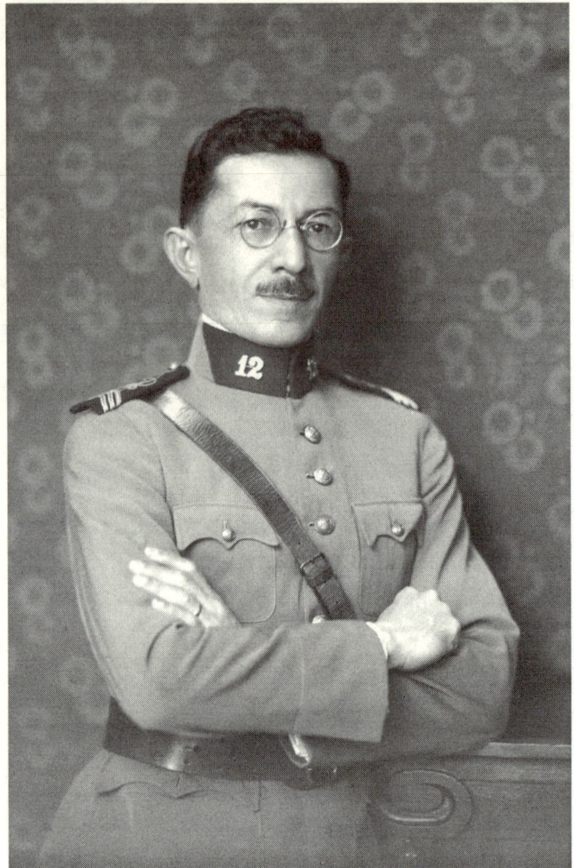

FIGURE 17. Major Luiz Thomaz Reis, undated. Acervo do
Museu do Índio / FUNAI—Brasil.

geographical, industrial, and scientific conquests."[44] Photography and film not only projected modernity but were part of it. More than mere documentation of the commission's progress, the technologically produced images were enactments of it.

This problematizes what Jay Ruby calls the "absolute power of authorship" and alerts us the fact that the images cannot be seen in isolation.[45] Rather than articulating the artistry of the operator, photographs and films were mediated by Rondon and took into account the needs of the Republican regime that funded the commission. It is hardly surprising, then, that many of the photographs have become detached from their creators and that, in cases where they are known, almost no information is available about the circumstances of their production.

This reinforces the images' "truth claim," since any indication of personal authorship could be seen to limit the objective value of the material.

This objective value was part of a broader relationship between science and visual technology. As Alison Griffiths demonstrates, by the start of the twentieth century scientists in Europe and the United States made extensive use of the photographic and cinematographic camera to "bolster the accuracy and impartiality of what they had observed."[46] Anthropologists were especially attracted to photography, which became "the darling child" of the discipline.[47] For Pinney, photography's "quantifying and reality apprehending qualities perfectly suited the realist and quantitative aspirations of anthropology."[48] Photography achieved rapid and widespread legitimation and application within anthropology soon after its invention. In the 1840s, French physician and naturalist E. R. A. Serres added daguerreotypes of "physical characters of indigenous types" to his collection of anatomical specimens. Similarly, Harvard naturalist Louis Agassiz commissioned photographer J. T. Zealy in 1850 to produce daguerreotypes of African-born slaves in South Carolina as part of Agassiz's anthropometric studies of human development.[49] Photography was immediately recognized as a vital medium for recording different places and peoples, and it became an indispensable research tool for anthropologists.

Film too was incorporated into anthropological fieldwork and intellectual tenets. Griffiths foregrounds the filmmaking efforts of Alfred Cort Haddon and Walter Baldwin Spencer as "some of the earliest examples of ethnographic filmmaking."[50] In 1898 (only two years after the apparatus's introduction), Haddon took a moving-picture camera on his expedition to the Torres Straits. Overcoming a lack of knowledge of the new medium and considerable technical and logistical problems, Haddon shot four and a half minutes of footage of the field and of Mer Islanders and Australian aborigines performing native dances and demonstrating fire making. Three years later, Spencer took a "kinematograph" on his expedition to central Australia.[51] By the 1910s more anthropologists were taking up the film camera, recognizing its usefulness as a research tool. For scientists like Frederic Starr and Franz Boas, film's mechanical eye opened up visual phenomena otherwise closed to the unaided senses, and its "facility of repeatability" also offered the anthropologist access "to minute details about their subject only detectable through repeated viewings."[52]

As Griffiths has shown, these ethnographic views were paralleled and even preceded by popular culture.[53] *Cartes de visite,* postcards, stereoscopes, museum displays, world's fairs, and early movies offered audiences visions of distant peoples and places, visually evoking the encounter with an ethnographic Other. These popular visions traded on a desire and curiosity to see geographical and corporeal difference and were inscribed in a topographical and bodily gesture that was bound up with what Fatimah Tobing Rony calls "fascinating cannibalism" (after Susan Sontag), referring to a fascination with seeing Other places and peoples.[54]

Disseminated in the press and in movie theaters, Rondon's visual documentation of the expeditions also moved from the scientific into the popular domain, where it expressed and satisfied a curiosity with seeing the country's unknown backlands and inhabitants. The commission then used photographs and films to provide a "truthful" account of the peoples and lands encountered, while also trading on a popular fascination with Brazil's Other lands and peoples.

THE LEXICAL SPACE OF PHOTOGRAPHY AND FILM

Photographs and films produced by Rondon shared an ethnographic focus in their depiction of Brazil's distant places and peoples, and the thematic focus of the two media overlapped. Nevertheless, photographs and films also manifested what Pinney calls different "lexical spaces."[55] Pinney writes that while photography and film involve similar visual technical phenomena, they also represent distinct styles of *stillness* and *movement,* something Christian Metz also stresses when he notes that film engages orders of perception that are missing from photography, most notably motion.

Motion was foregrounded as a key motive for the commission's adoption of the film camera. Moving pictures were seen as ideal for reproducing the practices of indigenous communities, something that still photography could not capture. Amílcar Armando Botelho de Magalhães, for instance, noted, "We all know the advantages of photographic documentation. . . . Who is not aware of the delights of leafing through images that reproduce the natural beauty of the scenes and landscapes of our expeditions? Cinematography, however, has a greater status, and in the Rondon Commission it is more important because of its ability to document the customs of our aborigines, their festivities, dances, and burial ceremonies."[56] The commission's interest in film derived from its ability to capture the movement of indigenous peoples' social rituals and to register and replay their minute details that were invisible to the naked eye. It was clearly believed that film's mobile lexicon was more suited to recording the "realism of motion and the psychological reality of interpersonal relations."[57] This was in keeping with the broader application of film in international scientific contexts. Early ethnographic filmmaking was devoted to recording the movements of aboriginal peoples.[58] The first films by Haddon and Spencer, for instance, featured ritual dances as well as daily activities, including industry and leisure. The Rondon Commission followed this ethnographic tradition, turning the movie camera on the bodies and practices of indigenous peoples. Like foreign scientists, in searching for a means of documenting the bodies of native inhabitants the commission privileged movement, which was provided by the movie camera.

Film's movement also provided it with the feeling of an unmediated and instantaneous view of the land and people, cementing its indexical credibility. Whereas photographs were divested temporally and spatially from their referent, the cinema seemed embedded in the time and space recorded, providing a sense of "an ethnographic present."[59] The moving pictures thus imbued the images with an eyewitness immediacy that was missing in the still photographic documents. So while film and photography both coexisted and participated in the wider discursive needs of the Rondon Commission, they were used in different ways. In the film *Rituais e festas Bororo* (Rituals and festivities of the Bororo; dir. Luiz Thomaz Reis, 1917), for instance, the movie camera was utilized to focus on the indigenous community of the Bororo, its very title invoking an ethnographic gaze. Such movies depicted what Maciel refers to as "the dangerous and adventurous, the unusual and the exotic," and thus satisfied a popular desire to see what Griffiths calls "wondrous difference."[60] Photography's lexical space, on the other hand, was employed to document the expedition's advance through the region and to chart the arduous labor of the men working on the line.

PHOTOGRAPHING LIFE ON THE LINE

Photographs largely focused on the expedition's journeys across the terrain, documenting the environments encountered, including huge waterfalls and dense jungles. Pictures of tropical expanses showed the potential of the region and its future prospects. Here the excessive wildness projected by photographers conveyed the Amazon's untapped fertility, which could be read as a blank space for improvement. Indigenous peoples were strikingly absent from these photographs, which instead presented unoccupied landscapes, devoid of native inhabitants, a strategy that isolated the indigenes from their lived environment. Emptied of human traces, the hinterlands appeared as places that were simply "out there," ready and ripe for conquest.

While the indigenous were significantly absent from photographic landscapes, expeditionary members were frequently present in them. Photographers often placed soldiers in images of the vast landscapes. Included to provide a sense of scale, in the photographs the isolated men are dwarfed by nature, which appears monumental (figure 18). The miniaturized figures thus convey the grand scope of the expedition's work and portray its labor as an epic struggle of man versus nature. This was often stressed in written accounts in newspapers. Articles with headlines like "Attacked by Indians" and "Dangers in Mato Grosso" reported on the harsh conditions that expeditions faced—diseases, hunger, and attacks by savage tribes—calling attention to the men's heroism and the personal risks they ran in their battle against nature.[61]

Such stories and accompanying photographs could have suggested the fragility of the campaign, whose progress was threatened by the excessive nature. The wilderness that features in photographs could then emerge as a signifier of resistance to the project of state capture and the modern sublimation of nature. To counter this, Reis and other photographers carefully portrayed the labor of industry in taming the savage backlands. Many photographs gave prominence to technology and

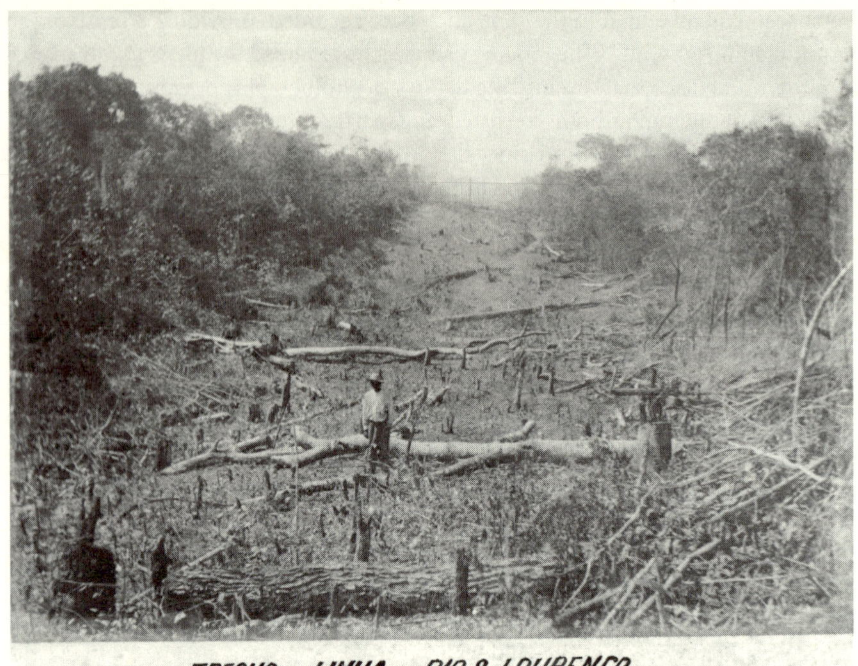

FIGURE 18. Men dwarfed by nature, 1922. Acervo do Museu do Índio / FUNAI—Brasil.

to the expeditions' scientific, technological, and mechanical resourcefulness. The machinery used to set up the telegraph line was often featured. Operated by soldiers, the machinery was shown as bringing civilization to the wild terrain, something that was posited as an act of modern and human intervention (figure 19). Photography thus visualized technology's conquest of nature and its ability to create a new national space. This conquest was often present in photographs, like that of figure 20, which depicted Rondon as the first inhabitant in an empty land, in what was literally a rite of territorial possession, a foundational act of occupation.

Pictures of telegraph stations represented the apex of this occupation, revealing places where nature had been turned into civilized outposts of the nation (figure 21). The commission's photographs were thus inscribed with an evolutionary narrative; they depicted a region transformed by technology, suggesting civilization's irreversible advance. This narrative was present in the organization of photographs in albums produced by the commission. Numbered photographs were assembled and archived in commemorative albums like *Photographias da construção, expedições e explorações* (Photographs of the construction, expeditions and explorations, 1922), which, published on the centenary of independence, was intended to

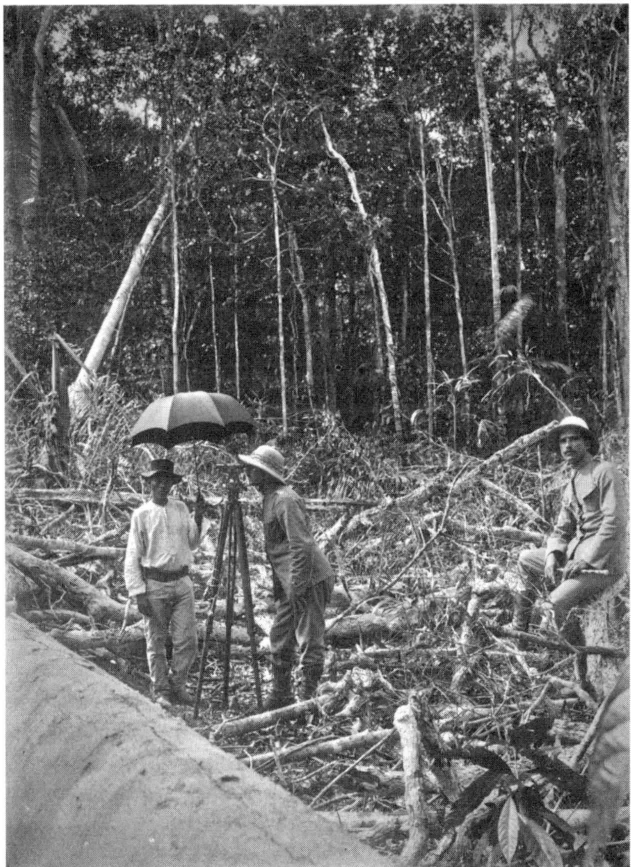

FIGURE 19. The telegraph in the field, 1922. Acervo do Museu do
Índio / FUNAI—Brasil.

construct a national visual memory of Rondon's efforts. The books depicted the
expedition's labor as a linear chronicle that began with its encounter with the dense
jungle and proceeded through to the final conquest of the virgin land, demonstrated by images of telegraphic garrisons, as well as towns constructed in the
former wilderness. Explanatory captions guided this progress, helping to fix the
images' order. Textual as well as visual details then projected the advancement of
civilization in the backlands and helped lead readers/viewers through to the con-
clusion of state capture. The photographs' narrative organization challenges Pinney's assertion of photography's "truncated stillness" versus what he distinguishes
to be "film's temporal regime and narrative chain of signification."[62] Carefully conveying the taming of the Amazon, the commission's photos and their organization

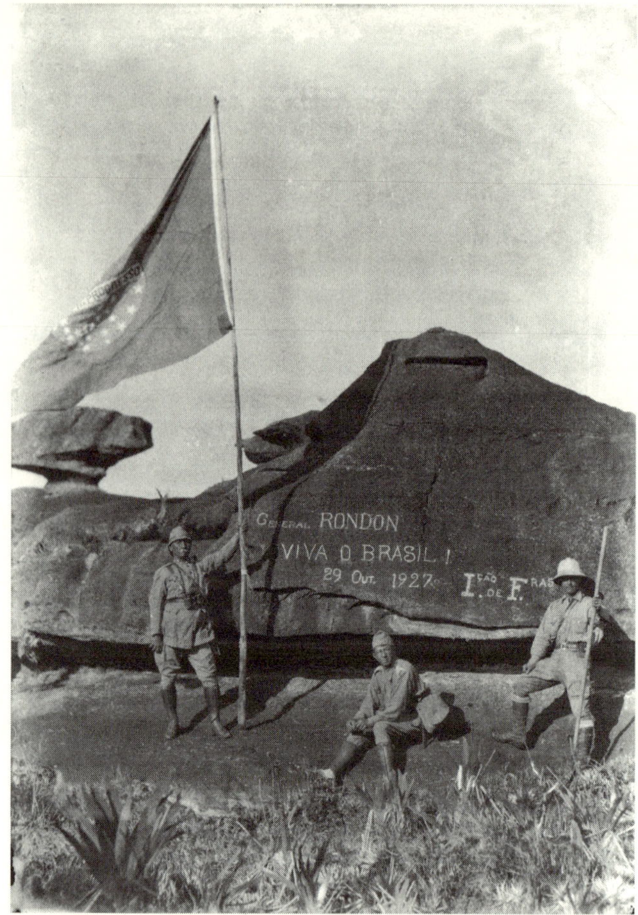

FIGURE 20. Rondon's conquest of space, 1927. Acervo do Museu do
Índio / FUNAI—Brasil.

projected emphatic narratives of progress. Photography was imbued with a narrative lexicon that visualized the advancement of civilization in the tropics.

If photographic depictions of Rondon's expeditions were yoked to a story of
progress and modernity, they also drew on pictorial conventions from painting,
especially landscape painting.[63] In their depiction of untamed nature, many photographs used an iconography established by European landscape painting that
was produced in seventeenth-century Brazil, emulating its pictorial grammar.
Compositions of expansive tropical landscapes and enormous waterfalls reveal an
artistic idiom that owed much to Romantic painters like E. F. Schute. These paintings communicated the sublime (that is, terror at the energy and grandeur of the

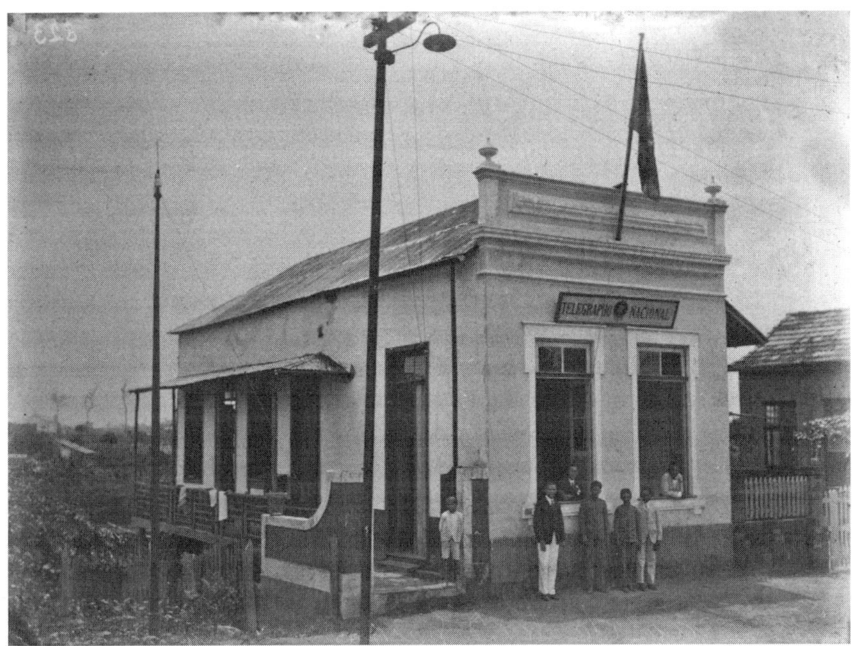

FIGURE 21. Telegraph outpost in Mato Grosso, 1922. Acervo do Museu do Índio / FUNAI—Brasil.

natural forces combined with sheer beauty). The grand scale of nature was sometimes provided in the paintings by the inclusion of lone figures placed within the natural scenes, a trope that the commission's photographers emulated. This dialogue with painting then inserted the photographic gaze at the tropics within well-known iconographic traditions, which helped to render the unknown and unfamiliar land known and familiar, providing viewers with an imaginative control over them. By using a well-known artistic language, photographers domesticated the Amazon to construct an image that enraptured but did not threaten.

The photographs, like the painterly conventions they drew upon, conjured up the intense pleasure and fear of the sublime. For Edmund Burke and Immanuel Kant the sublime is the individual or collective response to a confrontation with phenomena outside the imagination's ability to comprehend. Usually, this is associated with the greatness of the natural world, which offers danger and dramatic visual prospects. The sublime is, then, about a representation of limitlessness, an appreciation of something so great it overwhelms our power to understand it. In his *Critique of Judgment,* Kant divides the concept of the sublime into the mathematically and the dynamically sublime. The former involves a sense of magnitude, an awe that comes with experiencing something absolutely great. This experience, though, rests on the relational, subjective character of judgment. Unlike Burke, who located the sublime in the grand, terrifying objects themselves, Kant argued that it was in the appreciation of objects by a judging subject. Objects become sublime because we judge them in relation to other objects. This relational character was key to the images of the Rondon Commission's work in the field, which function by having a comparative pole—tropical nature being tamed by the men's technological work.

This sublime appeal was not limited to the land. Spectacular images of machinery and surveying instruments used in the expeditions presented what David Nye calls a "technological sublime," "an essentially religious feeling aroused by the confrontation with impressive objects that evoke a sense of individual powerlessness."[64] The commission's portraits of modern machines were not intended to be beautiful or scenic; they were awesome, powerful, and overwhelming. The photographs created an aura around technology and showed man's ability to manufacture a modern sublime. The commission's portrayal of the telegraph and infrastructural technologies, then, invoked the sublime not through the grandeur of nature but through the work of humankind. The technological sublime, however, was not a product solely of the commission. As noted, images of technological works proliferated during the Republic as the new regime sought to project its technological mastery of the natural world. The erection of buildings and the construction of roads, bridges, and railways—in fact, the ability to remake landscapes and force nature to conform to technology—were ways in which the sublime was produced as a spectacle of the modern power of the Republican regime. Visual depictions of the technological sublime were therefore an effort to use modern machinery to represent the rule of the Republic's order and became evidence of the supremacy of its civilizing mission. The issue of power implicit in this is reminiscent of Kant's conception of the dynamically sublime. Here the sublime is experienced as overwhelming not through a sense of its absolute greatness but through a sense of powerlessness that individuals feel when faced with something so overwhelming. Images of new technologies produced by the commission, in keeping with the wider representation of the technological subjugation of the natural world, asserted the new state's power of modernity by invoking feelings of submission to its extension.

The reemergence of the sublime during the Republic was perhaps to be expected. Positivist scientists, engineers, and military men were not rational technicians; they embraced transcendental ideas. Positivism was more than a scientific doctrine; it was a seen as a moral and religious dogma. A member of Brazil's Positivist Church since 1881, Rondon firmly subscribed to this belief. Speaking of positivism, he pronounced:

> The dogma of positivism is a science, because like science it is universal and relative and can be proved. It studies the universal order in order to perfect it. It improves science in order to improve mankind. It is also a religion of love, a religion of order, a religion of progress. I believe that man and the world are governed by natural laws.

I believe that science integrated man into the universe. I believe that science, art, and industry will transform the earth into a paradise for all men, with no prejudice of race, belief, or nation. I believe in the laws of sociology founded by Auguste Comte and therefore in the incorporation of the peoples and of nations considered uncivilized into modern society. I believe that the mission of all intellectuals is above all to elevate the unfortunate masses so that they may be incorporated into society.[65]

Subscribing to Comte's "religion of humanity," Rondon believed that positivism was a moral regenerator that could "serve mankind by bringing progress to the world."[66] This belief underlay Rondon's dedication to fully integrating the Amazon into modern Brazil through infrastructural development. Technology was thus part of a sacred endeavor, something that was registered in the sublime images of machinery in the commission's photographs. Their overwhelming spectacle of technology projected the political and spiritual regeneration of Brazil, which Rondon and others believed could be brought about by technological intervention.

In addition to depicting the expedition's progress across uncharted lands, photographs documented life in the camps. Panoramic shots provided overviews of the camps' organization and intimate scenes that portrayed the details of life in the field. Panoramas were designed to show the scope of the campaign to a home audience. A sense of order pervades these photos, which show troops inhabiting neat rows of white tents, in clear contrast to the surrounding dark, dense fields. The grids of tents and the discipline they symbolized imposed a naturalized semblance of visual order onto the rugged terrain and expressed the men's control and command of the landscape. Such photographs were projective: they forged an image of the Amazon as a place where order was being imposed by the commission and where the resistance of nature was being overcome by the disciplined expeditionary forces.

Most of the photographs of life in the field portrayed everyday scenes. Images of officers relaxing after a day's work, enjoying meals and leisure activities, registered working conditions, documenting how the men engaged with and inhabited the land (figure 22). The images were made to appear spontaneous, with the men seemingly oblivious to the camera. For Maciel, "They reveal an aim to present casualness and tranquility, as if the photographer had inadvertently caught them conversing at the end of the day."[67] The presence of images of men looking directly at the lens, however, shows that the images were staged, constructed, rather than objective.

Dressed in uniforms, the soldiers are identified with props of civilization: books, family portraits, chairs, tables, cups, saucers, even guitars. The carefully managed mise-en-scène underscores a performative dimension to the images, which simulate scenes of refinement. The staging of modernity in the jungle suggests a need to compulsively assert and reassert the commission's labor in the face of the potential for nature to "unmake" civilization. It was this potential that Alberto Rangel underscored in his 1904 book *Inferno verde* (Green hell),

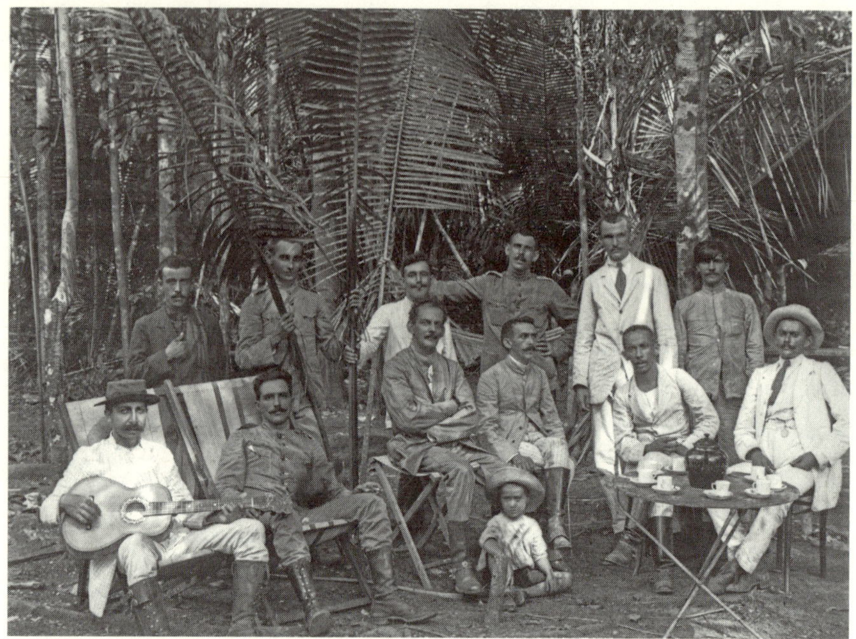

FIGURE 22. Military men relaxing after work, 1922. Acervo do Museu do Índio / FUNAI—Brasil.

which documented the Amazon as a place whose nature destroyed all intruders. This destruction is carefully disavowed in the Rondon Commission's photographs, yet their conscientious mimicry of modernity points to an unseen excess that threatens to displace the mission to conquer the *sertão*. The modern thus becomes a convention and mode of representation that is anxiously repeated through a constructed visual order.

Images of life in camp suggest the commission's leisure and civility in the dangerous hinterlands. Grouped together, they convey a sense of civilized camaraderie among soldiers. These photographs countered the sensational stories of the harsh environmental and working conditions that soldiers had to contend with, which had started to circulate in the press.[68] Wounds, attacks from indigenous peoples, pests, food shortages, and illnesses were common. One health official at the time estimated that 80 to 90 percent of the workers contracted terminal illnesses, and Maciel estimates that at any given time malaria incapacitated 25 percent of the personnel.[69] Diacon notes that the constant fear of illnesses created "a dark and potentially explosive emotional brew among commission soldiers," with frequent fights and even fatal shootings taking place in the camps.[70] Added to this were severe working conditions. Of the six thousand soldiers assigned, most were illiterate and poor and many were criminals, with the commission functioning as a quasi-penal colony. Up to half of the soldiers served against their will and were harshly treated. While corporal punishment had been abolished by the army in 1874, it remained central to Rondon's disciplinary measures. Rondon forcibly recruited many of the men, and they were frequently subjected to beatings, akin to torture, by the commander. Desertions were consequently common. In December 1907, a third of the men disappeared; and in July 1908, 158 soldiers abandoned the expedition. Rondon was aware that such desertions and news of mistreatment and harsh conditions countered ideas of the commission's order.[71] Civilized images of everyday scenes refuted these real working conditions and promulgated instead an image of camaraderie and leisure.

Rondon was often included in these photographs of life on the line (figure 15). Photographers produced numerous portraits of the colonel in the field alone. Looking off into the distance and surrounded by maps, surveys, and other scientific props, Rondon was pictured as a reflective and determined man, engaging the powers of reason in leading the campaign. He was depicted as an upright gentleman, suitably dressed in his pristine uniform and seated outside of a tidy tent, often with two faithful dogs by his side, a clear sign that this was a man who could tame the natural world. Such posed images gave the leader an aura of knowledge and provided the expeditions an aura of seriousness and authority. In some pictures Rondon appears among other expeditionary officials. In these he is placed either at the center of the image or standing over the other men, projecting the image of a great protector and provider for his platoon or of a superior who breaks military protocol to share a table with his subalterns. Any suggestion that Rondon might be a violent commander who subjected his soldiers to cruelty is completely absent in these images, which instead show a leader imbued with a sense of civil comradeship.

These photographs of life on the line and the expedition's advance were thus crafted to belie complaints that appeared in the press, which recounted the conditions of working on the frontier. To counter these stories, photographers portrayed the expeditions as orderly yet relaxed affairs, pervaded by a climate of solidarity. These images went out of their way to show the expedition's ability to civilize the harsh hinterlands, testifying to the conquest of the frontier lands and the ability to settle the tropics. Such tropical projections were clearly allied to the aims not just of the expedition but also of the Republic to create a new order for the nation and bring the distant lands into the narrative of progress. Photography's lexicon was thus employed to project and chart this progress. Photographs visually charted the national narrative for urban individuals to see and follow. Films too projected this national narrative. As the next chapter examines, film's scopic drive focused on the Amazon's topography and the expedition's advancement through the land. It also zoomed in on indigenous peoples encountered, people otherwise absent from the still photographs.

7

The Expedition Films of Major Luiz Thomaz Reis

While Cândido Rondon used photography early on, film became part of his expeditions only after 1912, when the commission employed military officer Major Luiz Thomaz Reis (1878–1940) to head the Central Office's photography and film section established that year. The movie camera had, however, been used before Reis's employment. In 1907, the year that the construction of the telegraph from Mato Grosso to the Amazon began, Rondon contracted numerous commercial filmmakers to record the commission's work in the tropics. This early deployment of film coincided with the "movie fever" that was part of the belle epoque of Brazilian cinema (examined in Part I). With movie theaters proliferating in Rio and domestic filmmaking flourishing, Rondon turned his attentions to the moving pictures, seeking to capitalize on the cinematic craze. He commissioned filmmakers from Casa Musso, a photography and film studio in Rio that had produced photos and movies of Brazil's new public works.[1] These initial cinematic endeavors, however, failed. As Reis noted, "The results were not successful because of the harshness of the *sertão*."[2]

Rondon, nevertheless, did not give up on his goal of producing cinematic images of the commission's labor and contracted Reis to pursue this more earnestly. To rectify previous mistakes, Reis was sent to London and Paris in 1912 to purchase "the necessary and, at that time, best equipment."[3] He acquired Williamson 16mm cameras, which had been specially developed in England for reconnaissance work in the field. He also purchased developing materials and seven thousand meters of film stock from Lumière Tropical.[4] Reis also took lessons in how to "operate a movie camera at Paris's Pathé Studios."[5] The commission was therefore in possession of the best equipment and, through Reis, was fully versed in filmmaking techniques needed for the particular conditions of the tropics. As Amílcar

Armando Botelho de Magalhães, head of the Central Office, observed, "The most modern filmmaking processes were utilized, and the Rondon Commission had at its disposal the necessary equipment for the effective completion of its movies."[6]

Reis's trip to Europe coincided with the end of the belle epoque. The vibrant production of domestic films that had characterized the previous years ceased abruptly in 1912 when European and especially North American distributors arrived in Brazil and made a concerted effort to control the exhibition sector. The appearance of branches of Hollywood studios that bought out local distributors essentially wiped out national production. That Reis was able to purchase new equipment and learn how to make movies during this bleak period of Brazilian cinema testifies to the commission's commitment to film. It also highlights how its cinematic pursuits were free from the vicissitudes of the market dominated by foreign movies. Funded by the War Ministry and the Ministry of Public Works, and supported by Rondon and Magalhães, who both believed in the power of the moving pictures, Reis's cinematic ventures played a key role in the Rondon Commission and were carried out without the pressures felt by Brazil's commercial filmmakers.

By 1930 Reis has completed nine feature-length films: *Os sertões de Mato Grosso* (The backlands of Mato Grosso, 1912–13), *Rondônia* (1912), *De Santa Cruz* (From Santa Cruz, 1917), *Rituais e festas Bororo* (Rituals and festivities of the Bororo, 1917), *Indústria da borracha em Minas Gerais e Amazonas* (The rubber industry in Minas Gerais and the Amazon, 1917), *Inspeção do nordeste* (Inspection of the Northeast, 1922), *Ronuro, selvas do Xingú* (Ronuro, the jungles of Xingú, 1924), *Viagem ao Roraima* (Journey to Roraima, 1927), *Parimã, fronteiras do Brasil* (Parimã, frontiers of Brazil, 1927).[7] The films charted the military expeditions into the Amazon region; they recorded the commission's inspection of the territory and highlighted its industrial potential. They also documented the soldiers' contact with indigenous peoples, including the Bororo. Only four of these completed films (*The backlands of Mato Grosso; Rondônia; Rituals and festivities of the Bororo; and Journey to Roraima*) are extant today. Many exist only as fragments (*Parimã, Fronteirs of Brazil; and Ronuro, the jungles of Brazil*) and some (*From Santa Cruz; and The Rubber industry in Minas Gerais and the Amazon*) are completely absent.

This cinematic gap is counterbalanced by Reis's extensive accounts of his cinematic undertakings in the field. In his field notes Reis records his efforts to overcome the considerable difficulties of filming in the Amazon. The hot and humid environment was particularly challenging. As Reis reported, "The temperature did not provide us with the necessary conditions to process the chemical baths. . . . Another problem was the number of small insects, like mosquitoes, that attacked the film and stuck to the gelatin, hindering our work. Nature triumphed everywhere."[8] Detailing the technical and logistical difficulties of filming in the inhospitable climate, Reis framed the filmmaking process as a struggle between civilization and nature, inscribing it within the commission's broader discourse. To overcome these complications and ensure that the cinematic technology triumphed, Reis undertook detailed studies on how to film in the tropics and how to develop movies onsite. He noted, "Since this was the first time that this was undertaken in the *sertão*, I carefully studied the emulsion and its developing times in the hot and humid area . . . ; this led me to construct specially prepared wooden apparatuses to develop the films locally."[9] These concerted efforts to overcome practical and technical difficulties testify to the commission's commitment to film and affirm Reis's dedication to his cinematic labor.

Responsible for all of the commission's filmmaking activities, Reis became known as "Rondon's Filmmaker." His responsibility afforded him relative independence to carry out his work in contrast to photographers on the expeditions. Indeed, Reis's reports indicate that he was given near freedom in the filmmaking process, receiving orders of *what* he should film but, according to Maciel, no instructions "in *how* to film."[10] Consequently, Reis considered his filmic work as art. Referring to himself as an "expeditionary artist," Reis conceived of his films as artistic creations as well as militaristic productions.

Reis often seemed torn between the creative and expeditionary demands of his labor. He wrote, "The expeditionary artist undertakes two excursions, while the military officer assumes only one. The forced marches and constant need to keep moving forward are a genuine sacrifice for the artist who does not have the opportunity to repose and collect his sentiments in order to coordinate elements of his work. I don't like those urgent journeys, especially when there is art to be obtained." Stating that artistic creation required time to allow for a emotional engagement, something that the pace of the expeditions' forward march did not permit, Reis pointed to a tension between the commission's advancement in the field and his creative work. As he observed, "Cinema is an instrument of investigation and of registering reality, but it is also important for the filmmaker's artistic elaboration."[11]

Reis, therefore, considered individual freedom from the expedition's collective progress as the foundation of his cinematic art. It was not simply a case of using the camera to objectively "obtain" scenes from reality. Coordinating all of the aspects of film production, Reis's personal intervention was fundamental; hence his assertion on the need to rest and consider his sentimental engagement with scenes, unencumbered by the progressive pace of the expeditions. The subjectivity of artistic representation was clearly a concern for "Rondon's filmmaker," whose independent creations made sentiment and the vagaries of sensuous encounters with the external world key to the "objective" medium of film. Reis's work thus blurred what are commonly perceived to be strict boundaries between objectivity and subjectivity and between science and art. Reis's approach did not so much threaten the commission's rational drive and its use of visual technology as introduce a subjective, sentimental element into it.

Reis's independent and creative investment in his films at times led to conflicts with military leaders. The filmmaker's reports document his frustration with officials who commented on and attempted to interfere in his work. Officers objected to Reis's depiction of naked indigenous women, criticizing it as immoral and as threatening to the norms of Brazilian propriety. They suggested omitting such "objectionable" scenes and even proposed clothing female indigenes. Reis dismissed these complaints on scientific and artistic grounds. Scientifically, he noted that nudity was ethnographically correct, even if it offended traditional sensibilities. The filmmaker thus argued that the scenes were true to life, in keeping with the commission's scientific dictates. This suggested that the naked women were to be seen as specimens of real tribal life, a view that stripped them of all feminine (and sexual) qualities. Artistically, Reis pointed out that depictions of female nudes were a historic form and a great tradition in art. The filmmaker thus placed his work within the conventions of high art, justifying the depiction of nudity artistically as well as arguing for its scientific accuracy. Reis defended his films simultaneously as illustrations of the commission's intellectual labor *and* as art. His work as an expeditionary artist suggested an interpenetration of art and science, pointing to the difficulty of separating film's scientific and artistic uses. This blurring of the boundary between the seemingly mutually exclusive disciplines of science and art underscores Reis's dialogue with the lexicon of different fields, both of which allowed him to defend his work in the face of criticism.

Given the stresses that the expeditions placed on Reis's work, it is unsurprising that he often traveled independently. On his cinematic expeditions, Reis purposefully set out to record different scenes of the backlands, from the flora and fauna to the commission's encounters with indigenous peoples. In one of his reports, he refers to his desire to film wild animals in motion, including a leopard, "something never before undertaken in Brazil." He adds that this task had to be "executed properly and in accordance with the opinion of experts," revealing an awareness of film criticism as well as a consideration of film language.[12] Here Reis aimed to capitalize on the lexis of film to "record the realism of time and motion."[13] Effectively seeking to document motion in real time, rather than to film a static object, Reis gave temporality and movement precedence over mimesis as signifiers of authenticity and the profilmic real.

Rondon's filmmaker, however, never managed to document the dynamism of any animals. His reports repeatedly refer to the camera's inability to capture the unpredictable actions of fauna. The bulky equipment was too conspicuous and filming too noisy to capture animals unawares, so they repeatedly escaped being framed by the movies. Wildlife thus frustrated the sovereignty of Reis's filmic gaze and escaped the cinema's predatory aspiration. This inability to cinematically sublimate wildlife was a constant disappointment for Reis, and he complained that he was left with registering "nothing of interest cinematographically, apart from a few views of the river, but they are always the same. Not an animal, nothing of interest."[14] Concerned with presenting cinematic scenes that would interest spectators, the expeditionary filmmaker went out of his way to track down fascinating moments. Reis thus carefully created the region as an exciting place for viewers, seeking to wow them with a variety of images of the territory so different from their own, rather than to provide them with images that were "the same." The Amazon was therefore inscribed as a space of alterity, its difference considered the source of visual wonder.

This "wondrous difference" (to use Griffiths's words) underscores a sensationalist aspect to Reis's films. The director aimed to provide spectators with extraordinary views of a tropical reality that would evoke an emotional rather than an intellectual engagement. In her work on popular sensationalism in Brazilian literature at this time, Alessandra El Far states that writers also appealed to the public's emotions as they filled their work with "unusual situations" that could elicit "a variety of novel perceptions."[15] For El Far, this sensationalism reflected changes in sensory perceptions driven by modernity. Reis keyed into this sensationalism, which was a reflection and an expression of modern sensibilities.[16] Setting out to cinematically manufacture the Amazon as a sensational landscape of exotic sights, he intended to shock the spectator with novel images. Reis's movies in this sense gravitated toward an "aesthetics of astonishment," their spectacle catering to a "cinema of attractions."[17] The filmmaker thus conceived of his films not only as art and science but also as a popular spectacle. This was in keeping with the dissemination of news and images of the commission's work by the Central Office, which also placed the expeditions before a popular gaze. Reis's films then encompassed different ways of looking at the Amazon that were in tune with art, science, *and* entertainment. They engaged in a complex interpenetrating cultural circuit of signs that encompassed the popular, the artistic, and the scientific. For Rondon's filmmaker, boundaries between cinema as science, art, and spectacle were not clearly delimited.

CINEMATIC TRAVELOGUES: MAPPING THE COMMISSION'S TERRITORIAL ADVANCE

While film was unable to capture tropical wildlife, it was successful in charting the commission's movement through the Amazon. This was often registered cartographically, with the camera operating as "locational machinery."[18] This form of cartography is explicit in *Journey to Roraima* (1927). Reis made the movie shortly after Rondon assumed the position of inspector of frontiers, and in it he charts the military's inspection of the northern state. The film begins with a map of Brazil. A white pointer indicates the itinerary that the film will follow as it tracks the expedition's progress into Roraima. This opening makes visible the commission's process of mapping the unknown territory. Cartographers marched alongside soldiers, charting the area for reconnaissance, for general information, and as a tool of civilization. They produced large-scale plans that became a means by which the region's resources could be explored and utilized and land tenure could be demarcated, controlled, and enforced. This systematic collection and production of knowledge about the area was supplemented by surveys that codified information about the region's potential, enabling the Republic to see it as a whole and to get better control of it. Imbued with a "strategic design," cartography thus became a means of appropriation and state capture of the region.[19] It marked the boundaries of the nation-state, while expanding and establishing the sovereignty of its "space discipline."[20]

Cinema became an agent in this cartographic traversal. *Journey to Roraima*'s opening underscores the film's "mapping impulse," establishing a relationship between the camera and the expedition's movement through the remote region.[21] A *mise en abyme* that introduces and duplicates the movie itself, the initial scene immediately locates the spectator within a mobile adventure of the frontier lands as the film navigates the expedition's trajectory, mapping its journey for the viewer to traverse cinematically. This is emphasized in panoramic views of landscapes that immediately follow the initial map shot. Taken from the point of view of the expedition arriving on an incoming boat, the sequences replicate the commission's journey upriver, making spectators participate in its movement of penetration and expansion into the region. Indeed, locating the camera at eye level, Reis invites the viewer to see the land as one of the officers on the boat. These panoramic views and traveling shots shift to numerous close-ups and panning shots of the land, as the camera visually explores the space and expands the spectator's depth of field.

Movement and mobility are thus central to *Journey to Roraima* and its cartographic practice. In the film, Reis capitalized on the ontologically kinetic status of the moving pictures to enact and replicate the expedition's movement through the *sertão* and place viewers within it. Film thus differed from the commission's photographs: while the static images printed in newspapers allowed individuals in cities to glimpse fragments of the backlands, bringing the distant region into their gaze, movies plunged viewers into the midst of the unknown terrain, letting them see and participate in the military's exploration of the hinterlands from the comfort of their own seats.

This form of armchair traveling inserts Reis's expedition films into the tradition of the travelogue. As Charles Musser argues, travel was "one of the most popular and developed" forms in early European and North American films, in which traveling through foreign lands was an extensive practice.[22] Tom Gunning notes that early travel films grew out of popular culture. Movies by the Lumières, Pathé-Frères, and others modeled themselves on travel literature, which detailed adventures into unknown places, taking readers on journeys around the world in *x* days and feeding a fascination to explore distant lands.[23] Early films developed this popular desire to prospect the world as an explorer, offering immediate views of the formerly inaccessible. Their annihilation of space and time gave rise to a panoramic perception, as distant places were made to appear instantly accessible.[24]

Griffiths links this panoramic perception to an infant travel industry and an aspiration to know distant places. In Europe and the United States it coincided with a broader trade in images of exotic lands in *cartes de visite,* postcards, and stereographs, which fostered what Lynne Kirby calls a "touristic consciousness."[25] This consciousness went hand in hand with Europe's acquisition of new territories, and accounts of travel at distant sites manifested colonial perspectives. Seen in this way, early travel films exhibited a historical bond with colonialism, and their mobile gaze was complicit in a drive to apprehend the world through cinematic representation. As travelogue filmmaker Burton Holmes put it, "To travel is to possess the world."[26]

Many of Reis's films for Rondon key into this sense of travel; indeed, a geographic itinerary is inscribed into the title of many of his movies, like *The Sertões of Mato Grosso, Rondônia, Ronuro: Jungles of the Xingú,* and *Journey to Roraima.* By transporting spectators to different geocultural locations in Brazil, these expedition films enact a virtual gaze and a sense of visual possession that is central to early cinema's travelogues. In *Journey to Roraima,* for example, the camera tracks the shoreline. Panning across the terrain, the lens visually scans the land. In these mobile shots the viewer's eye commands whatever falls within its gaze and the land is turned into an object of visual purchase by the camera. In the film, nature is shown, or presented, to the cinematic eye, and the tropical terrain is opened up before the spectator. Such shots condition the viewer to see the land as a place to be explored and taken over, incorporating a sense of visual prospecting and scopic possession, or what Fatimah Tobing Rony calls a "visual fantasy of dominance."[27]

These prospective views are also present in Reis's 1912 film *The Sertões of Mato Grosso.* Like *Journey to Roraima* this film includes traveling shots taken from a boat that are interspersed with pans across vast riverbeds. *The Sertões,* however, also includes panoramic shots taken from mountaintops that reveal vast landscapes. Such cinematic scenes give the spectator a commanding view of the territory displayed, which they share with Rondon and the other military men depicted. These extensive sequences are followed by numerous close-ups of officers presenting fruits to the camera, displaying the "exuberance" (as an intertitle states) of the land surveyed. *Os sertões* clearly sets out to project the natural promise of Mato Grosso as ripe for exploration and exploitation. In scanning the region's spatial prospects, viewers are invited to look at its prospects in a temporal sense: to see potential for resources to be developed and lands to be peopled. The pleasures of Reis's cinematic vision are firmly linked to commercial interests.

NEW BODYSCAPES

Film was also used to record the bodies and practices of indigenous peoples encountered by the expeditionary forces. Indeed, for Reis this was the movie camera's key advantage over photography, as he stated, "Few of us are unaware of the advantages of photographic documentation, . . . which can reproduce the natural beauty and landscapes of the explorations. Cinematography possesses greater distinction because of its ability to document the customs of our aborigines, their practices, dances, and funeral ceremonies."[28] While photography could reproduce vistas of natural locations, cinema could furnish information about various ethnic groups. Indigenous peoples feature in many of Reis's movies, such as *The Sertões of Mato Grosso, Rondônia, Journey to Roraima,* and *Rituals and Festivities of the Bororo,* now considered Brazil's first ethnographic films.[29]

Reis's cinematic documentation of indigenous groups fed into Rondon's own concerns. By 1907, the military leader began to see the nation-building implications of his telegraphic work. That is, he began to feel that the telegraph could be something more than a military instrument to secure and protect borderlands. The commission's work, he believed, could help incorporate indigenous peoples into the nation and promote the migration of coastal Brazilians into Mato Grosso's fertile lands. In other words, it could spark the physical, emotional, and affective unification of the nation. In addition to exploring and mapping the land so as to promote its effective occupation and exploitation, Rondon set out to get to know indigenous inhabitants, in an effort to ultimately turn them into Brazilians. This, he stated, was a "primordial necessity of the development of the Patria."[30]

The Sertões of Mato Grosso, Rondônia, Journey to Roraima, and *Rituals and Festivities of the Bororo* fed into this new focus. The film *Rondônia* documented the commission's expedition through the Juruena river valley, which is inhabited by the Nhambikwara peoples. The film begins with an establishing shot that pans across the Serra do Norte, presenting the landscape to viewers. It then cuts to a static shot of a group of Nhambikwara Indians who, led by Rondon, walk slowly toward the camera. The film then focuses almost exclusively on the Nhambikwara. Close-ups, medium long shots, and static takes of the indigenes mark much of the movie, as the camera sets out to capture their faces and bodies. In these sequences the Nhambikwara's bodies stand out as objects of visual pleasure, evidencing an exhibitionist quality to the film's display of the natives. This exhibition of Brazil's indigenous bodies was by no means new. Representations of the country's natives began during the colonial period, with European explorers' written and visual accounts of their encounter with Other peoples in the New World. These adventurers often took back more than tales and depictions of Brazil's indigenes. It was also common for them to return with indigenes who were exhibited in Europe for courtly amusement. In 1644, for instance, Johan Martius, governor of Brazil's Dutch possessions, took a contingent of Tapuya Indians with him to the Netherlands. Once there, the natives were made to perform war dances at courtly events and were forced to recreate Albert Eckhout's 1640 painting *Dance of the Tapuya Indians.*[31]

As Stephen Greenblatt has demonstrated, this European practice of exhibiting inhabitants from the New World was extremely popular in the sixteenth and seventeenth centuries and even became a source of income. "What spectators get for their money is the experience of wonder in the presence of the alien; they see and perhaps touch a fragment of a world elsewhere, a world of difference."[32] During the nineteenth century, such shows became institutionalized as a public form of entertainment throughout Europe. Exhibitors regularly paraded indigenes in circuses and dime shows, and world fairs recreated entire native villages for visitors, allowing Europeans to see indigenous folks in their "natural habitat." These displays created and satisfied a desire to see difference, one that was registered culturally, racially, and anatomically.

The fascination with seeing indigenes was not restricted to Europe. From the nineteenth century onwards, the country's native populations were often displayed for Brazil's urban inhabitants in a variety of media. Stereographs, postcards, *cartes de visite*, and ethnographic illustrations of indigenous "types" were increasingly mass-produced, finding their ways into the homes and hands of Brazilians.[33] Indigenous peoples were also displayed in cities as forms of entertainment. *Cronista* João do Rio, for example, documented a live show in São Paulo in 1905 that featured Bororo Indians, "who were paraded like tamed bears."[34]

Indigenes were also part of Brazil's exhibitions. Walter Garbe's photographs of the Botocudo of the state of Espirito Santo featured in the 1908 National Fair. The same event included life groups of São Paulo State's Cayuá, Coroado, Kaingang, and Xavante peoples. Organized by the Paulista Museum, these dioramas transplanted in situ the recreations of native villages that were displayed in international museums. The origins of these scale recreations can be traced to the *tableaux vivants* and waxworks. By the second half of the nineteenth century they had become a regular attraction at the world's fairs, where they aimed to stimulate the exotic and popularize ethnographic knowledge.[35] Knowledge was indeed a key goal in the staging of Indian life groups in Brazil's 1908 Fair. A report by Hermann von Ihering, the Paulista Museum's director, highlights how he sought to educate spectators with his life groups. He noted that the various "tribes were each represented by two or three Indian figures. Each group was organized in such a way to show the respective Indians in their habitats and characteristics of the tribe they represented, and they were surrounded by utensils and characteristic weapons."[36] Ihering set out to present the human effigies with their environments and artifacts in a way that was ethnographically correct as well aesthetically pleasing. The recreated context and added articles in this way reduced what Mark Sandberg calls the "object-ness" of the wax works, providing them with an air of authenticity.[37] The displays consequently enmeshed paradoxical discourses of truth and artifice, science and entertainment. In fact, the intention was to make viewers not just enjoy seeing cultural difference but also acquire knowledge about indigenous "types."

The dioramas thus sought to bring enlightenment to Brazil's urban inhabitants and functioned "as a window onto knowledge."[38] These life groups were hugely successful. They were one of the most popular attractions at the fair and won a prize for the best display.

The display of Brazilian natives at the 1908 fair may seem anachronistic. As Sven Schuster points out, the event's primary concern was to represent national progress, that is, modernity, for domestic audiences. Ideas of a Brazilian modernity, however, were combined with the celebration of a pre-Columbian past, an example of modernity's production and reproduction of the archaic and traditional.[39] For Schuster, spectacles of indigenes were part of this past. Alongside indigenous life groups, the fair exhibited a range of pre-Columbian objects from the country's museums, like the Paulista Museum, which specialized in national history, ethnology, and ethnography. They also presented Indianist paintings by Brazilian Romanticist artists, which generally portrayed Rousseau-inspired "noble savages." The construction of this Brazilian antiquity aimed to forge an image of Brazil's glorious past. It also provided an official narrative of national modernity as the result of a long-term teleological process, taking "ancient" indigenous cultures as its historical starting point. This narrative simultaneously invoked the indigenous and dismissed it in the name of progress. Placing images of natives and habitat groups as part of Brazil's history, viewers were invited to see the country's indigenes as relics of the past, not inhabitants of the present. Indigenous peoples were thus set in a different and distant temporal order, and the displays manifested what Johannes Fabian has famously referred to as a "denial of coevalness."[40]

The film *Rondônia* dialogues with this popular fascination with seeing Brazil's indigenous peoples. It also keys into contemporary tropes. Filming individuals naked and relatively still in profile and frontal shots or standing in formation, the film borrows from the language of anthropological and anthropometric photography. Photography nourished a new scientific interest in collecting and classifying information about the physical variations between human populations and aligned it with studies of human evolution, which in Europe set out to prove imperialist notions of white superiority by showing physical and scientific evidence of racial primitiveness and inferiority. Shots of the Nhambikwara in *Rondônia* follow the guidelines of anthropometric photography: staged poses, bodies unadorned by cultural markers, faces laid bare. Such scenes turn the natives into quantifiable objects and racial specimens and transform the spectator into a scientific observer. Intertitles reinforce this affinity with anthropometry. Captions such as "Warrior Girl from the Nhambikwara" fix and classify the individuals for viewers who are invited to adopt the gaze of an anthropologist scrutinizing the bodies displayed.

The film's dialogue with anthropometric photography is unsurprising. Scientists on the commission took numerous photographs of the indigenous peoples encountered as part of an endeavor to document and classify Brazil's various populations. Photographs of indigenes were included in anthropometric records produced by the commission, which included extensive measurements of their height, their weight, their cranial vault, the length of their nose, and even the width of their nostrils. This physical classification corresponded to a growing interest in race. Andermann notes that it responded to the rising demand for raw materials, which called for the spatial expansion of the zones of production and for the maintenance of low labor costs following abolition.[41] Scientific assessment of the physical qualities and capabilities of particular "types" in this context was linked to the need for a native workforce that could be coerced. The modern "spectacle of race" was physical and biological, not cultural and historical as it had been in the country's Romantic past.[42]

RITUALS AND FESTIVITIES OF THE BORORO

Rondônia's close-ups of faces and bodies demonstrate what Griffiths calls "an observational approach."[43] This approach is central to Reis's film *Rituals and Festivities of the Bororo*. The documentary was recorded in 1917 when Magalhães "organized a study of the Bororo Indians of São Lourenço, a tribe that maintains its dignified rituals that deserve be registered."[44] It was at that moment that Reis "made it my duty to film the Bororo's rituals."[45]

As Luciana Martins points out, the Bororo—their practices and bodies—were a object of fascination from the end of the nineteenth century.[46] Accounts of their lives and customs captivated scientists and adventurers who sought to profit from the popular attractions of images of primitives.[47] Expeditions to Mato Grosso by a number of European travelers produced a wealth of images of the Bororo. Artists such as Aimé-Adrien Taunay and Hercule Florence, for instance, depicted scenes of their everyday life: "people returning from hunting, listening to a storyteller's account of a jaguar hunt, performing daily activities."[48] Years later, Brazilian photographer Marc Ferrez produced numerous portraits of the Bororo. For Martins this visual archive of the Bororo aimed at the "commercial taste for the exotic."[49] While Reis's film caters to this desire for the exotic, it is also very specific in its depiction of the Bororo rituals, focusing on their funeral ceremony. In *Rituals,* the Bororo are not just physical spectacles to be observed; their practices are presented as repositories of vibrant information about their cultural difference.

Given the importance of funeral ceremonies for the Bororo, this focus is hardly surprising. According to Sylvia Caiuby Novaes, "Bororo conceptions of society and the individual are dramatized and made numerous through their funeral rituals. Of all of the events that mark the life cycle of the Bororo, death is the most celebrated."[50] Reis's film is divided into two parts: the first depicts everyday practices such as fishing, pottery, and weaving, and the second focuses on the funeral ritual. The daily activities initially portrayed, however, are implicated in the Bororo burial ceremony, which, as the title indicates, is the main focus of the film. Collective practices like fishing that are documented in the movie are fully part of the funeral ritual.

The film opens with an intertitle that informs the viewer, "After the swelling of the rivers, the tribe celebrates the *Jure,* the festival of happiness, beginning with fishing." The film then cuts to an establishing shot of a river followed by numerous pans of the landscape. A second intertitle announces, "Fishing takes place at dawn. It is conducted with nets and takes several days. The Indians travel to the bays in canoes. They cover the mouth of the river with straw mats. After having cut off the bay they beat the water with a liana *timbó,* which produces a narcotic effect in the water." The lengthy title provides viewers with detailed information regarding the fishing practices depicted, inscribing meaning through internal contextualization. Such extensive captioning is prevalent throughout *Rituals,* in which written words mediate ethnographic knowledge for audiences. The intertitles thus constitute a master narrative that seeks to assert a truth over the images. Meaning is therefore not present in the visual presentation of the Bororo, it is circumscribed through writing. This circumscription belies the medium's "truth claim" and foregrounds a semantic instability in the visual code.

After these opening sequences, the film presents numerous close-ups of Bororo men and women organizing the funeral rites: body painting, preparing feathered clothing and ornaments, all "symbolic practices." The camera then focuses on the ceremony itself. Intertitles present the viewer with different stages of the event, providing a narrative of the ritual, from the covering of the deceased with straw mats through to the ceremonial dance. In this part of the film, close-ups are replaced by long takes, which feature little editing and hardly any camera movement. These longer sequences allow the spectator to peruse the contents of the frame, much as they could a still photograph. In this regard, Reis's film challenges Christopher Pinney's distinction between photography and film, specifically his assertion of the difference between the photograph's "surplus of meaning" and cinema's "constraint of meaning through narrative chains of signification."[51] For Pinney, the viewer of still photography is able to scrutinize the image at leisure and has complete control over it. By contrast, the film spectator is trapped within a temporal chain of narrative causality, a context in which he or she is unable to intervene. In *Rituals,* however, the long takes with no camera movement and little editing remove the film's cause-effect logic and offer the spectator few clues of the anticipation and recollection linked to narrative cinema.[52] Instead, the sequences allow for a contemplative reading that makes the very act of viewing similar to that of looking at a still image.

This relatively unconstrained inspection of the filmic image by the spectator is reminiscent of Roland Barthes's idea of the photographic *punctum*—a detail or partial object, like the position of a hand or particulars of clothing, that grabs and holds the viewer's attention.[53] For Barthes, the *punctum* is not present in film, where the lexical movement of the cinematic image goes against the *punctum's* blind field: "In front of the screen I am not free to shut my eyes; otherwise opening them again, I would not discover the same image; I am constrained to a continuous veracity."[54] Barthes description, however, pertains more to narrative film, whose system of editing depends on "syntagmatic concatenation," than to the long static sequences evidenced in the Reis's film.[55] For urban Brazilians who had never seen the country's native peoples and their customs, *Ritual's* long sequences contained a plethora of details that warranted close inspection.

Reis's film is a fascinating record of the Bororo funeral ceremony. It documents each stage of the ritual: the preparation of the space of the rite; adornments used; creation of the objects utilized; the manufacturing of clothes worn from straw; the funeral dance; the food; the *aijê* ritual that recreates a hunt; and the funeral itself. At almost ten minutes, the funeral dance takes up most of the movie. As Rony notes, scenes of indigenous dances were a staple feature in ethnographic films, which satisfied a popular and scientific interest with seeing indigenous bodies in motion. She writes, "The public as well as scientists were fascinated by the bodies of indigenous peoples. Dance films showed how those bodies moved."[56] Reis's film focuses carefully on the moving bodies of a group of Bororo men as they participate in the funeral dance. With little editing or camera movement, there is no intervention in these scenes. The static camerawork and the lack of direct engagement with the dancing men impart a sense of impartiality to the film and also detach the spectator from the action shown, which is presented as a spectacle: something to be watched at a distance. The dance is thus presented as an ethnographic display, an instance of cultural difference, that is removed from the viewer's world. The spectator is consequentially invited to engage in a form of voyeurism as the screen emerges as a site of something that is ordinarily unseen. Long sequences contemplate the men's frenetic bodily movements, as they move quickly from left to right across the frame. Their actions appear frenzied, wild, even animal-like, an impression that is reinforced by their animal skins, feathers, painted bodies, and spears. An explanatory title during the *aijê* ritual emphasizes this anthropomorphism, informing viewers that the men are imitating jaguars. These shots and the caption link the Bororo to the natural world. This association is invoked in a number of Reis's films, where the camera shifts from close-ups of native peoples to shots of the flora and even fauna. In the film *Rondônia* the Nhambikwara are filmed with animals as if to stress their affinity with the natural. The overall effect is to locate the indigenes in the natural realm, evoking a cinematic attraction of the distant and different—the indigenous are other in space and time. Indeed, the final caption of *Rituals* stresses this temporal and spatial distancing, noting, "We had the impression of the remote times of the Discovery." Reis's film imagines the Bororo as existing in an earlier, pre-Columbian age and projects a view of the natives and their practices as detached from modern history. Spectators are consequently invited to regard the Bororo as relics of the past, much like the display of Indians in the 1908 national fair, manifesting their noncoevalness by treating the time of the other as "encapsulated in cultural gardens."[57]

The film's timeless depiction of the Bororo elides the reality of their history of contact, colonization, and historical process. The indigenous group had extensive contact with Salesian priests who established missions in Mato Grosso in 1883. Referred to as agricultural settlements, the missions focused on labor, aiming to assimilate the indigenous into the region's rural economy. The Salesian colonies attracted many Bororo, not least because they provided them with protection from rival indigenous groups and especially "civilized" settlers.[58] Much of the Bororo's contact with outsiders was extremely violent. Rubber tappers and local *caudilhos* often attacked the natives in an effort to exploit their lands or their labor. In the early 1820s, for instance, a six-year battle against the western Bororo on the eastern side of the Paraguay river, led by landowner and military officer João Carlos Pereira Leite, left 450 Bororo dead and 50 imprisoned. These prisoners, later deemed to be "pacified," were used as forced labor on Leite's farm. In the late nineteenth century, the provincial government of Mato Grosso founded two military settlements near the São Lourenço river in order to integrate the Bororo. Lacking an effective integration system, the settlements degenerated: drunkenness, sex, and fighting led to fierce clashes between Indians and soldiers.

Far from isolated and distant, the Bororo—like other indigenous peoples in Brazil—thus had a long history of contact with "outsiders" that was violent and assimilationist. Reis's film, however, obfuscates this reality and evokes the indigenous peoples as remnants of a bygone era. In doing so, it posits the spectator as a transparent observer who gazes through a peephole into a distant past. Indeed, the final caption of *Rituals* evokes an almost a nostalgic, even Romantic, structure of feeling, rather than a spirit of scientific truth, as the film purports to transport viewers to a different time and place. In this sense *Rituals* expresses what Renato Rosaldo refers to as the nostalgia often found in colonizing enterprises.[59] This nostalgia recalls a particular culture prior to colonialism's modernizing changes and laments the very change that has been brought about. Rosaldo explains that this nostalgia occurs alongside a sense of mission, the white man's burden, where civilized nations stand duty-bound to uplift so-called savages. In this ideologically constructed world of progressive change, putatively static barbaric societies become a stable reference for defining the felicitous progress of civilization. In the process, the agent of change is posited in a position of innocence, which absolves him or her of culpability in the process and effects of colonial domination. Nostalgia uses a pose of innocent yearning to capture people's imaginations and conceal their complicity with domination. This nostalgic longing is undoubtedly present in Reis's film, which embodies what Rony calls "impulse taxidermy," "an attempt to preserve artificially a body, in order to snatch it away from the flow of time, to stow it neatly away."[60] In *Rituals,* the Bororo are pulled out of history. They are contained, admired, and studied in a timeless ethnographic moment, as the officers occupy a place of yearning for the simple times and innocent practices of Brazil's past. This foregrounds how, far from being true, the film constructed its indigenous subjects in ways that glossed over their history of contact and the complexity of their societies.

PROJECTING INDUSTRIOUS CITIZENS

Rondon and the commission by no means ignored the violence that the Bororo and other indigenous communities had been subjected to. In 1910, Rondon became the first leader of the Indian Protection Service (IPS)—a federal agency entrusted with protecting the indigenous. As director of the IPS he devised a positivist plan for white-Indian relations in the belief that he could "protect" the indigenes with a policy of pacification through assimilation. This policy fed into contemporary debates about the role of Brazil's indigenous peoples in modern Brazilian society. Discussions focused on whether priority should be given to coercing a native workforce or to repopulating the region with immigrant laborers. Ihering, director of the Paulista Museum, ardently defended repopulation. He argued that Indians were incapable of learning and that they were "indolent and indifferent and would not make a minimum contribution to our culture and progress."[61] In his 1905 article "Anthropology in the State of São Paulo," Ihering even recommended exterminating the state's Amerindian population, writing, "The Indians of the state of São Paulo do not represent an element of labor and progress. As in other states, no serious and continuous work can be expected from civilized Indians, and they are an obstacle for colonizing the backland regions they presently occupy; it seems there is no other means at hand than to eliminate them."[62] Ihering's racism echoed discussions about the racial inferiority of the indigenes put forward by intellectuals at the time. In 1911, physician and pioneering eugenicist Afrânio Peixoto wrote of the inevitable disappearance of the "subhuman races" of indigenes; and historian Silvio Romero critiqued indigenous populations, whom he regarded as "the lowest race on the ethnographic scale."[63] Viewing indigenous peoples as subraces, Romero insisted on a break with Indianism and its object as a precondition for Brazil's progress.[64]

Rondon, a native of Mato Grosso who claimed Terena and Bororo ancestors, had a markedly different attitude toward the indigenous. In a 1908 letter to João Baptista Lacerda, director of Rio's National Museum, Rondon argued for the natives' capacity for civilization. He stated, "As their rudimentary works prove, they all have ability in any art and industry to assimilate science providing we give them a thorough education. They are neither more barbarous nor subhuman than those who, proclaiming themselves to be civilized, do not hesitate to preach for the extermination of an entire race, under the pretext of civilization and progress."[65] In lectures Rondon relentlessly argued that the natives were ready for progress and could be assimilated into Brazil as productive workers. Many of the commission's films set out to demonstrate this. *Rituals*, for instance, carefully shows the indigenes' capacity for industry. In several shots the Bororo are depcited engaging in hard work, making food, carrying objects, and pushing boats. Scenes of men hunting and fishing also show their intimacy with the natural environment and demonstrate how they are able to make it productive. Close-ups of hands laboring and mid-shots of men and women creating items from natural materials depict them as workers and display the objects of their labor. Textual accompaniment emphasizes their skills, with one title observing, "Men using fibers to manufacture materials that are better than any made by machines." Such scenes portray the Bororo as industrious. One caption even describes the Indian peoples as "our workers, cooperating in our society."

Assimilation was the central aim of the IPS and of Rondon, who made it his key mission. The military leader argued, "I think the mission of the intellectual is to train the impoverished masses so that they may elevate themselves and be incorporated into society."[66] This assimilationist stance was fully in keeping with positivism. Positivists, like Rondon, believed that the indigenes were not racially subhuman but at an earlier evolutionary stage and that they could be elevated through assimilation, which was to be gradual and nonviolent, encouraged by peaceful demonstration, not force. The idea was not to exterminate Indians but to allow them to evolve gradually via fraternal contact with civilization.

The commission established and operated two residential posts to implement Rondon's assimilationist policy, one at Ponte de Pedra and another at Utiariti, both of which operated alongside telegraph stations. The posts included schools that taught reading, writing, and arithmetic to boys and girls, as well as gymnastics. Boys were taught shoe repair and telegraph skills. Girls received instruction in sewing and crochet. Many of the boys went on to become telegraphers, maintenance workers, and line inspectors for the commission. Rondon's peaceful assimilationist policy, of course, hid the essentially violent nature of his project: the conquest of the indigenes and their lands, which would lead to the extinction of their culture. As Diacon point out, "The development and application of an indigenist policy was carried out primarily to impose state power in the hinterlands."[67] Despite euphemisms such as *pacification*, *protection*, and *fraternity*, the commission ultimately helped the state extract Indian wealth and labor, using the same extraeconomic power as *caudilhos* and rubber estate owners. With great efficacy it robbed the indigenous of their languages, altered their dress, and succeeded in attacking the totality of native activities, inserting them in times and spaces quite different from the rhythms and limits of indigenous life.

The Sertões projects the IPS's policy of fraternity. The film records the commission's 1912 visit to the villages of Uauru and Meinaco, located on the edge of the Xingu river. In addition to documenting life in these villages and the practices of their inhabitants, the film records the encounter between soldiers and indigenes. Army officers, including Rondon himself, often appear in the frame interacting peacefully with native men and women. Such images countered stories of harsh attacks by indigenous groups on outsiders in the region, including members of the commission. These tales evoked familiar tropes of Indian barbarism and prevented migrants from settling in the region. The cinematic scenes thus helped to promote migration to and settlement in the hinterlands by presenting an image of the indigenous as amenable to "outsiders." They also suggested the IPS's success in taming the natives, which led to the agency functioning as "a great wall of state power between the Indians and local whites."[68]

Intertitles stress pleasant relations between the expeditionary officers and the indigenes. One shot showing expeditionary soldiers interacting with Uauru men and women is intercut with a caption announcing that the natives "exceed all others in beauty, docility, veneration, and helpfulness." Another informs viewers, "We were welcomed by a group of men, women, and children. They showed us their village and took us to a farm that is just over a kilometer from the port. There they served us fresh and tasty *beiju*." The exchange of presents, including food, between the officers and the indigenes is a common feature of these filmed encounters. Expeditionary soldiers are often filmed distributing clothes and tools to the natives, who happily accept them. Many shots display the Uauru wearing the clothes handed out. The indigenes are shown as ready and willing to accept the products of progress and to be civilized. One of the film's captions informs us that the Uauru have themselves asked for specific materials, many of which are useful for hunting and working the land: machetes, hoes, scissors, and even bullets for a Winchester gun. While *Rituals* depicts the Bororo as objects of a distant past, *The Sertões* by contrast shows them as eager to engage with the tools of modern industry and civilization.

The Uauru's request counters the idea of the isolated native presented in *Rituals*. It also provides invaluable insights into networks of exchange that the indigenous were actively engaged in. Travelers, missionaries, anthropologists, and government officials advancing into Mato Grosso took with them Bibles and trinkets for exchange of information, as well as sketchbooks, cameras, and film equipment. The performance of native rituals became a valuable commodity within a transaction economy that collapsed symbolic value into use value. Martins states that the extensive production of visual images of the indigenous was often part of the Indians' barter with the "civilized."[69] Enmeshed in this visual economy, the indigenes were active participants in projecting their own images, and their appearance in front of the movie camera was in part an indication of the degree of their acculturation into a civilized society.

The sequences of interaction in *The Sertões* depict the Uauru's comfort with the commission's soldiers. It also shows their remarkable ease in relation to the camera. Men, women, and children frequently laugh and smile at the lens as they perform daily routines like grinding manioc. Others stare at the camera, returning the voyeuristic gaze of the spectator. In such scenes, the indigenous are fully aware of being observed as objects of a scientific gaze and are complicitous in presenting a spectacle of their own lives for the viewer, revealing an oxymoronic style that Dean MacCannell calls "staged authenticity," which subverts the illusion of scientific voyeurism and objectivity.[70] Far from being an authentic reality, the Uauru culture displayed is a charade for the camera and the viewer.

Many of the indigenes in this film confidently pose for the camera, spoiling the assumed transparency of the observer. Such posing denotes a complicity between the subject and filmmaker that subverts the power relations between surveyed and surveyor and turns the distant spectator into a participant observer. It also brings to the surface the artificiality of the actions of the natives and the expedition members. This artificiality is marked in one particular scene in *Rondônia*. Following the intertitle "Shooting," a young Nhambikwara boy waits for instructions offscreen and then, on cue, picks up a bow and arrow and shoots. When finished, he gazes at the camera and smiles as if waiting to receive the filmmaker's approval. The scene reveals the boy performing a role that Reis and the commission demand of him. It serves as a reminder that the expeditionary films documented a cultural encounter between subjects and onlookers, instead of simply showing spectators of how indigenous people "really" look and how they make their lives in the "wild."

As a "performative primitive," to use Amy Staples's expression, the indigenous willfully and strategically impersonate the "primitive" for the camera, suggesting that they are part of a network of trading in images of the exotic.[71] For Fernando de Tacca this impersonation also determines the film *Rituals,* including its lengthy dance sequence. While there is no "return gaze" in this sequence, which appears impartial, Tacca notes that the ceremony is a staged performance. Against tradition, the Bororo agreed to enact the ceremony before sunset so that it could be filmed. They also agreed to perform outside certain activities normally conducted inside huts so that Reis could record them. Tacca notes that the film is a condensed performance of a ritual that takes place over several days. It is also organized linearly: the intertitles present viewers with a narrative of the ritual so that time acquires meaning in the narrative of the film, not in the anthropological importance of the events. The ceremony was thus modified for the movie. Magalhães himself noted that Rondon asked for the time of certain actions to be altered so that Reis could film them: "I learned that a woman's corpse that was buried near the village was disinterred every morning to be sprinkled with water and on the eight day taken to a distant lake. Only Colonel Rondon could change the time of this ceremony."[72] All of this suggests that the Bororo were accustomed to performing their role as natives with considerable flair. As previously noted, there was considerable interethnic contact in the region, and the Bororo in particular were in contact with missionaries and other visitors for decades. The visualization of the indigenous was part of this history of contact and was the result of a collaborative venture between "civilized" onlookers and natives. This collaboration was also part of Reis's films, where natives and soldiers alike performed for the camera in order to construct images of the indigenes and of the commission's work.

RECEPTION OF THE COMMISSION'S FILMS

The Rondon films were shown in schools and museums throughout Brazil. Rio's National Museum took a particular interest in the movies, which became part of its film archive in 1916. Anthropologist Edgar Roquette-Pinto established the archive in 1910, seeking to capitalize on public interest in the movies and to harness their pedagogical potential.[73] Pinto himself had accompanied Rondon on an expedition through northwest Brazil in 1912 and had filmed the Nhambikwara for his own work.[74] The anthropologist believed that cinema was an ideal "mode of registering indigenous cultures and could help research and impart knowledge of Brazil's reality."[75] Pinto thus stressed the efficacy of film as an instrument of scientific knowledge and as a vital mode of instruction. In keeping with Pinto's educational interest in cinema, the National Museum's Educational Office organized screenings of the commission's films in schools in order to provide children with information about their own country's flora, fauna, and peoples and customs.[76] Such shows aimed to turn cinematic spectatorship into visual pedagogy and were part of the museum's broader civic mission.

The commission's films were also screened commercially in movie theaters in Brazilian towns and cities. The screenings were hugely popular with urban audiences, who flocked to see moving pictures of the Amazon and its inhabitants. *The Sertões,* for instance, toured Brazil in 1915 and 1916.[77] The Central Office's publicity of the film generated media frenzy. Adverts and articles for it filled newspapers and generated huge public interest. In Rio people fought to gain access to the film's showing. It played for five days in eight movie theaters and was seen by an audience of twenty thousand, with a reported two thousand unable to obtain tickets.[78] Four thousand people viewed the film in one São Paulo theater alone. The commission decided to exhibit the film again in São Paulo in 1916 because so many patrons had been turned away from the initial showing.[79] *Rituals* had a similar reception; this somewhat surprised Reis, who remarked that the film "has received applause and great audiences everywhere it has been shown. The sequences showing the Utiarity and Bello waterfalls and the customs of the Bororo Indians have awakened much admiration, as have the scenes of the indigenous dance, which until now has been unknown in civilized centers."[80]

For Diacon the success of Reis's films may have been due in part to a much-publicized controversy that was unanticipated and unwanted by the commission: naked men and especially women in the films. Many schools canceled screenings because of the nudity.[81] A protest against the scenes of nudity in the film *The Sertões* disrupted the screening in Guaratinguetá in São Paulo State and led to police intervention. The same happened in Minas Gerais, where the local police banned the film "in deference to the good morals of the town."[82]

The controversy led the Central Office to print a warning in newspapers. An advertisement for *The Sertões*, for instance, included the following announcement "NOTICE: This film was seen in Rio de Janeiro by more than twenty thousand people in five days, men and women. After complaints from overly sensitive people, we have separated the fifth and sixth reels, so that those who do not want to see NAKED INDIANS can leave the theater. *We ask for nonattendance by children and women.*"[83] The films' portrayal of naked Indians clearly offended the sensibility of many Brazilians, who were concerned for the moral susceptibility of children and women. Reis was outraged by the reception and found opposition to his films ridiculous. In a letter to the newspaper *A Tribuna* he wrote: "The naked Indian causes no scandal because the naked Indian has no significance in terms of morality. . . . He or she is an ethnographic type and not a man without clothes."[84] In the face of objections Reis stressed the scientific basis of his display of nude indigenes, whom he referred to as specimens, not people. The public, however, did not agree with Reis. Rather than view the natives as objects of scientific curiosity, they saw them as humans and Brazilians. A review of *The Sertões* that appeared in the journal *O Diário* wrote of "our Indians" inhabiting "our jungles."[85] The ethnographic distance between surveyor and surveyed did not come into play for Brazilian indigenes and their popular audiences.

The controversy regarding the nudity of the indigenes foregrounds how popular reception of the films was emotional and subjective, rather than scientific and objective. While some reviewers referred to *The Sertões* as "instructive" and "an educational film," most highlighted its sentimental appeal.[86] A journalist for *A Tarde* waxed lyrical about the film, reporting, "it has been a long time since I have felt such strong and earth-shattering sensations, which unfold into so many ideas and feelings, so full of instruction, inspiration, and elevated pleasure. The solemn magnificence of our archaic forests, the suggestive importance of our waterfalls; the magical superiority of great rivers in the ancient unknown backlands, wide channels of civilization; the marvelous opulence of our wild fauna, of indigenous life as it has always existed from its appearance in the Brazilian forests, the majesty of our incomparable nature."[87] The embodied observation articulates emotional pride in the country's peoples and nature, now "seen" as a conduit for civilization.

The Central Office emphasized this pride in Brazil, marketing screenings of the movies as "great national films." Journalists too praised the films as nationalistic. For example, a review for *The Sertões* in *O Correio de Campinas* stated, "The moviegoing public rarely has the opportunity to see such real and dramatic scenes that speak to the national soul as these which end with a beautiful symbolic act—the raising of our flag, a symbol of national sovereignty in the very extremes of our frontiers."[88] Underscoring this patriotism was an emotional belief in national progress. The *Diário do Povo* in Maceió titled its review of *The Sertões* "Civilizing Brazil." Praising Rondon's "civilizing mission," it announced that the film was "the best document of the efforts and patriotism of the Rondon Commission" and added that "the entire nation should be grateful to him."[89] One journalist for *O Estado de São Paulo* went so far as to declare seeing the film as a patriotic act for all Brazilians interested in the county's progress: "This film depicts the inhabitants of our forests and backlands, their customs and their lives. . . . This beautiful film should be seen by all Brazilians who possess an interest in and love for all things that are related to and constitute part of the progress of our nation."[90]

Viewing the commission's films was thus stressed as a civic duty, and the portrayal of the Brazilian backlands and its native inhabitants in *The Sertões* and other films was seen as articulating not just national knowledge but also national sentiment. The Rondon films in this way evoked a unifying discourse, or a unifying impression that the nation was making tangible progress. In doing so, they helped to forge "a community of sentiment . . . a group that begins to imagine and feel things together."[91] By projecting the commission's nationalizing project, Reis's cinematic output aimed to visually, imaginatively, and affectively string the nation together.

SELLING A PRODUCT AND A PLACE ABROAD:
REIS IN NEW YORK

Commercial screenings of the commission's movies in Brazil were extremely successful; they made $10,000 in 1915 and 1916 alone, the equivalent today of $230,000. Financial profits prompted Magalhães to send Reis to the United States in order to negotiate the distribution and exhibition of the now extant film *De Santa Cruz* throughout North America. Reis arrived in New York in February 1918. He spent six months in the city, meeting various film companies and undertaking painstaking studies of the North American film market. He also attempted to find a publisher for a collection of Rondon's public lectures about the Amazonian expeditions.

Reis's journey to New York aimed to capitalize on the growing interest of the United States in Latin America in a context of Pan-Americanism. Brazil played a prominent role in Pan-Americanism, and US expansion was especially drawn to the country's hinterlands. Brazil's increasing participation in the world market during the Republic as a supplier of rubber and agricultural products, and the consequent extension of its export industry into the *sertão,* were accelerated by investment from foreign countries, including the United States.

US interest in Brazil and its backlands was evidenced by Theodore Roosevelt's celebrated journey to the interior in 1914. Originally scheduled to give a series of speeches in Rio, Roosevelt requested then-president Lauro Müller to arrange a safari through the Northwest. Instead of a hunting trip Müller proposed that Roosevelt join Rondon on his exploration of the River of Doubt, which had never been mapped or explored. The expedition started in Cáceres, on the Paraguay river, with fifteen Brazilian porters, Roosevelt's son Kermit, American naturalist George Cherrie, and Roosevelt and Rondon. Roosevelt's goal was to experience an adventure and help gather specimens for the American Museum of Natural History.

The expedition was fraught with problems from the start. Insects and illnesses like malaria beset all of the expeditionary members. Food provision was low, leading to constant hunger and infighting, and attacks from indigenous groups were a constant worry. Roosevelt himself was near death when a leg he had cut became infected. The former president recounted his arduous adventures in public lectures when he returned to the United States. He also described them in the book *Through the Brazilian Wilderness.* In his memoirs, Roosevelt describes the region and stresses its promise: "This is a fertile land, pleasant to live in, and any settler who is willing to work can earn his living here. There are mines; there is water-power; there is abundance of rich soil. The country will soon be opened by rail. It offers a fine field for immigration and for agricultural mining, and business development; and it has a great future."[92] Roosevelt additionally praises Rondon for "opening up this great and virgin land to scientific knowledge and agricultural settlement" and "civilizing the savages."[93]

Roosevelt's memoirs helped to publicize Rondon and his work beyond Brazil. The exhibition of *De Santa Cruz* in the United States sought to capitalize on and add to this publicity. It also aimed to secure additional profits from screenings and to attract more foreign "cooperation and investment" in Brazil, as Reis wrote in his account of his New York endeavors.[94] This task required significantly changing the Brazilian film in order to cater to the US market. The six-reel movie had originally included vistas of Rio and São Paulo, footage from the Rondon-Roosevelt expedition, and sequences of the Parecis Indians in northwestern Mato Grosso.[95] Reis renamed the film *Wilderness.* He edited it down, giving prominence to scenes of Roosevelt's visit and cutting sequences of Indians' nudity, since "the Americans are very particular when it comes to scenes of nudity."[96] He also rewrote the intertitles, using extracts from Roosevelt's book.

With Roosevelt's assistance and in collaboration with the American Geographical Society, *Wilderness* was screened at Carnegie Hall on May 15, 1918. Organized as part of a "Brazilian program," the screening was accompanied by an orchestra, which played Carlos Gomes's "O Guarani," "a patriotic song."[97] The show was attended by the Brazilian ambassador and Roosevelt, who gave a lecture before the film, in which he recounted his Amazonian adventures and spoke of Rondon's great achievements. The event sold out. An audience of 2,800 watched Reis's movie, including representatives from Metro, Fox, Paramount, Goldwyn, and Interocean film studios. Following the screening, Metro and Interocean expressed an interest in distributing *Wilderness.* They complained, however, that the film was not sensational enough to be a feature-length movie and requested that Reis cut it down so that they could distribute it as an educational short. Aware of the lack of profits from educational films, Reis returned to Brazil in July 1918 having failed to gain a distributor for the feature film.

His second task of finding a publisher for Rondon's lectures was also unsuccessful. In his report, Reis wrote that editors complained that Rondon's texts were written in "a style that is not very American. They explained that the American style consisted in giving it the air of an adventure story in the forest." He sarcastically went on, "It should have photographs of wild animals and Indians etc. and if possible something sensational, like Rondon surrounded by terrifying tribes shooting arrows at him, then after dragging him through the Santo Bello waterfall and precipitating his fall, a strong American star like George Walsh will appear and save the day shouting, 'Freedom!' This, I imagined, was the style they would appreciate."[98]

Reis's failures are indicative of the popular perception of Brazil in the United States. Americans clearly wanted sensational stories and images of peril and heroic feats. While Rondon and Brazil were keen to project Brazil as a space of progress, for Americans it remained a savage place of danger. The scientific and civilizing impulse underpinning the commission's work thus undermined its ability to sell its products and its labor in the United States, where Brazil was attractive in the popular imaginary as a place of difference.

PART FOUR

Modernism and the Movies

8

Modernismo's Literary Engagements with Film

In February 1922 a group of iconoclastic Brazilian writers, artists, and intellectuals gathered in São Paulo's Municipal Theater and declared Brazil's artistic independence. Their declaration inaugurated the Semana de Arte Moderna, or Week of Modern Art, and gave rise to what has become known as the Brazilian modernist movement, or *modernismo*. The Week of Modern Art featured prose readings, music concerts, art exhibitions, and discussions on aesthetic theory, and it officially marked the coronation of a movement that had been gaining strength over the previous decade.[1]

The multifaceted nature of the Week of Modern Art underscores *modernismo*'s multidisciplinary character. As Randal Johnson points out, "Brazilian modernism was a heterogeneous movement encompassing a multiplicity of aesthetic, cultural, social and political proposals."[2] Yet in spite of this heterogeneity its adherents were united around a common concern: the need to create a new art in and for Brazil. This concern underpinned what standard historiography has defined as the movement's "heroic" period, which extended from 1922 to 1930, after which the initial relatively coherent group splintered along different ideological, political, and aesthetic lines.[3] During this period *modernismo* was characterized by an opposition to traditional European models that had dominated Brazilian letters since the end of the nineteenth century. Parnassian poetry became a particular target of attack. Its strict metric rhyme schemes, rigidly stratified structures, and academic discourse based on a blind adherence to French culture were satirized at the Week of Modern Art as out of touch with the changes Brazilian society was undergoing. For the modernists, Parnassianism's mimicry of French literature was evidence of a colonial mentality, in which writers passively imported European forms wholesale. Moving away from such blind allegiance to foreign models, the modernists sought to create literary forms that would engage with and articulate the processes of modernization under way in Brazil and also decolonize Brazilian letters. So it was that in his 1926 "Brazilwood Manifesto" Oswald de Andrade advocated for a poetry for export that would reverse the historically imitative stance of Brazilian literature and the one-directional flow of artistic influence.

Emerging on the centenary of Brazil's independence from Portugal, *modernismo* thus aimed to create a new art that would register the country's transformations. These transformations were profoundly felt in São Paulo. The scarcity of imported goods during World War I stimulated industrial production in Brazil. After 1917, manufacturing industries proliferated in the city, which became the country's industrial center.[4] The city also experienced massive demographic shifts. From 1890 to 1920 its population rose from 64,935 inhabitants to 579,033, a growth fueled by migrants from the interior and immigrants from Europe and Japan.[5] These new inhabitants provided labor for industrial expansion. They also imported a tradition of political militancy that started to challenge established social structures and hierarchies. Strikes protesting low wages and poor working conditions mobilized thousands of workers in the late 1910s, evidencing a growing class consciousness.[6]

The beginnings of Brazilian modernism were located in these shifts in São Paulo's social and material landscape, which altered the definition of the city. As Nicolau Sevcenko writes, São Paulo's transformations provided the modernists with "keys for the internal reformulation of their works."[7] Writers and artists brought the metropolis into cultural production, thematically and aesthetically. Collections of poetry such as Mário de Andrade's *Paulicéia desvairada* (1922; translated as *Hallucinated City,* 1968) and novels like *Brás, Bexiga e Barra Funda* (1927) by Antônio de Alcântara Machado took São Paulo's changing topography as their energizing and organizing inspiration. These texts helped to concretize a connection between São Paulo and *modernismo,* a connection that perfectly fits what Andreas Huyssen refers to as the "geography of classical modernism," which "is primarily determined by cities and the cultural experiments and upheavals they generated."[8]

Yet if the geography of Brazilian modernism is linked to São Paulo's changing spaces, it also reflects broader changes to the role and place of writing and the writer in Brazil. During the Republic, the institutional structures underlying literature—that is, the "lettered city," Angel Rama's term for the urban intellectuals who wrote the Americas' literature and laws—were being transformed in real and metaphoric senses. Urban transformations, like those in São Paulo, were allied to changes in higher education. University reforms in the late 1910s meant that the traditional degrees in laws and medicine held by the elite no longer guaranteed the same role in society and politics, and the antioligarchic reformers clamored for the rights of the underprivileged.[9] Néstor García Canclini points to contradictions in this.

"Confronted with the illiteracy of half of the population and with pre-modern economic structures and political habits . . . literary habits were conditioned by questions about what it means to make literature in societies that lack a sufficiently developed market for an autonomous cultural field to exist."[10] Though hardly successful in creating a shared nation, since Brazil was still characterized by the class and race divisions that split the elite from the masses (noted by Mário in his 1942 assessment of the movement), *modernismo* did "create new aesthetic trends within an incipient cultural field."[11] Daryle Williams refers to the Week of Modern Art as the beginning of the erosion of the ivory tower, as "new cultural practices, institutions, and ideas undermined the viability of an intellectual class isolated from society" and as these popular developments made the "medieval image of the scholar-in-the-turret" seem antiquated.[12] In this respect, the movement was characterized by a vanguardist drive toward what Vicky Unruh (after Peter Bürger) calls "the rehumanization of art"—an active reengagement of art with everyday life.[13]

Film was not part of *modernismo*'s Week of Modern Art. While cinema was received and perceived as "modern" in Brazil, the medium was absent from the gathering in 1922. This absence is not surprising. Ismail Xavier affirms that there were no "modernist" filmmaking practices in Brazil at this time, testifying to what he highlights as a divorce between theory and praxis.[14] Filmmakers like Humberto Mauro belonged to popular sectors of society and, seeing their work as entertainment, rarely theorized their activities as artistic endeavors. Consequently, magazines like *Cinearte,* which championed film art, contained few theoretical contributions from those making films. It was journalists and intellectuals, like Adhemar Gonzaga and Pedro Lima, who promoted discussions of the cinema's aesthetic qualities.

Cinema, however, was by no means extraneous to *modernismo*. A number of modernist authors wrote about the medium in the press throughout the 1910s and 1920s. Oswald de Andrade (1890–1954) discussed movie screenings in his column "Teatro e salões" (Theaters and salons) published in the *Diário de São Paulo* from 1909 to 1911 and in the journal *O Pirralho* from 1910 to 1911; Giulherme de Almeida (1890–1969) worked as a film critic for the *Estado de São Paulo* between 1926 and 1942; and Mário de Andrade (1893–1945) penned film reviews for different journals throughout the 1920s. This journalistic engagement with film was far from new. Brazilian authors began writing about cinema in the press shortly after the medium's first screening in Rio in 1896. Writers like Olavo Bilac and João do Rio commented on the new technology in newspapers at the start of the twentieth century, noting—with much fascination—its ability to mimetically record everyday reality.[15]

This early engagement with film rarely went beyond journalistic accounts. Brazilian writers initially interacted with the medium in nonliterary texts, documenting its appearance in the country and commenting on its novel effects in newspaper articles. Rarely did they allow their fascination with cinema to enter into more "serious" literary endeavors. Somewhat hesitant about the new medium, they shrank from developing a more intimate liaison with it. This began to change in the 1920s when modernist writers started to include references to film and adopt cinematic forms in their literary texts. Oswald de Andrade, Antônio de Alcântara Machado, and Mário de Andrade especially turned to cinema as a medium that could update their writing. The movies thus provided these modernist writers with a new vocabulary that could refashion writing. Brazilian literature "lost the syntax of its heart and trousers," as Oswald de Andrade puts it in *Serafim ponte grande* (1933; translated as *Seraphim Grosse Pointe*, 1979), with the appearance of texts such as his own *Os condenados* (The condemned, 1922) and *Memórias sentimentais de João Miramar* (Sentimental memoirs of João Miramar, 1924), Mário de Andrade's *Paulicéia desvairada* (translated as *Hallucinated City*, 1922) and *Amar, verbo intransitivo* (Love, intransitive verb, 1927), and Antônio de Alcântara Machado's *Pathé-Baby* (1926), which appropriated the techniques of film.[16]

These authors' literary appropriation of cinema testifies to the emergence of new conceptions regarding the medium after World War I. By the 1920s there was a widespread awareness in Brazil that cinema had a language of its own, that rather than simply reproducing reality, the camera produced it according to its own logic. This consciousness of film's particular vocabulary was fostered by the emergence of new venues that specialized in the critique of cinema. Popular movie magazines, like *Cinearte,* made people conscious of film's style and form and altered the status of the medium in Brazil, so that it started to be seen as an art form.

The proliferation of discussions of film's artistic values was reinforced by discourses regarding cinema as what Ricciotto Canudo termed "a seventh art." This discourse developed in France and became influential throughout Europe. Discussions took place in the context of wider deliberations over art, central to avant-garde movements like cubism, Dada, surrealism, primitivism, and futurism. From these deliberations sprang polemical debates over the nature and function of the movies, which began to query the tendency to think of cinema as an art of the real (as mimetic representation) and to consider its formal and stylistic systems.[17] Periodicals like *Le Cinéma* (1919) and *Cinéa* (1921) and *ciné-club*s like the Club des amis du septième art (1921) opened up a space for French intellectuals to raise questions about alternative film forms and methods of realization, as well as the medium's purpose.

Canudo, Louis Delluc, Léon Moussinac, Emile Vuillermoz, and Germaine Dulac, among others, started to discern and articulate theories regarding the cinema's unique aesthetics—its difference from other arts, especially from its closest cognate, the theater. For these critics, film's key characteristic was that it told a story, which was constructed through editing. Some writers, like Delluc, argued that the cinematic narrative was grounded in and could express the reality of everyday life. Others, like Vuillermoz, claimed it could communicate an interior reality, that film was as a mode of subjective expression.[18] These ideas foregrounded the medium's cognitive power: film could reveal the world to the spectator. Key to this revelatory potential was Delluc's concept of *photogénie* (literally "created by light"). It assumed that the "real" (the factual and natural) was the basis of film representation but stressed that the camera transformed the real. This transformation was facilitated by several features of the camera and its technical components, especially framing, mise-en-scène, and lighting. As Richard Abel writes, "*Photogénie* allowed people to see ordinary things as they had never been seen before."[19] In other words, it defamiliarized the familiar. Close-ups, for instance, could isolate and magnify objects of everyday life and reposition them. Such techniques stripped film from its exclusively narrative function. Disruptive of the space-time of the story, *photogénie* contained the potential for a modernist aesthetic and fueled speculations about developing non-narrative films.

These theoretical elaborations regarding the medium's specificity legitimated film as art. As a sign of its acceptance as an artistic form, literary and intellectual journals began to open their pages to the cinema. Le Corbusier and Amédée Ozenfant's *L'Esprit Nouveau* (1918–1925) embraced film, publishing pieces by Delluc and others. Authors too turned to cinema as a source of inspiration and production. At a speech delivered at Paris's Théâtre du Vieux-Colombier in November 1917, Guillaume Appollinaire called film a "new means of artistic expression" and encouraged poets to embrace it.[20] Many took up Apollinaire's challenge. Philippe Soupault and Yvan Goll wrote a hybrid form of cinematic poetry.[21] Jules Romain and Blaise Cendrars also embraced film, adopting the techniques and structure of screenplays in their prose.[22]

This adoption was matched by a growing interest in cinema by artists who began to utilize its uniqueness as art. Jean Epstein, René Clair, Francis Picabia, and Fernand Léger, for example, made the most of the cinema's non-narrative qualities to create avant-garde films. What interested these artists was not film's storytelling abilities but its plastic qualities—the mechanics of the medium, which occupied a principal role in their films. Linked to such qualities was the cinema's ability to represent what Abel calls "the mechanical of modern life."[23] This was also a feature of contemporary theoretical discussions, which were marked by a belief that mechanical dislocation and rapidity could produce new perceptions and new subjects. A product of the machine age, film, it was believed, not only reflected the experience of modernity but also could produce new sensibilities.

These ideas were central to Epstein's theoretical elaborations. For him cinema's *photogénie* meant that film did not just reproduce reality but intervened in it by revealing the world's internal structures.[24] The medium, in this sense, could foster what Walter Benjamin would later call "the optical unconscious" and could create a reflexive reengagement between art and everyday life.[25] This revelatory potential resonated with surrealists. Influenced by Freudian ideas, artists like Robert Desnos believed that cinema could reveal and explore the nonrational operations of the unconscious.[26] By doing so, the medium had the power to overturn the laws of logic and social convention, which could be the first step toward the transformation of the world.[27] The cinema's potential to manifest hidden aspects of the real also had an impact on Soviet theorists, like Dziga Vertov. For Russian filmmakers, film could expose internal material aspects of reality, that is, dialectical processes of sociohistorical human relations and forms of production. Unmasking these was the basis of Soviet montage theory and practice and became an aesthetic and sociopolitical project.

Brazil's modernist writers were familiar with these new ideas regarding film art. French literary and film journals circulated in Brazil and were read by many *modernistas*.[28] *L'Esprit Nouveau* had a particular influence on the young, with Mário de Andrade in particular citing the journal's articles in his writings.[29] Many modernists also regularly traveled to Paris, where they came into contact with avant-garde intellectuals and learned about theoretical discussions of film. French writers too traveled to Brazil and met *modernistas*. Cendrars, for example, was a regular visitor to Brazil.[30] He first visited in 1924 and was given a warm welcome by leading modernists. Inspired by the city's dynamism, he proposed the idea of producing a promotional film with Oswald de Andrade, whom he had met in Paris the year before. Oswald would be responsible for the script, while Cendrars would be the director.[31] The film was never produced, but Cendrars's proposal testifies to the intimate contact that Brazilian modernists had with French intellectuals and how film was part of that contact.[32]

Like French writers, many modernists turned to the art of film to reshape Brazilian letters. Film's influence on *modernismo* was evidenced by the centrality of a movie camera in its journal *Klaxon*, published in 1922. The magazine featured a simple black and white geometrical image of a movie camera at the top of its pages and on its back cover, equating the movement's modernity with the cinematic apparatus. This incorporation of film was part of *modernismo*'s wider evocation of technology. The very title, *Klaxon*, was drawn from technology, and the publication's geometric and abstract graphics also invoked the industrial. Demonstrating a futurist regard for technology, the modernists' artistic production was reconceptualized as a machine-like activity, which film inspired.

The cinema thus augured new artistic possibilities for formal experimentation. As the modernist manifesto printed in *Klaxon* declared, "The cinema is the most representative art form of our era. It is necessary to learn from it."[33] Cinematic lessons were part of the movement's attempt to break away from traditional cultural forms. This was clearly expressed in the manifesto, which opposed the "tragedy, sentimentality, and technical romanticism" of theater actress Sarah Bernhardt and celebrated the "rationality, dynamism, activity, and vitality" of movie star Pearl White. A leading actress in Hollywood's serial melodramas, Pearl White represented a stark departure from the "lachrymose sentimentalism" of traditional femininity. She embodied a new aesthetic ideal that was mobile, energetic, and popular.[34] The reference to Pearl Young, the intrepid actress, displayed little of the moral concern over the public display of women explored in chapter 4. If anything, the celebration of the movie star flies in the face of bourgeois moralities. Cinema thus provided modernists with possibilities for an artistic experimentation that was allied with social critique.[35] In this capacity the medium represented what Esther Gabara calls "a modern ethos" that challenged dominant sociopolitical mores.[36] This ethos articulated a "critical nationalism," to use Mário's term: that is, a politics that criticized the Republic's modernizing project, which was driven by a positivist narrative of progress imported from Europe.[37] Marked by "a new historical consciousness," writers set out to critique the Republic's European-inspired modernity, which involved countering its colonial logic of unilinear development and its diffusionist drive—questioning "hierarchies embedded in an official notion that aimed to spread civilization" from the urban center to the periphery.[38] Upsetting the linearity of Republican modernity was central to *modernismo*'s ethos, since it repressed Brazil globally, casting it as an unrealized but promising future potential or as a relic from a primitive past. Republicanist discourses in this sense reiterated a global project of modernity, which placed Brazil in what Doreen Massey calls "history's queue": forever occupying an exegetical horizon of difference as it attempted to mimic and catch up to a universal model.[39]

Recognition of such asymmetrical relationships fed into *modernismo*'s turn against dominant culture in Brazil. Its antagonistic ethos also keyed into a crisis of the universality of civilization following World War I, which put an end to the faith in progress.[40] In Brazil, this crisis took on particular political and aesthetic shadings and required literary and representational strategies in tune with the experiences and subjectivities created by colonization.[41] This was evident in *modernismo*'s articulation of a primitive order as a form of opposition to the homogeneous continuum of progress, revealing a hybrid consciousness. Resistance through hybridism was at the heart of Oswald's 1928 "Cannibalist Manifesto," which proposed the selective consumption of foreign forms and the creative mixing of the local and the global by the irrational savage. What was at stake in such cultural "cannibalism" was the disruption and rejection of modernity's logical order and progress through the rearticulation of a repressed past and the active consumption of modern methods.

The "Cannibalist Manifesto's" repudiation of evolutionary time was evidenced in its very form, which Haroldo de Campos refers to as Oswald's "semiological transgression of order."[42] The montage of unrelated fragments making up the reality of Brazilian life begins to reveal a different order. Contradictions between different "facts" appear on the page as the natural and technological, the barbaric and the cosmopolitan, come into dialectical struggle. Oswald's manifesto then not only deconstructs Brazil's dominant modern narrative but also constructs a new dynamic identity by juxtaposing the country's distinct elements to create a new whole. This ability to juxtapose different elements was of course central to film syntax, as montage brought together different times and spaces on the screen. For European vanguard artists, editing contained the potential for radical transformation in that it destroyed and reconfigured the temporal-spatial coherency of the real world and could allow viewers to see and experience it in new ways. This ability to break away from a sequential order and to reshape reality was seized upon by modernists like Oswald as a means of undermining the Republic's narrative of progress, and the movies were part of the young iconoclast's project to enable Brazilians "to see with free eyes."[43]

Modernismo's appropriation of the techniques of cinema thus participated in and contributed to its critical nationalism. But if this was influenced by French theorists, it was primarily mediated by US cinema. The movies that energized modernists' writings were not those of the European avant-garde but those of North America. For the modernists American cinema stood for modernity: the discarding of stifling traditions and cultures. Hollywood thus represented a counterdiscourse for the iconoclasts. It also functioned as what Miriam Hansen has termed a vernacular modernism, providing modernists with "a sensory reflexive experience of modernity and modernization." It was "the single most expansive discursive horizon in which the effects of modernity were reflected, rejected or denied, transmuted or negotiated."[44]

Modernismo's embrace of Hollywood movies can be traced to their attempt to cross the "great divide" between everyday culture and literature—to break through the narrowly conceived boundaries of literary production.[45] It also reflected the broader celebration of Hollywood evident in fanzines like *Cinearte*. Unlike *Cinearte*, however, modernists paid little attention to national cinema, evidencing what Xavier calls "the separation between Brazilian cinema and the other sectors of our culture."[46] *Modernismo*'s disregard of national production is not unexpected given the virtual absence of Brazilian films on domestic screens due to Hollywood's hegemony. Foreign cinema's dominance, however, was never a subject of discussion for the writers. As Xavier observes, Oswald and others never critiqued the "colonial situation" of Brazil's cinematic landscape, in which Hollywood's supremacy relegated the country to being an importer of movies and forced filmmakers to mimic its forms in an effort to compete with imported products.[47] Indeed, in his only review of a Brazilian film, *Do Rio a São Paulo para casar* (From Rio to São Paulo for a wedding; dir. José Medina, 1922), Mário praised its Hollywood style, writing, "Transplanting the North American art to Brazil. Great benefit. Sincere applause."[48] While Oswald advocated for "a poetry for export" that would reject Parnassianism's mimetic traits, this literary argument never made it to the modernists' engagements with film.

CINEMATIC SIMULTANEITY AND MODERN LIFE IN
MÁRIO DE ANDRADE'S WRITINGS

Mário de Andrade was the modernist writer who most engaged with film.[49] The author regularly frequented São Paulo's movie theaters and "watched with much interest films exhibited in the city."[50] It is hardly surprising, then, that both his journalistic essays and his literary works are littered with references to movies he has seen. Mário's engagement with the movies, however, went beyond mere quotation. As he himself affirmed, "Writing modern art does not mean representing the exterior aspects of contemporary life: cars, cinema, concrete. If these words frequent my work it is not because I think I am writing something modern with them, but because, being modern, they have a reason for being in my work."[51] Stressing an affinity between his literature and film, Mário was "was not content to simply be another enchanted spectator. . . . He learned to analyze what the screen showed him."[52]

Mário's engagement with film paralleled his broader interest in visual technology. Gabara has foregrounded the writer's interaction with photography.[53] The author collected and took hundreds of photographs. Yet photography was more than a means to represent modern life; it was also a rich mine of new aesthetic concepts. More than simply representing the world objectively, the camera opened up new potentials for formal experimentation. Mário's interest in photography fed into his fascination with film. The author never became involved in filmmaking, perhaps because of the difficulty of obtaining film stock in a country dominated by foreign imports. Nonetheless, he grappled with film closely as both writer and critic. In his articles for *Klaxon*, Mário praised cinema's ability to cater to numerous people as a means of attacking the "artistic prejudices" of traditional art.[54] The popular form of the movies could thus have a liberatory function, helping Brazilian letters to break away from traditional literature and bring writing into an everyday realm. Consequently the author referred to the medium as "a tenth muse, born this century, the cinematographic muse."[55]

If this muse was born in the twentieth century, it was also conceived in Hollywood. Mário's cinematic essays dwelt on US movie stars, most notably Charlie Chaplin.[56] Mário wrote three articles on Chaplin for *Klaxon,* in which he praised the actor's "creative genius."[57] Mário's admiration for Chaplin echoed European intellectuals' fascination for the English star-director. By 1920, the Little Tramp emerged as the hero of the European avant-garde.[58] Artists extolled his gestural performances, seeing his somatic body as the embodiment of modernity. In 1927, Epstein, for instance, remarked upon Chaplin's "photogenic neurasthenia," observing that "his entire performance consists of the reflex actions of a nervous, tired person."[59] Mário's engagement with Chaplin had a different orientation. In his article "A Lesson from Carlito," Mário echoes the Europeans' affirmation of Chaplin's incarnation of modern times, noting that the star "reflects, in the form of a superficial caricature, the twentieth-century man."[60] The Brazilian poet, however, critiques this: "Carlito, with his magnificent exaggerations, comprehended life as aesthetics. Burlesque aesthetics of course. This was a mistake. He created a life outside of life itself. He suffered from aestheticism, the worst sin of modern artists."[61] For Mário, Chaplin's burlesque features have become parodies that no longer articulate a sensory disposition linked to eternal human truths. This changed, he observed, in the 1921 film *The Kid,* which evoked a universal humanism. For Mário, with this film Carlito "became immense and immortal."[62]

It is tempting to read Mário's reception of the Little Tramp as conservative: Chaplin and the popular culture he emblematized can be praised only if he assumes eternal artistic dimensions, and this would entail covering up the burlesque and popular culture of the star's early performances. In extolling Chaplin's humanism in *The Kid,* however, Mário sees the performer as communicating the experience of the twentieth-century man across all boundaries, social and international, making him representative of unity in the consciousness of modern life. Chaplin thus embodies a collective experience, capable of detonating the hierarchies of progressive modernity.

The Brazilian poet's reception of Chaplin undoubtedly drew upon the star's public persona of humanitarian solidarity with the poor. Jason Borge notes that Chaplin's "picture personality . . . disseminated through magazines and newspapers . . . showcased Chaplin as an emblem of the artistic and social potential of film."[63] Mário's interpretation conveys an understanding of the presence that Chaplin gives to the marginalized within a modern space dominated by order and progress. While a foreign import, for Mário the Little Tramp was far from reconciled to the hegemonic vision of a foreign-inspired Republican civility. Instead, Chaplin showed how popular cinema, Hollywood included, could be a counter-discourse when it illustrated that part of the population that Jacques Rancière calls the *demos*—those who have neither voice nor representation.[64]

In his extensive review of *The Kid* Mário goes to great lengths to defend the film against criticism by Parisian Dadaist Celina Arnault that was published in the journal *L'Action.* Referring specifically to the film's dream sequence, in which Chaplin sports a set of angel wings, Arnault wrote, "The public doesn't want to dream at the cinema: it wants to see realities, live them. . . . But Charlot's poet dreams poorly. . . . This smells strongly of bad literature!"[65] Expressing not so much distaste for a dream sequence as for how Chaplin achieved it, Arnault charges the actor-director with abandoning a style grounded in everyday popular life—reality and the circus—for the mock-natural devices of conventional art. With his giant baroque wings Chaplin "ascended to his position above his subjects, who in turn admiringly gazed and were reaffirmed by his cinematic separateness as a representation of art."[66] Disagreeing with Arnault, Mário ardently defends the sequence. "Carlito dreamed what he had to dream, necessarily, sadly: an angelic happiness disturbed by the astute subconscious of real suffering and the difficult."[67] For Mário, Chaplin's dream emanates from the reality of his situation as a member of modern society's underclass and destabilizes its civilized contours. By rupturing modern civility, Chaplin reveals the cinema to be critically embedded within, rather than removed from, everyday modern life.

The Little Tramp, then, could help people to see modern life differently. The possibility of seeing modernity otherwise was central to Mário's review of Robert Wiene's 1920 film *The Cabinet of Dr. Caligari*. The review was part of Mário's "Crônicas de Malazarte" (Chronicles of Malazarte) that appeared in the journal *América Brasileira* from 1923 to 1924. The series was penned by Mário's heteronym Malazarte (a play on *mala arte*, meaning bad art), described by Telê Ancona Lopez as "a caustic critic who represents the adventurous avant-garde, irreverent experimenters with new solutions for art."[68] The review begins with Malazarte announcing his avant-garde status, which is reinforced by his embrace of film: "I am a modernizer! I celebrate the happiness of westerns and have become a film entrepreneur." He goes on, "I heard so much about *The Cabinet of Dr. Caligari* that I rented it."[69] Rather than praising the German expressionist film, however, Malazarte denounces it as "rubbish!" At this point, Mário intervenes. He states that Malazarte "was wrong to dislike *The Cabinet of Dr. Caligari*," adding that it is "one of the best works of art we have seen in film today." He foregrounds the movie's expressionism, which he refers to as "anticinematic," meaning antirealist. For him, this distortion of reality is a lesson for modern art: "What we seek and want to see in a work of art is not the visually realistic representation of the external world, but its internal conflicts in terms of shapes, lines, colors and syntheses, a new artistic order."[70] The writer recognizes *The Cabinet of Dr. Caligari*'s style as conveying the subjective experience of life through objective means and acknowledges a dialogue between the film's aesthetics and the goals of art as it seeks to express modern life.

For Mário, then, film language could help the artist capture the modern experiential field and register changes in perceptive structures brought about by modernization, especially in cities like São Paulo. Transformations in urban perceptions are central to his collection of poems *Hallucinated City*. This 1922 ode to São Paulo discovers the urban landscape as "a realm of human experience that is worthy of being interpreted via poetry."[71] The collection has three parts: the first, "Prefácio interessantíssimo" (Very interesting preface), is an impressionistic commentary on aspects of modern art that lays out a new theory of lyricism; the central corpus consists of twenty-one poems inspired by São Paulo; the final part is "As enfibraturas do Ipiranga" (The moral fibrature of Ipiranga), which imagines the city as a massive oratorio. The fragmented nature of the collection recalls the role of editing in film, and Benjamin's idea that mechanical reproduction transforms the reception and function of art by catalyzing a shift from a conception of the work of art as a totality to a theory of multiple works and practices.

This new conception of art is outlined in the preface to *Hallucinated City*, in which Mário self-consciously examines the artistic notions underlying the collection's creation. The poet's ideas are underwritten by music-based metaphors. Poetic verse, Mário affirms, lags behind musical composition, which for centuries preferred harmonic over melodic structures, understood as the horizontal arrangement of consecutive sounds, containing intelligible thought.[72] In *Hallucinated City*, he proposes a sensation of harmonic verse, a simultaneous superimposition of elements, which is created by juxtaposing disconnected phrases to create a "poetic polyphony."[73] "We made words with no immediate connection between them follow each other: these words, from the simple fact of not linking to each other intellectually or grammatically, superimpose themselves to others, in our sensation, forming not melodies but harmonies."[74]

Hallucinated City's musical analogy is in keeping with Mário's early training in São Paulo's conservatory and forecasts his subsequent achievements as a musicologist. It also engages European theories. Indeed, Mário's analogy between music and poetry was indebted to the theoretical elaborations of poet and cineaste Epstein, whose writings in *L'Esprit Nouveau* he was familiar with.[75] The particular essay by Epstein that caught his attention was "Le phénomène littéraire." From its discussion of simultaneism, Mário understood that to capture the experience of the modern city, art must record a rapid succession of sounds by way of registering the constantly changing affective states visited on the poet and the reader in the kaleidoscopic outside world.[76] The synthesis of noises was a means of comprehending the modern landscape through movement. From this, Mário imagined a play with words—a free association—that would operate on a deeper level than their denotative meaning, oscillating between the conscious and subconscious. Only the logic of the subconscious could guide the poet, motivating the inexplicable associations. The simultaneous sounds implied the replacement of a logical, rational conscious order by the subconscious order.[77] Indeed, the subconscious was the basis of Mário's lyricism, as he noted: "When I feel the lyrical impulse, I write everything that my subconscious cries out, without thinking."[78]

In his "Very Interesting Preface" Mário expressed his debt to Epstein's theory of simultaneism: "In December and November I received issues 11 and 12 of the magazine *L'Esprit Nouveau*: my ramblings in this 'Very Interesting Preface.' Epstein, continuing his study of 'The Literary Phenomenon,' observed a modern harmonism that he called simultaneism."[79] While Mário couched these ideas in musical terms in *Hallucinated City*, Unruh notes that "visual qualities" are essential to the collection's musicality.[80] The sequence of poems that follow the preface accumulate not just sounds but also visual impressions of São Paulo to reveal a dynamic portrait of the city that the writer impresses on the reader.[81] What Mário calls the "simultaneous association of images" is a key determinant of *Hallucinated City*; it underlies Mário's poetic polyphony and provides a rhythm for the collection.[82]

This rhythm is not structured by rhyme or meter (as in Parnassianism), which are radically rejected in favor of free verse, but by the relationships between different sounds and images—their conflicts and syntheses.[83]

Hallucinated City's visuality suggests a homology between poetry and film. Mário himself referred to the collection's cinematic quality in "A escrava que não é Isaura" (The slave who is not Isaura), where he related its simultaneism to "modern technology: the telegraph, the steamship, the telephone, and the movies."[84] Film, like technical forms of communication, could bring together different times and spaces. The perceptual paradigm of cinema thus included a changed spatial and temporal consciousness, what Lynne Kirby describes as "an orientation to synchronicity and simultaneity."[85] These new perceptions were premised on discontinuity: the physical, social, and visual disorientations caused by the modern transformations of space and time.

Film thus stimulated a simultaneist mode of consciousness. Epstein, a key influence for Mário, set out to formulate the possibility of integrating this new cinematic mode into poetry. In *La poésie d'aujourd'hui* he isolated formal features of modernist writing and compared them to new perceptual properties and to the cinema's technical possibilities. Modernist poetry, Epstein argued, was largely the transcription of the modifications of modern life taking place in the bodily subconscious, the importance of which was disclosed through the movies.[86] The physiological possibility of seeing everything at once could be directly paralleled by film technology's quick succession of shots approximating "the simultaneism of the perfect circle."[87] Epstein believed that cinema provided poets with the aesthetic tools that could consciously express the subconscious experience of modernity.[88]

For Mário, film also provided poetry an operational mode for externalizing the internalization of modern stimuli. In "The Slave Who Is Not Isaura" he praised the medium's relationship to the external world: "Representing the immediate features of life and nature with more precision than art and the written word (and bear in mind that the cinema is still a young art, we do not know how it will develop), representing life as no art form has managed to, she has been the Eureka! for the pure arts."[89] The writer here seems to point to film's mimetic capacity, its ability to record real life. In a letter to poet Manuel Bandeira, however, he noted that cinema documented not an external reality but something deeper: "I did not lose the photographic machine, or rather the cinematographic of my subconscious. Here I am in everyday life. Only yesterday photographs and more photographs began to be revealed within me! It is on the screen of blank pages that the very modern film of a poem began to develop!"[90] Born from the profound I, the unconscious takes cinematic images of everyday life, which reveal themselves in the critical mind of the poet, who then transcribes them onto paper in an altered but recognizable form. All of this is reminiscent of João do Rio's redefinition of writing. In 1909 the *cronista* described the man of letters as having "a huge cinematograph in his skull operated by imagination: one need only close one's eyes to see the movie unraveling in one's cortex at an unbelievable speed."[91] For Mário, however, the aim was not simply to reproduce the poet's emotional experience but to "recreate in the spectator the analogous commotion of what [the poet] first felt."[92] The modernist aesthetic was to explode cinematographically from the world into the poem and from the poem into the reader/viewer.

Hallucinated City adheres to this, presenting a highly subjective map of the city from the viewpoint of "a wandering artist."[93] Since the artist is obeying a subconscious order, the map does not follow a rational or logical route through São Paulo. Like a movie, the collection splices together different scenes, conflating the coherent logic of time and space. Buildings, transportation sites, shops, parks, and movie theaters occupy the rambling mind of the poet. Numerous neighborhoods (Brás, Mooca, Bom Retiro) come into play with each other. Urban locations clash with an abandoned countryside. Different social classes are brought together in a kaleidoscopic whole: aristocrats, the bourgeoisie, workers, and poor people come into contact. The collection thus portrays the city as a simultaneous multitude of different times, people, and places. For Charles Perrone, the result is a hermetically confusing cartography that "effectively configures the multiplicity of the city."[94] In doing so it creates an urban space that is at odds with the Republican ideal of progress. *Hallucinated City*'s spontaneous and surprising collision of different sights and sounds, people, and places subverts the ordered ideology that underpinned Republican modernity. The collection's mapping of São Paulo, in this sense, "errs" (to quote Gabara) from the official route of modernity and produces *um desvairismo*—an errant and erroneous urban cartography. Film and its simultaneity thus provided Mário with a mechanistic process for expressing the subjective experience of the modern metropolis and for altering its official geography.

FILM, AURA, AND AUTHENTICITY IN OSWALD DE ANDRADE'S WORKS

Oswald de Andrade also recreated the geography of modernity in his novels by using the cinema's lexicon. In his review of Oswald's *The Condemned* published in *Klaxon,* A. de Couto Barros writes that the 1922 novel "inaugurates an unknown cinematographic technique."[95] Critics have subsequently reiterated Barros's cinematic appraisal of the work. Mário da Silva Brito writes that Oswald's novel brought "a new film method to Brazilian fiction."[96] Campos also foregrounds the text's innovative cinematic form, and Antonio Candido states that *The Condemned* "initiated (in Brazil at least) a cinematographic technique."[97] Candido adds that the novel's filmic form reveals "less a process of counterpoint than of discontinuity, an attempt to use the simultaneity that obsessed modernism and had as its major theorist Mário de Andrade."[98]

The Condemned thus transfers to fiction the poetic theory of simultaneism developed by Mário. The novel depicts the lives of three São Paulo residents: Alma, who lives with her grandmother; João do Carmo, who works at the Estação da Luz train station; and Jorge, who owns an atelier in the city center. Through these protagonists' stories, *The Condemned* depicts the changing city of São Paulo, documenting its modernization in a cinematic style. Juxtaposing different fragments in a technique reminiscent of film montage, the novel's syncopated style systematically ruptures the novelistic discourse, reconceptualizing realism for the twentieth century.[99] Oswald took this cinematic experimentation further in his novels *Sentimental Memoirs of João Miramar* (1924) and *Seraphim Grosse Pointe* (1928). Indeed, for Campos the innovative style of these works reveals "the presence of montage in their narrative discontinuity, the simultaneous superimposition of different features . . . sliced up into disparate pieces, which confront and puncture, interpenetrate, and fold into each other, not in a linear sequence, but as moving parts. . . . The prose participates intimately in the analogical syntax of film."[100] Like *The Condemned,* these novels are indebted to cinematic montage for their use of simultaneity, evidenced in their fragmented style. Yet if *João Miramar* and *Seraphim* demonstrate the filmic style of Oswald's earlier film-novel, they also bring a new element to their cinematic focus. Far from appropriating the objective gaze of *The Condemned,* Oswald's later novels express a personal reflection. In *João Miramar* and *Seraphim,* movie montage is brought into dialogue with autobiography and the construction of a literary self, which is the real subject of these novels. In them, the filmic is brought to bear on the very question of the self, especially the authorial self, as the works cinematically project a form of self-exposure.

Because of the connections between them, critics like Candido and Campos have regarded *João Miramar* and *Seraphim* as a pair. Radically experimental in structure and style, the works display modernist strategies to reformulate Brazilian realism. But as tales of two men with literary pretensions they also expose the state of the country's artistic landscape and in doing so explore new creative personas. Both novels are structured through an autodiegetic narration, revealing a form of self-observation. *João Miramar* portrays in a fictionalized editor's preface and 163 brief segments the unfinished life of its bourgeois protagonist-author, João Miramar. The segments sequentially encompass episodes from João Miramar's life as he pens his memoirs: early schooling, adolescence, sexual initiations; wanderings and get-togethers in São Paulo with friends; European journeys and contact with the Parisian avant-garde; mother's death; courtship, marriage, and the birth of a child; the search for a vocation and work as a journalist; marriage problems and infidelities, divorce and the death of his wife; the decision to abandon writing his memoirs. The fragments are populated by the author and his family, friends, and acquaintances, as well as by important Brazilian cultural and historical figures. They also include letters, speeches, obituaries, public announcements, and an interview. This interplay of different linguistic registers reveals a cinematic structure, with distinct fragments edited together to create the whole.

Seraphim shares *João Miramar*'s thematic structures and features. The novel recounts the story of Seraphim through a collage of fragments that deal with his childhood, education, and marriage; his social life, marriage problems, and divorce; his European travels; and his death and commemoration by friends. It too engages in a linguistic polyphony: the fragments appropriate various literary traditions, including nineteenth-century realism, romance, travel literature, and the picaresque. The novel also incorporates nonliterary forms: letters, recipes, dictionary entries, and epigraphs, along with newsreels and film scripts. *Seraphim*'s interplay of distinct linguistic idioms constitutes parodic appropriations of different literary modes and reveals what Campos terms a "permanent and vivifying nonconformism" to any one tradition.[101]

In both *João Miramar* and *Seraphim* cinematic montage is utilized to project a repertoire of youthful education and friendship, sentimental and erotic initiations, and relations between the self and society. The novels build up a portrait of their heroes' lives, using markers of the Bildungsroman and shaping readers' expectations of accounts of individual formation.[102] Beyond these markers, the works identify their key protagonists as writers. In *João Miramar,* editor Machado Penumbra's preface introduces the writer to the reader, portraying him as an innovator and evoking the modernist movement's project of invention. João reinforces this portrait of the man as artist through his own elicitation of different writing styles. *Seraphim* likewise identifies its hero with the world of letters, building up his characterization through literary allusions, references to artistic friends, and vanguardist travel. Both men thus present their lives through literary constructions, consciously reproducing their experiences through fiction. The fictional quality of their life stories is reinforced by the texts' montage of the diverse literary styles and genres that constitute their autobiographies. Further, the protagonists, constituted from an accumulation of textual conventions, acquire the disjointed quality of the works themselves, and their subjectivities are continually displaced. Consequently, the heroes' identities prove empty and vacuous; as Unruh notes, Oswald's characters possess "no interiority at all."[103] This is particularly noticeable in *João Miramar.* The title "Sentimental Memoirs" promises intimate revelations, but the narrator rarely turns inwards. Instead, he records characters and situations around him. This absence of interior reflection undermines the formative Bildrungsroman that *João Miramar* and *Seraphim* draw on. Indeed, the events that constitute the protagonists' lives are "cumulative, not causal," and both heroes fail to explain the core of their existence.[104]

The novels therefore feature heroes that are ultimately "without any character," to quote Mário's novel *Macunaíma.* In *João Miramar* and *Seraphim* the cinematic interplay of different texts defers any secure characterization among the endless citations that produce no concrete identity for their narrator-protagonists. Subjectivity is instead exposed as an endless filmic replay of texts, and the protagonists' innermost identities become fictions to display. Two passages from *João Miramar* are particularly illustrative of this. The first is a scene in which Miramar speaks of his passion for Gisella Doni. "Musicians walked in, and the first idle faces installed themselves in the back seats of the audience. I secretly desired Gisella. Steps filled confused scales of flutes and affirmative violins. The audience was witness to my love."[105] The prose projects montage-like shots of the event, which are exhibited in nonhierarchical succession. The revelation of love, the tuning of the orchestra, and the arrival of the audience all take place simultaneously. Here love is simply an object of display, just like a scene at the movies. The second scene is Miramar's marriage to Célia. Inspired by a drawing by a Parisian architect, their wedding is patterned on furniture, interior decoration, clothes, and travels, forging a perfect life for a couple.[106] Married life is thus a reproduced image to be shown off. This sense of "lives on show" is suggested in the opening of *Seraphim*: "I appear to the reader. A ball player. Character in a display window."[107] Rather than representational, the style is presentational and reveals the work's divestiture of any personal characterization or depth.

While the protagonists of *João Miramar* and *Seraphim* both create their own stories, their identities prove strikingly superficial; replicated fragments with no roots, they are like stars in a movie of their own making. This emptiness extends to their status as writers. Being or becoming an author amounts to little more than a projection of citations each man accumulates throughout his lifetime. This lack of an authorial identity is underscored by João's fragmented, unfinished memoirs, which show no intention of vindicating the narrator and echo Machado de Assis's perverse use of the genre in *Memórias póstumas de Brás Cubas* (The posthumous memoirs of Brás Cubas, 1881). What is revealed here is the death of the classical narrator or writer and the demise of the auratic status of traditional letters.

Flora Süssekind links this demise to modernization and the emergence of a new technological context in Brazil, which included film.[108] With the start of the Republic, the appearance of new technologies like cinema "transformed the behaviours and perceptions of people."[109] They also had an impact on literary life, helping to reconceptualize the value of the work of art. In an age of mechanical reproduction, what Benjamin called art's cult value, a measure of authenticity, decreased, just as the aura of the artwork died. As Süssekind demonstrates, many Brazilian writers confronted this demise with a move in the opposite direction, attempting to affirm authorial subjectivity. The turn of the century onwards saw a proliferation of memoirs and autobiographies.[110] Examples include nostalgic novels like Raul Pompéia's *O Ateneu* (The Atheneum, 1888), Joaquim Nabuco's *Minha formação* (My formation, 1900) and Léo Vaz's *O professor Jeremias* (The professor Jeremias, 1919), which attempted to reconstruct the figure of the narrator. The use of memory in these works is an attempt to avoid the "death of the author" by nostalgically reconstructing an authorial self and to strive for singularization, just at a time when writing was being reduced to a reproduced image. Using cinematic techniques, Oswald parodies this literary use of reminiscences in *João Miramar* and *Seraphim.* Refusing to allow personal memories any sort of aura, in these novels he takes on the mechanically reproduced language of film and reveals authorial memoirs as a game of surfaces, with the identity of the writer displaced in the endless montage of fragmented texts. Oswald's use of the cinematic language in these novels corrodes memory and the idea of literature as pure subjectivity.

Oswald's autobiographies thus reveal the writer to be what Süssekind calls "surface only" characters.[111] All of this is part of the novels' sharp critique of Brazilian society and literature. The protagonists in both works live out a vacuous social existence. João Miramar himself admits to this: "Célia thought I should have an ennobling vocation. I had none at all."[112] This emptiness is evidenced in Seraphim's life, which includes gossip and social gatherings. For Candido, the novels satirize elite society, specifically "the rich bourgeoisie, whose emptiness, conventions, and shocking sterility travel round the world."[113]

Literature is enmeshed in this satirical attack. Both novels lampoon men of letters by revealing their vocation to be a shallow film-like reproduction of genres and styles. The narrators themselves refer to their literary careers as vacuous. João Miramar informs us that as an aspiring artist he has nothing important to do. This trivial literary existence is present too in *Seraphim.* The self-involved protagonist spends his days meeting friends, undertaking extramarital exploits, and thinking about what book he would like to write. If these are novels without any characters, they are also books without real authors. The protagonist-narrators spend their existence reproducing social conventions and literary styles, and they ultimately produce nothing, socially or artistically. Their impotence is a damning critique of modernity and its narrative of progress, which, led by the country's bourgeois elite, is shown to be unproductive.

Criticism of the superficial reproduction of literature was of course central to Oswald's manifestos, which attacked traditional Brazilian letters, especially Parnassianism, as mere mechanical imitation. As he noted in his "Brazilwood Manifesto," "There was no need to invent a machine for making poetry—we already had the poet."[114] For Oswald, Brazil lacked its own literary identity. It was characterless because it had "neither its own civilization nor an awareness of cultural tradition."[115] This lack articulated the country itself, which, while emphasizing a desire for autonomy, still remained subservient to foreign influences. Thus Oswald's literary criticism also constitutes a critique of the country's elite who, importing a foreign model of modernity, superficially reproduced a universal narrative that maintained the country in a perennial stance of attempting to catch up with a superior blueprint.

For Oswald, the answer is not to reclaim an auratic authenticity in writing. The writer is aware that mimetic production of reality is not possible in a modern technological age and that the continuity between reality and writing has been disrupted. Instead he seems to suggest using new technologies, like cinema, to remove the cloak of superficiality and register the contradictions and heterogeneity of Brazilian modernity. As he writes in the "Cannibalist Manifesto," "What impeded the truth were clothes, the raincoat between the interior and the world. A reaction against the clothed man. American cinema will inform us."[116] The adoption of film as technique, then, is a means of giving up timeworn methods that have become shallow, and the attack on past literary styles, on subjectivity, and on a writing that sacralizes its own place has a key accomplice in the cinema. Rather than attempting to cover up literature's self-displacement, its loss of aura, Oswald revels in it, incorporating mechanical forms of reproduction, like film, to produce a new Brazilian literature.

PATHÉ-BABY'S KINO-EYE

Antônio de Alcântara Machado considered film to be key in creating a new Brazilian literature. On March 24, 1925, he embarked on an eight-month trip to Europe and visited a number of cities, including Lisbon, Madrid, Paris, London, Milan, and Barcelona. While abroad the writer documented his metropolitan experiences in a series of journalistic essays, or *crônicas* (chronicles) published in the *Jornal do Commércio* that year. The essays provided Brazilian readers with accounts of Machado's impressions of the European capitals he traveled to, constituting a literary travelogue of his foreign expedition. They were collectively published in a book in 1926 under the title *Pathé-Baby.*

Machado's journey rehearses *modernismo's* touristic ties to Europe. Sérgio Luiz Prado Bellei and Canclini name travel to Europe as the formative experience of the movement's writers and artists.[117] Unruh too notes that "the European sojourn, actual or literary, had become a standard step in a would-be artist's formation and for many writers . . . the transatlantic experience provoked a discovery and reengagement with [Brazilian] culture."[118] Journeys to Europe were very much part of *modernismo's* search for new Brazilian artistic aesthetics. Not surprisingly the transatlantic journey is a frequent motif in modernist writing. In *João Miramar* and *Seraphim,* for instance, Oswald's pseudoauthors both undertake pilgrimages to Europe as a form of artistic apprenticeship.

Machado's travelogue replays the literary value of European travel for Brazilian modernism. In doing so it stages the journey to cosmopolitan cities through what John Ruskin terms "a contemplative abstraction from the world," that is, the formalization of the sensation of traveling through a land one does not understand.[119] The opticality of the *crônicas'* detached observation is evoked by the book's title: *Pathé-Baby,* the name of a movie camera. The collection's title foregrounds the

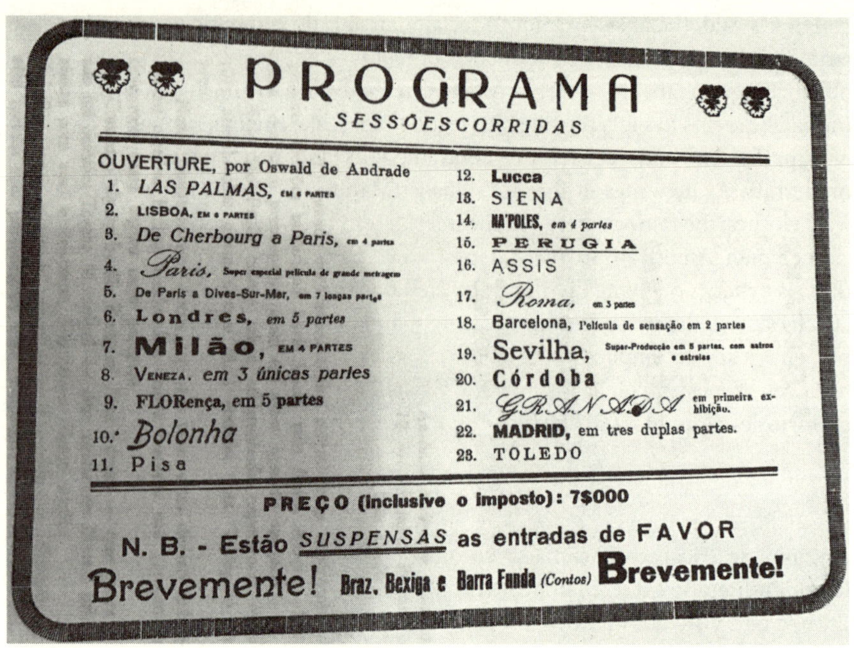

FIGURE 23. Contents page for *Pathé-Baby*, 1929. Author's personal collection.

omnipotence of a cinematic gaze in Machado's documentation of foreign capitals. London, Paris, Madrid, and other European cities are viewed through the eye of a movie camera—their streets, parks, and people projected onto the page in short cinematic shots. The book's graphic design reinforces this filmic focus. The cover depicts the interior of a movie theater whose screen displays the title of the book and the name of its author. Readers are consequently conceived of as spectators of *Pathé-Baby*'s urban movies, a role that is reinforced by the table of contents, which is laid out as a film program. In it each literary *crônica* is cast as a movie to be screened for the reader-viewer, following an overture by Oswald de Andrade (figure 23). The program perfectly illustrates what Unruh refers to as the performative stance of the Latin American vanguard, whose texts were perceived as activities to be played out for audiences.[120] *Pathé-Baby*'s mediated essays virtually perform cinematic cities, revealing an analogous relationship between the *crônica* and film, and also between the city and film. The *crônica,* cinema, and urban space—their imbrication is central to *Pathé-Baby*'s European travelogue.

The Brazilian *cronica* had established a link with the city and film well before Machado embarked for Europe. Beatriz Resende foregrounds a special relationship between the literary genre and urban space.[121] She notes that this relationship took on particular relevance in response to the processes of urbanization at the start of the twentieth century. The expansion of population in cities like Rio and São Paulo made them unfamiliar places for many inhabitants and were made even stranger by the influx of new technologies, like trams, that altered ways in which the urban was perceived and experienced. For Resende the *crônica* developed as a historical genre to register the "new life" of Brazil's cities.[122] Here, their writers, or *cronistas,* took on the role of tour guides. Charting different aspects of the changing cities, they helped readers make sense of urban spaces and made their unknown qualities less threatening. In this guise, the *cronistas* were Brazil's counterpart to the Parisian *flaneurs,* pivotal for Benjamin. Strolling through unknown streets, much like tourists, the *cronistas,* like the *flaneurs,* collected images of changing public spaces. They watched and interpreted the city: its crowds, architectural and human configurations, signs and images, sounds and tempo.

Highlighting and praising spaces of and practices in the city, the *cronistas* justified and articulated a new urban identity for Republican Brazil, helping to concretize the country's symbolic shift from tradition to modernity. The *cronista's* art form in this sense emerged as what Michel de Certeau calls "a spatial practice," as it contributed to the construction of an urban ideal. Renato Cordeiro Gomes describes this practice as highly subjective.[123] In documenting life in the city, the *cronistas* did not stand back and apart from real spaces, they came into contact with material reality and provided readers with personal accounts of it. It is this highly personal aspect of the *crônica* that Antonio Candido emphasizes, describing it as an intimate literary form that partakes of the context it simultaneously registers.[124] The Brazilian *cronistas* thus gave shape to *and* were part of the transformations of the country's urban landscape.

By the start of the twentieth century, film was part of Brazil's new urban landscape. It is hardly surprising, therefore, that *cronistas* increasingly began to discuss the new medium in their journalistic essays, commenting on its novelty and popularity. In a *crônica* written in 1906, for instance, Olavo Bilac commented on the cinema's newness, and João do Rio too stressed the movies' modernity. For him, however, film was not only a contemporary medium but also analogous to the activity of the *cronista.* So it was that he titled his 1909 collection of *crônicas Cinematógrapho de letras* (Cinematograph of letters). The *crônica,* he wrote, "has evolved toward the cinematograph. It was once reflection and commentary, the reverse of the sinister, unclassifiable animal known as the editorial. It turned into illustration and caricature. Later it was a retouched photograph, albeit a living one. With the frenetic hurry of us all, it is now cinematographic—the cinematograph of letters, the novel of the projectionist who is a secondary character dragged along by events."[125] The writer of *crônicas* as a projectionist, and *crônicas* as movies: these are the analogies of João do Rio's book, and this is how the author conceived of the activity of the *cronista.* Walking through different urban sites, the writer offered readers vistas of the city, projecting what were tantamount to sightseeing tours of urban spaces. Characterized by the author's roving eye, the *crônica* merged visuality with a sense of travel in its projections of modern landscapes. The *cronista* thus embodied the cinematic eye of the camera and its ability to present audiences with moving pictures.

Machado too regarded his work as a *cronista* as homologous to a filmmaker's, as the title of his collection suggests. *Pathé-Baby*'s ambulatory texts present readers with filmic snapshots of distant metropoles, allowing them to read, or see, their foreign topographies. In *Pathé-Baby*, however, the *crônicas*' cinematic projections are far from subjective. In contrast to João do Rio's anecdotal prose, which delights in an intimate language, Machado's language is sparse in its urban documentation:

> Noise. Dust. Lost of people. The policeman blows his whistle, raises his baton, the traffic stops so that the woman and the pram can cross, calmly. Two seamstresses chatter. A family on its way to the sleepy benches in the Bois. A one-armed man selling pins. The laughter of a blonde with green circles under her eyes. An English man's Kodak. Two lovers. Israelites showing off their Legion of Honor rosette. Monocles. Paris passes.[126]

Here Paris is described through simple flashes; it appears in an amalgamated montage of urban views. Machado clearly converses with the cinema and adopts the language of film in his narrative technique. In doing so, he transforms the literary genre of the *crônica*. Abandoning personal impressions, the author opts for a concise and economical language that systematically clears the texts of all emotion. The distinct urban scenes are disembodied of all individual perception as subjective expression is replaced by an automatized gaze. Indeed, in Machado's *crônicas* there is no sign of the projectionist-writer, not even "as a secondary character dragged along by the events." It is the camera that takes over the prose, and the collection presents us with different cityscapes from the point of view of what Soviet filmmaker and theorist Dziga Vertov called a "kino-eye," the "mechanical eye" of film.[127] For Vertov the film camera has the power of sight and the capacity to reveal things to the spectator. In *Pathé-Baby* Machado too bestows the movies, not the writer, with the ability to display and expose things to the reader/spectator.

The "poetics of impersonality" evident in Machado's collection was practiced by other modernist writers.[128] Beginning with a letter written by "Mário de Andrade" to "Mário de Andrade," *Hallucinated City*, for instance, effaces the author through a form of polylogue. As noted, Oswald does this as well by adopting autobiographical personae in *João Miramar* and *Seraphim*. In *Pathé-Baby* the author is subjected to assassination by the mechanics of film. The assassination underscores a challenge to the hegemony of Brazil's lettered city and writers' exceptional agency with the appearance of a new technological landscape. The death of the author is foregrounded by the relationship between the written word and the illustrations that adorn the collection's pages. Each of *Pathé-Baby*'s chapters (corresponding to cities

2. LISBOA

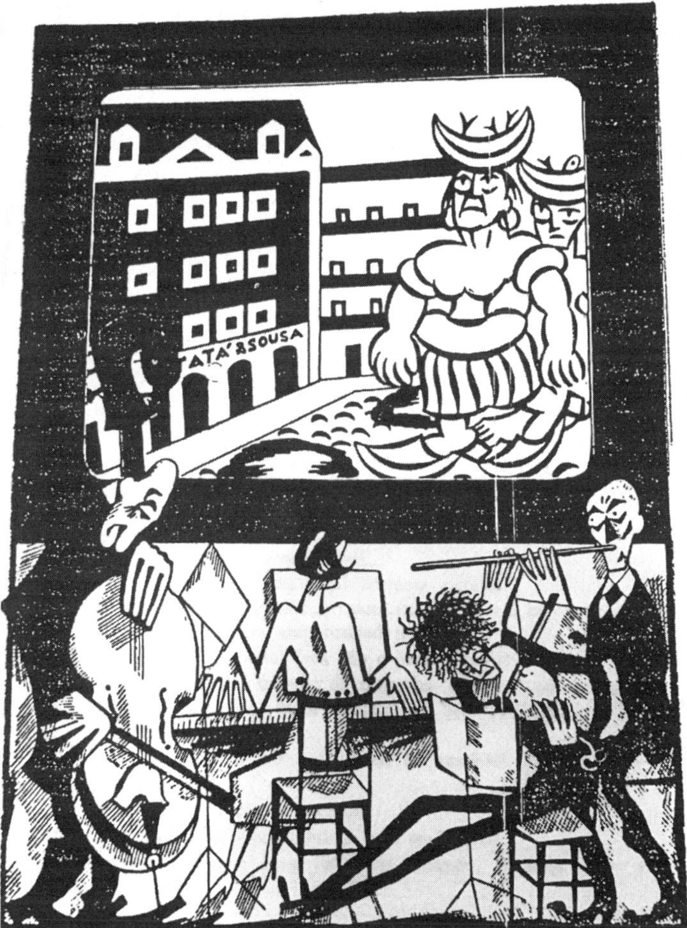

FIGURE 24. Illustrations in *Pathé-Baby* by Paim. Author's personal collection.

visited) has its own illustrated title page, created by graphic artist Antônio Paim Vieira. Reproducing the book's cover, the images depict the inside of a movie theater featuring a screen showing scenes of the city that is chronicled. Beneath the screen is an orchestra (figure 24). The chapters all reproduce this graphic, yet with slight variations. In the first six chapters, the orchestra is composed of four musicians: a pianist, a bass player, a violinist, and a flutist. From chapter 7 (Milan) onwards, the violinist has disappeared and the pianist has abandoned his instrument. After chapter 18, only the bass player remains. The repetition and alteration of the illustration suggest the passing of time: "It is as though the musicians stop playing their instruments as the screenings progress, suggesting a possible change in music."[129] This provides the illustrations collectively with their own narrative, which distracts the reader's attention from the written texts.

Distraction from the written word by images was characteristic of Brazil's illustrated magazines at the time. Antônio Dimas observes that by the start of the twentieth century editors were so fascinated by the expressive possibilities of graphic design and photography that they "attempted to illustrate everything, so that the written text was often relegated to a quite secondary plane." This left a mark on *crônicas* published in magazines, which began to use rich vocabulary, emphatic wording, and ornamental rhetoric. "It is as though language, facing the increasing eminence of images, resorted to hyperbole, excessive ornamentation, and preciosity."[130] Machado does not succumb to this taste for ornamentation. He embraces the analogy of the *crônica* as a cinematograph, and his collection's mechanical eye provides its own images of the city.

Readers of *Pathé-Baby* are thus invited to visually consume the collection of *crônicas,* much as they would a movie. Indeed, the film program that opens the book purports to allow the reader to enter a theater to see *Pathé-Baby,* after having paid an entrance fee of "7$000 (inclusive of tax)" (figure 23). Like a trip to the movies, Machado's collection is assigned a price, and access to it depends on the consumer having paid the amount allotted. The book is thus conceived of and promoted as a commercial product and a form of entertainment that is sold to the public. The analogy here highlights the reconceptualization of writing and reveals a new brand of intellectual: the professional writer who sells his or her literary merchandise. This suggests a new view of literature, which is now a source of income. Writing has escaped the ivory tower and is thrust into the street and the mass market, becoming another reproduced product in a landscape of cultural leisure, which includes film. This redefinition of writing relied on the recognition of the masses, something that was key to Machado's writing. Many of his texts incorporate the people, especially the urban working class. The collection of short stories *Brás, Bexiga e Barra Funda,* for instance, focuses on São Paulo's Italian immigrants who inhabit the working class neighborhoods of the book's title. In *Pathé-Baby* it is the book's visual literacy, forged through the medium of film, that composes its popular ethos.

In its cinematic guise, *Pathé-Baby* does not induce only vision; as Ana Paula Rodrigues Dias points out, the collection also evokes sound.[131] Depicting a group of musicians, the book's cover and inside illustrations underscore an element of the aural in the cinematic presentation of the European cities. In this capacity, the collection of *crônicas* is suggestive of the city-symphony films, like *Man with the Movie Camera* (Dziga Vertov, 1929), that constituted a key part of cinematic production for the vanguard of the interwar period. Mobilized by the dynamism of modern metropoles and constructed along the basis of musical theory, these films reproduced the urban experience without an advancing narrative. Disconnected fragments, musical compositions, and disassociative montage expressed urban sensibilities and subjectivities and registered what Georg Simmel termed "the mental life of the metropolis."[132]

This sort of visual and aural depiction of the city is evident in Mário's *Hallucinated City.* Indeed, Perrone notes that the poems express the diversity of São Paulo through sight and sound.[133] The culmination of this organizational rationale of accumulating the visual and the auditory is the final oratorio, "The Moral Fibrature of Ipiranga." The musical number is characterized aesthetically and socially. It includes the "Orientalismos convencionais" (Conventional Orientalisms), in which writers and artists are played by a chorus of sopranos, contraltos, baritones, and basses; the "Senectudes tremulinas" (Palsied decrepitudes), in which millionaires and the bourgeoisie are represented by a chorus of castrati; "Sandapilários indiferentes" (Indifferent pallbearers), in which workmen and poor people are performed by basses and baritones; "Juvelididades auriverdes" (Green-gilded youths), also identified as "we" and sung by tenors; and a soprano soloist, "Minha Loucura" (my madness). The piece is organized by an escalating chain of confrontations between the different social groups in the city, their divergent voices and their concomitant aesthetic stances played out in the diverse musical styles. The juxtaposition of different music and sights expresses the social and aesthetic heterogeneity of the metropolis, which is performed for the reader as a grand urban symphony.

Pathé-Baby too educes city-symphony movies in its formal construction of European urban panoramas. As in the film genre, images of cities are taken from different angles in an effort to express through the rhythm of the cinematic sequences the accelerated movement of the different human and mechanical activities. The cinematic prose is consequently hybrid, as the following portrait of Sienna illustrates:

> ALBERGO E RISTORANTE LE TRE DONZELLE *(di sopra) del nuovo proprietario signor Teri Gino.* A squinting blond family. PREMIATA FABBRICA DI PARAFULMINI. It has not rained for six months. A dogfight. The sun slides perpendicularly. PURGANTOLO *É l'ideale dei purganti (non disturba affato).* Flies. Flies.[134]

The impersonal and objective camera zooms in on ordinary everyday details: the sun, flies, two dogs fighting. It also focuses on posters and billboards, which are marked out in capital letters, and captures music, registered in italics. The fragmented style expresses the dynamic pace and intensity of the Italian metropolis.

The dynamism and speed of modern life are often conveyed in sequences where the city is viewed from aboard public transportation, such as trains:

> A Whistle. No: two whistles. Red signal lights.

> Quick, the train runs, it rolls with noises, screeching. Without nostalgia.

> Cherbourg disappears.[135]

With places rapidly disappearing from sight, such sequences capture the diso-rienting ephemerality of modern urban life. As Leo Charney discusses, cinema encapsulates the ephemeral, as scenes that flash up on the screen rapidly disappear from sight.[136] *Cronista* João do Rio noted and praised film's transient nature: "That was an interesting movie, you say. And two minutes later you have forgotten it."[137] Carrying no recollection or memory of the past, the cinema elicits a sort of dis-tracted attention that exists only in the moment. *Pathé-Baby* simulates a form of distraction for its readers. The short vignettes and their multitude of images and sounds take the spectator on rapid tours around each city and then quickly move on to the next place. The collection thus embodies the rapid scene changes of film as different images flit by on the pages.

The collection's montage of different views and sounds, then, conveys the vitality of the European cities visited, in a manner similar to cinematic symphonies like *Man with a Movie Camera*. In Vertov's film, however, the camera projectionist, Boris Kauffman (Vertov's brother), is often shown operating the camera, and the film title itself indicates human agency behind the cinematic lens. As noted earlier, human agency is absent in *Pathé-Baby*, which adopts a mechanized gaze in its focus on Europe. This objective focus on different cities is reminiscent of the ethnographic stance of travelogue films. From cinema's beginnings, European companies like Lumière and Pathé sent filmmakers to far-flung places around the world accumulat-ing images of distinct places and peoples. Movies of India, Africa, and Latin America were projected to audiences in Europe, offering them glimpses of the margins and letting them see "strange" civilizations. The camera thus explored different geograph-ical territories in ways that drew clear boundaries between the subject looking and the object being looked at. In touring different landscapes these films discovered Otherness, made it exotic and often acted as agents of an imperialist obsession. The touristic drive—the gaze of exploration—was not always a mere expression of curios-ity in cinematic travelogues. As Ella Shohat and Robert Stam have shown, this mode of discovery was also directed toward taking possession, conquering sites and their inhabitants, with the travelogue exhibiting a historical bond with colonialism.[138]

Pathé-Baby very much embodies the touristic gaze of the travelogue. The *crôni-cas* enable readers to become vicarious travelers throughout Europe and discover its varied cityscapes. They provide readers with cinematic panoramas of faraway European places, bridging the distance between here and there, the margins and the center. In doing so they reconfigure the spatial relations between Brazil and Europe and also challenge the viewing positions implicit in the ethnographic gaze of the travel film. European people and places emerge as objects of Machado's abstracted contemplation and are framed as trifles of curiosity.

Brought closer by the camera eye, the European "object" loses its aura and authority. Indeed, in many instances the cities and the people are depicted as unpleasant and inferior.

Mud in the Tejo. Horrible morning with a gray sky. A thick drizzle falls. Cold. Wind. The boat skips along the waves; it descends, ascends, descends, ascends. A jumping ball of rubber.

– How much longer until we reach land?
– God knows!

A spit completes the polite reply.

Finally. Disinfection Port. It needs its own disinfection. Filthy. Covered in mud. Fishing boats and sailboats tied up. Fishermen wearing red caps, red caps. Bad smell.[139]

In this synthesis of phrases, Lisbon is portrayed as unclean and putrid, and Lisbonites are presented as rude. Brazil's former colonial capital is clearly shown to be wanting. It is uncivilized. Maintaining an ethnographic distance from the Portuguese metropole, *Pathé-Baby* recasts the city and its inhabitants as primitives discovered by the camera. It thus reverses the colonizing gaze of the travelogue and undermines colonial discourse by overturning the supposed superiority of European civilization. A number of European capitals receive similarly unpleasant portrayals. In Barcelona "the air is putrefied," Cherbourg is "boring," and London is described as chaotic.[140] The collection's cinematic focus in this way defamiliarizes Europe, which is not displayed as a civilization that Brazil should emulate.

Pathé-Baby thus constructs a new way of looking at Europe, introducing what Oswald referred to as the "new perspective" that radically altered cultural relations between Brazil and European countries. Brito Broca notes that "after 1922 there was a veritable exodus of modernists for Paris. They all sought to use their experiences in Europe in the research they were undertaking. No one, however, thought it necessary to dismiss Europe in order to be modernist. Hence the revolutionary spirit of Machado's 'films.' Going to Europe in order to see its deficiencies was original."[141] By breaking away from the previous stance of emulating Europe, Machado's book produces a new national consciousness. Indeed, citing lines from Antônio Gonçalves Dias's patriotic *Canção do exílio* (Song of exile), the collection ends with a moral:

> Our skies have more stars
> Our valleys have more flowers
> Our forests have more life
> Our lives have more love.[142]

Provoking a discovery and reengagement with Brazil and Brazilian culture, the cinematic journey around Europe seeks to end the country's self-exile and alienation. Machado thus asserts a new subjectivity and a new identity for modern Brazilian history and for the modern Brazilian writer—all through the gaze of the *Pathé-Baby* camera.

9

The Cine-Poetry of Mário Peixoto's *Limite*

Ismail Xavier's assertion that Brazil lacked a modernist cinema displaying avant-garde tendencies is disproved by Mário Peixoto's *Limite*, which was filmed in 1929.[1] Robert Stam includes the film in his overview of Brazil's marginal cinema and hails it as "a landmark within the history of the country's cinematic avant-garde."[2] That Xavier overlooks Peixoto's film is not surprising. *Limite* first publicly screened in Rio's Capitólio theater on May 17, 1931. Disappointed by negative reviews, Peixoto withdrew his film from circulation, and for the next forty-six years *Limite* was virtually inaccessible, "viewed only by a small inner circle of critics, artists, and students."[3] It was not until 1978, after Plínio Süssekind and Saulo Pereira de Mello rescued the film from physical deterioration, that *Limite* was finally released. For decades, Süssekind and Mello undertook painstaking work to preserve and restore Peixoto's vanguard film, along with written and archival materials associated with it. Their endeavors were enhanced by Walter Salles, who founded the Mário Peixoto Archive in 1996, located within his production company Videofilmes in Rio. Curated by Mello and his wife Ayla, the archive led to a new interest in *Limite*, evidenced in a series of publications about Peixoto's avant-garde film.

This new appreciation of *Limite*, however, involves more than seeing it simply as an experimental film. Newspaper critics, scholars, and aficionados have repeatedly voted it the best Brazilian film of all time. In 1988, for instance, *Limite* was deemed the Best National Film by a jury of Brazilian critics selected by the Cinemateca Brasileira; and in 2015 the Association of Brazilian Film Critics declared it the greatest Brazilian film ever made. *Limite*'s coveted national status may seem anomalous given dominant assessments of Peixoto's movie, which have tended to stress its transcendence of national themes and styles. Mello, for one, writes that it is more related to world cinema than Brazilian culture, affirming that *Limite* "has no homeland."[4]

Such assessments refer to *Limite*'s hermetic remove from the national. The film has been foregrounded, not as delving into the country's reality and exploring Brazil's sociopolitical conditions, but as presenting what Carlos Calil calls an intimate or intimist portrait of the "human drama of the universal condition."[5] This universality may explain *Limite*'s restricted impact, which contrasts greatly to Brazilian literary experiments of the 1920s and '30s. As Walter Salles notes, "*Limite*, the film that heralded modernity in Brazilian cinema, left no successors—only confused admirers—unlike the 1922 Week of Modern Art, which profoundly modified art, poetry and literature. Both the three days of the Week of Modern Art and the first showing of *Limite* were snubbed by critics at the time. Yet, the movement led by Mário and Oswald de Andrade had such a momentum that, after the week, nothing would ever be the same. This would not be the lot of Peixoto, the solitary creator."[6] Not viewed as part of the broader movement that was revolutionizing the arts, *Limite* went unnoticed in São Paulo and had no influence on contemporary filmmaking taking place there or elsewhere in Brazil.

Limite's intimist mode contrasts to the regionalist focus that marked late 1920s and '30s Brazilian cinema. Movies produced outside the Rio–São Paulo axis in Minas Gerais, Campinas, Recife, and Cataguases, like *Aitaré na praia* (Aitaré on the beach; dir. Gentil Roiz, 1925), *O vale dos martirios* (Valley of martyrs; dir. Almeida Fleming, 1927), *Entre as montanhas de Minas* (Among the mountains of Minas; dir. Igino Bonfioli and Manoel Talon, 1928), *Tesouro perdido* (Lost treasure; dir. Humberto Mauro, 1927), *Sangue Mineiro* (Blood of Minas Gerais; dir. Humberto Mauro, 1929), and *Braza dormida* (Dormant embers; dir. Humberto Mauro, 1928), depicted the regional settings of their production while adopting the narrative conventions of Hollywood's classical cinema. Journalists praised the films' localism, with one writer for the *Correio da Manhã* noting that *Valley of Martyrs*, filmed in the small town of Ouro Fino, allowed viewers to "appreciate beautiful landscapes, the life of the interior, so characteristically ours, which speaks to the Brazilian soil."[7] Promotional material for the film emphasized its national content, declaring that its regionalism was "the true consecration of the Brazilian film industry and a legitimate source of pride for every Brazilian whose heart thrills for the fatherland."[8] The regional focus of such Hollywood-inflected dramas was clearly received and promoted as a source of pride and was seen as the basis of what a Brazilian cinema should be.

This pride in seeing Brazil projected on the screen was underwritten by a spirit of confidence following the introduction of sound in 1928. Foreign movies, no longer understood by Brazilian audiences, would, it was believed, simply self-destruct and end foreign companies' monopoly of the domestic market.[9] This belief was shared by anxious Hollywood studios, which began to fear the loss of world markets, since language barriers could potentially cut off all but English-speaking audiences and restrict US products to British territories. The initial years of synchronization did, in fact, disrupt the American industry's global reach as it attempted to grapple with problems of translation. In Brazil, this temporary disorder, along with the delay in transitioning to the sound technology due to the high costs required for upgrading production and exhibition equipment, led to several years of experimenting with the silent medium.[10] The year 1928 thus "seemed to open up a new phase for Brazilian cinema in which numerous silent films were produced and exhibited, and led to a wave of optimism concerning the future of the country's cinema."[11]

This optimistic belief was reinforced by the popular and critical success of *Cinearte* critic Adhemar Gonzaga's first film, *Barro humano* (Human clay), released in 1928. The silent movie tells the tale of a young girl who decides to earn a living outside the home and meets with hostility and prejudice. The leading roles were played by Eva Schnoor and Carlos Modesto, whose offscreen romance and subsequent marriage reinforced their status within Brazil's star system and helped bolster *Human Clay*'s popularity. The film's success, however, was also boosted by its regionalism. Critic Octávio Mendes's praise, for instance, went beyond the photogenic aspects of the movie's stars to focus on its location, citing in particular "our familiar settings."[12] A writer for the *Correio da Manhã* also celebrated the film, noting, "I believe that I am not mistaken when I state that it represents the most perfect work that has been produced in Brazil to date. Thanks to a group of courageous young men, cinema in Brazil is beginning to be a reality, when once it seemed like an almost impossible dream."[13] *Human Clay*'s commercial and critical success seemed to indicate the maturation of Brazil's silent narrative cinema, something that was reinforced by the popularity of Mauro's *Dormant Embers*, released the following year.

Limite's intimate film style does not evidence the national mode of these Brazilian regional films, and it had no impact on these cinematic productions. Neither did it influence subsequent filmmaking. Without having seen the film, Glauber Rocha, in his 1964 book *Revisão crítica do cinema brasileiro*, dismissed *Limite* as an inadequate model for Cinema Novo's search for a national cinema that sought to establish "a continuous dialogue with reality."[14] While Rocha recognized the audacious language of Peixoto's film, he viewed it as representing a cosmopolitan film modernism that imitated the French avant-garde, and he aligned *Limite* with the dynamic of cultural colonization. Consequently, he declared that any attempt to trace the genealogy of modern Brazilian cinema to Peixoto would be a "suicidal attempt, moving toward a future of sterile experiences, disconnected from the living source of our people, sad and starving in an exuberant landscape." *Limite* was, Rocha concluded, "the product of a decadent bourgeois intellectual branded with good taste, inwardly and entirely withdrawn from reality."[15] The director positioned Mauro's regional films instead as corresponding to aesthetic modernism and a tradition of Brazilian cinema that could be recuperated for a national film history.

Rocha's remarks speak to the canon of Brazil's modernist cinema, which has been established and determined in the name of a nationally rooted cultural tradition and patrimony to be reproduced. Here the focus on local realities, as manifested in Mauro's films, represents a unique and powerful expression of a Brazilian cinema. Within this canon, *Limite* appears as an exception and an aberration. The experimental film has entered the history of Brazilian cinema only as what Mello calls "a departure from the general rule."[16] Yet while Peixoto's intimist film tautologically gestures toward itself, it nevertheless evidences modernist practices, revealing what Vicky Unruh refers to as Brazilian modernism's double gesture, in which texts "evoke temporally and site specific" references that reflect the involvement of vanguard artists in artistic developments in the contexts in which they worked.[17] Crucial here is *Limite*'s engagement with critical debates regarding cinema that were taking place in the late 1920s and '30s in Brazil and beyond.

PEIXOTO AND FILM DEBATES

A key locus for these debates in Brazil was the country's first *ciné-club*, the Chaplin Club. Founded in Rio on June 13, 1928. by Octávio de Faria, Plínio Süssekind Rocha, Cláudio Mello, and Almir Castro, the club's main objective was "to study cinema as art" rather than to view it as a popular form of entertainment with roots in theatrical vaudeville, in Brazil the *teatro de revista*.[18] The discussion regarding film as art was not restricted to the Chaplin Club. Since 1926, the fanzine *Cinearte*, as the publication's title highlights, had been championing cinema as an artistic medium. As noted in chapter 4, for *Cinearte*'s writers, the art of the moving pictures resided in Hollywood's classic model.

The Chaplin Club's conception of cinema's artistic qualities departed radically from *Cinearte*'s. The group was influenced not by Hollywood but by discussions concerning film as art that had developed in post–World War I France.[19] Influenced by these discussions, the Chaplin Club regularly met to debate film's artistic qualities and organized screenings of what they considered great silent movies. Their emphasis on silent film was important given the onset of the talking pictures. While studios were investing in sound, the Cariocan cinephiles felt there was more to be gained from exploring film as a visual art form, freed from the tyranny of the word. They were strongly opposed to synchronized movies, which they viewed as "a return to the initial days in which cinema was confused with filmed theater." This regressive move, they believed, ignored the true nature of the medium. The members ardently declared, "Cinema is art. Black and white art. Silent art. Dynamic art. Visual art. It does not need the colors of real life. It does not need the theater's words. It does not need opera's music. It does not need the psychological complexity of the novel. Real art does not require anything from the other arts. Real art simply exists on its own."[20] The Chaplin Club thus championed the ideal

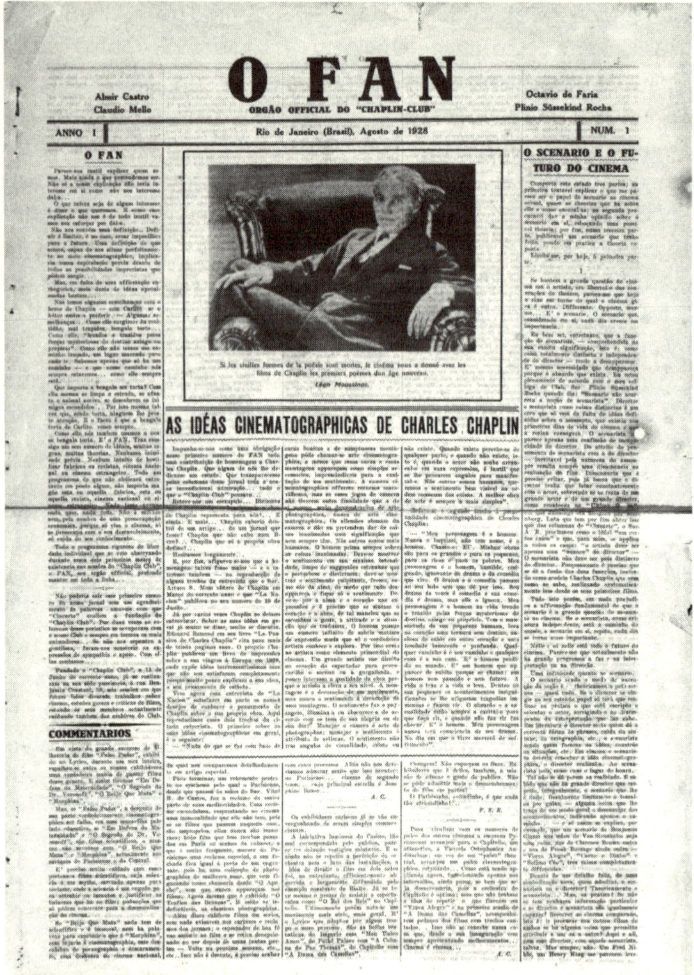

FIGURE 25. Chaplin Club's *O Fan* magazine, 1928. Acervo Cinemateca Brasileira, Secretaria do Audiovisual do Ministério da Cultura.

of a "pure cinema," entirely autonomous from other cultural forms—an ideal that had been elaborated and discussed by French theorists and filmmakers, especially Germaine Dulac, for whom "film should divest itself of all elements not particular to it."[21] As the name of the club attests, it was Charlie Chaplin and his staunch defense of silent film that became the group's inspiration.

The group's discussions on the art of silent film were published in their journal *O Fan* (The Fan; figure 25). Despite its name, *O Fan* was by no means a fanzine.

Unlike *Cinearte,* the Chaplin Club's publication had no advertisements, printed few photographs, and had no interest in Hollywood and its stars. Its pages were densely filled with serious analyses of European and North American silent productions, paying close attention to their language and form. It printed articles on the oeuvre of directors like D. W. Griffiths and F. W. Murnau, praising their individual mastery and their status as auteurs worthy of serious study. *O Fan* also included discussions of international books and articles, which introduced new ideas about filmmaking. These included the work of Léon Moussinac, whose writings on cinematic rhythms in *La naissance du cinéma* gave rise to ample deliberations in the journal's initial issues, as well as texts by Dulac and others. They also encompassed manifestos by Soviet filmmakers Sergei Eisenstein, Dziga Vertov, and Vsevolod Pudovkin, which were critiqued by Octávio de Faria and others.

O Fan testifies to the Chaplin Club's intimate engagement with and knowledge of novel theories about film art that were emerging globally. The cinephiles were avid readers of North American and European publications, like *Picture Play* (1915), *Cinéa* (1921), and *Close-Up* (1927). They were also conversant with works by Ricciotto Canudo, Dulac, Louis Delluc, Jean Epstein, Abel Gance, and others, which were often discussed in the pages of their journal. This testifies to the circulation of novel ideas regarding film, especially film art, in Brazil, which proposed alternatives to Hollywood's classical model adopted by regional filmmakers and promoted by *Cinearte.*

The Chaplin Club therefore developed a new forum of serious discussion about the art of cinema, which for Faria and the others was silent. They decried the talkies as attacking the purity of film's visual discourse and, worse still, as taking the medium back to its popular origins in the theater. Silent cinema was thus defended as a high art as opposed to a popular cultural form. Their journal reflected this antipopulist sentiment. Unlike the commercial fanzine *Cinearte, O Fan* was far from mainstream. Its dense articles and essays were written strictly for cinephiles who were well versed in international film theory; indeed, the publication's writers expressed no interest in catering to a broad readership. Consequently, the journal "had a restricted circulation and was dedicated only to those who were interested in cinema as an art form."[22] This limited reach did not concern the members of the Chaplin Club. As Xavier notes, "*O Fan* knew that it was read by almost no one and that it had no influence in the future of film, but it was not troubled by this."[23] Far from opening up a public forum about film, the Brazilian *ciné-club* conceived of itself as an alternative specialized space for those who truly understood and appreciated the art of the silents.

While Peixoto was not formally part of the Chaplin Club, his close contact with Faria and Süssekind made him aware of new artistic discussions concerning cinema, which laid the groundwork for the idea of making his own silent film. Indeed, Peixoto noted that *Limite* was made only after "lessons" from Faria.[24] *Limite* was, then, part of the new network of theoretical debates of the time, and the Chaplin Club's discussions were "the roots of the [film's] inception."[25]

All of this was supplemented by Peixoto's own contact with European experimentations in film. Independently wealthy, Peixoto had traveled widely in Europe, where he became conversant with the cinematic avant-garde. In fact, Süssekind recalls that Peixoto became profoundly fascinated with the cinema during his days as a student in England in 1927 and a trip to Paris the following year, where he was exposed to artistic films that were flourishing among Soviet, German, Russian, and French directors.[26] These experiments opened Peixoto up to a world of film beyond Hollywood's narrative movies, revealing a different cinematic syntax. Aware of experimental movies being made in Europe and familiar with theories regarding film from his contact with the Chaplin Club, Peixoto set out to rethink Brazil's cinematic discourse beyond the country's Hollywood-inspired regional movies.

VISUAL CONFINEMENT IN *LIMITE*'S PURE CINEMA

Although *Limite* was influenced by cinematic debates circulating in 1920s Brazil, the film's development was also catalyzed by a specific visual stimulus. While on a trip to Paris in 1929, Peixoto caught sight of the cover of a *Vue* magazine that featured a photograph by Hungarian André Kertész depicting a woman facing the camera and embraced by a handcuffed man (figure 26). Peixoto recalled that the photo "profoundly reverberated in me."[27] He promptly purchased the magazine, returned to his hotel, and, seized by an uncontrollable impulse, wrote the first draft of the scenario for *Limite* that evening. Peixoto's film was thus inspired by Kertész's photograph, which became what Mello calls its protoimage.[28] *Limite* filmically adapts Kertész's photo, which establishes the movie's theme: limitations.

An image, not an event or story, was therefore key to *Limite*'s conception. Indeed, the beginning of the movie reproduces Kertész's photograph, which informs and structures its very language and development (figure 27). Departing radically from Hollywood's classical cinema, Peixoto's film has no narrative. As Mello writes, *Limite* "is not a story, it is a vision."[29] Dismissing conventional causality, the film instead "affirms, reaffirms and reiterates obsessively the film's protean image."[30] Formally devised and structured down to its smallest detail, *Limite*'s scenes, or visions, emerge as altered variations of the opening reproduced photograph, which are not subordinated to a narrative logic. In-camera techniques, such as fades, dissolves, superimpositions, and long sequences devoid of action, reinforce *Limite*'s rejection of linearity. The virtual absence of intertitles (there are only three in the entire film) also underlines the importance of the visual over the narrative. Consequently, editing is employed not to create a story, but to connect different images and scenes together morphologically. In this sense *Limite* functions in terms of what filmmaker Maya Deren calls verticality rather than horizon-

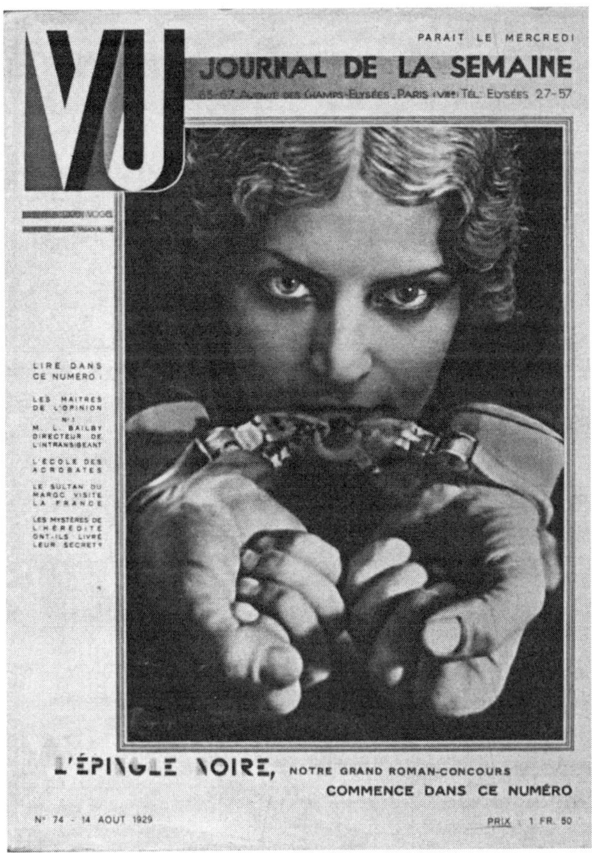

FIGURE 26. Cover of *Vue* magazine by André Kertész, 1929.
Acervo Cinemateca Brasileira, Secretaria do Audiovisual do
Ministério da Cultura.

tality. For Deren, films' horizontal development is guided by a logic of action, which leads to the development of a story. This logic is central to Hollywood cinema, which borrows narrative conventions from literature. Eschewing such narrative conventions, *Limite* dispenses with horizontal development, favoring the paradigmatic over the syntagmatic.[31]

Free from the confines of narrative, Peixoto can be seen to have accomplished the pure cinema that Dulac in 1927 had demanded: "Every cinematic drama, whether created by forms of movement or by human beings in a state of crisis, *must* be visual and not literary."[32] According to Dulac, "A real film cannot be able to be told, since it must draw its active and emotive principle from the images formed of unique visual tones. Can you tell a painting? Can you tell a sculpture? Of course

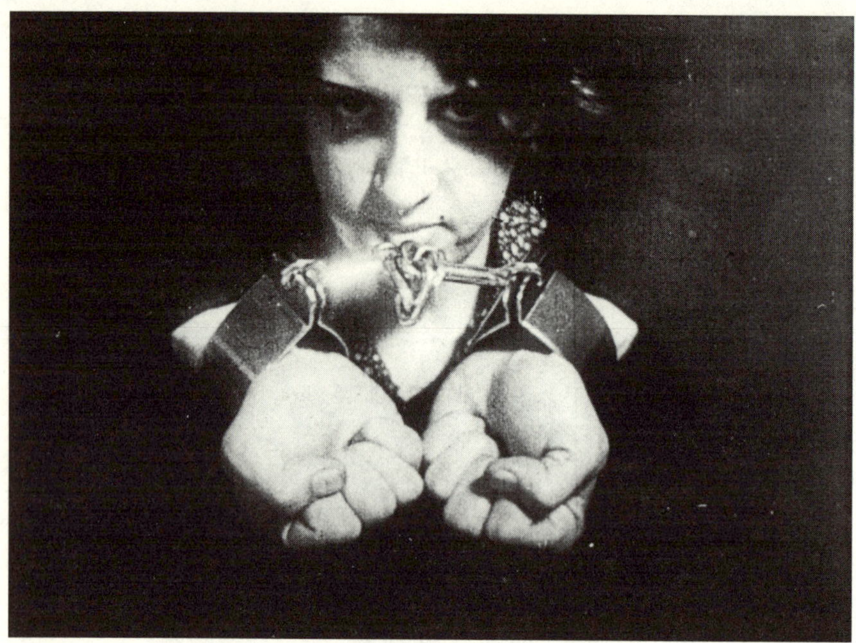

FIGURE 27. André Kertész photograph reproduced in *Limite*, 1930. Acervo Cinemateca Brasileira, Secretaria do Audiovisual do Ministério da Cultura.

not."[33] Dulac argued that rhythm and movement, expressed in the image and between images, were key aspects of film's specific visual syntax. The real film-maker, she stated, should "divest cinema of all elements not particular to it and seek its true essence in the consciousness of movement and visual rhythms."[34] According to Dulac, rhythm and movement were two plastic and aesthetic elements that coordinated shots into an ensemble and made pure cinema analogous to poetry.

In its visual exploration of the theme of limitations, *Limite* adopts the rhythmically oriented variations identified by Dulac. It experiments with movement within the film's images, employing audacious camerawork, as well as rhythms between them, through montage. Eccentric framing, disorientingly outsized close-ups, and graphic compositions are used throughout the film in an expressionistic manner. The camerawork oscillates between extremely long slow takes and frenetic pans and rapid movements. The editing places shots in diverse syntagmatic contexts, structurally varying their meaning. Visual analogies and associative montage link distinct situations and objects together in a technique that evokes Eisenstein's principle of intellectual montage. These rhythmic variations work together visually in a poetic way, and the series of images are to be interpreted collectively, as Peixoto himself noted: "The whole is held up with a total freedom of vision and so, all the parts fit together and complement each other as in a chain, with the detailed, clear precision of the finest poetry."[35] Accompanying this poetic precision is a musical score, arranged by Brutus Pedreira (who also acts in the film), in which modern compositions complement the images.

Brazilian critics have reinforced Peixoto's own poetic analogy of *Limite*. Calil, for instance, refers to *Limite*'s "lyrical camera," and William Drew writes that the film is "akin to poetry but with images rather than words."[36] Mello too likens *Limite*'s cinematic purity to poetry, referring to it as a "cine-poem."[37] *Limite* is, Mello contends, "a poetic moment of pure cinema."[38] Rather than relate a story dealing with the key theme, Peixoto's poetic movie seeks to express the feeling of limitations. Indeed, Peixoto noted that the film offers the spectator an experience that cannot be captured by language but must be "felt as an aura, with the eyes as a gateway."[39] Characterizing *Limite* as a "desperate scream," Peixoto suggests that it aims for resonance, not comprehension, and that viewers should subjugate themselves to the images, which are the "anguished cords [*sic*] of a synthetic and pure language of cinema."[40]

For some critics, this emphasis on resonance over comprehension is indicative of the movie's surrealist tendencies. Noting that *Limite* was contemporaneous with Luis Buñuel's *Um chien Andalou* (1929), Sérgio Lima, for instance, includes the film in his overview of French surrealism's influence on Brazilian cinema.[41] While *Limite*'s visual rather than narrative structure may have a dreamlike reverie and an oneiric quality reminiscent of surrealism, Peixoto's minutely organized film reveals very little of André Breton's automatism. As Michael Korfmann points out, it results from "a carefully planned and executed idea, rather than coming from the basic principle of a chance outcome."[42] Peixoto's stress on the film's resonance instead underscores the emotional qualities of his cine-poem. *Limite* latches onto subjective expression and symbolic impression, which envelop the viewer in a network of sensations. The movie's images are thus "structured in terms of their symbolic meaning rather than narratively. . . . Their meanings, rhythm, framing, the acting, camera angles are determined by a symbolic intention."[43] In other words, the film's images, its pure language, are governed by *Limite*'s symbolic expression of the key organizing theme, that of limitations, which is to be felt.

LIMITE'S ORGANIZATION AND STRUCTURE

Limite is then subjective expression rather than rational comprehension. It aims for resonance, as its pure language ensconces the viewer in a screen space of visual confinement. This confinement is evoked by a situation: three castaways—two women and a man—are aimlessly adrift in a boat. Captured in static shots, the passengers are inactive. They each recall episodes that drove them to the present situation. We know nothing else about these characters. How they got there and how they found themselves together in this predicament are never divulged to us. Their stories tell us nothing about them, and the figures are not developed with a view to generating spectatorial identification. *Limite* thus rejects the psychological realism of Hollywood's classical cinema as it disavows the characters' identities. Its protagonists remain unnamed throughout the film. In typical expressionist style, they are abstracted from social categories; they and their stories are to be interpreted not as part of the characters' psychology or as symbols of a social reality but as expressions of the idea of limitation.

The protagonists' stories emerge as flashbacks from the present time of the boat, which encloses them and their narratives. In this real time the camerawork is minimalist and graphic. At times the camera pans slowly, but the scene is largely composed of long static shots that visually capture, in close-up, the anguish of the marooned figures on the boat. This is punctuated by the melancholic sounds of Erik Satie's *Gymnopédie*. Satie's composition progresses from and alternates between two major seventh chords, a deliberate and measured limitation of sounds that aurally reinforces *Limite*'s key theme. This is also emphasized by the mise-en-scène. In the opening sequence, the edges of the boat and lines of the horizon are always visible. Functioning as barriers for the characters and the camera, these lines and edges create a sense of claustrophobia, so that the spectator is forced to experience the physical and spatial imprisonment that engulfs the figures and structures their stories.

The first story tells of an anonymous woman (played by Olga Breno) who flees from prison on a train only to find herself in a new situation of oppression, working as a seamstress in a factory. In the opening shot of this sequence, the woman appears behind bars. The film then cuts to an extremely low shot, which reveals a door opening and the woman's feet emerging. The camera tracks her feet as the woman leaves prison, and the film follows her flight: her walk through the town, her trek through the countryside, her journey on a train, and her entrance into the factory. The movement in the woman's journey away from the prison evokes an escape from confinement. This is particularly present in the train journey. Composed of a series of extreme close-ups of the train's wheels, the rapid actions of the locomotive's mechanics contrast to the slow pace and inactivity of the opening sequence on the boat and appear to communicate mobility and progress. This is immediately countered, however, by lengthy scenes of the woman wandering along endless country paths that seem to go nowhere. The woman's escape is far from liberatory. While taking her to new and different places, the character remains in a state of confinement.

This confinement is registered by the mise-en-scène. The prison bars are evoked throughout this sequence in visual analogies. Hedges, telegraph lines, and fences that mark the woman's aimless journey visually imprison her, and the bars on the factory windows where she labors at her sewing machine also echo her initial incarceration. Peixoto employs extreme close-ups and high angle shots of the woman at work to communicate the oppressive nature of her labor and its psychological effects, with the tight framing adding to the sense of her confinement. In these scenes, the careful placement of fashionable dress patterns brings to mind the specific gender politics of this oppression, that is, the larger context in which Brazilian women were increasingly compelled to leave the cloistered space of the home for labor. The discourse of freedom that impelled this shift in women's place in modern Brazilian society is contradicted here by the repressive images of the woman at work. The sequence is thus not just thematically expressive of the character's inner life but also social: it reveals the source and reality of the limitations depicted.

Successive shots—spools, buttons, scissors, measuring tape—all bathed in a dusty light, evoke the tedium of the woman's work. These round objects are visually analogous to the train's wheels, evoking a circle of directional constraints. A dissolve also merges these objects to the barred windows in the factory, linking the tools of the woman's labor to her oppression. While this use of associative montage is similar to that evidenced in Soviet films, like Vertov's *Man with a Movie Camera*, its social politics is not. Vertov's film, and its obsession with speeding cars and trams, celebrates the modern machine age as liberatory. In Peixoto's film, modern industry, the train and the factory, is imprisoning. The accompanying musical score, Claude Debussy's *Quartet in G-Minor* reinforces this. Confined to four connected movements that are repeated, the music's circularity and underlining cyclical structure provides an aural rendition of the film's imagistic rendering.

The second woman's tale exhibits similar stifling elements, associated this time with domestic life and marriage. Her flashback begins with a visit to a seaside village to purchase fish. After a prolonged walk through the village, the woman (played by Tatiana Rey) arrives home where her alcoholic husband, a cinema pianist, awaits her. Extreme close-ups of her and her husband's wedding rings visually echo the handcuffs of the film's protoimage and become symbols of claustrophobia: the rings bind the couple together. In this film, unlike Hollywood movies, sexual and familial relations are not celebrated; they are depicted as restrictive. As in the first story, the mise-en-scène evokes this claustrophobia. Doors, windows, walls, stairway bannisters, and fences imprison the second woman and give the sequence a feeling of confinement that registers her psychological state of mind. Peixoto thus employs mise-en-scène in a way similar to expressionist filmmakers to demonstrate what Dulac called "interior expression," that is, the interior expression of souls.[44] The camerawork reinforces this. Toward the end of this sequence, the female character heads toward the sea, which she observes from a high vantage point, evidently contemplating suicide. Her torment is communicated in a sequence of frenzied shots. The camera tilts and rotates at extreme angles and pans frenetically across the landscape, expressing the woman's desperation and her desire to break away from her confined existence. Indeed, mirroring the woman's state of mind, the camera appears to want to break free from the film's confinement. This is complemented by the musical score, Alexander Borodin's *Notturno Quartet No. 2 in D Major,* whose counterpoint registers tumult.

This second story is not restricted to the woman's tale. The camera abandons her to focus on her husband (played by Brutus Pedreira). His narrative takes us to a movie theater where he works as a pianist. The film screened is Chaplin's *The Adventurer* (1917). Watched by an audience depicted as a montage of laughing mouths, the comedy recapitulates in microcosm *Limite*'s structuring theme. The clip shows Charlie tunneling out of prison only to discover that he is at the feet of a guard. He escapes one place of incarceration to encounter another. For Mello this sequence is underscored by a "vulgarity" in its depiction of the movie audience.[45] Peixoto does seem to deride the laughing spectators and their carefree acceptance of Chaplin's film as entertainment. Debussy's piano solo, *Golliwogg's Cake Walk,* which accompanies this scene, underpins this derision. The composer wrote the popular ragtime piece for his three-year old daughter, and it captures the naïveté of childhood and of children's games. Peixoto thus appears to mock the spectators' blithe reaction and contrasts it to the close-ups of the pianist's tormented face and the sentiment of Chaplin's film.

The sequence's disdain for the cinematic masses is reminiscent of Siegfried Kracauer's criticism of "the little shop girls" who "go to the movies." In his essay, Kracauer catalogs the ways in which the film industry recasts oppression into more appealing forms of adventure, romance, and comedy. Yet film's unreal fantasies are, Kracauer argues, "the daydreams of society in which actual reality comes to the fore."[46] In Peixoto's film, the clip from Chaplin's comedy mirrors the limitations of *Limite*'s characters, yet the the diegetic audience watching it appears unaware of this as it embraces its surface distractions. Peixoto thus reveals the distracting nature of Hollywood's cinematic products, and resists it by associating Chaplin's own imprisonment with that of the pianist and the film's other protagonists.

In the third sequence, the man (played by Raul Schnoor) tells his story. A handheld camera follows his promenade along a beach and in the countryside with a woman whose face we never see. The opening scenes depict love and happiness, which are complemented by the music: an allegro by Maurice Ravel. The man accompanies the woman home and then walks to a cemetery where he visits a grave, that of his former wife who has died. There he encounters another man (played by Peixoto) who tells him that the woman he has just been with is his wife and has leprosy. The man escapes the cemetery and flees through the countryside. Ravel's allegro is replaced by Cesar Franck's *Chorale No. 3,* whose agitated sounds communicate disquiet. The images reinforce this. Gnarled trees, a series of chaotic shots, and extreme close-ups of the man screaming register his inner torment, and frenzied pans express his dizziness. The camera circles around the character and the landscape frantically. The freedom the man's new relationship had given him from the anguish after his wife's death has been thwarted and his future has been frustrated through physical disease. The man collapses on to the ground. The camera abandons him to focus on the vast sky, its wide expanse a symbolic contrast to the character's restricted horizon.

The man's limited existence is therefore visually expressed. As in the other stories, shots of nature, like cacti and palms, as well as of buildings, visually imprison him, their straight lines confining him. These shots, moreover, reveal a decaying landscape that evokes death, which a succession of crosses from the cemetery serves to emphasize. The funereal atmosphere is starkly evoked in a series of low-angle shots of twisted trees, which are shown in negative film. Here Peixoto experiments with and exploits the actual plastic properties of cinema. Using negative photograph techniques utilized by Dada artists in films like Man Ray's *Return to Reason* (1923), Peixoto recognizes film not just as a system of representation but also as a material system. The bleach-white appearance of trunks and branches against a black sky seems to abstract them from nature and reality. This is not pure abstraction, however: the negative images evoke a funereal mood and a sense of foreboding for this particular sequence and the film as a whole. As Mello writes, "Nature is permeated by death. . . . The entire world—roads, the landscape, decadent ruins, hedges, doors, trees—everything is marked by decadence and death."[47]

Limite thus registers the vanishing of time in its final story. There is no progression into the future for its male figure. The man's efforts to constitute a new life have been fruitless. This lack of progress characterizes all of the stories in *Limite*. It is evidenced in the fruitless sexual and familial bonds, which are stifling and unproductive. It is also evoked by the characters' endless journeys that go nowhere, the imprisoning mise-en-scène, and the circular objects that symbolize cyclicality and the futility of flight. The three stories are thus thematically and visually connected, something that is reinforced by Peixoto's use of dissolve shots, which merges the tales together. They are also temporally and spatially connected. The individuals' stories emanate from the present time-space of the boat to which they, and the film, return. As Mello states, "Everything in the film converges on the boat, where serene resignation is permeated with a feeling of imminent doom. The rhythms, the feeling of hopelessness, and the tragic fate of the characters derive from the very limitations of existence. They are overcome by an increasing awareness of their own inutility, boxed in a situation in which any action is pointless."[48]

All attempts made by the three figures to escape their confined existence have been futile. Their ineffectiveness is registered in the camerawork in the boat sequence, which is marked by long static shots. Everything in the boat evokes restrictions: the camerawork, the mise-en-scène, the characters' inaction, and Satie's melancholic music. The boat therefore symbolizes the restrictions that *Limite* visually and thematically explores and seeks to convey. This restricted state, however, ends with a climactic tour-de-force storm sequence, which consists of seven shots of crashing waves, frenetically edited to suggest a tempest on the sea. The storm formally and thematically brings the film to an end. Formally, the rapidly edited shots lead to a crescendo that breaks the film's slow rhythm and cadence, which has only brought anxiety. Thematically, it is an analogue of the characters' despair at their limited existence, which finally brings it to an end. Only the first woman survives the storm, as she clings to a piece of driftwood, seeking not to escape but only to survive. Escape is, it seems, impossible, and human limitations are an inevitable part of life. As if to reinforce this, *Limite* ends by reproducing its protoimage: Kertész's photograph from *Vue* magazine, bringing us back full circle to its beginning and enclosing *Limite* in its visual origins. The film thus resists closure in the conventional cinematic sense. Indeed, *Limite* refuses to adhere to the rules of narrative film. The film begins with no conflict and ends with no resolution, and it repudiates the causal linearity associated with classical cinema's productive temporality. Instead, *Limite* takes the viewer into the three figures' situations and minds, expressing them in a pure cinematic language that distances the spectator from the events depicted. The distance forces spectators to accept the situations rather than analyze them, even if they are not understood. As Peixoto himself stated, *Limite* "is a state, not an analysis."[49]

The film is consequently marked by an evacuation of rationality. It is also characterized by a sense of stasis rather than advancement toward a resolution. For William Drew, this stasis and absence of rational analysis reveals *Limite*'s "implied criticism of the modern civilizational project," which links the film to the wider zeitgeist of the European and Brazilian avant-garde.[50] As noted in chapter 8, postwar Europe saw a questioning of the legacy of the Enlightenment and its foundation as the model of rationality and historical agency under the direction of universal progress. Artistic movements like surrealism, expressionism and primitivism challenged the fundamentals of Western civilization and sought out new aesthetics that could represent a different order. Film theorists and practitioners keyed into this, refusing a narrational form of dominant discourse, the kind of authoritative narrative organization associated with classical Hollywood, in favor of the language of pure cinema. These experiments in art and film upset the linear notion of temporality, reflecting an end to the previous faith in the rationality of European history.

This crisis was also felt in Brazil, where it ushered in a new era in which the progressive narrative that had allowed the new nation to project itself as part of the wider world started to be questioned and critiqued. Writers and artists belonging to Brazilian modernism began to explore the limits of a national response to this crisis of civilization and the logic of unilinear order and progress, which had placed them either as relics of a primitive past or as potentials for an unrealized future. Mário de Andrade and Oswald de Andrade most notably engaged in what Esther Gabara calls a critical nationalism, undermining a positivist rationality imported from Europe.[51] Peixoto's film *Limite* can also be read as a response to the crisis of liberal modernity, as Drew suggests. Its axiomatic refusal of narrativity, of the pressures of closure and the fulfillment of rational interpretation, stages a rejection of signification and of the liberal and progressive order. Venturing outside the tradition of mainstream Hollywood cinema emulated by Brazilian filmmakers of the time, it challenges the linear mode and disrupts the referentiality of language and of images, what Pier Paolo Pasolini called the language of reality.[52]

It was this challenge—*Limite*'s refusal to visually refer to real Brazil and Brazilian society—that Rocha critiqued and dismissed. For Rocha, *Limite*'s heuristic opacity is evidence of its failure to produce social knowledge of Brazil, something the Cinema Novo director resolutely condemned. Yet *Limite*'s failure to produce knowledge and its undoing of analysis can be interpreted as an active refusal to commit to dominant narratives and their vision of progress. Indeed, the film's digression from linearity and its insistence on the poetics of a pure cinema suggest the rejection of the dominant liberal history that Republican Brazil had embraced since the late 1880s, with Peixoto participating in the critical nationalism that Gabara theorizes as evident in *modernismo*. Refusing to duplicate universal narratives of progress, *Limite* digresses from the formal terms of futurity and emerges as a destabilizing force that produces a different cinema, one that, as in a poem, is to be seen, felt, and evoked, not understood. In this capacity, Peixoto's film reveals what Jacques Rancière calls a subjective political value: it creates innovative, detached forms and aesthetics that are nevertheless part of the social fabric of culture, national and international.[53]

Peixoto's film thus registers a wider disorder and a lack of faith in a progressive narrative. In doing so, it suggests a different role and place for Brazilian film, one that goes beyond the conventional Hollywood narratives evidenced in the country's regional filmmaking traditions. His experimentation was in keeping with contemporary cinematic debates disseminated by the Chaplin Club in Brazil, debates that Peixoto engaged with and synthesized. While the film does not include obvious national markers, it nevertheless evokes time- and place-specific references that reflect Peixoto's involvement in contemporary artistic developments and discussions. *Limite*'s engagement with new ideas regarding film allows its viewer to see film "with new eyes," to use Oswald's term, and his film dealing with limitations paradoxically gives spectators freedom of vision, releasing them from the horizontal confines of Hollywood and from imported narratives of modernity.[54]

10

Fabricating Discipline and Progress in *São Paulo, Symphony of a Metropolis*

Mário Peixoto's *Limite* was not the only avant-garde film made in late 1920s Brazil. Other filmmakers were also influenced by cinematic experimentations taking place in Europe. City-symphony films like Paul Strand's *Manhattan* (1921), Alberto Cavalcanti's *Nothing but Time* (1926), Dziga Vertov's *Man with a Movie Camera* (1926), and especially Walter Ruttmann's *Berlin: Symphony of a Great City* (1927) inspired a number of filmmakers in Brazil. Humberto Mauro made a short film *Sinfonia de Cataguases* (Symphony of Cataguases) in 1929 about his native town, and that same year Hungarian immigrants Adalberto Kemeny and Rodolfo Lustig made the feature-length *São Paulo, a sinfonia da metrópole* (São Paulo, Symphony of a metropolis). Inspired by Ruttmann's cine-symphony, the latter was a cinematic homage to what Paramount's press releases referred to as the "thundering rhythm of progress" in São Paulo (figure 28).

São Paulo was probably modeled on its German predecessor, Ruttmann's *Berlin*, which Kemeny and Lustig would likely have seen when they lived and worked as filmmakers in the German city prior to arriving in Brazil in 1928.[1] Like *Berlin,* the Brazilian film eschews a formal plot and psychological realism to chart a day in the life of the Paulista metropolis, beginning at dawn and ending at dusk. It also deploys a combination of everyday images, montage, kaleidoscopic projection, and camera trickery to articulate the intensity of 1920s São Paulo. Taking inspiration from Ruttmann, Kemeny and Lustig's film thus registers an intimate relationship with the city. It also expresses a homology between urban experience and cinematic spectatorship, characterized by diffusion and distraction. All of this was part of what Georg Simmel theorized as the great impact of modern cities at the end of the nineteenth century on what he called mental life. For Simmel, forms of

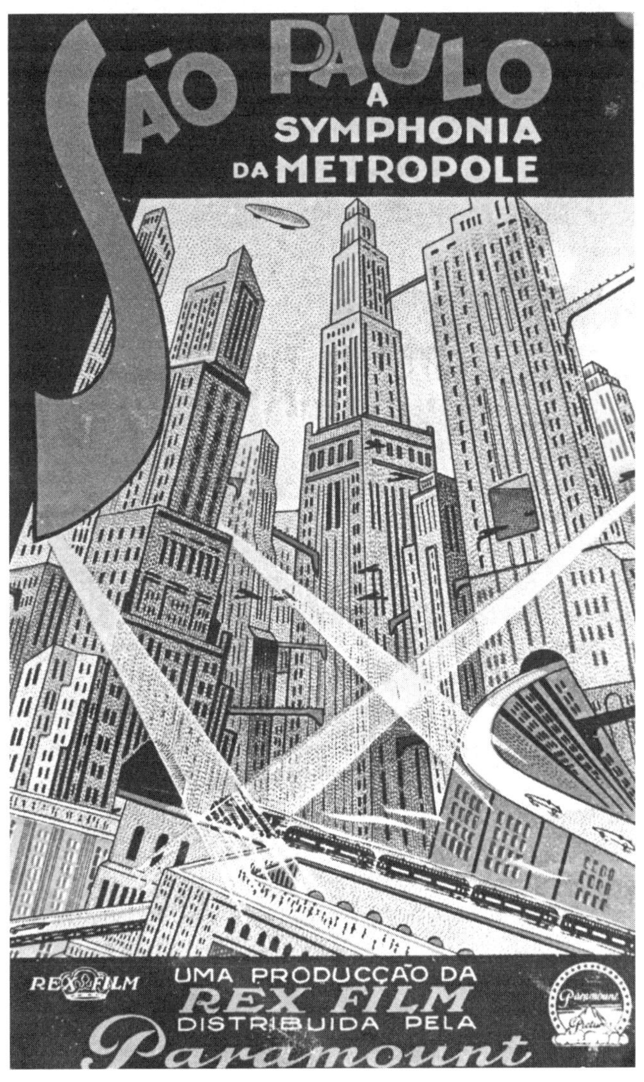

FIGURE 28. Poster for *São Paulo, Symphony of a Metropolis*, 1929.
Acervo Cinemateca Brasileira, Secretaria do Audiovisual do Ministério
da Cultura.

perceptions were disordered and reconfigured by new methods of industrial production, cityscapes, techniques of social regulation, means of transportation, and forms of communication. With their montage of everyday scenes, city-films articulated and responded to these new sensory perceptions as they projected urban locations on the screen. In doing so, they provided a mediating pedagogy between the reality of the metropolis and its imaginary place in everyday mental life.

Kemeny and Lustig's *São Paulo* certainly articulated the experience of 1920s São Paulo. In doing so, however, their film keyed into contemporary discourses regarding the city's growing significance in Brazil's First Republic. Their film thus mediated a particular pedagogy of urban life, for it sought to project São Paulo as a modern metropolis that was part of the Republic's national narrative of order and progress and also integral to its future.

The imagined configurations of São Paulo's future identity were bound up with the expansion of the coffee business that was occurring from the late nineteenth century onwards.[2] Capital accumulation from this growing market produced spectacular results. Railway lines were developed, transforming the city into a key export site. This process led to an increased demand for industrial goods, stimulating investment in industry. Between 1915 and 1919, 5,490 industries were established in Brazil, mainly in São Paulo, which became the "national metropolis of industry."[3] Working opportunities offered by these new businesses attracted migrants and immigrants, altering the city's demographic makeup. When the Republic dawned in 1889, São Paulo was a small city of 64,934 inhabitants. By the start of the twentieth century, this number had expanded to 270,000. In 1920, the population had risen to 579,000, and by 1934 it had reached 1,120,000, making the city Brazil's largest.[4] New industries and the population boom fostered the development of train and tram lines close to outlying factories, giving rise to working-class neighborhoods like Lapa, Bom Retiro, Belém, and Mooca. There was also a growing speculation in real estate. In 1912, ambitious speculators, foreign investors, and local property owners formed the Cia. City, which started to sell exclusive lots to the elite. Fashionable suburbs such as Consolação, Higienópolis, Santa Cecília, and Paulista, with grand avenues and exclusive mansions, were constructed to the west and south of the center.[5] The city's map was thus radically and rapidly redrawn, as its cartography expanded to incorporate outlying land. As commentator Firmino Pinto stated at the time, "We are witnessing almost daily the opening of new roads and creation of new neighborhoods."[6]

The first decades of the new century also saw urban reforms in São Paulo's center that aimed to replace the city's colonial fabric with a functional, structured, and modern urban design.[7] Under the auspices of Prefect Antônio da Silva Prado (1899–1911), the center was reformed. Parks were constructed, streets widened, and new thoroughfares built. Viaducts were made, and old public buildings were reconstructed and new ones erected, all of which "came to project the image of

[São Paulo] as a modern city."[8] As Candido Malta Campos notes, these reforms were part of the Republic's broader urban politics, which aimed to provide the country's principal cities with a more modern and civilized identity.[9] It was this urban politics that at the start of the twentieth century led to Rio's dramatic makeover, which, modeled on Haussmann's Parisian reforms, transformed the city into a tropical version of the French capital, its beaux arts architecture and grand boulevards concretizing Brazil's modernity. Prado's São Paulo reforms also borrowed from the French city's design, as evidenced in the Municipal Theater, inaugurated in 1911, whose architectural reference was the Palais Garnier Opera House in Paris. As the twentieth century progressed, however, São Paulo's French patrimony was left behind as politicians and architects sought out new modern models.

By the time of the prefecture of Washington Luís Pereira de Sousa (1914–17) the city's blueprint for modernity no longer came from Europe but from North America.[10] Seized by what Nicolau Sevcenko calls "a Yankee enthusiasm," a new generation of engineers and architects began to dismiss the beaux arts style and promote and implement an architecture of verticalization.[11] With the centenary of independence approaching, this new architectural model was, it was argued, more suitable for the growing metropolis, since it was "directed toward the future."[12] New skyscrapers, like the Edífcio Sampaio (1924) and Edifício Martinelli (1929), came to dominate São Paulo's topography, providing it with a dramatic new skyline.[13] The city expanded not just outwards but also upwards, its modern image cemented in a vertical urbanism. This vertical extension was a symbolic representation of São Paulo's power and reach, its ability to conquer the sky. Rising skyscrapers of steel and aluminum romanticized the power and intensity of the twentieth-century city.[14] Literal embodiments of the feats of modern engineering, they loomed large as visual icons of São Paulo's progress and prospects. Adopting the tall architecture of North American metropoles like New York, the city dramatically announced its transformation from an agricultural backland into a modern metropolis.

By the 1920s, São Paulo had spectacularly grown in stature and significance. As Sevcenko writes, "From a peripheral nucleus composed of a free-floating population, it became the most dynamic economic pole of the country and its political center, the place where the destiny of the Republic was decided."[15] The cinema was bound up with these transformations. The first screening of the medium took place in São Paulo's center on August 7, 1896.[16] The session was attended by politicians, dignitaries, and journalists, who watched a number of European films including Lumière's *Arrival of a Train at a Station*. The next day a writer for the newspaper *O Estado* praised the cinematograph's "illusion of reality."[17] Filmmakers soon capitalized on the cinema's realism, projecting everyday scenes of São Paulo. The first film made in the city was *O Círcolo Operário Italiano em São Paulo* (São Paulo's Italian Workers' Group, 1901). Directed by Affonso Segreto, the movie recorded Italian immigrants' celebrations of the anniversary of the unification of Italy. Other urban actualities followed, such as *Procissão do Corpo de Deus* (Procession of the Body of God; n. dir., 1903), *Carnaval Paulista* (São Paulo's carnival; n. dir, 1909) and *Inauguração da exposição de animais do posto zootécnico* (Inauguration of the exhibition of animals at the zoo; n. dir, 1910). Such films provided spectators with views of occasions taking place in the city, but, as Rubens Machado Jr. notes, "They displayed little concern with projecting the urban landscape."[18] In many of these early movies the city hardly appears at all, with the camera focusing on events and their elite participants.

These movies reveal what Machado refers to as "the predominance of a human over a physical São Paulo."[19] This human focus changed in the late 1920s as filmmakers increasingly began to turn their attention to the city that was being modernized. *Cinejornais,* or newsreels, particularly documented São Paulo's changing topography. Between 1921 and 1935, fifty-one newsreels were shown in São Paulo.[20] Zooming in on new buildings and sites, they provided spectators with panoramas of the developing city. The *cinejornais* consequently functioned as what Machado refers to as "a form of urban propaganda disguised as actuality news." This promotional mode became a lucrative business for producers. Filmmakers were "acutely aware that São Paulo's municipal authorities were profitable clients, and they accordingly engaged in an intense flair for urban publicity."[21] Directors recorded São Paulo's modern image in the hope of earning a living from their cinematic activities by securing contracts from the state and its sociopolitical elites. The "realism" of the *cinejornais* thus masked propagandistic objectives, as filmmakers set out to promote São Paulo in order to sell their cinematic labor.

São Paulo's newsreels acquired their own denomination: dubbed *cavações,* literally "excavations," they became known as a means by which domestic filmmakers could dig out a living for themselves from their surrounding landscape. Such efforts were a result of imported cinema's dominance of the exhibition sector. Faced with this hegemony, filmmakers focused on producing newsreels, like *Rossi Atualidades* (1921–31), *Atualidades Serrador* (1925–30), and *Revista Serrador* (1927), which were paid for by commercial organizations or state institutions.[22] Newsreels proliferated in São Paulo as filmmakers capitalized on the city's modernization by seeking out alliances with industrial or governmental organizations.[23] Randal Johnson writes that "this type of production sustained Brazilian cinema during these years."[24] It also often proved profitable. In 1921, Rossi Atualidades, established by Italian immigrant Gilberto Rossi, received a ten-year contract from São Paulo's governor Washington Luís to document the city's modernization.[25] The opening intertitle in the company's first newsreel for Washington Luís explicitly noted this intention, stating that it would "reveal the progress of the state of São Paulo" and serve as "propaganda." Rossi's newsreels provided spectators with numerous panoramas of the metropolis in an attempt to impress upon them its progress.

The *cavações* were thus "completely linked to the city's political and financial elite, on whom filmmakers were entirely dependent."[26] As a result, they were strongly marked by what Paulo Emílio Salles Gomes refers to as early Brazilian cinema's "ritual of power, as their production was linked to the social and political elite." [27] This ritual of power was not just "crystallized around important people," such as military leaders, presidents, journalists, and writers, as Gomes states; in the *cavacões* of São Paulo it was also crystallized in the space of city itself, in new buildings, roads and parks. [28]

This institutional use of film articulated and responded to changes taking place in the city's cinematic landscape. São Paulo's growth during the 1910s and '20s paralleled the rising popularity of the moving pictures. Moviegoing became a favored pastime of the city's expanding population, especially its rural and international transplants, and by the 1920s São Paulo had become Brazil's largest film market, surpassing the capital Rio. [29] In response, the 1920s saw an upsurge in the construction of movie theaters in the city. Grand picture palaces, like those in North America, were inaugurated, many located not in the fashionable center, which had previously housed the city's cinemas, but in populous working-class neighborhoods like Brás, Mooca, and Bom Retiro. [30] In 1927 Brás, for instance, had seven cinemas, while the city center had eight and the elite suburb of Santa Cecília only one. [31] Sheila Schvarzman notes that after World War I, film in São Paulo was increasingly "geared towards the suburbs and to the working class." [32]

As elsewhere in Brazil, US feature films dominated São Paulo's movie theaters and the screening of domestic movies was a rare phenomenon. Seeking to find a foothold in the exhibition market, filmmakers began to focus on local surroundings. The city became an important setting for fiction films like *Exemplo regenerador* (Regenerating example; dirs. Gilberto Rossi and José Medina, 1919) and *Fragmentos da vida* (Fragments of Life; dirs. Gilberto Rossi and José Medina, 1929), whose dramas incorporated new trams, roads, and buildings. This "cinema of locality" was key to the *cavações*. [33] Filmmakers like Rossi not only recorded local occasions in newsreels but also captured the cityscape. Along with carnival parades and government events, they documented urban sites, turning the metropolis into a cinematic event. This cinema forged a "vernacular modernism," in Miriam Hansen's term, which addressed domestic spectators by engaging with local modernization processes. Projecting the emerging metropolis's new identity, the newsreels enabled new inhabitants to visualize their own place in it, helping to forge them as modern urban citizens.

The *cavações* in this sense offer a particular example of the homology between cinema and the city. Kemeny and Lustig draw upon this homologous relationship in *São Paulo*. While modeled on European city-symphony films, their film also uses the form and content of the *cavações*, perhaps as an attempt to capitalize on the opportunities the genre could afford the filmmakers. In its adoption of the *cavação* the film evidences what Ismail Xavier calls the "rhetoric of the guided tour," mapping scenes of urban modernity. [34] In its touristic re-presentation, *São Paulo* produces and promotes a progressive image of the metropolis. It also creates a new symbolic subject in and for it, the workers, who emerge on the stage of visibility. In Kemeny and Lustig's film, the body of the workers and the body of the city are mutually constitutive, both fabricating an industrial vision of São Paulo's progress. São Paulo's working class were thus not just spectators of the Paulista city-symphony film but also its key subject.

São Paulo thus foregrounds a new relationship between the working class and the cinema in Brazil. Historians of early cinema in Europe and the United States have long highlighted the special relationship between early moving pictures and working people. For Hansen the movies carried the potential to function as an "alternative public sphere" for workers by furnishing an intersubjective context in which they could recognize fragments of their own experience. Although Kemeny and Lustig's film recognizes and includes São Paulo's working class, its potential to function as an alternative public sphere is complicated by the film's engagement with the form of the *cavação* and its ties to the city's social and political elite. While *São Paulo* privileges the city's working inhabitants, it contains and constrains them narratively in a hegemonic vision of an ordered and progressive modernity. In doing so it constitutes a mediating pedagogy between the elite's ideal vision of the city and the mental imaginaries of São Paulo's workers.

NEW BODIES IN/OF THE CITY

São Paulo begins slowly. We see the Paulista capital's empty streets, its closed shops and buildings. An early morning electric tram rushes toward the city center. Animated by the modern form of transport, São Paulo, at first asleep, gradually wakes up and comes to life. Streets are cleaned, stores are opened, and people make their way to work. More than an abstract formal consideration, *São Paulo*'s opening, with the tram ride into the city, enacts the daily commute of many Paulistas from outlying neighborhoods and reflects the fact that the metropolis is composed of working people. In this sense, the opening sequence builds upon the opening intertitle, which promises to present "a film of the city, a film that will show Paulistas the grandeur of this superb metropolis, which was vertiginously built thanks to the constructive energy of its people."

Kemeny and Lustig portray this constructive energy in a number of sequences that document individuals engaged in various forms of labor. We see men clocking into a factory and operating different industrial equipment—turning wheels and pulling levers. We witness them managing conveyor belts that manufacture food items and newspapers; we view women typing, street vendors hawking their wares, drivers chauffeuring people around the city, and construction workers erecting buildings. Working bodies abound in the film, which carefully charts the processes of work.

Images of labor were a common feature of São Paulo's *cavações,* which often recorded the working class, especially their relationship to machinery.[35] They were also prevalent in the European city-symphony films that influenced Kemeny and Lustig. Yet in *São Paulo*, unlike these other films, there are no long shots or medium shots of human bodies at work. The Paulista film instead zooms in on workers' hands moving precisely and purposefully as they operate different machines. Such scenes reveal a controlled and collective use of machinery. Individuals' actions are repetitive, rigid, and disciplined. Indeed, their activities appear identical and seem to replicate the mechanical movements of a machine, evidencing the productive force of their bodies.

This visual and rhythmic analogy between workers' actions and industrial equipment points to the influence of machinism in Kemeny and Lustig's film: that is, the belief that machines can alter reality and produce a new man.[36] This belief developed in the United States at the end of the nineteenth century and was linked to a new conception of the human body as a machine that was part of an industrial system of production. The productivist vision of the machine and the human body influenced the organization of work, giving rise to attempts by F. W. Taylor and others to measure and quantify labor power in order to harmonize people with the industrial workplace to ensure efficiency and productivity. This led to what Malcolm Turvey calls a "re-enchantment of technology . . . , the idea that the integration of human beings and technology would create a 'new people.'"[37] These new people would be able to coordinate their movements with the precision of a machine, and their daily lives would be governed by self-discipline.

As Meily Assbú Linhales points out, machinism, linked to social positivism, took root in 1920s Brazil, especially in São Paulo, where it was central in establishing the IDORT (Instituto de Organização Racional do Trabalho; Institute for the Rational Organization of Labor). Taking cues from Taylor, politicians and engineers like Armando de Sales Oliveira and Roberto Mange conceived of individuals as "mechanical parts . . . , capable of being prepared for industry." These conceptions were "indicators of modernizing precepts regarding the fabrication of . . . a disciplined body that was oriented to production and efficiency."[38] In Brazil, machinism thus articulated and responded to a desire to forge a modern industrial workforce.

Sevcenko notes that the belief in the body as a machine was so prevalent in 1920s São Paulo that it influenced the wider cultural landscape, becoming linked to "the physical mobilization of its population."[39] In this climate, "a sports fever" took over the city.[40] Journalists and writers endorsed athleticism as a civilizing endeavor that could produce a dynamic and disciplined body. Authorities too encouraged physical activities as a means of "fortifying the nation."[41] Jorge de Moraes, for instance, argued for obligatory physical education in schools and promoted the creation of recreational facilities as a means of "energizing characters," making them stronger and more efficient, or, as Linhales writes, "more capable of carrying out labor."[42] Aiding corporal discipline, sport was to create a new people who were in tune with the industrial rhythms of labor.

Work and sport come together in *São Paulo*. In addition to featuring images of laboring bodies, the film includes numerous sequences of sporting bodies. As elsewhere in the world, sport was a key subject of Brazil's early actualities, which frequently documented local sporting events, including soccer matches. Such team sports are notably absent in Kemeny and Lustig's movie, which zooms in on individuals doing athletic activities like swimming and running in their leisure time. In these sequences, women and especially men openly exhibit their corporal prowess for the camera. The camera does not focus on any particular part of the sportsmen's bodies; it shows them in their entirety. In doing so, it invites a fetishistic contemplation of the athletic bodies.

The film links São Paulo's sporting activities to ideas regarding its ability to forge a dynamic people, with one intertitle explicitly announcing that "sports culture forms new generations full of energy and strength." This strength is registered in the controlled movements of the sportsmen and women depicted, which, like those of the workers, appear almost machine-like. This impression is reinforced by the artful film editing, which manipulates shots of bodies in motion. Trickery abounds in these sporting sequences. Kemeny and Lustig utilize reverse motion in their depiction of divers at a swimming pool, for instance, revealing men and women diving backwards out of the water. They also deploy split screens and superimpositions to depict a multitude of sporting actions in one time and space. Such tricks rupture the film's illusion of reality and call attention to the machinations of the cinema, revealing a homology between the fabrication of bodies and the fabrication of film. Athletic exhibitionism is thus an iteration of the corporeal dynamics of a new people and also of the visual dynamics of the modern medium of film, both of which can be controlled and modified, or "assembled under a new law."[43]

Kemeny and Lustig's projection of "new people" is present in other scenes. The film includes a lengthy sequence of São Paulo's state penitentiary, which was inaugurated by Washington Luís in 1912 as part of his wider modernization of the penal system.[44] An intertitle introduces the prison as an "institute of regeneration unequaled in the world," adding, "Here the prisoner is not condemned but morally infirm and will be cured by the system of rehabilitation to which he will be submitted." The role of the prison is not to punish criminals but to rehabilitate them by changing their behavior. Consequently, the sequence elides the predictable visual iconography of incarceration that Alison Griffiths notes was a feature of many US and European carceral silent movies.[45] There are no barred windows, wire fences, chains, prison stripes, or aimless bodies moving in exercise yards or assembled in mess halls. Nor are there shots of corporal punishment or any attempts to portray what Griffiths calls "incarceration's recalibration of space."[46] In fact, prison cells, obvious symbols of containment and deprivation, are absent in this sequence of *São Paulo*. The penitentiary is projected not as a punitive space but as a space of reform, in which control is enacted through labor rather than corporeal punishment. The sequence depicts prisoners laboring in workshops, manufacturing shoes, furniture, and clothes. It also shows them carrying out agricultural work. The grim realities of incarceration are absent; instead, convicts are little different from the workers outside, and the penitentiary appears as a reflection of the city beyond its walls.

The prison is thus depicted as a space of correction that regulates the criminal body and changes it by making it work. Labor is imbued with a transformative power that can mold individuals and make them useful. An intertitle announces added advantages to the penitentiary's reformist agenda: "The fruits of the labor of those who redeem their errors contribute in a noteworthy way to meeting the costs of the institute." Reform is productive *and* profitable, and the carceral system is positioned as an ancillary to modern capital accumulation.

The penal colony's role in capital accumulation is, the film shows, dependent on the efficient administration of the accumulation of the men's physical labor. In addition to working, the inmates are represented parading and doing exercises in formation, their ordered movements an obvious symbol of their physical regulation. These scenes are bound up with the fetish value of seeing the convicts embody the principles of penal control and discipline through marching. They also reinforce the penitentiary's militaristic regime. An intertitle tells us that the correction system "instills discipline as an element of order and makes inmates comprehend that discipline will enable them to succeed when the prison doors are opened to them." The prison's military order therefore turns the inmate into an individual capable of withstanding the discipline of modern society outside the prison. Labor and discipline, we are told, "redeem the mistakes committed" and "lead the man to social communion." Rather than segregation, the penitentiary produces and aids social integration. This is melodramatically depicted in scenes of family visits, which underscore the inmates' relationships to people beyond the space of the prison. One scene, captioned "An Emotional Hour," includes one of the film's few facial close-ups. Zooming in on the face of a convict holding his child, the close-up triggers an imaginary glimpse into the prisoner's interiority, shattering the otherwise distant and objective style of the film. In doing so, *São Paulo* points to the prison's power of self-transformation.

The city's educational institutions are also portrayed as producing new subjects. *São Paulo*'s day starts not just with men and women going to work but also with children going to school. Discipline is paramount in these sequences, which echo the depiction of regimented actions in both the prison and the workplace. Periodic shots of clocks intersperse the scenes, pointing to the students' punctuality. The young boys and girls do not linger or swagger on their journey. Accompanied by parents, they purposefully make their way to morning lessons, entering the building in an orderly line. The same order is evident inside the school building: seated at neat rows of desks, the students work diligently. Lunchtime too is an ordered affair. When one young boy drops trash on the playground floor, a peer admonishes him and he immediately places his litter in a bin, his civilized action caught in close-up. This object lesson in good behavior is clearly rehearsed. Gazing directly at the camera, the students perform civility for spectators. This performativity ruptures *São Paulo*'s realism. It also represents a stark departure from the European city-symphonies' lexicon, which aimed to capture the authentic life of the city unawares.[47] The scene purposefully stages schools' social pedagogy, demonstrating their power to proactively instill civil behavior in the city's future workers.

São Paulo, then, depicts state institutions as inculcating individuals in the forms of civic order that are deemed to be foundational for the modern industrial metropolis.[48] In doing so, the film normalizes public codes of conduct and promotes the institutions responsible for instilling them. It consequently functions as propaganda for local mechanisms associated with São Paulo's progress, presenting what Xavier calls "a boastful discourse" in its images and explanatory captions, which "idealize institutions and extol the state."[49] While *São Paulo* dialogues with Ruttmann and other modernist movies, it also conforms to the *cavações*' propagandistic parameters and performs the ideological labor of official institutions and industries. The film, in this sense, reinforces hegemonic ideas regarding the space of the metropolis, translating them into cinematic views.

In its propagandistic rhetoric, *São Paulo* elides the real experiences of São Paulo's workers and their material conditions of life. Social differences and relations, however, *are* at times glimpsed at in the film. Street scenes are marked moments of class differentiation. Kemeny and Lustig show the different ways people get to work: on foot, by public transportation, by car. They also cut between distinct ways that São Paulo's inhabitants have lunch: a packed lunch on the street, a snack at a *botequim*, a visit to an elegant restaurant. Distinctions are also legible in people's dress, from the formal suits of officer workers to the collarless shirts of street vendors. Such differences, however, are unified by views of the city that bring everyone together. In street scenes office workers and vendors mingle, forming an indistinguishable crowd. The film's projection of the people as a collective body of workers obscures social differences and elides social conflicts. As Machado writes, São Paulo "is shown to have no disjuncture and counterpoint."[50]

This projection of harmony makes *São Paulo* different from foreign city-films, especially *Berlin*. Walter Natter writes that Ruttmann made "the depiction of a highly contested urban place its central focus."[51] James Donald too foregrounds what he refers to as the German cinematic-symphony's "dark spaces," which undermine its utopian celebration of Berlin.[52] Portraits of prostitutes plying their trade and a woman committing suicide point to urban anonymity and isolation. Isolation and fragmentation are not present in Kemeny and Lustig's film, which instead constructs and celebrates an image of São Paulo as a place that is fabricated by the collective efforts of its workers and their disciplined actions and labor.

Interpellated by and integrated into the space of the modern industrial city, the working inhabitants are thus homogenized, their social differences and inequalities disavowed. Workers are united as beneficiaries of and contributors to a progress that is identified with the state. A particular scene is apposite here. Among images of workers going about their daily work, Kemeny and Lustig zoom in on a beggar. Using camera trickery, the movie superimposes a giant hand that descends from the sky to give the mendicant money, while a caption announces, "Prosperity opens its cornucopia to those on whom fortune has not shone." The message is clear: São Paulo's progress benefits everyone, and the state's economic advancement will overcome all social differences. The state and its working people are thus united through a common goal of progress. The film consequently enables the urban masses to see themselves on the screen not as working individuals but as part of a larger progressive narrative that is identified with the city of São Paulo.

THE COHERENT CITY

São Paulo's unity is not restricted to workers; it is also concretized in the modern cityscape. The film consistently depicts different parts of the metropolis as interdependent and interconnected via networks of transportation, circulation, and exchange. As the film and the day start, we see trams and buses crisscross the urban landscape, allowing people to traverse the entire city, from its outlying suburbs to the center. The dynamic interchange of transportation is reinforced in kaleidoscopic shots that bring different places together on the screen on one time, projecting the dynamic heterogeneity of the city as a whole (figure 29). Products too navigate the metropolis's vast geography. Vans zip around the city delivering goods to stores and neighborhood homes; street vendors run around different areas selling their wares to an array of consumers. One of the first sequences shows a machine operator churning out bottles of milk for the day's breakfast. Kemeny and Lustig then chart the product's movement from the factory to suburban homes, via delivery trucks. In doing so the directors effectively map the city through the circulation of its industrial products, making visible the supply chain of the product and its domestic consumption. Production and consumption form a single unit in the fabrication of São Paulo, where modern industry is a connecting force.

São Paulo thus emerges as a circulatory system defined by accumulation and exchange, and as such a materialization of the time-space compression associated with modernity. Streets, described in *São Paulo* as arteries of the city, are key to this. More than mere setting, they bring eclectic places and people together, creating an organic whole. Traveled by a never-ending stream of trams, buses, and cars, São Paulo's streets are defined by circulation and constant movement, overcoming any static idea of place. Within the city-film itself there is no place of home, as in interior family settings. Residences are shot only from the outside, adding to the

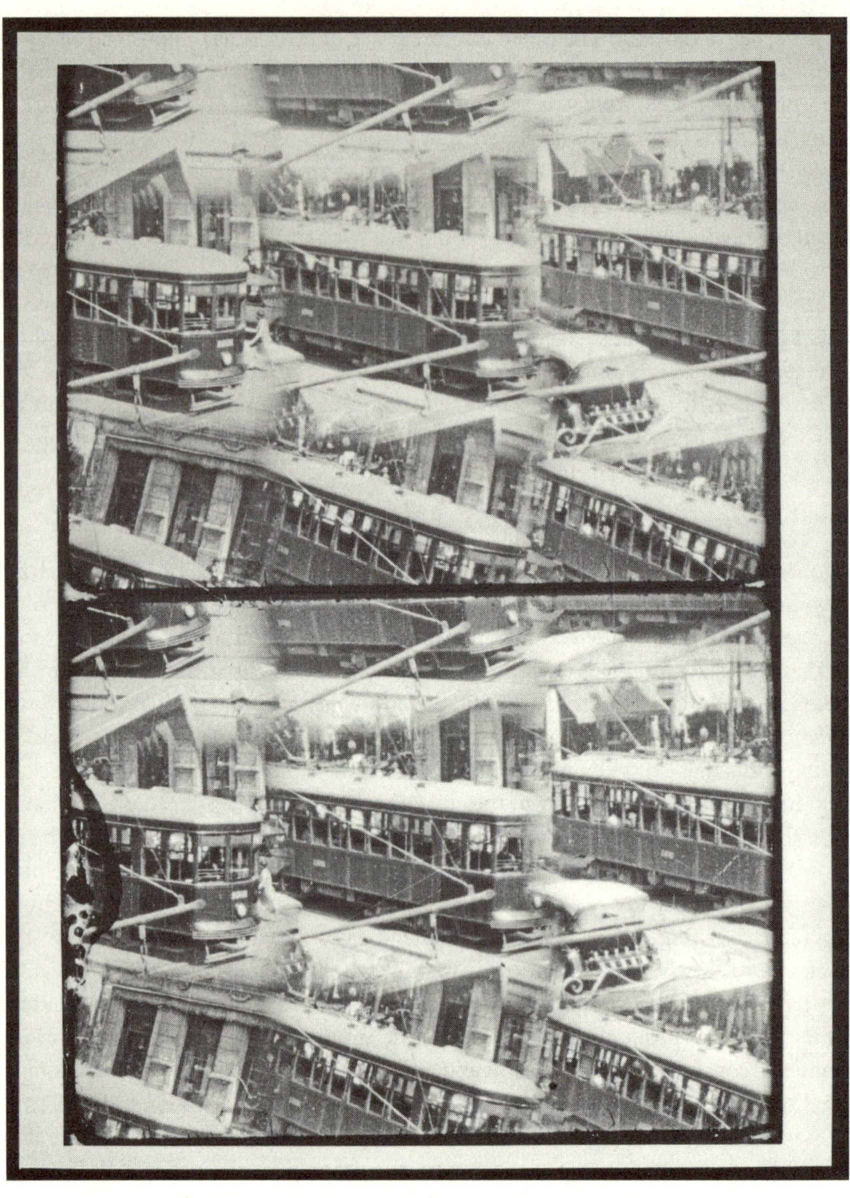

FIGURE 29. Kaleidoscopic images in *São Paulo, Symphony of a Metropolis*, 1929. Acervo Cinemateca Brasileira, Secretaria do Audiovisual do Ministério da Cultura.

sense of perpetual motion. The city is constantly on the move. Like the European city-films, *São Paulo* thus offers an illustration of the acceleration of everyday life brought about by modern industry and the pure sensation of speed in transportation networks. The kaleidoscope effects, in which a multitude of trams and buses fill the screen simultaneously, exaggerate this condensation of space and communicate the rapidity of urban living and its cult of distraction.

Communication networks play a role in condensing the city space. Kemeny and Lustig chart the production, circulation, and consumption of morning and afternoon newspapers, whose distribution spans the vast city. Benedict Anderson has illustrated how the newspaper's mass circulation created a collective experience of simultaneity that Benjamin termed "a homogenous empty time." In *São Paulo,* such homogeneity is evident in the press's wide urban reach, which pulls the city's vast landscape together spatially and temporally. The radio, telephone, and telegraph also appear as connecting forces. High-angle shots of a radio megaphone towering over the city stress the media's all-encompassing reach.

High-angle panoramic shots feature prominently in *São Paulo.* Placed on the top of buildings, the camera often slowly scans the urban horizon, bringing the city into full view and producing a coherent image of the metropolis. This camerawork functions as what Xavier calls "an expressive visualization of an economy of scale," which "admires and creates for admiration the amounts of places and things implicated in the modern industrial city."[53] Such descriptive shots aim to produce a gasp of admiration and appreciation of the vast attractions of the industrial metropolis. The horizontality of these shots is matched with verticality, as the camera gazes not just across the landscape but also down at it, a visual sign of the heights the metropolis has reached. São Paulo's verticality is stressed in numerous tilts up and down of skyscrapers being constructed, revealing the city's powerful conquest of space. These vertical and panoramic shots exemplify a regime of spatial and visual control of the city. The film's ubiquitous movement across the breadth of the metropolis adds to this sense of control, as it seems to render the entire city transparent, obliterating any obscurity, or to use Donald's term, dark spaces. *São Paulo*'s montage of fragmented and distracted views is subsumed by a more conventional descriptive camerawork that brings the city into complete view as a totality.

The spectator is fully woven into this will to visibility. While *São Paulo* offers its spectators different views of the city, it undoes the effect of its multiperspectival field by making spectators identify with the camera as the locus of an all-seeing eye. Indeed, the movie's unpsychologized sequences and lack of close-ups thwart identification with the workers depicted, who remain objects of contemplation for the lens's ubiquitous gaze. The camera consequently operates as what Jean-Louis Baudry refers to as "a sort of relay," inviting the spectator to identify "less with what is represented, the spectacle itself, than with what stages the spectacle, makes it seen."[54] Kemeny and Lustig's film thus promotes what Christian Metz calls primary identification rather than secondary identification, producing the identification of one's own gaze with that of the camera. This identification process stabilizes the spectator's distracted perceptual field and allows him or her to occupy a unified and coherent position vis-à-vis the flow of urban images on the screen. The camera's visual plenitude is shared by the viewer, who is brought into the coherent space forged by the film and delights in visual mastery over the space gazed at.

In its ample use of panoramas and tilts, *São Paulo* provides the spectator with time to contemplate the urban space depicted in order to admire it. This contemplation clearly aims to produce a sentiment of pride in the city displayed. Instilling pride in spectators was a key objective of the film, evidenced in its effusive captions. An initial intertitle states that the film "is a preliminary piece of work but one that will delight those who see themselves in it. Brazilians, you will feel the symphony of São Paulo in this film, which is your symphony!" Promotional material also described *São Paulo* as "the film that all Brazilians will watch with pride and enthusiasm because it depicts the very immense and stunning symphony of the agitated life of the new Brazil!" This excessive rhetoric is reflected in the slow contemplative shots of urban locations that aim to instill civic pride in its viewers.

Such contemplation is very different from the distracted form of reception elicited by the film's montage of urban vistas, inspired by Ruttmann. The extensive use of *São Paulo*'s intertitles adds to this difference. Unlike European city-symphony films, *São Paulo* makes extensive use of explanatory titles. A total of 183 captions carefully cohere the disparate urban images, uniting them in a narrative that tells a story of São Paulo's development. The film thus disciplines the distracted perceptions of the metropolis and of the cinema by utilizing a narrative norm whose teleological impetus is progress. Viewers are expected not just to enjoy following this narrative but also, as the opening intertitle states, "to delight in seeing themselves in it." Spectators are thus willed to see themselves reflected in the city-symphony, to narcissistically visualize themselves as similar to the disciplined bodies of the workers and urban citizens projected.

The extensive use of intertitles thus carefully guides the film's urban rhetoric for viewers and helps to interpellate them into the metropolis's vision of progress. The intertitles therefore contain any residuals or excesses that could counter *São Paulo*'s coherent and hegemonic view of the city. As Xavier observes, such residuals were often unwittingly exposed in São Paulo's *cavações,* which revealed the realities of poverty and their distribution among different classes. Panoramas displayed a mixture of new cars and old carts. Long shots showed distracted and undisciplined bodies, working children wearing dirty clothes and barefoot, and unhygienic landscapes.[55] The intrusion of "uncivilized" objects, peoples, and places into these films led contemporary commentators to dismiss the *cavações. Cinearte* critic Adhemar

Gonzaga, for example, severely critiqued the newsreels whose unscripted realism could allow for the incursion of unmodern images. The critic condemned "the dirty medium of the *cavadores*" and dismissed the filmmakers as "pirates, imbeciles who are ignorant of cinema and are even thieves."[56]

Such uncivilized sights are absent in *São Paulo,* whose guided rhetoric takes viewers on a disciplined tour of São Paulo's spaces of order and progress. Working-class neighborhoods like Brás and Mooca are absent in the movie, and there is no visual depiction of urban violence, the city's social movements, or trade unions. Instead the film restricts itself to focusing on industries, state institutes, beautified streets, buildings, modern forms of communication, and elite suburbs. Shots of the workplace are also carefully guided to avoid any socially conflictive elements. Working people are elided as the camera zooms in on their laboring hands, and the portrayal of poor workers and exploitative working conditions is avoided. Contingent happenings and all their details are absent in Kemeny and Lustig's movie, whose organization evidences principles of careful selection. Indeed, there is very little spontaneity in *São Paulo,* which is geared toward celebrating a proud vision of the metropolis's progress rather than capturing the city unawares.

São Paulo's cinema of locality thus promotes the state's narrative of progress, firmly inscribing the metropolis within a broader national ideology. The film purposely links the metropolis's history to wider Brazilian history in a sequence portraying the Museu de Ipiranga, named after its location near where Emperor Pedro I proclaimed Brazilian independence on the banks of the Ipiranga river. The sequence takes the viewer on a tour of the museum's artwork, including Pedro Américo's 1888 painting *Independência ou morte* (Independence or death), which represents the proclamation of Brazil's independence from Portugal. As the camera settles on Américo's painting, the piece literally comes to life. Actors recreate the battle for independence led by Paulista politician José Bonifácio de Andrade e Silva. This dramatic departure from the city's present time and space is unambiguous: the Brazilian nation was born in São Paulo, as Kemeny and Lustig vividly show viewers. The Paulista film thus reveals São Paulo's role as a driving force in the country's national narrative and places the metropolis as a defining agent in Brazil's history.

The scene has clear pedagogic intentions. Dramatizing the city's memory, it teaches spectators, including new migrants and immigrants, about São Paulo's national heritage and patrimony, helping to instill civic pride. This was especially important given class conflicts associated with the conditions of industrialization and the radical activism of new immigrant laborers. Strikes protesting low wages and poor working conditions mobilized thousands of laborers in São Paulo in 1917, 1918, 1919, and 1920, openly challenging power structures and creating conflicts in the city. The film's recreation of the past helps mobilize workers as part of an urban community, bringing them collectively into São Paulo's national history. The didactic scene thus masks the tumultuous class politics of São Paulo by focusing the eye on the aesthetic representation of the metropolis's role in Brazil's historical formation.

The sequence illustrates ways in which the film interpellates the people into São Paulo's time-space, figuring them as part of its progressive teleology. This is explicit in *São Paulo*'s ending. As dusk falls, an intertitle announces: "Shadows grow. The day ends in a tumultuous activity, as it did yesterday and as it will tomorrow." The caption is followed by a shot of a worker gazing at the horizon. A caption reads, "The man who subjugates nature according to the will of iron accompanying the force of progress contemplates his superb work." Another intertitle then speaks of the city's future: "Their fecund labor will make a new Brazil emerge, bigger, more powerful, upon whose immense, active, and glorious territorial expansion quiver the most beautiful and strongest of flags." This is followed by a shot of an hourglass, which dissolves into a spinning globe, dissolving in turn into the image of the globe on the Brazilian flag, on which is written the nation's positivist ideology: "Order and Progress." It is this ideology that brings the film's multiple views of São Paulo and its workers together in a coherent narrative.

São Paulo's urban celebration was lauded in the press. Critic Guilherme de Almeida wrote that it was "the first national film that has managed not to embarrass us, but on the contrary to make us proud." He goes on to proclaim the film to be "splendid propaganda for us! It is much better than any publicity than anyone can read, any discourse anyone can hear, or poster anyone can see. This intelligent film will be understood and felt in other lands, by other people. The state government would do well to acquire it to exhibit at fairs, exhibitions, and any foreign places where São Paulo should appear."[57] Praising the film's propagandistic qualities, Almeida sees its value in promoting São Paulo and recommends its purchase by the state. *São Paulo* can thus contribute to the city's progress by attracting a foreign gaze and interest. This attraction rests on the city's progressive image and its future promise, which is produced by the disciplined bodies of its workers, inculcated by the regulatory mechanisms of the city's industrial and state institutions.

The workers' visible entrance onto the screen in this film therefore in no way carries the potential to forge what Hansen calls an alternative public sphere. Their place in the Brazilian city-symphony projects the hegemonic positivist discourse of national progress, eschewing the critical nationalism that modernist writers and Mário Peixoto saw in the medium of cinema. The film's political conformism is fully in keeping with the *cavações*' conservative stance. Given the dominance of foreign film, local producers were unable to finance their trade through returns on exhibition and so relied on creating links to São Paulo's upper classes that were keen to promote their names, organizations, and institutions in newsreels. As Bernardet writes, domestic filmmakers were entirely dependent on the social and political elites: "The ideology that underlines these films is that of the elite," and their values are "official ones."[58] Such loyalties benefited these filmmakers or *cava-dores*. For these largely first-generation immigrants, the *cavações* became means of great social mobility.[59] By projecting official images of modernity, the *cavações* enabled immigrant directors like Kemeny and Lustig to make a cinematic living for themselves *and* assert their affiliation to Brazil. In creating São Paulo's image of industrial discipline, they thus fabricated their own role in the city.

Postscript

Toward New Cinematic Foundations

Adalberto Kemeny and Rodolfo Lustig's dependency on São Paulo's industrial and political elite to produce *São Paulo, Symphony of a Metropolis* was not exceptional. By the late 1920s American films occupied 80 percent of the Brazilian market, leaving little space for local production. Without full access to the domestic market, producers could not achieve adequate returns on their investments, and consequently the process of capital accumulation within the industry was stifled, as was production. Even the temporary disruption of the coming of sound did not end Hollywood's ubiquity in Brazil. In fact, the arrival of the talkies further entrenched US cinema's presence. The high costs of acquiring synchronized equipment meant that local investment lagged behind Hollywood and allowed the North American industry to maintain its hegemony. By the early 1930s, North American dubbing and subtitling techniques had proved popular among Brazilian audiences, and Hollywood increased its presence in the country. In the face of North America's dominance, domestic production was unstable and unprofitable, and local producers were mostly unable to attain a sufficient return on their investments to allow them to develop on a larger scale. *Cavações*, which were paid for by industrial and political organizations, were thus the most viable option for those, like Kemeny and Lustig, seeking to make a living from filmmaking. Support from sources beyond the film industry was essential.

Given this situation, it is hardly surprising that the 1920s saw calls for state support of national cinema. In 1924, Mário Behring, who would become a journalist for the film magazine *Cinearte*, suggested that the Republican government should take measures to support a national film industry.[1] Behring's concern did not extend to the production of feature films. Instead he favored documentaries and newsreels that would provide propaganda for Brazil. Such films, he argued, would be pedagogically useful in the attempt to stimulate good working habits and would help to forge a civilized citizenry.[2] For Behring, cinematic production and spectatorship were linked to the instilling of patriotism, something that would clearly benefit the modernizing Republican state, so he called upon the state to institute official policies regarding a national cinema. Stressing the important role that film could play in the nation, in 1925 Behring, along with Adhemar Gonzaga, called upon the government to revise customs tariffs on raw film stock, whose costs equaled those of printed film stock. They also argued for the compulsory exhibition of one Brazilian film per month.[3]

Such calls were not officially heeded by the Republican regime. While filmmaking endeavors were embraced by Brazil's social and political elite and were bound up with the national discourse of progress, the state had virtually no active role in the film industry during this period. Nevertheless, as this book has showed, cinematic activities, both on and off the screen, were closely linked to the Republic's project of modernity, as the medium played a role in projecting and forging the foundations of a civilized nation. This projection was not straightforward, as films and filmmakers tempered the desire for a worldly modernity to Brazil's social traditions, revealing the complex mediations and hybridity that Barbero and Canclini have theorized as key to Latin American modernity. Films and film culture produced during the First Republic, then, evidence and allow us to apprehend the hybrid formations of Brazilian modernity, notwithstanding the regime's lack of intervention in the film industry.

The absence of state intervention in Brazilian cinema changed in the 1930s, which inaugurated a new phase in the development of a domestic cinema. The year 1930 saw the demise of the First Republic in a coup that brought Getúlio Vargas's populist government to power and would soon see the establishment of the authoritarian *Estado Novo* or New State. The coup consolidated the social and political power of the urban middle sectors and the industrial bourgeoisie. The "New" Republic that ensued witnessed a concentration of power in the hands of the federal government that had been absent in the more dispersed federalism of the First Republic. It created conditions, in short, for the transformation of the agriculturally based oligarchic state of 1889–1930 to the bourgeois state of 1930–45.[4]

Over the ensuing years the Vargas regime tightened its grip on the media, including film. Recognizing cinema's pedagogical potential and the role that it could play in transmitting a national ideology and fostering a sense of belonging to the national community, Vargas passed the first legislation supporting national cinema, making it compulsory to screen one Brazilian short in each movie program. In a 1934 speech given as president of the Associação Cinematográfica de Produtores Brasileiros (Brazilian Film Producers Association), Vargas stated, "Cultivating the land, polishing the intelligence and tempering the character of its citizens, adapting them to the necessities of their habitat, is the primary duty of the

State. Among the most useful educational agents available to the modern state is the cinema." He added, "Film can be truly essential. It will bring together, through its incisive vision of facts, the different human nuclei dispersed in the vast territory of the Republic. The cinema will become a book of luminous images though which our coastal and rural populations will learn to love Brazil, and it will raise confidence in the fortunes of our fatherland. For the many who do not read, it will be the perfect pedagogical tool, the easiest and most impressive. For the educated, for those responsible for the success of our administration, it will be an admirable teaching method."[5] Vargas thus saw film as a means of reaching the country's illiterate and as an instrument of national unification.

Responding to the cinema's educational and patriotic potential, in 1937 Vargas established the INCE (Instituto Nacional de Cinema Educativo; National Institute for Educational Cinema), under the leadership of Edgar Roquette-Pinto, one of a series of measures aimed at co-opting popular performers and actors in the construction of a nationalist ideology. With its slogan "Educational cinema in Brazil must be the school for those who never went to school," it produced pedagogical films for distribution in schools and cultural institutions across Brazil.[6] The regime also made it compulsory for movie theaters to show these short movies before every screening of a commercial feature film.

Film was thus officially adopted during Vargas's New Republic as a means of inculcating nationalistic values and unifying the country's vast territory and distinct cultures. It was also used to project the nation to foreign spectators. Many of INCE's documentaries traveled abroad to world's fairs, showcasing Brazil's accomplishments in modern industry, as well as its tropical exuberance. In 1939 the Departamento de Imprensa e Propaganda (Department of Press and Propaganda) was established to promote the production of films that valorized the natural beauty of the nation and the achievements of the state. This projection was central to the *Cinejornal Brasileiro* newsreels, which centered on a patriotic discourse around the figure of Vargas. The shorts recorded official celebrations and national events attended by the president and other state officials. Another dominant theme was modernity, with the films showcasing industrial progress and public works, like the construction of dams, highways, and road tunnels. They also displayed the country's prolific resources and its sugar and coffee industries. Cinematic production during the New Republic thus continued to project the "ritual of power," that is, the depiction of the country's presidents and politicians, and the "splendid cradle," the celebration of the country's natural wonders, that according to Paulo Emílio Salles Gomes was key to Brazil's silent films. Thus while the Vargas regime ushered in a new era in Brazilian cinema, in which the film industry became directly implicated in the concerns of the state, its visual syntax had already been founded during the First Republic.

Yet it is important to point out that the visual politics of the New State differed from those of the First Republic. The First Republic saw the first hegemonic attempt to articulate the nation as modern, but it did not interpellate the people in ways remotely comparable to the Vargas regime, which relied heavily on cinema, as its direct intervention in the film industry testifies. Prior to the coup that brought Vargas to power, the people were not projected as beholders of the nation. While films and film culture articulated the discourses of the social and political elite, they were not populist. Filmmakers and journalists writing for magazines like *Cinearte* excluded the popular from their modern cinematic visions, which carefully adapted progress to the desires of the traditional elite. A major change took place in Brazilian cinema after 1930 as popular culture appeared onscreen. Indeed, along with newsreels and documentaries disseminating images of the nation, popular films proliferated, benefiting from the government's interest in the medium. Key here were the *chanchadas,* musical comedies that drew on the popular carnival and the radio, two media used to "propagate the nationalist and centralizing ideas of the Vargas period."[7]

The *chanchadas'* links to carnival expanded on the tradition of the *carnavalescos,* or carnival films, that were popular in Rio during the belle epoque, discussed in chapter 3. They also and at the same time exploited Hollywood musicals that were well known in Brazil. Movies like *Alô alô Brasil* (dir. Wallace Downey, 1935) and *Alô alô carnaval!* (dir. Adhemar Gonzaga, 1926) promoted carnival songs and incorporated stars of the radio, while also adopting the template of the North American musical. Recognizing the inability to perfectly copy North America's technically superior musicals, however, the *chanchadas* eschewed elite cosmopolitan visions to focus instead on everyday life, stories, and people.[8] The films thus not only incorporated the popular but also appealed to everyday shared experiences and emotions. With their slapstick and saucy humor the *chanchadas* appealed to everyone, men and women, children and adults. In doing so they helped to forge the collective sentiment that was key to Vargas's fostering of *brasilidade.* As Catherine Benamou observes, the *chanchadas* were in synchrony, at least nominally, with the cultural policies of the central state apparatus.[9]

So just as a new character, the people-nation, made its appearance on the political stage, so the people entered the cinematic screen. Kemeny and Lustig's film is significant in this respect. Filmed in 1929, the film portrays São Paulo's workers, including laborers, in its collective vision of the industrial metropolis. Although the film disavows their particular social and material realities, it nevertheless represents a change in Brazil's cinematic landscape as it brings into focus a new actor previously marginalized by filmmakers. This shift testifies to the emergence of a new cinematic era for Brazil that accompanied a rewriting of the European-inflected narrative of progress, which was the very foundation of the First Republic. The year 1930 thus sees the formation of a new relationship between cinema and modernity in Brazil, revealing a new narrative in and for the country's film history and bringing with it new foundational films.

NOTES

INTRODUCTION

1. João do Rio, "Cinematógrafo de letras," in *Cinematógrafo* (Porto: Chadron, 1909), x.

2. *Jornal do Brasil,* July 10, 1896, n. pag.; *A Notícia,* July 9, 1896, n. pag.

3. Advertisement for film show in Máximo Barro, "As primeiras projecções em São Paulo," *Filme Cultura* 47 (1986): 57.

4. Leo Charney and Vanessa Schwartz, introduction to *Cinema and the Invention of Modern Life* (Berkeley: University of California Press, 1995), 1.

5. Ana M. López, "Early Cinema and Modernity in Latin America," *Cinema Journal* 40, no. 1 (2000): 49.

6. Néstor García Canclini, *Hybrid Cultures: Strategies for Entering and Leaving Modernity,* trans. Christopher L. Chiappari (Minneapolis: University of Minnesota Press, 1995), 46.

7. Angel Rama, *The Lettered City,* trans. John Charles Chasteen (Durham, NC: Duke University Press, 1996), 99.

8. Jeffrey Needell, "The Domestic Civilizing Mission: The Cultural Role of the State in Brazil, 1808–1930," *Luso-Brazilian Review* 36, no. 1 (1999): 1.

9. Nicolau Sevcenko, "Peregrinations, Visions and the City: From Canudos to Brasília, the Backlands Become the City and the City Becomes the Backlands," in *Through the Kaleidoscope: The Experience of Modernity in Latin America,* ed. Vivien Schelling and trans. Lorraine Leu (New York: Verso, 2000), 75–108.

10. Needell, "Domestic Civilizing Mission," 5.

11. Roberto Schwarz, *As idéias fora do lugar* (São Paulo: Companhia das Letras, 2014).

12. Canclini, *Hybrid Cultures,* 47.

13. Jesús Martín Barbero, *Communication, Culture and Hegemony: From the Media to Mediations* (London: Sage Publications, 1993).

14. Brito Broca, *A vida literária no Brasil, 1900*, 2nd ed. (Rio de Janeiro: J. Olympio, 1960).

15. Miriam Hansen, "Fallen Women, Rising Stars, New Horizons: Shanghai Silent Film as Vernacular Modernism," *Film Quarterly* 54, no. 1 (2000): 10–22.

16. Miriam Hansen, "Early Silent Cinema: Whose Public Sphere?," *New German Critique* 29 (1983): 147–84.

17. For more on the factory gate genre, see Tom Gunning, "Pictures of Crowd Splendor: The Mitchell and Kenyon Factory Gate Films," in *The Lost World of Mitchell and Kenyon: Edwardian Britain on Film*, ed. Vanessa Toulmin, Simon Popple, and Patrick Russell (London: BFI, 2004), 49–58.

18. Francisco Foot Hardman notes such abstractions in photographs of factories during this period in *Nem patria, nem patrão! Memória operária, cultura e literatura no Brasil* (São Paulo: UNESP, 2002), 61.

19. In Vicente de Paula Araújo, *A bela época do cinema brasileiro* (São Paulo: Perspectiva, 1976), 107–8.

20. In ibid., 151.

21. Paulo Emílio Salles Gomes, "A expressão social dos filmes documentais no cinema mudo brasileiro (1898–1930)," in *Paulo Emílio—Um intellectual na linha de frente: Coletânea de textos de Paulo Emílio Salles Gomes*, ed. Carlos Calil and Maria Teresa Machado (São Paulo: Editora Brasiliense; Rio de Janeiro: Embrafilme, 1986), 325.

22. Ibid., 326.

23. Jens Andermann, *The Optic of the State: Visuality and Power in Argentina and Brazil* (Pittsburgh, PA: University of Pittsburgh Press, 2007), 210.

24. P. Gomes, "Expressão social," 324.

25. Ibid., 324.

26. Jean Claude Bernardet, *Cinema brasileiro: Propostas para uma história*, 2nd ed. (São Paulo: Companhia de Bolso, 2009), 103.

27. Eduardo Morettin, "Cinema e estado no Brasil: A Exposição Internacional do Centenário da Independência em 1922 e 1923," *Novos Estudos CEBRAP*, no. 89 (2011): 137–48.

28. "Viagem ao Brasil," *Estado de São Paulo*, October 23, 1928, 7.

29. Benedict Anderson, *Imagined Communities: Reflections on the Origin and Spread of Nationalism* (New York: Verso, 1991).

30. Doris Sommer, *Foundational Fictions: The National Romances of Latin America* (Berkeley: University of California Press, 1991).

31. Ibid., 9.

32. Renato Ortiz, *A moderna tradição brasileira* (São Paulo: Brasiliense, 1988).

33. Sommer, *Foundational Films*, 19.

34. André Bazin, "In Defense of Mixed Cinema," in *What Is Cinema?*, vol. 1, trans. Tim Barnard (Montreal: Caboose, 2009), 53.

35. Esther Gabara, *Errant Modernism: The Ethos of Photography in Mexico and Brazil* (Durham, NC: Duke University Press, 2008), 26.

36. For more on these discussions, see Randal Johnson, "Brazilian Modernism: An Idea Out of Place?" in *Modernism and Its Margins: Modernity from Spain and Latin America*, ed. Anthony Geist and José Monleon (New York: Garland Press, 1999), 188–214.

37. Dilip Gaonkar, ed., *Alternative Modernities* (Durham, NC: Duke University Press, 2001).

38. See Arjun Appadurai, *Modernity at Large: Cultural Dimensions of Globalization* (Minneapolis: University of Minnesota Press, 1996), and Andres Huyssen, "Geographies of Modernism in a Globalizing World," *New German Critique* 34, no. 1 (2007): 6–18.

39. Zhang Zhen, *An Amorous History of the Silver Screen: Shanghai Cinema, 1896–1937* (Chicago: University of Chicago Press, 2005), xv.

40. Jennifer M. Bean and Diane Negra, introduction to *A Feminist Reader in Early Cinema*, ed. Jennifer M. Bean and Diane Negra (Durham, NC: Duke University Press, 2002), 8.

41. Alison Butler, "New Film Histories and the Politics of Location," *Screen* 33, no. 4 (1992): 425.

42. José Inácio de Melo Souza, *Imagens do passado: São Paulo e o Rio de Janeiro nos primórdios do cinema* (São Paulo: SENAC, 2003); Eduardo Morettin, *Dimensões históricas do documentário brasileiro no periodo silencioso* (São Paulo: Associação Nacional de História, 2005); Samuel Paiva and Sheila Schvarzman, eds., *Viagem ao cinema silencioso do Brasil* (Rio de Janeiro: Azouge, 2011).

43. López, "Early Cinema and Modernity," 49.

44. Andrew Higson, "The Concept of National Cinema," in *Film and Nationalism,* ed. Andrew Williams (New Brunswick, NJ: Rutgers University Press), 57.

45. Ana M. López, "Facing Up to Hollywood," in *Reinventing Film Studies,* ed. Christine Gledhill and Linda Williams (New York: Edward Arnold, 2000), 419–38.

46. Timothy Mitchell, *Rule of Experts: Egypt, Techno-Politics, Modernity* (Berkeley: University of California Press, 2002).

47. Todd A. Diacon, *Stringing Together a Nation: Cândido Mariano da Silva Rondon and the Construction of a Modern Brazil, 1906–1930* (Durham, NC: Duke University Press, 2004).

48. Fernando J. Rosenberg, *The Avant-Garde and Geopolitics in Latin America* (Pittsburgh, PA: University of Pittsburgh Press, 2006).

1. EARLY CINEMA AND NATIONAL IDENTITY IN BRAZIL

1. López, "Early Cinema and Modernity," 99.

2. Ibid., 101.

3. Carlos Roberto de Souza, "Resgate do cinema silencioso," liner notes for *Resgate do cinema silencioso,* DVD (São Paulo: Cinemateca Brasileira, 2008), 3.

4. Giuliana Bruno, *Streetwalking on a Ruined Map: Cultural Theory and the City Films of Elvira Notari* (Princeton, NJ: Princeton University Press, 1993), 147.

5. Alex Viany, *Introdução ao cinema brasileiro* (Rio de Janeiro: Ministério da Educação e Cultura, 1959); Adhemar Gonzaga, *70 anos de cinema brasileiro* (Rio de Janeiro: Expressão Cultura, 1966); Paulo Emílio Salles Gomes, *Cinema: Trajetória no subdesenvolvimento* (São Paulo: Paz e Terra 1973).

6. Viany, *Introdução ao cinema brasileiro,* 33.

7. López, "Facing Up to Hollywood," 419.

8. In Randal Johnson and Robert Stam, "The Shape of Brazilian History," in *Brazilian Cinema,* ed. Randal Johnson and Robert Stam (New York: Columbia University Press), 22.

9. P. Gomes, *Cinema,* 11.

10. Michel Foucault, *The Archeology of Knowledge* (New York: Pantheon, 1972), 118.

11. As Michel de Certeau stresses, "it is impossible to eliminate from the labor of historiography the ideologies that inform it." *The Writing of History,* trans. Steven Rendall, European Perspectives (New York: Columbia University Press), 28.

12. Antonio Candido, "Literature and Underdevelopment," in *On Literature and Society,* trans. Howard S. Becker (Princeton, NJ: Princeton University Press, 1995), 119.

13. Roland Corbisier, *Formação e problema da cultura brasileira* (Rio de Janeiro: Textos Brasileiros de Filosofía, 1958). See Randal Johnson, *The Film Industry in Brazil: Culture and the State* (Pittsburgh, PA: University of Pittsburgh Press, 1987), for more on the relationship between cinema, intellectual ideas, and the state.

14. López, "Facing Up to Hollywood," 421.

15. See Johnson, *Film Industry in Brazil.*

16. Bernardet notes that in the '50s and '60s film criticism assumed a predominantly political role. Jean-Claude Bernardet, *Historiografia clássica do cinema brasileiro: Metodologia e pedagogia* (São Paulo: Annablume, 1995), 196.

17. Pierre Bourdieu, *The Field of Cultural Production: Essays on Art and Literature,* ed. Randal Johnson (New York: Columbia University Press, 1993), 196.

18. Gomes's study was influenced by and engaged with contemporary diagnoses of Brazil, notably the work of historian Caio Prado Júnior and economist Celso Furtdao, who examined Brazil's historical evolution from its roots in a colonial past. See Caio Prado Júnior, *História econômica do Brasil* (São Paulo: Editora Brasiliense, 1959), and Celso Furtado, *A economia brasileira: Contribução à análise do seu desenvolvimento* (Rio de Janeiro: A Noite, 1954).

19. Ismail Xavier, *Allegories of Underdevelopment: Aesthetics and Politics in Modern Brazilian Cinema* (Minneapolis: University of Minnesota Press, 1997), 121.

20. Paulo Emílio Salles Gomes, "Cinema: Trajetória no desenvolvimento," *Argumento,* no. 1 (October 1973): 55–67.

21. Glauber Rocha, introduction to *Revisão crítica do cinema brasileiro* (São Paulo: Cosac e Naify, 2003), 33.

22. Carlos Diegues, "Ciclos ou crises," in *Cinema brasileiro: Idéias e imagens* (Porto Alegre: Editor da Universidade, 1988), 96.

23. Jacques Derrida, *Archive Fever: A Freudian Impression,* Religion and Postmodernism (Chicago: University of Chicago Press, 1996), 33; Paulo Emílio Salles Gomes, "Pequeno cinema antigo," in *Cinema,* 7.

24. C. Souza, "Resgate," 2.

25. Bernardet, *Historiografia clássica,* 22.

26. Ibid., 34–49.

27. Xavier, *Allegories of Underdevelopment.*

28. These accounts also assume Hollywood to be a monolithic entity, ignoring different processes of production within studios, especially for B movies and marginal genres.

29. Bernardet, *Historiografia clássica,* 9.

30. Ibid., 65.

31. Jennifer Bean and Diane Negra, introduction to *A Feminist Reader in Early Cinema* (Durham, NC: Duke University Press, 2002), 7.

32. Christine Geraghty, "Cinema as a Social Space: Understanding Cinema-Going in Britain, 1947–1963," *Framework Journal* 42, published online January 1, 2000, http://docs.wixstatic.com/ugd/32cb69_dea4296d45c2450bbf7aa65cf5e35d97.pdf.

33. Douglas Gomery and Robert C. Allen, *Film History: Theory and Practice* (New York: Knopf, 1987), 38.

34. Tom Gunning, "Early Cinema as Global Cinema: The Encyclopedic Ambition," in *Early Cinema and the "National,"* ed. Richard Abel, Giorgio Bertellini, and Rob King (Bloomington, IN: John Libbey, 2008), 11.

35. Jonathan Auerbach, "Nationalizing Attractions," in Abel, Bertellini, and King, *Early Cinema*, 18.

36. Richard Abel, "Booming the Film Business: The Historical Specificity of Early French Cinema," in *Silent Film,* ed. Richard Abel (New Brunswick, NJ: Rutgers University Press 1996), 109.

37. Mark Shiel, "Cinema and the City in History and Theory," in *Cinema and the City: Film and Urban Societies in a Global Context*, edited by Mark Shiel and Tony Fitzmaurice (Oxford: Blackwell, 2001), 10–11.

38. Tom Gunning, "Early Cinema," 11.

39. Ella Shohat and Robert Stam, *Unthinking Eurocentrism: Multiculturalism and the Media* (New York: Routledge, 1994), 100.

40. Gilles Deleuze and Félix Guattari, *A Thousand Plateaus: Capitalism and Schizophrenia* (Minneapolis: University of Minnesota Press, 1987).

41. Eric Hobsbawm, *Age of Empire: 1875–1914* (London: Abacus, 1989), 40–41.

42. Gaonkar, *Alternative Modernities,* 1. Deleuze and Guattari also highlight the relationship between nationalism, imperialism, and capitalist modernity when they write that flows of capital would dispatch themselves to the moon if capitalist nation-states were not there to bring them back to earth. This is key to what they highlight as the social axiomatic of modern nations, in which capitalism is continuously reterritorializing with one hand what it is deterritorializing with the other. Capital modernity's international mobility and ceaseless movement are thus always grounded by the nation. *Anti-Oedipus: Capitalism and Schizophrenia* (Minneapolis: University of Minnesota Press, 1983), 257–59.

43. Brazil became independent from Portugal in 1822. Until the start of the Republic in 1889, the country was ruled by emperors Pedro I and Pedro II, descendants from the former Portuguese rulers. The Republic thus signaled the end of Portugal's imperial presence.

44. Jeffrey Needell, *A Tropical Belle Époque: Elite Culture and Society in Turn-of-the-Century Rio de Janeiro* (New York: Cambridge University Press, 1987), 21.

45. Canclini, *Hybrid Cultures,* 71.

46. Mona Domosh, *American Commodities in an Age of Empire* (New York: Routledge, 2006).

47. Sevcenko, "Peregrinations," 89.

48. Nicolau Sevcenko, *Literatura como missão: Tensões sociais e criação cultural na Primeira República* (São Paulo: Editora Brasiliense, 1983), 93.

49. Lima Barreto, *Os Bruzundangas* (São Paulo: Editora Brasiliense, 1956), 106.

50. Sevcenko, "Peregrinations," 89.

51. Bernardet, *Historiografia clássica,* 17; J. Souza, *Imagens do passado,* 71.

52. Anthony D. King, *Colonial Urban Development: Culture, Social Power, and Environment* (London: Routledge and Paul, 1976), 67. King stresses that discussions of modernity are primarily temporal, not spatial, positing a narrative that focuses on development and locates the epicenter of modern progress in Europe.

53. Charney and Schwartz, introduction to *Cinema*, 3.

54. Huyssen, "Geographies of Modernism," 191.

55. A. King, *Colonial Urban Development*, 69.

56. Felix Driver and David Gilbert, *Imperial Cities: Language, Display and Identity* (Manchester: Manchester University Press, 2003); Jane Jacobs, *Edge of Empire: Postcolonialism and the City* (London: Routledge, 1996).

57. Anthony King, *Urban Colonialism and World Economy: Cultural and Spatial Foundations of the World Urban System* (London: Routledge, 1990), 78.

58. Huyssen, "Geographies of Modernism," 191.

59. Ibid., 68.

60. Doreen Massey, "A Global Sense of Place," in *Space, Place, Gender* (Cambridge: Polity Press, 1994), 146.

2. CINEMATIC VISTAS OF RIO DE JANEIRO'S WORLDLY MODERNITY

1. Charney and Schwartz, introduction to *Cinema*, 2.

2. Needell, "Domestic Civilizing Mission," 1.

3. Beatriz Sarlo, "Buenos Aires in the 20s and 30s," in *Mediating Two Worlds: Cinematic Encounters in the Americas*, ed. John King, Ana M. López, and Manuel Alvarado (London: BFI, 1993), 165.

4. The shift from rural to urban also mirrors the move from literary romanticism to realism, presenting a shift in style, aesthetics, and location.

5. See James Donald, *Imagining the Modern City* (Minneapolis: University of Minnesota Press, 1999); Charney and Schwarz, *Cinema*; and Bruno, *Streetwalking*.

6. Lilia Moritz Schwarcz, *The Emperor's Beard: Dom Pedro II and the Tropical Monarchy of Brazil*, trans. John Gledson (New York: Hill and Wang, 2004).

7. Sevcenko, *Literatura como missão*, 28.

8. Broca, *Vida literária*, 4.

9. Danilo Gomes, *Uma rua chamada Ouvidor* (Rio de Janeiro: Prefeitura da Cidade do Rio de Janeiro, 1980), 36.

10. *Jornal do Commércio*, July 17, 1890, n. pag.

11. Alice Gonzaga, *Palácios e poeiras: 100 anos de cinemas no Rio de Janeiro* (Rio de Janeiro: Record, 1996), 52.

12. Needell, *Tropical Belle Époque*, 162–64.

13. Ibid., 163.

14. Afrânio Peixoto, *As razões do coração* (Rio de Janeiro: F. Alves, 1925), 184.

15. López, "Early Cinema and Modernity," 49.

16. Tom Gunning, "The Cinema of Attractions: Early Film, the Spectator, and the Avant-Garde," *Wide Angle* 8, nos. 3–4 (1986): 63–70.

17. Ibid., 64.

18. Miriam Hansen, "Early Cinema, Late Cinema: Permutations of the Public Sphere," *Screen* 34 no. 3 (1993): 197–210.

19. Flora Süssekind, *Cinematograph of Words: Literature, Technique, and Modernization in Brazil*, trans. Paulo Henrique Brito (Stanford, CA: Stanford University Press, 1997), 23.

20. López, "Early Cinema and Modernity," 52.

21. Paulo Roberto Ferreira, "Do kinetoscópio ao omniographo," *Filme Cultura* 47 (1986): 19.

22. López, "Early Cinema and Modernity," 53.

23. V. Araújo, *Bela época,* 94–95.

24. López, "Early Cinema and Modernity," 52.

25. In V. Araüjo, *Bela época,* 106.

26. Jeffrey Ruoff, introduction to *Virtual Voyages: Cinema and Travel,* ed. Jeffrey Ruoff (Durham, NC: Duke University Press, 2006), 1.

27. Olavo Bilac, "Contemporary Illness," Appendix 1 in Conde, *Consuming Visions,* 181.

28. Bruno, *Streetwalking,* 76.

29. López, "Early Cinema and Modernity," 52.

30. P. Gomes, "Pequeno cinema antigo," 9.

31. *Gazeta de Noticias,* September 29, 1907, 1.

32. P. Gomes, "Pequeno cinema antigo," 11.

33. Needell, *Tropical Belle Époque,* 32.

34. Ibid., 39.

35. Mayor Pereira Passos had worked on Paris's reforms under Baron Haussmann. See Larry Benchimol, *Pereira Passos: Um Haussmann tropical. A renovação urbana da cidade do Rio de Janeiro no início do século XX* (Rio de Janeiro: Prefeitura da Cidade do Rio de Janeiro, 1990).

36. Sevcenko, *Literatura como missão,* 31.

37. Broca, *Vida literária,* 3

38. Sevcenko, "Peregrinations," 89.

39. Needell, *Tropical Belle Époque,* 40.

40. T. J. Clark, *The Painting of Modern Life: Paris in the Art of Manet and His Followers* (New York: Knopf, 1985); Vanessa R. Schwartz, *Spectacular Realities: Early Mass Culture in Fin-De-Siècle Paris* (Berkeley: University of California Press, 1998).

41. Gilberto Freyre, *The Mansions and the Shanties: The Making of Modern Brazil* (Berkeley: University of California Press, 1987), 278.

42. Antônio Dimas, *Tempos eufóricos: Análise da Revista Kosmos, 1904–1909, ensaios* (São Paulo: Ática, 1983).

43. *Fon-Fon!,* April 11, 1908, 22.

44. V. Araújo, *Bela época,* 24.

45. P. Gomes, "Expressão social," 327.

46. P. Gomes, *Cinema,* 40.

47. Sevcenko, *Literarura como missão,* 30.

48. William Rowe and Vivien Schelling, *Memory and Modernity: Popular Culture in Latin America* (London: Verso, 1991), 38; Zuenir Ventura, *Cidade partida* (São Paulo: Companhia das Letras, 1994).

49. Rama, *Lettered City,* 3.

50. Hansen, "Early Silent Cinema," 147–84.

51. Needell, *Tropical Belle Époque,* 46.

52. Ibid., 46.

53. Sevcenko, *Literatura como missão,* 45.

54. Needell, *Tropical Belle Époque,* 40.

3. ALTERNATIVE URBAN PROJECTIONS IN
EARLY NARRATIVE FILMS

1. Sevcenko, *Literatura como missão*, 25.

2. López, "Cinema and Modernity," 63.

3. Niterói is a city in Rio State.

4. Michel de Certeau, *The Practice of Everyday Life*, trans. Steven Rendall (Berkeley: University of California Press, 1984), 96.

5. Stephanie Dennison and Lisa Shaw, *Popular Cinema in Brazil, 1930–2001* (Manchester: Manchester University Press, 2004), 9.

6. Tiago de Melo Gomes, *Um espelho no palco: Identidades sociais e massificação da cultura no teatro de revista dos anos 1920* (Campinas: UNICAMP, 2004), 32.

7. Flora Süssekind, *As revistas do ano e a invenção do Rio de Janeiro* (Rio de Janeiro: Nova Fronteira, 1986), 17.

8. See Maria Inez Turazzi's *Poses e trejeitos: A fotografia e as exposições na era do espetáculo* (Rio de Janeiro: Rocco, 1995).

9. Roland Barthes, *The Rustle of Language*, trans. Russell Howard (Berkeley: University of California Press, 1992), 141.

10. Süssekind, *Revistas do ano*, 109.

11. Dennison and Shaw, *Popular Cinema*, 13.

12. Sevcenko, *Literatura como missão*, 51.

13. López, "Early Cinema and Modernity," 65.

14. Miriam Hansen, *Babel and Babylon: Spectatorship and American Silent Film* (Cambridge, MA: Harvard University Press, 1991), 90.

15. Antonio Candido, "Dialectic of Malandroism," in *On Literature and Society*, 79.

16. Raimundo Magalhães Júnior, *O fabuloso Patrocínio Filho* (Rio de Janeiro: Civilização Brasileira, 1957), 65.

17. P. Gomes, "Expressão social," 325.

18. See Monica Pimento Velloso, *Modernismo no Rio de Janeiro: Turunas e quixotes* (Rio de Janeiro: Fundacão Getúlio Vargas, 1996), for more on the *jornal do falado*.

19. Foot Hardman, *Nem pátria, nem patrão!*, 125–30.

20. Sevcenko, *Literatura como missão*, 11.

21. Teresa Meade, *Civilizing Rio: Reform and Resistance in a Brazilian City, 1889–1930* (University Park: Pennsylvania State University Press, 1997), 31.

22. Sidney Chalhoub, *Cidade febril: Cortiços e epidemias na corte imperial* (São Paulo: Companhia das Letras, 1996), 25.

23. Furtado, *Economia brasileira*, 153.

24. Francisco Foot Hardman and Victor Leonardi, *História da indústria e do trabalho no Brasil: Das origens aos anos 20*, 2nd ed. (São Paulo: Ática, 1991), 185.

25. Paschoal Segreto, for instance, established distribution links with the film company Cines Italiana. Dora Film, circulated films to distributors in Brazil, and other Italian production companies (Ítalo-Americana, Carrari Film, Trento e Trieste, Ambrosio Cinema, Itala, Aquila, Milano, Pasquali) sent films to Brazil. See Bruno *Streetwalking*, 124.

26. P. Gomes, *Cinema*, 10.

27. Bernardet, *Cinema brasileiro*, 35.

28. Hardman and Leonardi, *História da indústria*, 195.

29. Roberto Schwarz, *Misplaced Ideas: Essays on Brazilian Culture*, ed. and trans. John Gledson (London: Verso, 1992), 21.

30. Hardmann and Leonardi, *História da indústria*, 193.

31. Maria Goés, *A formação da classe trabalhadora: Movimento anarquista no Rio de Janeiro, 1888–1911* (Rio de Janeiro: Jorge Zahar, 1988), 20–21.

32. Roberto Moura, *Tia Ciata a a Pequena Africa no Rio de Janeiro* (Rio de Janeiro: Prefeitura da Cidade do Rio, 1995), 13.

33. Jurandyr Noronha, *Pioneiros do cinema brasileiro* (São Paulo: Melhoramentos, 1997), 3.

34. Gonzaga, *Palácios e poeiras*, 95.

35. Ibid., 31.

36. *Gazeta de Notícias*, October 2, 1899, 4.

37. Gonzaga, *Palácios e poeiras*, 30–31.

38. *Gazeta de Notícias*, July 13, 1897, 2.

39. José Murilo de Carvalho, *Os bestializados: O Rio de Janeiro e a República que não foi* (São Paulo: Companhia das Letras, 1987), 143.

40. Cláudio Batalha, *O movimento operário na Primeira República* (Rio de Janeiro: Jorge Zahar, 2000), 15.

41. V. Araújo, *Bela época*, 105.

42. P. Gomes, *Cinema*, 31.

43. Bruno, *Streetwalking*, 131.

44. Michel Foucault, "Of Other Spaces," *Diacritics* 16, no. 1 (1986): 22–23.

45. Ibid., 25.

46. V. Araújo, *Bela época*, 116.

47. Robert Stam, *Tropical Multiculturalism: A Comparative History of Race in Brazilian Cinema and Culture* (Durham, NC: Duke University Press, 1997), 63.

48. *Gazeta de Notícias*, October 4, 1908, 8.

49. *Gazeta da Manhã*, September 30, 1910, n. pag.

50. *Gazeta da Manhã*, October 13, 1908, 6.

51. Boris Fausto's *Crime e cotidiano: A criminalidade em São Paulo, 1880–1924* (São Paulo: EDUSP, 1984).

52. Josefina Ludmer, *The Corpus Delicti: A Manual of Argentine Fictions*, trans. Glen S. Close (Pittsburgh, PA: University of Pittsburgh Press, 2004), 4.

53. Teresa Caldeira, *City of Walls: Crime, Segregation, and Citizenship in São Paulo* (Berkeley: University of California Press, 2000), 19.

54. Alessandra El Far, *Páginas de sensação: Literatura popular e pornográfica no Rio de Janeiro* (São Paulo: Companhia das Letras, 2004).

55. Ibid., 18.

56. Meade, *Civilizing Rio*, 6.

57. Ibid., 3.

58. José Inácio de Melo Souza, "As imperfeições do crime da mala," *Revista USP* 45 (2000): 159.

59. Lilia Moritz Schwarcz, *The Spectacle of the Races: Scientists, Institutions, and the Race Question in Brazil, 1870–1930* (New York: Hill and Wang, 1990), 26.

60. Walter Benjamin, "The Work of Art in the Age of Mechanical Reproduction," in *Illuminations*, ed. Hannah Arendt (New York: Schocken Books, 1986), 233–34.

61. Noël Burch, *A Life to Those Shadows*, trans. Ben Brewster (Berkeley: Universty of California Press, 1990), 72.

62. Thomas Holloway, *Policing Rio de Janeiro: Repression and Resistance in a Nineteenth-Century City* (Stanford, CA: Stanford University Press, 1993), 231.

63. "Relatório de policia," *Boletim de policia* 2, no. 3 (July 1908): 138.

64. Alan Sekula, "The Body and the Archive," *October* 39 (1986): 3.

65. Schwarcz, *Spectacle of the Races*, 191–208.

66. Ibid.

67. Chalhoub, *Cidade febril*, 186.

4. FILM AND FANDOM IN *CINEARTE* MAGAZINE

1. See Victoria de Grazia's *Irresistible Empire: America's Advance through Twentieth-Century Europe* (Cambridge, MA: Belknap Press, 2005), and Emily S. Rosenberg's *Spreading the American Dream: American Economic and Cultural Expansion, 1890–1945* (New York: Hill and Wang, 1982).

2. Kristen Thompson, *Exporting Entertainment: America in the World Film Market, 1907–1934* (BFI: London, 1985), 41.

3. J. Souza, *Imagens do passado*, 5.

4. Thompson, *Exporting Entertainment*, 52.

5. Ibid., 1.

6. Paramount established the Companhia de Pelliculas de Luxo da América do Sul in Rio 1916, Universal set up its office in 1921, MGM in 1926, Warner Brothers in 1927, and First National and Columbia in 1926. See Johnson, *Film Industry in Brazil*, 36.

7. Stam, *Tropical Multiculturalism*, 65.

8. *Moving Picture World*, October 1917, 861.

9. Ibid., 529.

10. *Cine-Mundial*, January 1916, n. pag.; quote's translation in Laura Isabel Serna, *Making Cinelandia: American Films and Mexican Film Culture before the Golden Age* (Durham, NC: Duke University Press, 2014), 28.

11. *Cine-Mundial*, January 1916, n. pag.; quote's translation in Serna, *Making Cinelandia*, 28.

12. *Moving Picture World*, October 1917, 778.

13. Ibid., 2.

14. De Grazia, *Irresistible Empire*, 284–336.

15. Thompson, *Exporting Entertainment*, 46–47.

16. De Grazia, *Irresistible Empire*, 3.

17. Domosh, *American Commodities*, 6.

18. Mary Ann Doane, "The Economy of Desire: The Commodity Form in/of the Cinema," *Quarterly Review of Film and Video* 11 (1989): 4.

19. Charles Eckert, "The Carole Lombard in Macy's Window," *Quarterly Review of Film Studies* 3 (1973): 7.

20. Ibid., 5, my emphasis.

21. Thompson, *Exporting Entertainment,* 121.

22. Ibid.

23. "Vida elegante" [Elegant life], *Careta,* November 20, 1914, n. pag.

24. The percentage of exports, for instance, rose from 16.2 percent in 1913 to 26.8 percent in 1926.

25. Micol Seigel, *Uneven Encounters: Making Race and Nation in Brazil and the United States* (Durham, NC: Duke University Press, 2009), 20.

26. Ibid., 20.

27. Mark Crinson, *Empire Building: Orientalism and Victorian Architecture* (London: Routledge, 1996), 2.

28. De Grazia, *Irresistible Empire,* 6.

29. Domosh, *American Commodities,* 7, 23.

30. Ibid., 4.

31. De Grazia, *Irresistible Empire,* 6.

32. Seigel, *Uneven Encounters,* 20.

33. Ibid., 20.

34. Ibid., 21.

35. De Grazia, *Irresistible Empire,* 299.

36. Serna, *Making Cinelandia,* 29.

37. F. Rosenberg, *Avant-Garde and Geopolitics,* 3.

38. Ibid., 4.

39. Hernani Heffner, "Breve histórico da imprensa especializada em cinema no Brasil," Ms. 14455, n.d., Acervo de Cinemateca do Museu de Arte Moderna, Rio de Janeiro.

40. Ismail Xavier, *Sétima arte: Um culto moderno. O idealismo estético e o cinema* (São Paulo: Perspectiva, 1978), 182.

41. *Cinearte,* no. 25 (1926): 5–6; *Cinearte,* no. 30 (1926): 20–22.

42. *Cinearte,* no. 9 (1926): 2.

43. *Cinearte,* no. 163 (1929): 27.

44. *Cinearte,* no. 160 (1929): 18.

45. *Cinearte,* no. 2 (1926): 9.

46. Richard Dyer, *Stars* (London: BFI, 1998), 21.

47. Paulo Emílio Salles Gomes, *Humberto Mauro, Cataguases, Cinearte* (São Paulo: Perspectiva, 1974), 295; Xavier, *Sétima arte,* 167.

48. João Luis Vieira, "O marketing do desejo," in *Quase catálogo 3: Estrelas do cinema mudo no Brasil, 1908–1930,* ed. Heloísa Buarque de Hollanda (Rio de Janeiro: Museu de Imagem e Som, 1991), 34–42.

49. See Marissa Gorberg, *Parc Royal: Um magazine na belle-époque carioca* (Rio de Janeiro: Ermakoff, 2013).

50. Susan Besse, *Restructuring Patriarchy: The Modernization of Gender Inequality in Brazil, 1914–1940* (Chapel Hill: University of North Carolina Press, 1996), 19.

51. Ibid.

52. The civil code of 1916 emphasized women's centrality to consumerism. The new code preserved husbands' supremacy within marriage, maintaining wives as legally incapacitated. When it came to consumerism, however, it authorized wives to make purchases on their own, granting them individual freedom as consumers. June Hahner, *Emancipating the*

Female Sex: The Struggle for Women's Rights in Brazil, 1850–1940 (Durham, NC: Duke University Press, 1990), 82.

53. Besse, *Restructuring Patriarchy*, 19.

54. João Luiz Vieira and Margareth Pereira, "Cinemas cariocas: Da Ouvidor à Cinelândia," *Filme Cultura* 47 (1986): 25–34.

55. Süssekind, *Cinematograph of Words*, 46.

56. *A Cigarra*, September 16–30, 1926, 30; quote's translation in Besse, *Restructuring Patriarchy*, 28.

57. Paulo Menotti del Picchia, "Arte moderna," in *Vanguarda européia e modernisno brasileiro*, ed. Gilberto Mendonça Teles (Rio de Janeiro: Vozes, 1976), 291; quote's translation in Vicky Unruh, *Performing Women and Modern Literary Culture in Latin America* (Austin: University of Texas Press, 2006), 201.

58. Beatriz Resende, "A volta de Mademoiselle Cinema," in *Mademoiselle Cinema: Novela de costumes do momento que passa* (Rio de Janeiro: Casa da Palavra, 1999), 9.

59. Besse, *Restructuring Patriarchy*, 24–32.

60. Madame Chrysanthème, *As enervadas* (Rio de Janeiro: Leite Ribeiro, 1922), 119.

61. Benjamin Costallat, *Mademoiselle Cinema: Novela de costumes do momento que passa* (São Paulo: Costallat e Micciolis, 1923), 118.

62. Andreas Huyssen, *After the Great Divide: Modernism, Mass Culture, Postmodernism*, Theories of Representation and Difference (Bloomington: Indiana University Press, 1986), 45.

63. Gaylyn Studlar, "The Perils of Pleasure? Fan Magazine Discourse as Women's Commodified Culture in the 1920s," *Wide Angle* 13, no. 1 (1991): 7.

64. Laura Mulvey, *Visual and Other Pleasures* (London: Palgrave Macmillan, 2009), 221–22.

65. Hahner, *Emancipating the Female Sex*, 115.

66. Besse, *Restructuring Patriarchy*, 2.

67. Maria Fernanda Bicalho, "The Art of Seduction: Representations of Women in Brazilian Silent Cinema," *Luso Brazilian Review* 30 (1993): 26.

68. *A Careta*, January, 17, 1915, n. pag.

69. Benedicto Bastos Barreto [Belmonte pseud.], *Assim falou Juca Pato: Aspectos divertidos de uma confusao dramatica* (São Paulo: Companhia Editora Nacional, 1933), 43–45; quote's translation in Besse, *Restructuring Patriarchy*, 29.

70. *Cinearte*, no. 142 (1928): 21.

71. *Cinearte*, no. 149 (1929): 26.

72. *Cinearte*, no. 41 (1926): 4.

73. *Cinearte*, no. 41 (1926): 34.

74. *Cinearte*, no. 26 (1926): 5.

75. Huyssen, *After the Great Divide*, 52.

76. Joli Jenson, "Fandom as Pathology: The Consequences of Characterization." in *The Adoring Audience: Fan Culture and Popular Media*, ed. Lisa A. Lewis (New York: Routledge, 1992), 10.

77. *Cinearte*, no. 27 (1926): 27, 5.

78. *Cinearte*, no 45 (1927): 29.

79. Ibid.

80. *Cinearte*, no. 203 (1928): 7.

81. Bicalho, "Art of Seduction," 22.

82. P. Gomes, *Humberto Mauro*, 336.

83. Ibid., 337.

84. *Cinearte*, no. 189 (1929): n.pag.

85. Xavier, *Sétima arte*, 119.

86. *Cinearte*, no. 113 (1928): 8.

87. *Cinearte*, no. 5 (1926): 1.

88. *Cinearte*, no. 21 (1926): 5.

89. The competition was organized by the Omega Film studio, established in Rio by American William Jansen for the film *Urutau* (1919). Thanks to Lisa Shaw for drawing this to my attention.

90. *Palcos e Telas*, June 10, 1920, n. pag.

91. Quoted in Ana Pessoa, *Carmen Santos: O cinema dos anos 20* (Rio de Janiero: Aeroplano, 2002), 52.

92. Ibid., 65.

93. Heloísa Buarque de Hollanda and Maria Fernanda Bicalho, "As atrizes," in Buarque de Hollanda, *Quase catálogo 3*, 29.

94. *Cinearte*, no 249 (1930): 13.

95. Ibid., 29.

96. Bicalho, "Art of Seduction," 23.

97. *Cinearte*, no. 189 (1929): 6.

98. *Cinearte*, No. 14 (1926): n. pag.

99. Shelly Stamp, *Movie-Struck Girls: Women and Motion Picture Culture after the Nickelodeon* (Princeton, NJ: Princeton University Press, 2000), 137; Hansen, *Babel and Babylon*, 54.

100. *Cinearte*, no. 108 (1928): 6.

101. *Cinearte*, no. 151 (1929): n.pag.

102. *Cinearte*, no. 174 (1929): 4.

103. Xavier, *Sétima arte*, 194.

104. Marina Maluf and Maria Lúcia Mott, "Recônditos do mundo feminine," in *República: Da belle-époque à era do radio*, ed. Nicolau Sevcenko (São Paulo: Companhia das Letras, 2001), 367–423.

105. Ibid., 179.

106. *Cinearte*, no. 225 (1930): 9.

107. Ibid.

108. *Cinearte*, no. 225 (1930): 9.

109. Stam, *Tropical Multiculturalism*, 66.

110. *Cinearte*, no. 14 (1926): 3.

111. Ibid.

112. *Cinearte*, no. 198 (1929): 28; quote's translation in Lisa Shaw and Stephanie Dennison, *Brazilian Cinema, National Cinemas* (London: Routledge, 2007), 119.

113. *Cinearte*, no. 42 (1926): 4.

114. *Cinearte*, no. 26 (1926): 5.

115. An exception was Benjamin de Oliveira (1870–1954). Oliveira made his name in the circus and also vaudeville plays in the late 1880s. In 1908 he starred in a cinematic adaption of

José de Alencar's *O Guaraní,* which he also directed. Oliveira is credited as being the first black film actor in Brazilian cinema. His career, however, was brief, and he appeared in just two more films in minor roles in the sound era: *Alma do Brasil* (Soul of Brazil; dir. Libero Luxardo, 1931) and *Inconfidência Mineira* (Conspiracy in Minas Gerais; dir. Carmen Santos, 1948).

5. BEYOND HOLLYWOOD

1. Jean-Claude Bernardet, *Cinema brasileiro,* 101.

2. López, "Facing Up to Hollywood," 424.

3. Bernardet, *Cinema brasileiro,* 101.

4. Roberto Schwarz, "Misplaced Ideas," 26–28.

5. Gomes, "Cinema: Trajetória," essay translated as "Cinema: A Trajectory within Underdevelopment," in *Brazilian Cinema,* ed. Randal Johnson and Robert Stam (New York: Columbia University Press, 1995), 245.

6. Homi K. Bhabha, "Of Mimicry and Man: The Ambivalence of Colonial Discourse," in *The Location of Culture* (London: Routledge, 1994), 128.

7. Roman de la Campa, *Latin Americanism* (Minneapolis: University of Minnesota Press), 113–14.

8. Canclini, *Hybrid Cultures.*

9. P. Gomes, *Humberto Mauro,* 144.

10. For Jobst Welge, narratives of familial decline reflect the experience of sociohistorical change in peripheral regions or nations, where tradition still holds currency. See *Genealogical Fictions: Cultural Periphery and Historical Change in the Modern Novel* (Baltimore: John Hopkins University Press, 2014).

11. The most obvious example of these novels in Brazil is Alencar's romanticist *Iracema,* examined by Doris Sommer, along with *O Guaraní,* also by Alencar. See chap. 5, "*O Guaraní* and *Iracema*: Brazil's Two-Faced Indigenism," in *Foundational Fictions.*

12. Bernardet, *Cinema brasileiro,* 141.

13. Ibid.

14. Welge, *Genealogical Fictions,* 14.

15. Sommer, *Foundational Fictions,* 183.

16. Gilberto Freyre, *The Masters and the Slaves: A Study in the Development of Brazilian Civilization* (Berkeley: University of California Press, 1986), 356.

17. Hansen, *Babel and Babylon,* 225–26.

18. Gomes, *Humberto Mauro,* 144; Luciana Corrêa Araújo, "Versão brasileira? Anotações em torno da incorporação do modelo norteamericano em filmes silenciosos brasileiros," in *Viagem ao cinema brasileiro,* ed. Samuel Paiva and Sheila Schvarzman (São Paulo: Azougue, 2011), 36.

19. Xavier, *Sétima arte,* 179.

20. L. Araújo, "Versão brasileira?," 35.

21. Gomes, *Humberto Mauro,* 166.

22. Ibid., 166.

23. L. Araújo, "Versão brasileira?," 36.

24. Jean-Claude Bernardet, *Trajetória crítica* (São Paulo: Polis, 1978), 214–15.

25. Ibid., 215.

26. Gomes, *Humberto Mauro,* 167.

27. L. Araújo, "Versão brasileira?" 40.

28. Joaquim Nabuco, *O abolicionismo* (Rio de Janeiro: Instituto Nacional do Livro, 1977), 130; quote's translation in Marcus Wood, *Black Milk: Imagining Slavery in the Visual Cultures of Brazil and America* (Oxford: Oxford University Press, 2013), 56.

29. Joaquim Nabuco, *Essencial* (São Paulo: Companhia das Letras, 2010), 42.

30. Freyre, *Masters and the Slaves,* 429.

31. Arthur Autran, "O personagem negro no cinema silencioso," *Sessões do Imaginário* 7 (2001): 7.

32. Gomes, *Humberto Mauro,* 166.

33. Maria Rita Galvão, *Crônica do cinema paulistano* (São Paulo: Ática, 1975), 61.

34. Significantly, there is little visual or written material on Lola Lys and her role in *Lost Treasure* in *Cinearte* and other fanzines of the time, though many other films were amply promoted, especially visually, in Brazilian publications. Perhaps this was due to her being Mauro's wife and to her simply filling in for the actress originally assigned to play the role, Eva Nil.

35. Gomes, *Humberto Mauro,* 149.

36. Bernardet, *Cinema brasileiro,* 102, 103.

37. Writers Mário de Andrade and Oswald de Andrade and painter Tarsila do Amaral all traveled to Minas Gerias in 1924.

38. Marilena Chauí, *Between Conformity and Resistance: Essays on Politics, Culture, and the State,* trans. Maite Conde (NewYork: Palgrave Macmillan, 2011), 3.

39. See Stam, *Tropical Multiculturalism.* João Carlos Rodrigues has sought to uncover the presence of black actors in the country's cinema in *O negro e o Cinema* (Rio de Janeiro: Globo, 1988).

40. Autran, "Negro no cinema brasileiro," 7.

6. PICTURING THE TROPICS

1. Lúcia Sá, introduction to *The Amazon: Land without History,* by Euclides da Cunha (Oxford: Oxford University Press, 2007), xii.

2. E. Cunha, *Amazon,* 4.

3. Ibid., 7.

4. Ibid., 44.

5. Susana Hecht, "The Last Unfinished Page of Genesis: Euclides da Cunha and the Amazon," *Historical Geography* 32 (2004): 50.

6. Sylvia Molloy, "The Politics of Posing," in *Hispanisms and Homosexualities,* ed. Sylvia Molloy and Robert Irwin (Durham, NC: Duke University Press, 1998), 143.

7. Luiz Costa Lima, *História, ficção, literatura* (São Paulo: Companhia das Letras, 2006), 104.

8. E. Cunha, *Amazon,* 17.

9. Ibid., 28–29.

10. Ibid., 28.

11. Quoted in Andermann, *Optic of the State,* 141.

12. The proposals were also fully in keeping with European ideas of technology as an instrument that could improve the colonies and their peoples and alleviate their

backwardness. Michael Adas, for instance, notes that "as early as the 1830s European colonial administrators and also missionaries viewed railroads, steamships and western machines in general as key agents in their campaigns to revive 'decadent' civilizations in Asia and uplift the 'savage' peoples of Africa." See *Machines as the Measure of Men: Science, Technology and Ideologies of Western Dominance* (Ithaca, NY: Cornell University Press), 224–25.

13. Warren Dean, *Brazil and the Struggle for Rubber: A Study in Environmental History*, Studies in Environmental History (Cambridge: Cambridge University Press, 1987), 56.

14. Andermann, *Optic of the State*, 126.

15. The relationship between technology and colonialism and imperialism has been explored in depth by a number of historians. See, for instance, Adas, *Machines as the Measure*, as well as Daniel Headrick's *The Tools of Empire: Technology and European Imperialism in the Nineteenth Century* (New York: Oxford University Press, 1981).

16. Amílcar Armando Botelho de Magalhães, quoted in Diacon, *Stringing Together a Nation*, 149.

17. Deep Kanta Lahiri Choudhury, *Telegraphic Imperialism: Crisis and Panic in the Indian Empire* (London: Palgrave Macmillan, 2010), 6.

18. Laura Antunes Maciel, *A nação por um fio: Caminhos, práticas e imagens da "Comissão Rondon"* (São Paulo: FAPESP, 1998), 52.

19. Cândido Mariano da Silva Rondon, *Relatorio dos trabalhos realizados de 1900–1906 pelo Major de engenharia Cândido Mariano da Silva Rondon*, vols. 4–5 (Rio de Janeiro: Departamento da Imprensa Nacional, 1946), 11; quote's translation in Diacon, *Stringing Together the Nation*, 16.

20. See Nancy Stepan, *Picturing Tropical Nature* (Ithaca, NY: Cornell University Press), and Luciana Martins, *Photography and Documentary Film in the Making of Modern Brazil* (Manchester: Manchester University Press).

21. Diacon, *Stringing Together the Nation*, 4.

22. Maciel, *Nação por um fio*, 16.

23. Diacon, *Stringing Together the Nation*, 4.

24. Homi Bhabha, "The Other Question," in *Location of Culture*, 95.

25. Antonio Carlos de Souza Lima, *Um grande cerco de paz: Poder tutelar indianidade e formação do estado no Brasil* (Petropolis: Vozes, 1995), 55.

26. Ibid., 114.

27. Roland Barthes, *Camera Lucida: Reflections on Photography* (New York: Hill and Wang, 2010), 95–96.

28. Mitchell, *Rule of Experts*.

29. Süssekind, *Cinematograph of Words*.

30. Maciel, *Nação por um fio*, 80.

31. Diacon, *Stringing Together the Nation*, 134.

32. Bruno Latour, *Science in Action: How to Follow Scientists and Engineers through Society* (Cambridge, MA: Harvard University Press, 1987), 215–58.

33. Maciel, *Nação por um fio*, 185.

34. Tom Gunning, "What's the Point of an Index? Or Faking Photographs," in *Still/Moving: Between Cinema and Photography*, ed. Karen Beckman and Jean Ma (Durham, NC: Duke University Press, 2008), 41.

35. Walter Benjamin, "A Short History of Photography," in *Selected Writings*, vol. 2, *1931–1934*, ed. Michael W. Jennings, Howard Eiland, and Gary Smith (Cambridge, MA: Harvard University Press, 1996), 242.

36. André Bazin, "The Ontology of the Photographic Image," in *What Is Cinema?*, 15.

37. Christopher Pinney, "Classification and Fantasy in the Photographic Construction of Caste and Tribe," *Visual Anthropology* 3, nos. 2–3 (1990): 284.

38. *Gazeta de Notícias*, March 18, 1917.

39. *Jornal do Commércio*, November 3, 1911. See also Diacon, *Stringing Together the Nation*, 137.

40. Diacon, *Stringing Together the Nation*, 138.

41. Maciel, *Nação por um fio*, 188.

42. Denise Portugal Lasmar, *O acervo imagético da Comissão Rondon* (Rio de Janeiro: Museu do Índio, 2011), 223. Maciel also refers to the photographers in *Nação por uma fio*, 195–98.

43. Maciel, *Nação por um fio*, 194.

44. Liuz Thomas Reis, "Nosso álbum," in *Photografias da construção, expedições e explorações desde 1900 a 1922 encaminhado ao Exmo. Sr. General de Divisão Fernando Setembrino de Carvalho, D. Ministro d'Estado dos Negócios da Guerra*, 2 vols. (Rio de Janeiro: Ministro d'Estado, 1922).

45. Jay Ruby, "The Moral Burden of Authorship in Ethnographic Film," *Visual Anthropology Review* 11, no. 2 (1995): 80.

46. Alison Griffiths, *Wondrous Difference: Cinema, Anthropology, and Turn-of-the-Century Visual Culture* (New York: Columbia University Press, 2002), 91.

47. Ibid., 87.

48. Pinney, "Classification and Fantasy," 260.

49. Griffiths, *Wondrous Difference*, 89.

50. Alison Griffiths, "Knowledge and Visuality in Turn of the Century Anthropology: The Early Ethnographic Cinema of Alfred Cort Haddon and Walter Baldwin Spencer," *Visual Anthropology Review* 12, no. 2 (1996): 19.

51. Ibid.

52. Griffiths, *Wondrous Difference*, 296.

53. Ibid.

54. Fatimah Tobing Rony, *The Third Eye: Race, Cinema, and Ethnographic Spectacle* (Durham, NC: Duke University Press, 1996), 10.

55. Christopher Pinney, "The Lexical Spaces of Eye-Spy," in *Film as Ethnography*, ed. Peter Ian Crawford and David Turton (Manchester: Manchester University Press, 1992), 26.

56. Amilcar Armando Botelho de Magalhães, *Pelos sertões do Brasil* (São Paulo: Companhia Editora Nacional, 1941), 372.

57. Pinney, "Lexical Spaces," 27.

58. Rony, *Third Eye*, 33–35.

59. Griffiths, *Wondrous Difference*, 116.

60. Maciel, *Nação por um fio*, 256.

61. *Jornal do Commércio*, November 21, 1915, n. pag.; *Noite*, November 20, 1915, n. pag.

62. Pinney, "Lexical Spaces," 26.

63. James Ryan notes that expeditionary photography, for all of its claims to and pretensions of objectivity, was never entirely distinct from landscape painting. See *Photography and Exploration* (London: Reaktion, 2013), 78.

64. David Nye, *American Technological Sublime* (Cambridge, MA: MIT Press, 1994), xiii.

65. Quoted in Maciel, *Nação por um fio*, 19.

66. Diacon, *Stringing Together the Nation*, 84–85.

67. Maciel, *Nação por um fio*, 19.

68. Diacon, *Stringing Together the Nation*, 224.

69. Ibid., 63.

70. Ibid., 67.

71. Ibid., 64.

7. THE EXPEDITION FILMS OF MAJOR LUIZ THOMAZ REIS

1. Erico J. Siriuba Stickel, *Uma pequena biblioteca particular: Subsídios para o estudo da iconografia no Brasil* (São Paulo: EDUSP, 2004), 431.

2. Quoted in Amílcar Armando Botelho de Magalhães, *Impressões da Commissão Rondon* (São Paulo: Brasiliana, 1942), 313.

3. Reis, quoted in Maciel, *Nação por um fio*, 253.

4. Luiz Felipe Miranda, *Dicionário de cineastas brasileiros* (São Paulo: Art Editora /Secretaria de Estado da Cultura, 1990), 275.

5. Ibid.

6. Quoted in Fernando de Tacca, *A imagética da Comissão Rondon: Etnografias fílmicas estratégicas* (Campinas: Papirus, 2001), 46.

7. Reis also worked independently of the Rondon Commission. In 1917 he made the publicity film *Rio Branco* for Asensi and Cia, one of the largest rubber-tapping companies in Mato Grosso and the Amazon.

8. Reis quoted in Maciel, *Nação por um fio*, 257.

9. Reis quoted in ibid.

10. Ibid., 259.

11. Reis quoted in ibid., 262.

12. Reis quoted in ibid., 264.

13. Pinney, "Lexical Spaces of Eye-Spy," 27.

14. Quoted in Maciel, *Nação por um fio*, 263.

15. El Far, *Páginas de sensação*, 28–29.

16. Süssekind, *Cinematograph of Words*, outlines the effects of these new sensibilities on literary production during this period.

17. Gunning, "Cinema of Attractions," 63–70.

18. Tom Conley, *Cartographic Cinema* (Minneapolis: University of Minnesota Press, 2007), 11.

19. Certeau, *Practice of Everyday Life*, xviii.

20. J. B. Harley, "Maps, Knowledge and Power," in *The Iconography of Landscape: Essays on the Symbolic Representation, Design, and Use of Past Environments*, ed. Denis E. Cosgrove and Stephen Daniels (Cambridge: Cambridge University Press, 1988), 280.

21. Teresa Castro, "Cinema's Mapping Impulse: Questioning Visual Culture," *Cartographic Journal* 46, no. 1 (2009): 9.

22. Charles Musser, "The Travel Genre in 1903–1904: Moving towards Fictional Naratives," in *Early Cinema: Space, Frame, Narrative,* ed. Thomas Elesaesser (London: BFI, 1990), 123.

23. Gunning, "Early Cinema," 11–16.

24. Lynne Kirby, *Parallel Tracks: The Railroad and Silent Cinema* (Durham, NC: Duke University Press, 1997), 7.

25. Ibid., 42.

26. Quoted in ibid., 112.

27. Rony, *Third Eye,* 82.

28. Quoted in Maciel, *Nação por um fio,* 255.

29. Paulo Menezes, "Major Reis e a constituição visual do Brasil enquanto nação," *Horizontes Antropológicos* 14, no. 29 (2008): 194.

30. Quoted in Diacon, *Stringing Together the Nation,* 18.

31. Charles R. Boxer, *The Dutch in Brazil, 1624–1654* (Hamden, CT: Archon Books, 1973), 135.

32. Stephen Greenblatt, *Marvelous Possessions: The Wonder of the New World* (Oxford: Clarendon Press, 1991), 122.

33. Photographers Albert Frisch, Felipe Augusto Fidanza, Herman Meyer, and Marc Ferrez produced photographs of indigenous groups, including the Botocudo, Tikuna, Tapuya, and Bororo, both "on site" and in urban studios. See Boris Kossoy, *Dicionário histórico-fotográfico brasileiro: Fotógrafos e Ofício da Fotografia no Brasil (1833–1910)* (São Paulo: Instituto Moreira Salles, 2002).

34. João do Rio, *Cinematógrafo* (Porto: Chardron, 1909), 349.

35. Jens Andermann, "Tournaments of Possession: Argentina and Brazil in the Age of Exhibitions," *Journal of Material Culture* 14, no. 3 (2009): 72.

36. Hermann von Ihering, "O museu paulista nos annos de 1906–1909," *Revista do Museu Paulista* 8 (1911): 13.

37. Mark Sandberg, "Effigy and Narrative: Looking into the Nineteenth-Century Folk Museum," in Charney and Schwartz, *Cinema,* 331.

38. Donna Haraway, *Primate Visions: Gender, Race, and Nature in the World of Modern Science* (New York: Routledge, 2006), 29.

39. Sven Schuster, "The Brazilian Native on Display: Indianist Artwork and Ethnographic Exhibiits at the World's Fairs: 1862–1889," *Journal of the International Association of Research Institutes in the History of Art,* no. 127 (September 2015): n. pag., www.riha-journal.org/articles/2015/2015-jul-sep/schuster-the-brazilian-native-on-display.

40. Johannes Fabian, *Time and the Other: How Anthropology Makes Its Object* (New York: Columbia University Press, 2002), 35.

41. Andermann, *Optic of the State,* 68.

42. Schwarcz, *Spectacle of the Races,* 61–65.

43. Griffiths, *Wondrous Difference,* 186.

44. Reis quoted in Maciel, *Nação por um fio,* 259.

45. Reis quoted in ibid.

46. Martins, *Photography and Documentary Film,* 160.

47. Ibid., 181.

48. Ibid., 172.

49. Ibid., 174.

50. Sylvia Caiuby Novaes, "Funerais entre os Bororo: Imagens da refiguração do mundo," *Revista de Antropologia* 49, no. 1 (2006): 287.

51. Pinney, "Lexical Spaces of Eye-Spy," 27.

52. Ibid., 38.

53. Barthes, *Camera Lucida*, 43.

54. Ibid., 55.

55. Pinney, "Lexical Spaces of Eye-Spy," 38.

56. Rony, *Third Eye*, 65.

57. Fabian, *Time and the Other*, 153.

58. Martins, *Photography and Documentary Film*, 168–69.

59. Renato Rosaldo, "Imperialist Nostalgia," *Representations* 26 (1989): 107–22.

60. Rony, *Third Eye*, 101.

61. Hermann von Ihering, "Extermínio ds indigenas ou dos sertanejos," *Jornal do Commércio*, December 15 1908, n. pag.; quote's translation in Andermann, *Optic of the State*, 69.

62. Hermann von Ihering, *Anthropology of the State of São Paulo, Brazil* (São Paulo: Duprat, 1904), 202.

63. Quoted in Diacon, *Stringing Together the Nation*, 123.

64. Quoted in Andermann, *Optic of the State*, 94.

65. Quoted in Tacca, *Imagética da Comissão Rondon*, 7.

66. Quoted in Maciel, *Nação por um fio*, 16.

67. Diacon, *Stringing together the Nation*, 116.

68. Ibid.

69. Martins, *Photography and Documentary*, 198.

70. Dean MacCannell, "Staged Authenticity: Arrangements of Social Space in Tourist Settings," *American Journal of Sociology* 79, no. 3 (1973): 407–8.

71. Amy Staples, "The Last of the Great (Foot-Slogging) Explorers: Lewis Cotlow and the Ethnographic Imaginary in Popular Travel Film," in Ruoff, *Virtual Voyages*, 210.

72. Magalhães, *Impressões da Commissão Rondon*, 40.

73. Rosana Elisa Catelli, "Dos 'naturais' ao documentário: O cinema educativo e a educação do cinema entre os anos 1920 e 1930" (PhD diss., Universidade Estadual de Campinas, 2007), 145.

74. Maciel, *Nação por um fio*, 252.

75. Edgar Roquette-Pinto, *Rondônia* (São Paulo: Companhia Editora Nacional, 1975), 74.

76. Fernando de Azevedo, *As ciências no Brasil*, 2 vols., 2nd ed. (Rio de Janeiro: Editora UFRJ, 1994), 1:209.

77. It was shown in São Paulo, in Rio, and in Minas Gerais in 1915. In 1916 it was shown in northern cities, including Maranhão.

78. Maciel, *Nação por um fio*, 287–88.

79. Diacon, *Stringing together a Nation*, 151.

80. Reis quoted in Maciel, *Nação por um fio*, 267.

81. Diacon, *Stringing Together a Nation*, 150.

82. Ibid., 151.

83. "Os sertões de Mato Grosso" advertisement, unidentified, undated news clipping from the Cinemateca Brasileira.

84. *Tribuna,* November 20, 1915, n. pag.

85. *Diário,* August 9, 1916, n. pag.

86. *Jornal do Commércio,* March, 19, 1916, n. pag.

87. *Tarde,* April 13, 1916, n. pag.

88. *Correio de Campinas,* February 1, 1915, n. pag.

89. *Diário do Povo,* November 11, 1916, n. pag.

90. *Estado de São Paulo,* November 29, 1915, n. pag.

91. Appadurai, *Modernity at Large,* 7.

92. Theodore Roosevelt, *Through the Brazilian Wilderness* (New York: Create Space, 2009), 49.

93. Ibid., 104, 93.

94. Luiz Tomaz Reis, "Relatório apresentado pelo Primeiro Tenente Luiz Thomaz Reis da sua excursão aos Estados Unidos da America no Norte, 1918," diary from New York trip, Cinemateca Brasileira, D147/2, n. pag.

95. Maciel, *Nação por um fio,* 264.

96. Reis, "Relatório," n. pag.

97. Ibid., n. pag.

98. Ibid., n. pag.

8. *MODERNISMO*'S LITERARY ENGAGEMENTS
WITH FILM

1. See Mário da Silva Brito, *História do modernismo brasileiro: Antecedentes da Semana de Arte Moderna* (São Paulo: Saraiva), 1958), for an analysis of transformation taking place in Brazilian letters before 1922.

2. Randal Johnson, "Brazilian Modernism," 188.

3. Ibid.

4. Ibid., 189.

5. Nicolau Sevcenko, *Orfeu extático na metrópole: São Paulo, sociedade e cultura nos frementes anos 20* (São Paulo: Companhia das Letras, 1992), 108.

6. Ibid., 142; Johnson, "Brazilian Modernism," 190.

7. Sevcenko, *Orfeu extático,* 18.

8. Huyssen, "Geographies of Modernism," 189.

9. Gabara, *Errant Modernism,* 24.

10. Canclini, *Hybrid Cultures,* 47.

11. Ibid., 53.

12. Daryle Williams, *Culture Wars in Brazil: The First Vargas Regime, 1930–1945* (Durham, NC: Duke University Press, 2001), 36.

13. Vicky Unruh, *Latin American Vanguards: The Art of Contentious Encounters,* Latin American Literature and Culture (Berkeley: University of California Press, 1994), 21.

14. Xavier, *Sétima arte,* 151.

15. See Conde, *Consuming Visions.*

16. Oswald de Andrade, *Serafim Ponte Grande*, 4th ed., Coleção Múltipla (São Paulo: Globo, 1984), 143.

17. Richard Abel, preface to *French Film Theory and Criticism: A History/Anthology*, vol. 1, *1907–1929* (1988; repr., Princeton, NJ: Princeton University Press, 1993), xiii.

18. Richard Abel, "Photogénie and Company" (Part II introduction), in Abel, *French Film Theory*, 1:106.

19. Ibid., 110.

20. The lecture was published the following year as "The New Spirit and the Poet." See *The Selected Writings of Guillaume Apollinaire*, trans. Roger Shattuck (London: Harvill, 1950), 237.

21. Writer Philippe Soupault was active in Dada and later founded surrealism with André Breton. He wrote about poetry and created a number of cine poems, beginning in 1918 with "Indifference: A Cinematographic Poem." Yvan Goll also wrote what he termed *Kinodichtung* (cine poems), like "The Chaplinade" (1920). See Christopher Wall-Romana, *Cinepoetry* (New York: Fordham University Press, 2013), for more about this cinematic literature.

22. Jules Romains published a mock-film script entitled *Donogoo Tonka* in 1919, and Blaise Cendrars wrote *La fin du monde filmée par l'Ange N.D.* (The end of the year filmed by the angel of Notre Dame) in 1919. Cendrars's engagement with film went beyond literary experimentation. He worked closely with Abel Gance on his two films *J'accuse* and *La roue* and also wrote film criticism, collectively published as *L'ABC du cinéma* (1926). See Wall-Romana, *Cinepoetry*, and Mary Ann Caws, "Blaise Cendrars: A Cinema of Poetry," in *The Inner Theater of Recent French Poetry: Cendrars, Tzara, Péret, Artaud, Bonnefoy*, Princeton Essays in European and Comparative Literature (Princeton, NJ: Princeton University Press, 1972).

23. Abel, "*Cinégraphie* and the Search for Specificity" (Part III introduction), in *French Film Theory*, 204.

24. Tom Gunning, preface to *Jean Epstein: Critical Essays and New Translations*, ed. Sarah Keller and Jason N. Paul (Amsterdam: Amsterdam University Press, 2012), 21.

25. Benjamin, "Work of Art," 161.

26. In 1923 Robert Desnos articulated an explicit surrealist theory of cinema in his *Paris-Journal* review column.

27. Abel, "Cinégraphie," 205.

28. Xavier, *Sétima arte*, 154.

29. See Mario Helena Grembecki's *L'Esprit Nouveau* (São Paulo: ISEB, 1969).

30. Cendrars visited Brazil three times, in 1924, 1926, and 1927–28. See Alexandre Eulálio and Carlos Augusto Calil, eds., *A aventura brasileira de Blaise Cendrars: Ensaio, cronologia, filme, depoimentos, antologia, desenhos, conferências, correspondência, traduções* (São Paulo: EDUSP, 2001).

31. A translation of Cendrars's film *Censário* into Portuguese by Carlos Calil is reproduced in "O filme 100% brasileiro," *Revista IEB* 47 (2008): 201–14. See also Calil's essay "Cinema = cavação: Cendroswald Produções," *Revista IEB* 47 (2008): 3–28.

32. In 1926 Antônio de Alcântara Machado dedicated his 1926 cinematic *crônica Pathé-Baby* to Cendrars, "the great specialist in documentary film."

33. *Klaxon*, no. 1 (May 15, 1922): 2.

34. Ibid.

35. Unruh, *Latin American Vanguards,* 1.

36. Gabara, *Errant Modernism,* 5.

37. Ibid., 6.

38. F. Rosenberg, *Avant-Garde and Geopolitics,* 3–5.

39. Doreen Massey, "Globalization: What Does It Mean for Geography?" *Development Education Journal* 9 (2002): 3.

40. F. Rosenberg, *Avant-Garde and Geopolitics,* 22.

41. Huyssen, "Geographies of Modernism," 190.

42. Haroldo de Campos, "The Rule of Anthropophagy: Brazil under the Sign of Devoration," *Latin American Literary Review* 14, no. 27 (1986): 50.

43. Oswald de Andrade, "Manifesto of Pau-Brasil Poetry," trans. Stella M. de Sá Rego, *Latin American Literary Review* 14, no. 27 (1986): 184–87; originally published as "Manifesto da Poesia Pau-Brasil," *Correio da Manhã,* March 18, 1924.

44. Hansen, "Fallen Women, Rising Stars," 10.

45. Andreas Huyssen, *After the Great Divide,* viii.

46. This lack of interest in Brazilian film extended beyond São Paulo. The modernist group Verde in Cataguases, for instance, disregarded the work of local filmmaker Humberto Mauro in spite of knowing the Brazilian director. See Xavier, *Sétima arte,* 153.

47. Ibid., 141.

48. *Klaxon* 14 (1929): 14.

49. Xavier, *Sétima arte,* 148; João Manuel dos Santos Cunha, *A lição aproveitada: Modernismo e cinema em Mário de Andrade* (Cotia: Ateliê, 2011), 35.

50. J. Cunha, *Lição aproveitada,* 148.

51. Mário de Andrade, *Hallucinated City / Paulicéia Desvairada,* trans. Jack Tomlins (Nashville, TN: Vanderbilt University Press, 1968), 29.

52. Telê Porto Ancona Lopez, introduction to *Fotógrafo e turista aprendiz,* by Mário de Andrade (São Paulo: IEB, 1993), 8.

53. Photography is key to *O turista aprendiz* (The apprentice tourist), Mário's chronicles of his 1927 journey to the states of the Amazon and Pará, written for the *Diário Nacional.* In addition to documenting his journey Mário took about 540 photographs. He returned in 1928 and took a further 260 photographs. A posthumous volume was published in 2002 by Telê Porta Ancona Lopez, who was also responsible for an edited volume of his travel photographs published in 1993 as *Fotógrafo e turista aprendiz* (São Paulo: IEB, 1993).

54. *Klaxon,* no. 1 (1922): 1.

55. Mário de Andrade, "Crônicas de Malazarte," *Revista de Estudos Literários* 1, no. 1 (1993): 156.

56. Jason Borge notes that Chaplin had a profound impact on a number of writers, filmmakers, and actors in Latin America. "Replaying Carlitos: Chaplin, Latin American Cinema and the Paradigm of Imitation," *Journal of Latin American Cultural Studies* 22 (2013): 271–86.

57. *Klaxon* 6 (1922): 14.

58. Jennifer Wild, *The Parisian Avant Garde in the Age of Cinema, 1900–1923* (Berkeley: University of California Press, 2015), 225–75.

59. Jean Epstein, "Magnification," in Abel, *French Film Theory,* 1:238.

60. *Klaxon* 3 (1922): 14.

61. Ibid.

62. Ibid., 15.

63. Jason Borge, *Latin American Writers and the Rise of Hollywood Cinema* (New York: Routledge, 2008), 75.

64. Jacques Rancière, *Dissensus: On Politics and Aesthetics*, trans. Steve Corcoran (London: Continuum, 2010), 6.

65. Céline Arnauld, "Le Cinéma," *Cahiers de Philosophie et d'Art* (hors série, 1921), n. pag., quoted in Wild, *Parisian Avant Garde*, 271.

66. Ibid., quoted in Wild, *Parisian Avant Garde*, 271–72.

67. *Klaxon* 5 (1922): 13.

68. Lopez,introduction to M. de Andrade, *Fotógrafo e turista aprendiz*, 8.

69. M. de Andrade, "Crônicas de Malazarte," 157.

70. Ibid., 158.

71. David William Foster, "On Being São Paulo Otherwise in *Pauliceia desvairada*," *Iberoamericana* 19 (2005): 28.

72. M. de Andrade, *Hallucinated City*, 22.

73. Ibid., 21–23.

74. Ibid., 23.

75. Mário de Andrade, "A escrava que não é Isaura," in *Obra imatura* (Belo Horizonte: Martins, 1980). Mário cites Epstein as his inspiration (232).

76. José Suárez and Jack E. Tomlins, "Early Modernist Poetics and Early Poetry," in *Mário de Andrade, The Creative Works,* ed. José Suárez and Jack E. Tomlins (Lewisburg, PA: Bucknell University Press, 2000), 39.

77. M. de Andrade, "A escrava que não é Isaura," 242.

78. M. de Andrade, *Hallucinated City*, 13.

79. Ibid., 16.

80. Unruh, *Latin American Vanguards,* 48.

81. Charles Perrone, "Performing São Paulo: Vanguard Representations of a Brazilian Cosmopolis," *Latin American Music Review* 23, no. 1 (2002): 22.

82. M. de Andrade, "Escrava que não e Isaura," 256.

83. Ibid., 227.

84. Ibid., 266.

85. Kirby, *Parallel Tracks,* 6.

86. Christophe Wall-Romana, *Jean Epstein: Corporeal Cinema and Film Philosophy,* Verbal Arts: Studies in Poetics (Oxford: Oxford University Press, 2013), 22.

87. Jean Epstein, *La poésie d'aujourd'hui, un nouvel état d'intelligence* (Paris: Editions de la Siréne, 1921), 173, quoted in Wall-Romana, *Jean Epstein,* 22.

88. Epstein, *La poésie d'aujourd'hui,* quoted in Wall-Romana, *Jean Epstein,* 122.

89. M. de Andrade, "Escrava que não é Isaura," 258.

90. Mário de Andrade, *Cartas a Manuel Bandeira* (São Paulo: Editora Singular, 2009), 46.

91. Do Rio, *Cinematógrafo,* v.

92. M. de Andrade, "Escrava que não é Isaura," 203.

93. Charles Perrone's description; Perrone, "Performing São Paulo," 20.

94. Ibid., 22.

95. *Klaxon* 6 (1922): 15.

96. Mário da Silva Brito, "O aluno de romance Oswald de Andrade," in *Os condenados*, by Oswald de Andrade, ed. Mário da Silva Brito (Rio de Janeiro: Vera Cruz, 1941), n. pag.

97. Haroldo de Campos, "Miramar na mira," in *Metalinguagem e outras metas* (São Paulo: Civilização Brasileira, 1970), 30; Antonio Candido, "Estouro e libertação," in *Vários escritos* (São Paulo: Duas Cidades, 1970), 20.

98. Candido, "Estouro e libertação," 20.

99. Oswald himself, in a 1943 article, referred to *Os condenados* as "the first attempt of new prose." See Haroldo de Campos, "Miramar na mira." Mário also appropriated his own ideas of simultaneity in his prose in his 1927 novel *Amar, verbo instransitivo,* referring in a letter to fellow modernist, Sérgio Milliet, to the novel's fragmented style as "very cinematographic." See J. Cunha, *Lição aproveitada,* 200.

100. Campos, "Miramar na mira," 30.

101. Haroldo de Campos, "Serafim: Um grande não livro," prologue to *Serafim Ponte Grande,* 129.

102. Unruh, *Latin American Vanguards,* 115.

103. Ibid., 119–20.

104. Ibid., 120.

105. Oswald de Andrade, *Memórias sentimentais de João Miramar* (Rio de Janeiro: Civilização Brasileira, 1975), 21.

106. Ibid., 38.

107. Campos, *Serafim Ponte Grande,* 137.

108. Süssekind, *Cinematograph of Words,* 100.

109. Ibid., 12.

110. Ibid., 62.

111. Ibid., 72.

112. O. de Andrade, *Memórias sentimentais,* 42.

113. Candido, "Estouro e libertação," 21.

114. O. de Andrade, "Manifesto Pau Brasil."

115. Johnson, "Brazilian Modernism," 208.

116. Oswald de Andrade, "Manifesto Antropófago," *Revista de Antropofagia* 1 (1928): 3; translated by Leslie Bary as "Cannibalist Manifesto," *Latin American Literary Review* 19, no. 38 (1991): 40.

117. Sérgio Prado Bellei, "Brazilian Anthropophagy Revisited," in *Cannibalism and the Colonial World,* ed. Francis Barker, Peter Hulme, and Margaret Iverson (Cambridge: Cambridge University Press, 1998), 88; Canclini, *Hybrid Cultures,* 50.

118. Unruh, *Latin American Vanguards,* 133.

119. John Ruskin, *Praeterita* (Oxford: Oxford University Press, 1979), quoted in Rosalind Krauss, *The Optical Unconscious* (Cambridge, MA: MIT Press, 1993), 5.

120. Unruh, *Latin American Vanguards,* 26.

121. Beatriz Resende, "Rio de Janeiro: Cidade da crônica," in *Cronistas do Rio,* ed. Beatriz Resende (Rio de Janeiro: José Olympio, 1995), 35.

122. Ibid., 77.

123. Renato Cordeiro Gomes, *Todas as cidades, a cidade: Literatura e experiência urbana* (Rio de Janeiro: Rocco, 1994), 30; Certeau, *Practice of Everyday Life*, 96.

124. Antonio Candido, "A vida ao rés-do-chão," in *A crônica: O gênero, a sua fixação e as suas transformações no Brasil,* ed. Antonio Candido (São Paulo: Unicamp; Rio de Janeiro: Fundação Rui Barbosa, 1992), 14.

125. Do Rio, *Cinematógrafo*, vii.

126. Antônio de Alcântara Machado, *Pathé-Baby,* ed. Cecília de Lara (1926; facsimile ed., São Paulo: Arquivo do Estado de São Paulo, 1982), 65.

127. Dziga Vertov, *Kino-Eye: The Writings of Dziga Vertov*, ed. Annette Michelson, trans. Kevin O'Brien (Berkeley: University of California Press, 1984), 69.

128. Maud Ellmann, *The Poetics of Impersonality: T.S. Eliot and Ezra Pound* (Cambridge, MA: Harvard University Press, 1988), 3.

129. Ana Paula Dias Rodrigues, "António de Alcântara Machado com a câmera: Exploração geográfica e cinematográfica em *Pathé-Baby,*" *Cadernos de Semiotica Aplicada* 10 (2012): 8.

130. Antônio Dimas, *Tempos eufóricos: Análise da Revista Kosmos, 1904–1909, ensaios* (São Paulo: Atíca 1983), 8.

131. A. Rodrigues, "António de Alcântara Machado," 10.

132. Georg Simmel, "The Metropolis and Mental Life," in *On Individuality and Social Forms,* ed. Donald N. Levine (Chicago: University of Chicago Press 1971), 321.

133. Perrone, "Performing São Paulo," 24.

134. A. Machado, *Pathé-Baby,* 121.

135. Ibid., 41.

136. Leo Charney, *Empty Moments: Cinema, Modernity, and Drift* (Durham, NC: Duke University Press, 1998).

137. Do Rio, *Cinematógrafo*, vi.

138. Shohat and Stam, *Unthinking Eurocentrism.*

139. A. Machado, *Pathé-Baby,* 29.

140. Ibid., 52, 59, 85.

141. Cited in A. Rodrigues, "Antônio de Alcântara Machado," 6.

142. Antônio Gonçalves Dias, *Canção do exílio,* stanza 2, http://www.horizonte.unam.mx/brasil/gdias.html.

9. THE CINE-POETRY OF MÁRIO PEIXOTO'S *LIMITE*

1. Xavier, *Sétima arte*, 151.

2. Robert Stam, "On the Margins: Brazilian Avant-Garde Cinema," in Johnson and Stam, *Brazilian Cinema,* 311.

3. Bruce Williams, "The Lie That Told the Truth: (Self) Publicity Strategies and the Myth of Mário Peixoto's *Limite,*" *Film History* 17 (2005): 392.

4. Saulo Pereira de Mello, "Man's Fate," in *Ten Contemporary Views on Mário Peixoto's Limite,* ed. Michael Korfmann (Munster: Monsenstein und Vannerdat, 2006), 21.

5. Carlos Calil, "Mário Peixoto's Revelation," in Korfmann, *Ten Contemporary Views,* 33.

6. Walter Salles, "Free Eyes in the Country of Repetition," in Korfmann, *Ten Contemporary Views,* 18.

7. "Noticias do Cinema Brasileiro: *O valé dos martirios*," *Correio da Manhã*, February 3, 1927, n. pag.

8. "*O vale dos martírios*," press release / advertisement, 1927, Coleção Pedro Lima, Cinemateca Brasileira, reference number 549/24.

9. Johnson and Stam, "Shape of Brazilian Film History," in *Brazilian Cinema*, 26.

10. It wasn't until 1936 that sound became the norm in Brazilian cinema, and the years leading up to this were marked by a kaleidoscopic multiplicity of different cinematic styles.

11. Saulo Pereira de Mello, *Limite* (Rio de Janeiro: Rocco, 1996), 17.

12. *Cruzeiro*, May 25, 1929, 32.

13. *Correio da Manhã*, June 14, 1929, n. pag.; quote's translation in Shaw and Dennison, *Brazilian National Cinema*, 45.

14. Glauber Rocha, "Humberto Mauro e a situação histórica," in *Revisão crítica do cinema brasileiro* (São Paulo: Cosac e Naify, 2003), 54.

15. Ibid., 59.

16. Mello, *Limite*, 88.

17. Unruh, *Latin American Vanguards*, 83.

18. *Fan* 3 (1928): 2.

19. See, e.g., Ricciotto Canudo's "Reflections on the Seventh Art" [1923], in Abel, *French Film Theory*, 2:291–302.

20. *Fan* 3 (1928): 3.

21. Germaine Dulac, "Aesthetics, Objects, Integral *Cinégraphie*," in Abel, *French Film Theory*, 2:397.

22. Mello, "O Fan, o Chaplin Club e *Limite*," *Revista o percevejo* 5, no. 5 (1997): 58.

23. Xavier, *Sétima arte*, 201.

24. Mello, "Fan, o Chaplin Club," 62.

25. Mello, "Notas sobre a história de *Limite*," *Folha de São Paulo*, October 8, 1988, 3.

26. Peixoto spent a year at the Hopdene School in Willingdon near Eastbourne, Sussex, in 1927, when he was nineteen years old. His interest in film began there with a particular admiration for Fritz Lang, F. W. Murnau, Sergei Eisenstein, and Vsevolod Pudovkin. He returned to Europe the following year with the express intention of seeing the latest cinematic experiments unavailable in Brazil. See Michael Korfmann, "On Brazilian Cinema: From Mário Peixoto's *Limite* to Walter Salles," *Senses of Cinema* 40 (July 2006), http://sensesofcinema.com/2006/feature-articles/brazilian-cinema/#10.

27. Mello, "Notas," 4.

28. Ibid., 6.

29. Ibid., 5.

30. Mello, "Man's Fate," 5.

31. Maya Deren, "Poetry and Film: A Symposium," in *Film Culture Reader*, ed. P. Adams Sitney (New York: Praeger, 1970), 171–86.

32. Germaine Dulac, "Visual and Anti-visual Films," in *The Avant-Garde Film: A Reader of Theory and Criticism*, ed. P. Adams Sitney (New York: New York University Press, 1978), 31.

33. Ibid., 33–34.

34. Dulac, "Aesthetics, Objects," 397.

35. Mário Peixoto, "A Film from South America," in Korfmann, *Ten Contemporary Views*, 12.

36. Calil, "Mário Peixoto's Revelation," 32; William Drew, "The Counter Cinema of Mário Peixoto: *Limite* in the Context of World Film," in Korfmann, *Ten Contemporary Views*, 39.

37. Mello, *Limite*, 74.

38. Ibid., 95.

39. Peixoto, "Film from South America," 12.

40. Ibid., 13.

41. Sérgio Lima, "The Discovery of Surrealism in 1920 Rio de Janeiro: Notes on the Relationship between Surrealism and Cinema and between France and the Cinema of Brazil," in *Conscious Hallucinations: Filmic Surrealism*, ed. Claudia Dillmann (Frankfurt: Deutsches Filminstitut, 2014), 166.

42. Korfmann, introduction to Korfmann, *Ten Contemporary Views*, 8.

43. Mello, "Visão de *Limite*," unpublished essay, 3, given to the author.

44. Tami Williams, *Germaine Dulac: A Cinema of Sensations* (Champaign: University of Illinois Press, 2014), 156.

45. Mello, *Limite*, 60.

46. Siegfried Kracauer, "The Little Shopgirls Go to the Movies," in *The Mass Ornament: Weimar Essays* (Cambridge, MA: Harvard University Press, 1995), 292.

47. Mello, *Limite*, 58.

48. Ibid., 26.

49. Peixoto, "Film from South America," 12.

50. Drew, "Counter Cinema," 35.

51. Gabara, *Errant Modernism*, 31.

52. Pier Paolo Pasolini, "The Written Language of Reality," in *Heretical Empiricism*, trans. Ben Lawton and Louise K. Barnett (Bloomington: Indiana University Press, 1988), 197.

53. Jacques Rancière, *The Politics of Aesthetics: The Distribution of the Sensible* (2006; repr., London: Bloomsbury, 2013), 29.

54. Taken from O. de Andrade, "The Cannibalist Manifesto."

10. FABRICATING DISCIPLINE AND PROGRESS IN *SÃO PAULO, SYMPHONY OF A METROPOLIS*

1. While in Germany in the early 1920s, Lustig and Kemeny undoubtedly saw the publicity films Walter Ruttmann made for Julius Pinschewer, but they denied having seen his cine-symphony, or having known of its existence.

2. By 1925, coffee made up 71.1 percent of Brazil's exports, leading to São Paulo's growing national significance. See Warren Dean, *The Industrialization of São Paulo, 1880–1945* (Austin: University of Texas Press, 1969).

3. Johnson, "Brazilian Modernism," 189.

4. Sevcenko, *Orfeu extático*, 109.

5. Lúcia Sá, *Life in the Megalopolis: Mexico City and São Paulo* (London: Routledge, 2007), 12.

6. Quoted in Candido Malta Campos, *Os rumos da cidade: Urbanismo e modernização em São Paulo* (São Paulo: SENAC, 2002), 236.

7. Ibid., 12, 191–287.

8. Ibid., 13.

9. Ibid., 57.

10. Campos notes that from 1917 and the start of Washington Luís's prefecture, urban reformers and planners aimed to "free themselves from the Haussmann model dominant until then" (ibid., 219).

11. Sevcenko, *Orfeu extático*, 116.

12. Campos, *Rumos da cidade*, 229.

13. The Edifício Sampaio was inaugurated in 1929 after five years of construction. It had twelve floors and was fifty meters high, and was São Paulo's tallest building until the inauguration of the Edifício Martinelli. Construction on the Edifício Martinelli began in 1922 and it was inaugurated in 1929, with twelve floors. Work ended in 1934 when the building had twenty-four floors.

14. For more on the symbolic resonance of skyscrapers, see Stephen Graham, *Vertical: The City from Satellite to Bunkers* (London: Verso, 2016), 149–74.

15. Sevcenko, *Orfeu extático*, 108.

16. Vicente de Paula Araújo, *Salões, circos e cinemas de São Paulo*, Coleção Debates (São Paulo: Perspectiva, 1981), 13.

17. Ibid.

18. Rubens Machado Jr., "São Paulo em movimento: A representação cinematográfica da metrópole nos anos 20" (Master's thesis, University of São Paulo, 1989), 19.

19. Ibid., 20.

20. Bernardet, *Cinema brasileiro*, 38.

21. R. Machado, "São Paulo em movimento," 20.

22. Johnson, *Film Industry in Brazil*, 33.

23. Carlos Roberto de Souza, "Os pioneiros do cinema Brasileiro," *Alceu* 8, no. 15 (2007): 20–37.

24. Johnson, *Film Industry in Brazil*, 38. Gilberto Rossi, for instance, financed his feature films, like *O crime de cravinhos* (The crime of the cloves; dir., Artur Carrari, 1920), *O segredo do corcunda* (The hunchback's secret; dir. Alberto Tavares, 1924), *Exemplo regenerador* (Regenerating example; co-directed with José Medina, 1919), and *Fragmentos de vida* (Fragments of Life; co-directed with José Medina, 1929), using funds from his *cinejornais*.

25. Ibid., 21. Profits from the *cinejornais* enabled Rossi to produce feature films, like *O segredo do corcunda* (The secret of the hunchback, 1924).

26. Bernardet, *Cinema brasileiro*, 40.

27. Paulo Emílio Salles Gomes, "The Social Expression of Documentary Films in Silent Brazilian Cinema," in *Paulo Emílio Salles Gomes: On Brazil and Global Cinema*, trans. Amber MacCartney, ed. Maite Conde and Stephanie Dennison (Cardiff: University of Wales Press, forthcoming).

28. Ibid.

29. R. Machado, "São Paulo em movimento," 10.

30. See José Inácio de Melo Souza, *Salas de cinema e história urbana de São Paulo (1895–1930)* (São Paulo: SENAC, 2016), 236–37.

31. Sheila Schvarzman, "Ir ao cinema em São Paulo nos anos 20," *Revista Brasileira de História* 25 (2005): 158.

32. Ibid.

33. Gunning, "Pictures of Crowd Splendor," 52.

34. Ismail Xavier, "Progresso, disciplina fabril e descontração operária: Retóricas do documentário brasileiro silencioso," *ArtCultura* 11 (2009): 51.

35. Ibid., 46.

36. Central to constructivist theory, machinism influenced filmmakers like Dziga Vertov, who employed the machine as a model for his films. See Malcolm Turvey, *The Filming of Modern Life: European Avant-Garde Films of the 1920s*, October Books (Cambridge, MA: MIT Press, 2011), 135–63.

37. Ibid., 141–42.

38. Meily Assbú Linhales, "O sport no 'clima cultural' da década de 1920: A 'energização do caráter,'" *Anais do Congresso Internacional de Ciências do Esporte* 2 (May 2007): 3.

39. Sevcenko, *Orfeu extático*, 50.

40. Ibid., 51.

41. Laura Podalsky, introduction to *Sports Culture in Latin American History*, ed. David Sheinin (Pittsburgh, PA: University of Pittsburgh Press, 2015), 6.

42. Linhales, "Sport," 27.

43. Benjamin, "Work of Art," 234.

44. Fernando Salla, *As prisões em São Paulo, 1822–1940* (São Paulo: Annablume, 1999).

45. Alison Griffiths, *Carceral Fantasies: Cinema and Prison in Early Twentieth-Century America* (New York: Columbia University Press, 2016), 106.

46. Ibid., 8.

47. Martin Gaughan, "Ruttmann's Berlin: Filming in a Hollow Space?," in *Screening the City*, ed. Mark Shiel and Tony Fitzmaurice (London: Verso, 2003), 43.

48. R. Machado, "São Paulo em movimento," 50.

49. Ismail Xavier, "The Modern and the Contemporary: Two Representations of the Metropolis in Film," *Review: Literature and Arts of the Americas* 39 (2006): 189.

50. R. Machado, "São Paulo em movimento," 51.

51. Wolfgang Natter, "The City as Cinematic Space," in *Place, Power, Situation and Spectacle*, ed. Stuart C. Aitken and Leo E. Zonn (New York: Rowman and Littlefield, 1994), 204.

52. James Donald, *Imagining the Modern City* (Minneapolis: University of Minnesota Press, 1999), 78.

53. Xavier, "Progresso," 48.

54. Jean Louis Baudry, "Ideological Effects of the Basic Cinematographic Apparatus," in *Movies and Methods*, vol. 2, ed. Bill Nichols (Berkeley: University of California Press, 1982), 540.

55. Xavier, "Progresso," 52.

56. Adhemar Gonzaga, "Filmagem brasileira," *Para Todos*, October 10, 1925, 30.

57. Guilherme de Almeida, *Estado de S. Paulo*, May 25, 1929, quoted in Machado, "São Paulo em movimento," 138.

58. Bernardet, *Cinema brasileira*, 42.

59. Ibid.

POSTSCRIPT: TOWARD NEW CINEMATIC FOUNDATIONS

1. P. Gomes, *Humberto Mauro*, 302.

2. Ibid., 297.

3. Ibid., 316.

4. Thomas E. Skidmore, *Politics in Brazil, 1930–1964: An Experiment in Democracy* (New York: Oxford University Press).

5. Vargas quoted by Secretary Armando de Moura Carijó, *Relatório da diretoria: Associação ciematográfica de produtores brasleiros, biénio de 02/06/34 a 02/06/36* (Rio de Janeiro: Typografia do Jornal do Commércio, 1937), 66–68; quote's translation in Johnson, *Film Industry in Brazil,* 47.

6. Carlos Roberto Souza, introduction to *Catálogo: Filmes produzidos pelo INCE* (Rio de Janeiro: Fundação do Cinema Brasileiro, 1990), iii.

7. Mônica Rugai Bastos, *Tristezas não pagam dívidas: Cinema e política nos anos da Atlantida* (São Paulo: Olho d'Água, 2001), 6.

8. On "our creative incapacity for copying," see P. Gomes, "Cinema: A Trajectory."

9. Catherine Benamou, *It's All True: Orson Welles's Pan-American Odyssey* (Berkeley: University of California Press, 2007), 200.

FILMOGRAPHY

Aitaré na praia (Aitaré on the beach; dir. Gentil Roiz, 1925)

Alô alô Brasil (dir. Wallace Downey, 1935)

Alô alô carnaval! (dir. Adhemar Gonzaga, 1926)

A Avenida Central (Avenida Central; n. dir., 1910)

Avenida Central da capital federal (Avenida Central in the federal capital; n. dir., 1906)

As aventuras de Zé (The adventures of Zé; n. dir., 1908)

Barro humano (Human clay; dir. Adhemar Gonzaga, 1928)

O Brasil desconhecido (Unknown Brazil; dir. Paulino Botelho, 1926)

O Brasil grandioso (Magnificent Brazil; dir. Alberto Botelho, 1923)

O Brasil maravilhoso (Marvelous Brazil; dir. Alfredo dos Anjos, 1928)

O Brasil pitoresco (Picturesque Brazil; dir. Cornélio Pires, 1925)

Braza dormida (Dormant embers; dir. Humberto Mauro, 1928)

Brota do café (Coffee harvest; n. dir., 1925)

Os capadócios da cidade nova (The imposters of the new city; dir. Antonio Leal, 1908)

O carnaval da Avenida Central (Avenida Central's carnival; n. dir., 1906)

Carnaval Paulista (São Paulo's carnival; n. dir., 1909)

A carne (Flesh; dir. Leo Marten, 1924)

O caso dos caixotes (Case of the packages; n. dir., 1912)

Chegada de um trem em Cadouços (Arrival of a train in Cadouços; dir. Aurélio da Paz, 1894)

Chegada de um trem em Petrópolis (Arrival of a train in Petrópolis; dir. Vittório di Maio, 1897)

Círcolo Italiano Operário (Italian Workers Party; dir. João Stamato, 1910)

O Círcolo Operário Italiano em São Paulo (São Paulo's Italian Workers' Group; dir. Affonso Segreto, 1901)

O comprador de ratos (The rat buyer; dir. Antonio Leal, 1908)

O corso de Botafogo (Promenade in Botafogo; n. dir., 1909)

O crime da mala (The suitcase crime; dir. Francisco Serrador, 1912)

De Santa Cruz (From Santa Cruz; dir. Luiz Thomaz Reis, 1917)

Do Rio a São Paulo para casar (From Rio to São Paulo for a wedding; dir. José Medina, 1922)

Um drama na Tijuca (A drama in Tijuca; dir. Antonio Serra, 1909)

Embarque do general Hermes da Fonseca para a Alemanha (Hermes de Fonseca's departure for Germany; n. dir., 1908)

Entre as montanhas de Minas (Among the mountains of Minas; dir. Igino Bonfioli and Manoel Talon, 1928)

Erradicação da febre amarela no Rio de Janeiro (Eradication of yellow fever in Rio de Janeiro; n. dir., 1909)

Os estranguladores (The stranglers; dir. Antonio Leal, 1908)

Exemplo regenerador (Regenerating example; dirs. Gilberto Rossi and José Medina, 1919)

Fazenda Santa Catarina (Santa Catarina Farm; n. dir., 1927)

A festa da Penha no Rio (Festival in Penha, Rio; n. dir., 1908)

Festejos do General Roca (General Roca's celebrations; n. dir., 1901)

A filha do advogado (The lawyer's daughter; dir. Jota Soares, 1926)

Fragmentos da vida (Fragments of life; dirs. Gilberto Rossi and José Medina, 1929)

A gigolette (The gigolette; dir. Vittorio Verga, 1924)

Inauguraçao da estátua do Doutor João Mendes (Inauguration of the statue of Doctor João Mendes; dir. Antonio Campos, 1913)

Inauguração da exposição de animais do posto zootécnico (Inauguration of the exhibition of animals at the zoo; n. dir, 1910)

Indústria da borracha em Minas Gerais e Amazonas (The rubber industry in Minas Gerais and the Amazon; dir. Luiz Thomaz Reis, 1917)

Inspeção do nordeste (Survey of the Northeast; dir. Luiz Thomaz Reis, 1922)

Inundações de ontem em diversas ruas da cidade (Yesterday's flooding in various streets of the city; dir. Alberto Botelho, 1908)

Largo de São Francisco por ocasião de um meeting (São Francisco Square during a meeting; dir. Affonso Segreto, 1899)

Limite (Limit; dir. Mário Peixoto, 1930)

A mala sinistra (The sinister suitcase; dir. Antonio Leal, 1908)

Melhoramentos do Rio de Janeiro (Improvements of Rio; n. dir., 1906)

Mocidade louca (Crazy youth; dir. Felipe Ricci, 1927)

Morfina (Morphine; dir. Nino Ponti and Francisco Madrigano, 1928)

Nas entranhas do morro do castelo (In the belly of Castelo Hill; dir. Antonio Leal, 1909)

Nhô Anastácio chegou de viagem (Mr. Anastácio has arrived on a trip; dir. Júlio Ferrez, 1908)

Noivado de sangue (Blood courtship; n. dir., 1909)

Nos sertões do Brasil (In the Brazilian backlands; dir. Paulino Botelho, 1927)

O palácio do Catete (Catete Palace; n. dir., 1900)

Parada militar em 15 de November no Rio (Military parade on November 15 in Rio; dir. Paulino Botelho, 1909)

Parimã, fronteiras do Brasil (Parimã, frontiers of Brazil; dir. Luiz Thomaz Reis, 1927)

Passagem do Círculo Operário Italiano no largo de São Francisco de Paula (Procession of the Italian Workers Party in São Francisco de Paula Square; dir. Affonso Segreto, 1900)

Paz e amor (Peace and love; dir. Alberto Botelho, 1909)

Pela vitória dos clubes carnavalescos (For the victory of the carnival clubs; n. dir., 1909)

A posse do novo governo do estado (Inauguration of the new municipal government; dir. Gilberto Rossi, 1920)

Procissão do Corpo de Deus (Procession of the Body of God; n. dir. 1903)

Quando elas querem (When they love; dir. Eugênio Kerrigan, 1925)

Retribuição (Retribution; dir. Gentil Roiz, 1924)

Revolta da esquadra (Squadron revolt; n. dir., 1910)

Revolta no Rio (Revolt in Rio; n. dir., 1910)

Rituais e festas Bororo (Rituals and festivities of the Bororo; dir. Luiz Thomaz Reis, 1917)

Rondônia (dir. Luiz Thomaz Reis, 1912)

Ronuro, selvas do Xingú (Ronuro, the jungles of Xingú; dir. Luiz Thomaz Reis, 1924)

O roubo dos mil e quatrocentos contos (The robbery of 1,400 contos; dir. Paulino Botelho, 1912)

Um roubo na Casa Michel (Robbery at the Michel Department Store; dir. Antonio Campos, 1918)

Sangue Mineiro (Blood of Minas Gerais; dir. Humberto Mauro, 1929)

São Paulo, a sinfonia da metrópole (São Paulo, symphony of a metropolis; dir. Adalberto Kemeny and Rodolfo Lustig, 1929)

O segredo do corcunda (The hunchback's secret; dir. Alberto Tavares, 1924)

Os sertões de Mato Grosso (The backlands of Mato Grosso; dir. Luiz Thomaz Reis, 1912–13)

Sinfonia de Cataguases (Symphony of Cataguases; dir. Humberto Mauro, 1929)

Tesouro perdido (Lost treasure; dir. Humberto Mauro, 1927)

A uzina Estrellina (The Estrellina factory; n. dir., 1930)

O vale dos martirios (Valley of the martyrs; dir. Almeida Fleming, 1927)

Viagem ao Brasil (Journey to Brazil; n. dir., 1927)

Viagem ao Roraima (Journey to Roraima; dir. Luiz Thomaz Reis, 1927)

Viagem presidencial a Campos (Presidential visit to Campos; n. dir., 1916)

Vício e beleza (Vice and beauty; dir. Antonio Tibiriçá, 1926)

A vida do cabo João Candido (The life of Corporal João Candido; dir. Carlos Lambertini, 1912)

24 horas na vida de uma mulher elegante (Twenty-four hours in the life of an elegant lady; dir. Arturo Carrai, 1920)

Visita ao Brasil (Voyage to Brazil; n. dir., 1907)

Visita do Conselheiro Rui Barbosa à faculdade de direito (Counselor Rui Barbosa's visit to the law school; n. dir., 1909)

Abel, Richard. "Booming the Film Business: The Historical Specificity of Early French Cinema." In *Silent Film*, edited by Richard Abel, 109–24. Rutgers Depth of Field Series. New Brunswick, NJ: Rutgers University Press, 1996.

———. "*Cinégraphie* and the Search for Specificity" (Part III introduction). In *French Film Theory*, 195–223.

———, ed. *French Film Theory and Criticism: A History/Anthology, 1907–1939.* 2 vols. 1988. Reprint, Princeton, NJ: Princeton University Press, 1993.

———. "Photogénie and Company" (Part II introduction). In *French Film Theory*, 1:95–124.

———. Preface to *French Film Theory*, 1:xiii–xxii.

Abel, Richard, Giorgio Bertellini, and Rob King, eds. *Early Cinema and the "National."* Bloomington, IN: John Libbey, 2008.

Adas, Michael. *Machines as the Measure of Men: Science, Technology, and Ideologies of Western Dominance.* Ithaca, NY: Cornell University Press, 1989.

Allen, Jeane. "The Film Viewer as Consumer." *Quarterly Review of Film Studies* 5, no. 4 (1980): 481–99.

Almeida, Guilherme de. *Cinematographos: Antologia da crítica cinematográfica.* Edited by Danny Correia and Marcelo Tápia. São Paulo: UNESP, 2016.

Altick, Richard D. *The Shows of London.* Cambridge, MA: Belknap Press, 1978.

Amaral, Aracy A. *Artes plásticas na semana de 22.* São Paulo: Bovespa, 1992.

Andermann, Jens. *The Optic of the State: Visuality and Power in Argentina and Brazil.* Pittsburgh, PA: University of Pittsburgh Press, 2007.

———. "Tournaments of Possession: Argentina and Brazil in the Age of Exhibitions." *Journal of Material Culture* 14, no. 3 (2009): 333–63.

Anderson, Benedict. *Imagined Communities: Reflections on the Origin and Spread of Nationalism.* Rev. and extended ed. London: Verso, 1991.

Andrade, Mário de. *Cartas a Manuel Bandeira*. São Paulo: Editora Singular, 2009.

——. "Crônicas de Malazarte." *Revista de Estudos Literários* 1, no. 1 (1993): 156–60.

——. *Hallucinated City / Paulicéia Desvairada*. Translated by Jack E. Tomlins. Nashville, TN: Vanderbilt University Press, 1968.

——. *Obra imatura*. Obras Completas. São Paulo: Martins, 1960.

——. *O turista aprendiz*. Edited by Telê Porto Ancona Lopez. São Paulo: IEB, 1993.

Andrade, Oswald de. "Cannibalist Manifesto." Translated by Leslie Bary. *Latin American Literary Review* 19, no. 38 (1991): 40.

——. *Os condenados [I. Alma. II. A estrêla de absinto. III. A escada]*. Edited by Mário da Silva Brito. Obras Completas. Rio de Janeiro: Civilização Brasileira, 1970.

——. "Manifesto Antropófago." *Revista de Antropofagia* 1 (1928): 3.

——. "Manifesto da Poesia Pau-Brasil." *Correio da Manhã*, March 18, 1924.

——. "Manifesto of Pau-Brasil Poetry." Translated by Stella M. de Sá Rego. *Latin American Literary Review* 14, no. 27 (1986): 184–87.

——. *Memórias sentimentais de João Miramar*. Rio de Janeiro: Civilização Brasileira, 1975.

——. *Serafim Ponte Grande*. Coleção Múltipla. São Paulo: Globo, 1984.

——. *Telefonema*. Edited by Vera Chalmers. Obras Completas de Oswald de Andrade. São Paulo: Globo, 1996.

Apollinaire, Guillaume. *Selected Writings of Guillaume Apollinaire*. Translated by Roger Shattuck. London: Harvill, 1950.

Appadurai, Arjun. *Modernity at Large: Cultural Dimensions of Globalization*. Minneapolis: University of Minnesota Press, 1996.

——. *The Social Life of Things: Commodities in Cultural Perspective*. Cambridge: Cambridge University Press, 1986.

Araújo, Luciana Corrêa. "Versão brasileira? Anotações em torno da incorporação do modelo norteamericano em filmes silenciosos brasileiros." In *Viagem ao cinema brasileiro*, edited by Samuel Paiva and Sheila Schvarzman, 30–46. São Paulo: Azougue, 2011.

Araújo, Vicente de Paula. *A bela época do cinema brasileiro*. São Paulo: Perspectiva, 1976.

——. *Salões, circos e cinemas de São Paulo*. Coleção Debates. São Paulo: Perspectiva, 1981.

Armes, Roy. *Third World Film Making and the West*. Berkeley: University of California Press, 1987.

Auerbach, Jonathan. "Nationalizing Attractions." In Abel, Bertellini, and King, *Early Cinema*, 17–21.

Autran, Arthur. "O negro no cinema brasileiro silencioso." *Sessões do Imaginário* 7 (2001): 5–9.

Azevedo, Fernando de. *As ciências no Brasil*. 2 vols. 2nd ed. Rio de Janeiro: UFRJ, 1994.

Barbero, Jesús Martín. *Communication, Culture and Hegemony: From the Media to Mediations*. London: Sage Publications, 1993.

Barreto, Benedicto Bastos [Belmonte pseud.]. *Assim falou Juca Pato: Aspectos divertidos de uma confusão dramática*. São Paulo: Companhia Editora Nacional, 1933.

Barreto, Lima. *Os Bruzundangas: Sátira*. São Paulo: Editora Brasiliense, 1956.

Barro, Máximo. "As primeiras projeções em São Paulo." *Filme Cultura* 47 (1986): 52–59.

Barthes, Roland. *Camera Lucida: Reflections on Photography*. New York: Hill and Wang, 2010.

——. *The Rustle of Language*. Translated by Russell Howard. Berkeley: University of California Press, 1992.

Bastos, Mônica Rugai. *Tristezas não pagam dívidas: Cinema e política nos anos da Atlântida.* São Paulo: Olho d'Água, 2001.

Batalha, Cláudio. *O movimento operário na Primeira República.* Rio de Janeiro: Jorge Zahar, 2000.

Baudry, Jean Louis. "Ideological Effects of the Basic Cinematographic Apparatus." In *Movies and Methods: An Anthology*, edited by Bill Nichols, 2 vols., 2:531–42. 1976. Reprint, Berkeley: University of California Press, 1982.

Bazin, André. "In Defense of Mixed Cinema." In *What Is Cinema?*, 1:53–75.

———. "The Ontology of the Photographic Image." In *What Is Cinema?*, 1:9–16.

———. *What Is Cinema?* Vol. 1. Translated by Tim Barnard. Montreal: Caboose, 2009.

Bean, Jennifer. "Technologies of Early Stardom and the Extraordinary Body." *Camera Obscura* 16, no. 3 (2001): 9–56.

Bean, Jennifer, and Diane Negra. Introduction to *A Feminist Reader in Early Cinema*, edited by Jennifer Bean and Diane Negra, 1–28. Durham, NC: Duke University Press, 2002.

Bellei, Sérgio Prado. "Brazilian Anthropophagy Revisited." In *Cannibalism and the Colonial World*, edited by Francis Barker, Peter Hulme, and Margaret Iverson, 87–109. Cambridge: Cambridge University Press, 1998.

Benamou, Catherine. *It's All True: Orson Welles's Pan-American Odyssey.* Berkeley: University of California Press, 2007.

Benchimol, Jaime L. *Pereira Passos: Um Haussmann tropical. A renovação urbana da cidade do Rio de Janeiro no início do século XX.* Rio de Janeiro: Prefeitura da Cidade, 1990.

Benjamin, Walter. "Little History of Photography." In *Selected Writings*, vol. 2, *1931–1934*, edited by Michael W. Jennings, Howard Eiland, and Gary Smith, 507–31. Cambridge, MA: Harvard University Press, 1996.

———. *Reflections: Essays, Aphorisms, Autobiographical Writing.* Edited by Peter Demetz. New York: Schocken Books, 1986.

———. "The Work of Art in the Age of Mechanical Reproduction." In *Illuminations*, edited by Hannah Arendt and translated by Harry Zohn. New York: Schocken Books, 1986.

Bernardet, Jean-Claude. *Cineastas e imagens do povo.* São Paulo: Companhia das Letras, 2003.

———. *Cinema brasileiro: Propostas para uma história.* 2nd ed. São Paulo: Companhia de Bolso, 2009.

———. *Historiografia clássica do cinema brasileiro: Metodologia e pedagogia.* São Paulo: Annablume, 1995.

———. *Trajetória crítica.* São Paulo: Polis, 1978.

Besse, Susan. *Restructuring Patriarchy: The Modernization of Gender Inequality in Brazil, 1914–1940.* Chapel Hill: University of North Carolina Press, 1996.

Bhabha, Homi K. *The Location of Culture.* London: Routledge, 1994,

———. "Of Mimicry and Man: The Ambivalence of Colonial Discourse." In *The Location of Culture*, 121–31.

———. "The Other Question: Stereotype, Discrimination and the Discourse of Colonialism." In *The Location of Culture*, 94–120.

Bicalho, Maria Fernanda. "The Art of Seduction: Representations of Women in Brazilian Silent Cinema." *Luso Brazilian Review* 30, no. 1 (1993): 21–33.

Bilac, Olavo. "Contemporary Illness." Translated by Maite Conde. Appendix 1 in *Consuming Visions: Cinema, Writing, and Modernity in Rio de Janeiro*. Charlottesville: University of Virginia Press, 2012.

———. *Vossa insolência: Crônicas. Retratos do Brasil*. Edited by A. Dimas. São Paulo: Companhia das Letras, 1996.

Borge, Jason. *Latin American Writers and the Rise of Hollywood Cinema*. New York: Routledge, 2008.

———. "Replaying Carlitos: Chaplin, Latin American Cinema and the Paradigm of Imitation." *Journal of Latin American Cultural Studies* 22 (2013): 271–86.

Botelho de Magalhães, Amílcar Armando. *Impressões da Commissão Rondon*. 5th ed. São Paulo: Companhia Editora Nacional, 1942.

———. *Pelos sertões do Brasil*. São Paulo: Companhia Editora Nacional, 1941.

Bourdieu, Pierre. *The Field of Cultural Production: Essays on Art and Literature*. Edited by Randal Johnson. New York: Columbia University Press, 1993.

Boxer, Charles R. *The Dutch in Brazil, 1624–1654*. Hamden, CT: Archon Books, 1973.

Brito, Mário da Silva. "O aluno de romance Oswald de Andrade." In *Os condenados*, by Oswald de Andrade, edited by Mário da Silva Brito, n. pag. Rio de Janeiro: Vera Cruz, 1941.

———. *História do modernismo brasileiro: Antecedentes da Semana de Arte Moderna*. São Paulo: Saraiva, 1958.

Brizuela, Natalia. *Fotografia e império: Paisagens para um Brasil moderno*. São Paulo: Companhia das Letras, 2012.

Broca, Brito. *A vida literária no Brasil, 1900*. 2nd ed. Rio de Janeiro: J. Olympio, 1960.

Bruno, Giuliana. *Atlas of Emotion: Journeys in Art, Architecture, and Film*. New York: Verso, 2002.

———. *Streetwalking on a Ruined Map: Cultural Theory and the City Films of Elvira Notari*. Princeton, NJ: Princeton University Press, 1993.

Buarque de Hollanda, Heloísa, ed. *Quase catálogo 3: Estrelas do cinema mudo no Brasil, 1908–1930*. Rio de Janeiro: Museu de Imagem e Som, 1991.

Buarque de Hollanda, Heloísa, and Maria Fernanda Bicalho. "As atrizes." In Buarque de Hollanda, *Quase catálogo 3*, 27–34.

Buarque de Hollanda, Heloísa, Maria Fernanda Bicalho, and Patrícia Moran. "Vamps, ingênuas e flappers." In Buarque de Hollande, *Quase catálogo 3*, 7–19.

Burch, Noël. *A Life to Those Shadows*. Translated by Ben Brewster. Berkeley: University of California Press, 1990.

Butler, Alison. "New Film Histories and the Politics of Location." *Screen* 33, no. 4 (1992): 413–26.

Caldeira, Teresa. *City of Walls: Crime, Segregation, and Citizenship in São Paulo*. Berkeley: University of California Press, 2000.

Calil, Carlos. "Cinema = cavação: Cendroswald Produções." *Revista IEB* 47 (2008): 3–28.

———. "O filme 100% brasileiro." *Revista IEB* 47 (2008): 201–14.

———. "Mário Peixoto's Revelation." In Korfmann, *Ten Contemporary Views*, 49–57.

Campos, Candido Malta. *Os rumos da cidade: Urbanismo e modernização em São Paulo*. São Paulo: SENAC, 2000.

Campos, Haroldo de. "Miramar na mira." In *Metalinguagem e outras metas: Ensaios de teoria e crítica literária*, 2nd ed., 1–30. São Paulo: Civilização Brasileira, 1970.

———. "The Rule of Anthropophagy: Brazil under the Sign of Devoration." *Latin American Literary Review* 14, no. 27 (1986): 42–60.

Canclini, Néstor García. *Hybrid Cultures: Strategies for Entering and Leaving Modernity.* Translated by Christopher L. Chiappari. Minneapolis: University of Minnesota Press, 1995.

Candido, Antonio, ed. *A crônica: O gênero, a sua fixação e as suas transformações no Brasil.* Rio de Janeiro: Fundação Rui Barbosa, 1992.

———. "Dialectic of Malandroism." In Candido, *On Literature and Society*, 79–103.

———. "Estouro e libertação." In *Vários escritos*, 17–32. São Paulo: Duas Cidades, 1970.

———. "Literature and Underdevelopment." In Candido, *On Literature and Society*, 119–41.

———. *On Literature and Society.* Translated by Howard S. Becker. Princeton, NJ: Princeton University Press, 1995.

Canudo, Ricciotto. "Reflections on the Seventh Art" [1923]. In Abel, *French Film Theory*, 2:291–302.

Carijó, Armando de Moura. *Relatório da diretoria: Associação ciematográfica de produtores brasleiros, biénio de 02/06/34 a 02/06/36.* Rio de Janeiro: Typografia do Jornal do Commércio, 1937.

Carvalho, José Murilo de. *Os bestializados: O Rio de Janeiro e a república que não foi.* São Paulo: Companhia das Letras, 1987.

Castro, Teresa. "Cinema's Mapping Impulse: Questioning Visual Culture." *Cartographic Journal* 46, no. 1 (2009): 9–15.

Catelli, Rosana Elisa. "Dos 'naturais' ao documentário: O cinema educativo e a educação do cinema entre os anos 1920 e 1930." PhD diss., Universidade Estadual de Campinas, 2007.

Caulfield, Sueann. *In Defense of Honor: Sexual Morality, Modernity, and Nation in Early-Twentieth-Century Brazil.* Durham, NC: Duke University Press, 2000.

Caws, Mary Ann. *The Inner Theater of Recent French Poetry: Cendrars, Tzara, Péret, Artaud, Bonnefoy.* Princeton Essays in European and Comparative Literature. Princeton, NJ: Princeton University Press, 1972.

Certeau, Michel de. *The Practice of Everyday Life.* Translated by Steven Rendall. Berkeley: University of California Press, 1984.

———. *The Writing of History.* Translated by Steven Rendall. European Perspectives. New York: Columbia University Press, 1988.

Chalhoub, Sidney. *Cidade febril: Cortiços e epidemias na corte imperial.* São Paulo: Companhia das Letras, 1996.

Charney, Leo. *Empty Moments: Cinema, Modernity, and Drift.* Durham, NC: Duke University Press, 1998.

Charney, Leo, and Vanessa R. Schwartz, eds. *Cinema and the Invention of Modern Life.* Berkeley: University of California Press, 1995.

———. Introduction to Charney and Schwartz, *Cinema*, 1–14.

Chauí, Marilena de Souza. *Between Conformity and Resistance: Essays on Politics, Culture, and the State.* Translated by Maite Conde. New York: Palgrave Macmillan, 2011.

Chrysanthème, Madame [Cecília Moncorvo Bandeira de Melo]. *As enervadas.* Rio de Janeiro: Leite Ribeiro, 1922.

Clark, T. J. *The Painting of Modern Life: Paris in the Art of Manet and his Followers.* New York: Knopf, 1985.

Conde, Maite. *Consuming Visions: Cinema, Writing, and Modernity in Rio de Janeiro.* Charlottesville: University of Virginia Press, 2012.

Conley, Tom. *Cartographic Cinema.* Minneapolis: University of Minnesota Press, 2007.

Corbisier, Roland. *Formação e problema da cultura brasileira.* Rio de Janeiro: Textos Brasileiros de Filosofía, 1958.

Costallat, Benjamin. *Mademoiselle Cinema: Novela de costumes do momento que passa.* São Paulo: Costallat e Micciolis, 1923.

Crinson, Mark. *Empire Building: Orientalism and Victorian Architecture.* London: Routledge, 1996.

Cunha, Euclides da. *The Amazon: Land without History.* Library of Latin America. Translated by Ronald W. Sousa. Introduced by Lúcia Sá. New York: Oxford University Press, 2006.

Cunha, João Manuel dos Santos. *A lição aproveitada: Modernismo e cinema em Mário de Andrade.* Cotia: Ateliê Editorial, 2011.

Dean, Warren. *Brazil and the Struggle for Rubber: A Study in Environmental History.* Studies in Environment and History. Cambridge: Cambridge University Press, 1987.

———. *The Industrialization of São Paulo, 1880–1945.* Austin: University of Texas Press, 1969.

De Cordova, Richard. "The Emergence of the Star System in America." In *Stardom: Industry of Desire,* edited by Christine Gledhill, 17–29. London: Routledge, 1991.

De Grazia, Victoria. *Irresistible Empire: America's Advance through Twentieth-Century Europe.* Cambridge, MA: Belknap Press, 2005.

De la Campa, Roman. *Latin Americanism.* Minneapolis: University of Minnesota Press, 1999.

Deleuze, Gilles, and Félix Guattari. *Anti-Oedipus: Capitalism and Schizophrenia.* Minneapolis: University of Minnesota Press, 1983.

———. *A Thousand Plateaus: Capitalism and Schizophrenia.* Minneapolis: University of Minnesota Press, 1987.

Dennison, Stephanie, and Lisa Shaw. *Popular Cinema in Brazil, 1930–2001.* Manchester: Manchester University Press, 2004.

Deren, Maya. "Poetry and Film: A Symposium." In *Film Culture Reader,* edited by P. Adams Sitney, Praeger Film Books, 171–86. New York: Praeger, 1970.

Derrida, Jacques. *Archive Fever: A Freudian Impression.* Religion and Postmodernism. Chicago: University of Chicago Press, 1996.

Diacon, Todd A. *Stringing Together a Nation: Cândido Mariano da Silva Rondon and the Construction of a Modern Brazil, 1906–1930.* Durham, NC: Duke University Press, 2004.

Diegues, Carlos. "Ciclos ou crises." In *Cinema brasileiro: Idéias e imagens,* 96–100. Porto Alegre: Editor da Universidade.

Dimas, Antônio. *Tempos eufóricos: Análise da Revista Kosmos, 1904–1909, ensaios.* São Paulo: Ática, 1983.

Doane, Mary Anne. "The Economy of Desire: The Commodity Form in/of the Cinema." *Quarterly Review of Film and Video* 11, no. 1 (1989): 23–33.

Domosh, Mona. *American Commodities in an Age of Empire.* New York: Routledge, 2006.

Donald, James. *Imagining the Modern City.* Minneapolis: University of Minnesota Press, 1999.

do Rio, João. *Cinematógrafo*. Porto: Chadron, 1909.

Drew, William. "The Counter Cinema of Mário Peixoto: *Limite* in the Context of World Film." In Korfmann, *Ten Contemporary Views*, 57–87.

Driver, Felix, and David Gilbert, eds. *Imperial Cities: Landscape, Display and Identity*. Manchester: Manchester University Press, 2003.

Dulac, Germaine. "Aesthetics, Objects, Integral *Cinegraphie*." In Abel, *French Film Theory*, 2:389–97.

———. "Visual and Anti-visual Films." In *The Avant-Garde Film: A Reader of Theory and Criticism*, edited by P. Adams Sitney, 31–48. New York: New York University Press, 1978.

Dyer, Richard. *Stars*. London: BFI, 1998.

———. *White*. London: Routledge, 1997.

Eckert, Charles. "The Carole Lombard in Macy's Window." *Quarterly Review of Film Studies* 3, no. 1 (1973): 1–23.

El Far, Alessandra. *Páginas de sensação: Literatura popular e pornográfica no Rio de Janeiro, 1870–1924*. São Paulo: Companhia das Letras, 2004.

Ellmann, Maud. *The Poetics of Impersonality: T. S. Eliot and Ezra Pound*. Cambridge, MA: Harvard University Press, 1987.

Elsaesser, Thomas, ed. *Early Cinema: Space, Frame, Narrative*. London: BFI, 1990.

———, ed. A *Second Life: German Cinema's First Decades*. Amsterdam: Amsterdam University Press, 1996.

Epstein, Jean. "Magnification." in Abel, *French Film Theory*, 1:238.

———. *La poésie d'aujourd'hui, un nouvel état d'intelligence*. Paris: Editions de la Siréne, 1921.

Escorel, Eduardo. " A décima musa." *Novos Estudos CEBRAP* 35 (1993): 171–94.

Eulálio, Alexandre, and Carlos Augusto Calil, eds. A *aventura brasileira de Blaise Cendrars: Ensaio, cronologia, filme, depoimentos, antologia, desenhos, conferências, correspondência, traduções*. São Paulo: EDUSP, 2001.

Fabian, Johannes. *Time and the Other: How Anthropology Makes Its Object*. New York: Columbia University Press, 2002.

Fausto, Boris. *Crime e cotidiano: A criminalidade em São Paulo, 1880–1924*. São Paulo: Editora Brasiliense, 1984.

Featherstone, David, and Joe Painter, eds. *Spatial Politics: Essays for Doreen Massey*. Malden: John Wiley and Sons, 2013.

Ferreira, Paulo Roberto. "Do kinetoscópio ao omniographo." *Filme Cultura* 47 (1986): 14–22.

Foster, David William. "On Being São Paulo Otherwise in *Paulicéia desvairada*." *Iberoamericana* 19 (2005): 28–40.

Foucault, Michel. *Archaeology of Knowledge*. London: Routledge, 2002.

———. "Of Other Spaces." *Diacritics* 16, no. 1 (1986): 22–27.

Freyre, Gilberto. *The Mansions and the Shanties: The Making of Modern Brazil*. Berkeley: University of California Press, 1987.

———. *The Masters and the Slaves: A Study in the Development of Brazilian Civilization*. Berkeley: University of California Press, 1986.

Friedberg, Anne. *Window Shopping: Cinema and the Postmodern*. Berkeley: University of California Press, 1993.

Furtado, Celso. *A economia brasileira: Contribução à análise do seu desenvolvimento*. Rio de Janeiro: A Noite, 1954.

Gabara, Esther. *Errant Modernism: The Ethos of Photography in Mexico and Brazil*. Durham, NC: Duke University Press, 2008.

Galvão, Maria Rita Eliezer. *Cinema, repercussões em caixa de eco ideológica: As idéias de "nacional" e "popular" no pensamento cinematográfico brasileiro*. Edited by Jean Claude Bernardet. São Paulo: Editora Brasiliense, 1983.

———. *Crônica do cinema paulistano*. São Paulo: Ática, 1975.

Gaonkar, Dilip Parameshwar. *Alternative Modernities*. A Millennial Quartet Book. Durham, NC: Duke University Press, 2001.

Gaughan, Martin. "Ruttmann's Berlin: Filming in a Hollow Space?" In *Screening the City*, edited by Mark Shiel and Tony Fitzmaurice, 41–57. London: Verso, 2003.

Geist, Anthony L., and José Monleón, eds. *Modernism and Its Margins: Reinscribing Cultural Modernity from Spain and Latin America*. New York: Garland, 1999.

Geraghty, Christine. "Cinema as a Social Space: Understanding Cinema-Going in Britain, 1947–1963." *Framework Journal* 42. Published online January 1, 2000. http://docs .wixstatic.com/ugd/32cb69_dea4296d45c2450bbf7aa65cf5e35d97.pdf.

Gledhill, Christine. *Stardom: Industry of Desire*. London: Routledge, 1991.

Goés, Maria. *A formação da classe trabalhadora: Movimento anarquisto no Rio de Janeiro, 1888–1911*. Rio de Janeiro: Jorge Zahar, 1988.

Gomery, Douglas, and Robert C. Allen. *Film History: Theory and Practice*. New York: Alfred A. Knopf, 1987.

Gomes, Danilo. *Uma rua chamada Ouvidor*. Rio de Janeiro: Prefeitura da Cidade do Rio de Janeiro, 1980.

Gomes, Paulo Emílio Salles. "Cinema: A Trajectory within Underdevelopment." Translated by Randal Johnson and Robert Stam. In Johnson and Stam, *Brazilian Cinema*, 244–55.

———. *Cinema: Trajetória no subdesenvolvimento*. São Paulo: Paz e Terra, 1973.

———. "Cinema: Trajetória no subdesenvolvimento." *Argumento*, no. 1 (October 1973): 55–67.

———. "A expressão social dos filmes documentais no cinema mudo brasileiro (1898–1930)." In *Paulo Emílio—Um intellectual na linha de frente: Coletânea de textos de Paulo Emilio Salles Gomes*, edited by Carlos Augusto Calil and Maria Teresa Machado, 323–30. São Paulo: Editora Brasiliense; Rio de Janeiro: Embrafilme, 1986.

———. *Humberto Mauro, Cataguases, Cinearte*. São Paulo: Perspectiva, 1974.

———. "Panorama do cinema brasileiro: 1896/1966." In *Cinema*, 19–76.

———. "Pequeno cinema antigo." In *Cinema*, 1–19.

———. "The Social Expression of Documentary Films in Silent Brazilian Cinema." In *Paulo Emílio Salles Gomes: On Brazil and Global Cinema*, edited by Maite Conde and Stephanie Dennison, translated by Amber MacCartney. London: Cardiff: University of Wales Press, forthcoming.

Gomes, Renato Cordeiro. *Todas as cidades, a cidade: Literatura e experiência urbana*. Rio de Janeiro: Rocco, 1994.

Gomes, Tiago de Melo. *Um espelho no palco: Identidades sociais e massificação da cultura no teatro de revista dos anos 1920*. Coleção Várias Histórias. Campinas: UNICAMP, 2004.

Gonzaga, Adhemar. "Filmagem brasileira." *Para Todos,* October 10, 1925, 30.

Gonzaga, Alice. *Palácios e poeiras: 100 anos de cinemas no Rio de Janeiro.* Rio de Janeiro: Record 1996.

———. *70 anos de cinema brasileiro.* Rio de Janeiro: Expressão Cultura, 1966.

Gorberg, Marissa. *Parc Royal: Um magazine na belle époque carioca.* Rio de Janeiro: Edições Acadêmicas, 2015.

Graham, Stephen. *Vertical: The City from Satellites to Bunkers.* London: Verso, 2016.

Greenblatt, Stephen. *Marvelous Possessions: The Wonder of the New World.* Oxford: Clarendon Press, 1991.

Grembecki, Maria Helena. *Mário de Andrade e L'Esprit Nouveau.* São Paulo: ISEB, 1969.

Griffiths, Alison. *Carceral Fantasies: Cinema and Prison in Early Twentieth-Century America.* New York: Columbia University Press, 2016.

———. "Knowledge and Visuality in Turn of the Century Anthropology: The Early Ethnographic Cinema of Alfred Cort Haddon and Walter Baldwin Spencer." *Visual Anthropology Review* 12, no. 2 (1996): 18–43.

———. "Shivers down Your Spine: Panoramas and the Origins of Cinematic Reenactment." *Screen* 44, no. 1 (2003): 1–37.

———. *Wondrous Difference: Cinema, Anthropology, and Turn-of-the-Century Visual Culture.* New York: Columbia University Press, 2002.

Gunning, Tom. "The Cinema of Attractions: Early Film, the Spectator, and the Avant-Garde." *Wide Angle* 8, nos. 3–4 (1986): 63–70.

———. "Early American Film." In *The Oxford Guide to Film Studies,* edited by John Hill and Pamela Church Gibson, 255–17. New York: Oxford University Press, 1998.

———. "Early Cinema as Global Cinema: The Encyclopedic Ambition." In Abel, Bertellini, and King, *Early Cinema,* 11–16.

———. "Embarrassing Evidence: The Detective Camera and the Documentary Impulse." In *Collecting Visible Evidence,* edited by Jane Gaines and Michael Renov, 46–64. Visible Evidence. Minneapolis: University of Minnesota Press, 1999.

———. "Pictures of Crowd Splendor: The Mitchell and Kenyon Factory Gate Films." In *The Lost World of Mitchell and Kenyon: Edwardian Britain on Film,* edited by Vanessa Toulmin, Simon Popple, and Patrick Russell, 49–58. London: BFI, 2004.

———. Preface to *Jean Epstein: Critical Essays and New Translations,* edited by Sarah Keller and Jason N. Paul. Amsterdam: Amsterdam University Press, 2012.

———. "What's the Point of an Index? Or Faking Photographs." In *Still/Moving: Between Cinema and Photography,* edited by Karen Beckman and Jean Ma, 23–40. Durham, NC: Duke University Press, 2008.

Hahner, June E. *Emancipating the Female Sex: The Struggle for Women's Rights in Brazil, 1850–1940.* Durham, NC: Duke University Press, 1990.

Hansen, Miriam. *Babel and Babylon: Spectatorship and American Silent Film.* Cambridge, MA: Harvard University Press, 1991.

———. "Early Cinema, Late Cinema: Permutations of the Public Sphere." *Screen* 34, no. 3 (1993): 197–210.

———. "Early Silent Cinema: Whose Public Sphere?" *New German Critique* 29 (1991): 147–84.

———. "Fallen Women, Rising Stars, New Horizons: Shanghai Silent Film and Vernacular Modernism." *Film Quarterly* 54 (2000): 10–22.

Haraway, Donna Jeanne. *Primate Visions: Gender, Race, and Nature in the World of Modern Science.* New York: Routledge, 2006.

Hardman, Francisco Foot. *Nem pátria, nem patrão! Memória operária, cultura e literatura no Brasil.* São Paulo: UNESP, 2002.

———. *Trem-Fantasma: A Ferrovia Madeira-Mamoré e a modernidade na selva.* São Paulo: Companhia das Letras, 2005.

Hardman, Francisco Foot, and Victor Leonardi. *História da indústria e do trabalho no Brasil: Das origens aos anos 20.* 2nd ed. Série Fundamentos. São Paulo: Ática, 1991.

Harley, J. B. "Maps, Knowledge and Power." In *The Iconography of Landscape: Essays on the Symbolic Representation, Design, and Use of Past Environments,* edited by Denis E. Cosgrove and Stephen Daniels, 277–312. Cambridge: Cambridge University Press, 1988.

Headrick, Daniel R. *Power over Peoples: Technology, Environments, and Western Imperialism, 1400 to the Present.* The Princeton Economic History of the Western World. Princeton, NJ: Princeton University Press, 2010.

———. *The Tentacles of Progress: Technology Transfer in the Age of Imperialism, 1850–1940.* New York: Oxford University Press, 1988.

———. *The Tools of Empire: Technology and European Imperialism in the Nineteenth Century.* New York: Oxford University Press, 1981.

Hecht, Susanna B. "The Last Unfinished Page of Genesis: Euclides da Cunha and the Amazon." *Historical Geography* 32 (2004): 43–69.

Higashi, Sumiko. *Virgins, Vamps and Flappers: The American Silent Movie Heroine.* St. Albans: Eden Press, 1977.

Higson, Andrew. "The Concept of National Cinema." In *Film and Nationalism,* edited by Andrew Williams, 52–67. New Brunswick, NJ: Rutgers University Press.

Hobsbawm, Eric. *Age of Empire: 1875–1914.* London: Abacus, 1989.

Hobsbawm, Eric, and T. O. Ranger, eds. *The Invention of Tradition.* Past and Present Publications. Cambridge: Cambridge University Press, 1983.

Holloway, Thomas H. *Policing Rio de Janeiro: Repression and Resistance in a Nineteenth-Century City.* Stanford, CA: Stanford University Press, 1993.

Huyssen, Andreas. *After the Great Divide: Modernism, Mass Culture, Postmodernism.* Theories of Representation and Difference. Bloomington: Indiana University Press, 1986.

———. "The Geographies of Modernism in a Globalizing World." *New German Critique* 34, no. 1 (2007): 189–207.

Hyde, Ralph, and Barbican Art Gallery. *Panoramania! The Art and Entertainment of the "All-Embracing" View.* London: Barbican Art Gallery, 1988.

Ihering, Hermann von. *Anthropology of the State of São Paulo, Brazil.* São Paulo: Duprat, 1904.

———. "Exterminio dos indígenas ou dos sertanejos." *Jornal do Commércio,* December 15 1908, n. pag.

———. "O museu paulista nos annos de 1906–1909." *Revista do Museu Paulista* 8 (1911): 1–22.

Jacobs, Jane. *Edge of Empire: Postcolonialism and the City.* London: Routledge, 1996.

Jenson, Joli. "Fandom as Pathology: The Consequences of Characterization." In *The Adoring Audience: Fan Culture and Popular Media,* edited by Lisa A. Lewis, 9–29. New York: Routledge, 1992.

Johnson, Randal. "Brazilian Modernism: An Idea Out of Place?" in *Modernismo and its Margins: Modernity from Spain and Latin America*, edited by Anthony Geist and José Monleon, 188–214. New York: Garland, 1999.

———. *The Film Industry in Brazil: Culture and the State*. Pittsburgh, PA: University of Pittsburgh Press, 1987.

Johnson, Randal, and Robert Stam, eds. *Brazilian Cinema*. New York: Columbia University Press, 1995.

———. "The Shape of Brazilian History." In Johnson and Stam, *Brazilian Cinema*, 15–52.

Kant, Immanuel. *Critique of Judgment*. Translated by J. H. Bernard. New York: Barnes and Noble, 2005.

King, Anthony D. *Colonial Urban Development: Culture, Social Power, and Environment*. London: Routledge, 1976.

———. *Urban Colonialism and World Economy: Cultural and Spatial Foundations of the World Urban System*. London: Routledge, 1990.

King, John. *Magical Reels: A History of Cinema in Latin America*. Critical Studies in Latin American Culture. London: Verso, 1990.

Kirby, Lynne. *Parallel Tracks: The Railroad and Silent Cinema*. Durham, NC: Duke University Press, 1997.

Korfmann, Michael. Introduction to Korfmann, *Ten Contemporary Views*, 5–11.

———. "On Brazilian Cinema: From Mário Peixoto's *Limite* to Walter Salles." *Senses of Cinema* 40 (July 2006). http://sensesofcinema.com/2006/feature-articles/brazilian-cinema/#10.

———, ed. *Ten Contemporary Views on Mário Peixoto's "Limite."* Munster: Monsenstein and Vannerdat, 2006.

Kossoy, Boris. *Dicionário histórico-fotográfico brasileiro: Fotógrafos e Ofício da Fotografia no Brasil (1833–1910)*. São Paulo: Instituto Moreira Salles, 2002.

Kracauer, Siegfried. "The Little Shopgirls Go to the Movies." In *The Mass Ornament: Weimar Essays*, 291–306. Cambridge, MA: Harvard University Press, 1995.

Krauss, Rosalind E. *The Optical Unconscious*. Cambridge, MA: MIT Press, 1993.

Lahiri Choudhury, Deep Kanta. *Telegraphic Imperialism: Crisis and Panic in the Indian Empire, c.1830*. New York: Palgrave Macmillan, 2010.

Larkin, Brian. *Signal and Noise: Media, Infrastructure, and Urban Culture in Nigeria*. Durham, NC: Duke University Press, 2008.

Lasmar, Denise Portugal. *O acervo imagético da Commissão Rondon do Museu do Índio*. Rio de Janeiro: Museu do Índio, 2011.

Latour, Bruno. *Science in Action: How to Follow Scientists and Engineers through Society*. Cambridge, MA: Harvard University Press, 1987.

Levine, Robert M. *The History of Brazil*. Westport, CT: Greenwood, 1999.

Lima, Antonio Carlos de Souza. *Um grande cerco de paz: Poder tutelar indianidade e formação do estado no Brasil*. Petropolis: Vozes, 1995.

Lima, Luiz Costa. *História, ficção, literatura*. São Paulo: Companhia das Letras, 2006.

Lima, Sérgio. "The Discovery of Surrealism in 1920 Rio de Janeiro: Notes on the Relationship between Surrealism and Cinema and between France and the Cinema of Brazil." In *Conscious Hallucinations: Filmic Surrealism*, edited by Claudia Dillmann, 164–69. Frankfurt: Deutsches Filminstitut, 2014.

Linhales, Meily Assbú. "O sport no 'clima cultural' da década de 1920: A 'energização do cárater.'" *Anais do Congresso Internacional de Ciências do Esporte* 2 (May 2007): 1–22.

López, Ana M. "Early Cinema and Modernity in Latin America." *Cinema Journal* 40 (2000): 48–78.

———. "Facing Up to Hollywood." In *Reinventing Film Studies,* edited by Christine Gledhill and Linda Williams, 419–38. New York: Edward Arnold, 2000.

Lopez, Telê Porto Ancona. Introduction to *Fotógrafo e turista aprendiz,* by Mário de Andrade. São Paulo: IEB, 1993.

Ludmer, Josefina. *The Corpus Delicti: A Manual of Argentine Fictions.* Translated by Glen S. Close. Pittsburgh, PA: University of Pittsburgh Press, 2004.

MacCannell, Dean. "Staged Authenticity: Arrangements of Social Space in Tourist Settings." *American Journal of Sociology* 79, no. 3 (1973): 589–603.

Machado, Antônio de Alcântara. *Pathé-Baby.* Edited by Cecília de Lara. 1926. Facsimile ed., São Paulo: Arquivo do Estado de São Paulo, 1982.

Machado, Rubens, Jr. "São Paulo em movimento: A representação cinematográfica da metrópole nos anos 20." MA thesis, University of São Paulo, 1989.

Maciel, Laura Antunes. *A nação por um fio: Caminhos, práticas e imagens da "Comissão Rondon."* São Paulo: FAPESP, 1998.

Magalhães, R., Jr. *O fabuloso Patrocínio Filho.* Rio de Janeiro: Civilização Brasileira, 1957.

Maluf, Marina, and Maria Lúcia Mott. "Recônditos do mundo feminino." In *República: Da belle-époque à era do radio,* edited by Nicolau Sevcenko, 367–423. São Paulo: Companhia das Letras, 2001.

Martins, Luciana. *Photography and Documentary Film in the Making of Modern Brazil.* Manchester: Manchester University Press, 2013.

———. *O Rio de Janeiro dos viajantes: O olhar Britânico, 1800–1850.* Rio de Janeiro: Jorge Zahar, 2001.

Massey, Doreen. "Globalization: What Does It Mean for Geography?" *Development Education Journal* 9 (2002): 3–5.

———. "A Global Sense of Place." In *Space, Place, Gender,* 146–57. Cambridge: Polity Press, 1994.

Matta, Roberto da. *Carnivals, Rogues, and Heroes: An Interpretation of the Brazilian Dilemma.* Notre Dame, IN: University of Notre Dame Press, 1991.

Mattelart, Armand. *The Invention of Communication.* Minneapolis: University of Minnesota Press, 1996.

———. *Networking the World, 1794–2000.* Minneapolis: University of Minnesota Press, 2000.

McCabe, Susan. *Cinematic Modernism: Modernist Poetry and Film.* Cambridge: Cambridge University Press, 2005.

McNeill, Donald. "Skyscraper Geography." *Progress in Human Geography* 29 (2005): 41–55.

Meade, Teresa. *"Civilizing" Rio: Reform and Resistance in a Brazilian City, 1889–1930.* University Park: Pennsylvania State University Press, 1997.

Mello, Saulo Pereira de. "*O Fan,* o Chaplin Club e *Limite.*" *Revista o Percevejo* 5, no. 5 (1997): 58–68.

———. *Limite.* Artemídia. Rio de Janeiro: Rocco, 1996.

———. "Man's Fate." In Korfmann, *Ten Contemporary Views,* 33–49.

———. "Notas sobre a história de *Limite*." *Folha de São Paulo*, October 8, 1988, 3.

Mello, Saulo Pereira de, and Mário Peixoto. *Limite, filme de Mário Peixoto*. Film script. Rio de Janeiro: Funarte, 1979.

Menezes, Paulo. "Major Reis e a constituição visual do Brasil enquanto nação." *Horizontes Antropológicos* 14, no. 29 (2008): 231–56.

Miller, Angela. "The Panorama, the Cinema and the Emergence of the Spectator." *Wide Angle* 18, no. 2 (1996): 34–69.

Mindlin, José E. "Illustrated Books and Periodicals in Brazil, 1875–1994." *Journal of Decorative and Propaganda Arts* 21 (1995): 60–85.

Miranda, Luiz Felipe. *Dicionário de cineastas brasileiros*. São Paulo: Art Editora/Secretaria de Estado da Cultura, 1990.

Mitchell, Timothy. *Rule of Experts: Egypt, Techno-Politics, Modernity*. Berkeley: University of California Press, 2002.

Molloy, Sylvia. "The Politics of Posing." In *Hispanisms and Homosexualities*, edited by Sylvia Molloy and Robert Irwin, 141–60. Durham, NC: Duke University Press, 1998.

Monteiro, José Carlos. *Cinema brasileiro*. São Paulo: Ministério da Cultura, 1996.

Moreno, Antonio. *Cinema brasileiro: História e relações com o estado*. Niteroi: EDUFF/CEGRAF, 1994.

Morettin, Eduardo. "Cinema e estado no Brasil: A Exposição Internacional do Centenário da Independência em 1922 e 1923." *Novos Estudos CEBRAP*, no. 89 (2011): 137–48.

———. *Dimensões históricas do documentário brasileiro no periodo silencioso*. São Paulo: Associação Nacional de História, 2005.

Moreyra, Alvaro. *A cidade mulher*. Coleção Biblioteca Carioca 19. Rio de Janeiro: Prefeitura da Cidade do Rio, 1991.

Morse, Richard M., and Jorge Enrique Hardoy, eds. *Rethinking the Latin American City*. Baltimore: John Hopkins University Press, 1993.

Moura, Roberto. "A bela época (primórdios–1912), cinema carioca (1912–1930)." In *História do cinema brasileiro*, edited by Fernão Ramos, 12–24. São Paulo: Art Editora, 1987.

———. *Tia Ciata e a Pequena Africa no Rio de Janeiro*. Rio de Janeiro: Departamento Geral de Documentação e Informação Cultural, 1995.

Moya, Jose C. *Cousins and Strangers: Spanish Immigrants in Buenos Aires, 1850–1930*. Berkeley: University of California Press, 1998.

Mulvey, Laura. *Visual and Other Pleasures*. London: Palgrave Macmillan, 2009.

Musser, Charles. "The Travel Genre in 1903–1904: Moving towards Fictional Naratives." In *Early Cinema: Space, Frame, Narrative*, edited by Thomas Elesaesser, 123–33. London: BFI, 1990.

Nabuco, Joaquim. *O abolicionismo*. Rio de Janeiro: Instituto Nacional do Livro, 1977.

———. *Essencial*. São Paulo: Companhia das Letras, 2010.

Natter, Wolfgang. "The City as Cinematic Space." In *Place, Power, Situation, and Spectacle: A Geography of Film*, edited by Stuart C. Aitken and Leo Zonn, 203–28. Lanham, MD: Rowman and Littlefield, 1994.

Needell, Jeffrey. "The Domestic Civilizing Mission: The Cultural Role of the State in Brazil, 1908–1930." *Luso-Brazilian Review* 36, no. 1 (1999): 1–18.

———. *A Tropical Belle Époque: Elite Culture and Society in Turn-of-the-Century Rio de Janeiro*. Cambridge: Cambridge University Press, 1987.

Nina Rodrigues, Raymundo. *As raças humanas e a responsabilidade penal no Brazil.* Introduction by Afrânio Peixoto. Rio de Janeiro: Guanabara, Waissman, Koogan, 1935.

Noronha, Jurandyr. *Pioneiros do cinema brasileiro.* São Paulo: Melhoramentos, 1997.

Novaes, Sylvia Caiuby. "Funerais entre os Bororo: Imagens da refiguração do mundo." *Revista de Antropologia* 49, no. 1 (2006): 283–315.

Nye, David E. *American Technological Sublime.* Cambridge, MA: MIT Press, 1994.

Oettermann, Stephan. *The Panorama: History of a Mass Medium.* New York: Zone Books, 1997.

Orgeron, Marsha. "Making 'It' in Hollywood: Clara Bow, Fandom and Consumer Culture." *Cinema Journal* 42, no. 4 (2003): 76–97.

Ortiz, Renato. *A moderna tradição brasileira.* São Paulo: Editora Brasiliense, 1988.

Paiva, Samuel, and Sheila Schvarzman, eds. *Viagem ao cinema silencioso do Brasil.* São Paulo: Azougue, 2011.

Pasolini, Pier Paolo. "The Written Language of Reality." In *Heretical Empiricism,* translated by Ben Lawton and Louise K. Barnett, 197–222. Bloomington: Indiana University Press, 1988.

Peixoto, Afrânio. *As razões do coração.* Rio de Janeiro: F. Alves, 1925.

Peixoto, Mário. "A Film from South America." In Korfmann, *Ten Contemporary Views,* 11–16.

Perrone, Charles. "Performing São Paulo: Vanguard Representations of a Brazilian Cosmopolis." *Latin American Music Review* 23, no. 1 (2002): 60–78.

Pessoa, Ana. *Carmen Santos: O cinema dos anos 20.* Rio de Janiero: Aeroplano, 2002.

Phillips, Richard. *Mapping Men and Empire: A Geography of Adventure.* London: Routledge, 1997.

Picchia, Paulo Menotti del. "Arte moderna." In *Vanguarda européia e modernisno brasileiro,* edited by Gilberto Mendonça Teles, 287–92. Rio de Janeiro: Vozes, 1976.

Pimento Velloso, Monica. *Modernismo no Rio de Janeiro: Turunas e quixotes.* Rio de Janeiro: Fundacão Getúlio Vargas, 1996.

Pinney, Christopher. *Camera Indica: The Social Life of Indian Photographs.* Chicago: University of Chicago Press, 1997.

———. "Classification and Fantasy in the Photographic Construction of Caste and Tribe." *Visual Anthropology* 3, nos. 2–3 (1990): 259–88.

———. "The Lexical Spaces of Eye-Spy." In *Film as Ethnography,* edited by Peter Ian Crawford and David Turton, 26–49. Manchester: Manchester University Press, 1992.

———. *"Photos of the Gods": The Printed Image and Political Struggle in India.* New York: Oxford University Press, 2004.

Pinney, Christopher, and Nicolas Peterson, eds. *Photography's Other Histories.* Objects /Histories. Durham, NC: Duke University Press, 2003.

Podalsky, Laura. Introduction to *Sports Culture in Latin American History,* edited by David Sheinin. Pittsburgh, PA: University of Pittsburgh Press, 2015.

Prado, Caio. *História econômica do Brasil.* 5th ed. São Paulo: Editora Brasiliense, 1959.

Pratt, Mary Louise. *Imperial Eyes: Travel Writing and Transculturation.* New York: Routledge, 1992.

Rabinovitz, Lauren. *For the Love of Pleasure: Women, Movies, and Culture in Turn-of-the-Century Chicago.* New Brunswick, NJ: Rutgers University Press, 1998.

Rama, Angel. *The Lettered City.* Durham, NC: Duke University Press, 1996.

Ramos, Fernão. *História do cinema brasileiro.* São Paulo: Art Editora, 1987.

Rancière, Jacques. *Dissensus: On Politics and Aesthetics.* Translated by Steve Corcoran. New York: Continuum, 2010.

———. *The Politics of Aesthetics: The Distribution of the Sensible.* 2006. Reprint, London: Bloomsbury, 2013.

Rangel, Alberto. *Inferno verde: Cenas e cenários do Amazonas.* Introduction by Marcos Frederico Krüger. Manaus: Editora Valer, 2001.

Reis, Liuz Thomaz. "Nosso álbum." In *Photografias da construção, expedições e explorações desde 1900 a 1922 encaminhado ao Exmo. Sr. General de Divisão Fernando Setembrino de Carvalho, D. Ministro d'Estado dos Negócios da Guerra.* 2 vols. Rio de Janeiro: Ministro d'Estado, 1922.

Resende, Beatriz. "Rio de Janeiro: Cidade da crônica." In *Cronistas do Rio,* edited by Beatriz Resende. Rio de Janeiro: José Olympio, 1995.

———. "A volta de Mademoiselle Cinema." In *Mademoiselle Cinema: Novela de costumes do momento que passa,* 9–29. Rio de Janeiro: Casa da Palavra, 1999.

Rocha, Glauber. "Humberto Mauro e a situação histórica." In *Revisão crítica do cinema brasileiro,* 43–57. São Paulo: Cosac e Naify, 2003.

———. Introduction to *Revisão crítica do cinema brasileiro,* 33–42. São Paulo: Cosac e Naify, 2003.

Rodrigues, Ana Paula Dias. "Antônio de Alcântara Machadao com a câmera: Exploração geográfica e cinematográfica em *Pathé-Baby.*" *Cadernos de Semiótica Aplicada* 10 (2012): 1–14.

Rodrigues, João Carlos. *O negro brasileiro e o cinema: 1988, 100 anos de abolição—90 anos de cinema no Brasil.* Rio de Janeiro: Globo, 1988.

Romero, Sílvio. "Couto de Magalhaes e a influência dos selvagens no folklore brasileiro." In *Etnografia brasileira.* Rio de Janeiro: Laemmert, 1888.

Rondon, Cândido Mariano da Silva. *Relatório dos trabalhos realizados de 1900–1906 pelo Major de engenharia Cândido Mariano da Silva Rondon.* Vols. 4–5. Rio de Janeiro: Departamento da Imprensa Nacional, 1946.

Rony, Fatimah Tobing. *The Third Eye: Race, Cinema, and Ethnographic Spectacle.* Durham, NC: Duke University Press, 1996.

Roosevelt, Theodore. *Through the Brazilian Wilderness.* New York: Create Space, 2009.

Roquette-Pinto, Edgar. *Rondônia.* São Paulo: Companhia Editora Nacional, 1975.

Rosaldo, Renato. "Imperialist Nostalgia." *Representations* 26 (1989): 107–22.

Rosenberg, Emily S. *Spreading the American Dream: American Economic and Cultural Expansion, 1890–1945.* New York: Hill and Wang, 1982.

Rosenberg, Fernando J. *The Avant-Garde and Geopolitics in Latin America.* Pittsburgh, PA: University of Pittsburgh Press, 2006.

Rowe, William, and Vivian Schelling. *Memory and Modernity: Popular Culture in Latin America.* London: Verso, 1991.

Ruby, Jay. "The Moral Burden of Anthorship in Ethnographic Film." *Visual Anthropology Review* 11, no. 2 (1995): 77–82.

Ruoff, Jeffrey. Introduction to *Virtual Voyages,* 1–24.

———, ed. *Virtual Voyages: Cinema and Travel.* Durham, NC: Duke University Press, 2006.

Ryan, James R. *Photography and Exploration*. London: Reaktions Books, 2013.

———. *Picturing Empire: Photography and the Visualization of the British Empire*. Chicago: University of Chicago Press, 1997.

Sá, Lúcia. Introduction to *The Amazon: Land without History*, by Euclides da Cunha, xi–xiii. Oxford: Oxford University Press, 2007.

———. *Life in the Megalopolis: Mexico City and São Paulo*. London: Routledge, 2007.

Said, Edward W. *Culture and Imperialism*. New York: Knopf, 1993.

Saliba, Elias Thomé. *Raízes do riso: A representação humorística na história brasileira. Da Belle Époque aos primeiros tempos do rádio*. São Paulo: Companhia das Letras, 2002.

Salla, Fernando. *As prisões em São Paulo: 1822–1940*. São Paulo: Annablume, 1999.

Salles, Walter. "Free Eyes in the Country of Repetition." In Korfmann, *Ten Contemporary Views*, 25–33.

Sandberg, Mark. "Effigy and Narrative: Looking into the Nineteeth-Century Folk Museum." In Charney and Schwartz, *Cinema*, 320–62.

Sarlo, Beatriz. "Buenos Aires in the 20s and 30s." In *Mediating Two Worlds: Cinematic Encounters in the Americas*, edited by John King, Ana M. López, and Manuel Alvarado, 164–75. London: BFI, 1993.

Schelling, Vivian. *Through the Kaleidoscope: The Experience of Modernity in Latin America*. New York: Verso, 2000.

Schivelbusch, Wolfgang. *The Railway Journey: The Industrialization of Time and Space in the Nineteenth Century*. Berkeley: University of California Press, 1986.

Schnapp, Jeffrey T., and João César de Castro Rocha. "Brazilian Velocities." *South Central Review* 13 (1996): 105–56.

Schuster, Sven. "The Brazilian Native on Display: Indianist Artwork and Ethnographic Exhibits at the World's Fairs, 1862–1889." *Journal of the International Association of Research Institutes in the History of Art*, no. 127 (September 2015). www.riha-journal.org /articles/2015/2015-jul-sep/schuster-the-brazilian-native-on-display.

Schvarzman, Sheila. *Humberto Mauro e as imagens do Brasil*. São Paulo: UNESP, 2004.

———. "Ir ao cinema em São Paulo nos anos 20." *Revista Brasileira de História* 25 (2005): 153–74.

Schwarcz, Lilia Moritz. *The Emperor's Beard: Dom Pedro II and the Tropical Monarchy of Brazil*. Translated by John Gledson. New York: Hill and Wang, 2004.

———. *The Spectacle of the Races: Scientists, Institutions, and the Race Question in Brazil, 1870–1930*. New York: Hill and Wang, 1990.

Schwartz, Jorge. *Las vanguardias latinoamericanas: Textos programáticos y críticos*. Madrid: Cátedra, 1991.

Schwartz, Vanessa R. *Spectacular Realities: Early Mass Culture in Fin-de-Siècle Paris*. Berkeley: University of California Press, 1998.

Schwarz, Roberto. *As ideias fora do lugar*. São Paulo: Companhia das Letras, 2014.

———. *Misplaced Ideas: Essays on Brazilian Culture*. Edited and translated by John Gledson. London: Verso, 1992.

Seigel, Micol. *Uneven Encounters: Making Race and Nation in Brazil and the United States*. Durham, NC: Duke University Press, 2009.

Sekula, Alan. "The Body and the Archive." *October* 39 (1986): 3–64.

Serna, Laura Isabel. *Making Cinelandia: American Films and Mexican Film Culture before the Golden Age.* Durham, NC: Duke University Press, 2014.

Sevcenko, Nicolau. *Literatura como missão: Tensões sociais e criação cultural na Primeira República.* São Paulo: Editora Brasiliense, 1983.

———. *Orfeu extático na metrópole: São Paulo, sociedade e cultura nos frementes anos 20.* São Paulo: Companhia das Letras, 1992.

———. "Peregrinations, Visions and the City: From Canudos to Brasília, the Backlands Become the City and the City Becomes the Backlands." In *Through the Kaleidoscope: The Experience of Modernity in Latin America,* edited by Vivien Schelling and translated by Lorraine Leu. London: Verso, 2000.

Shaw, Lisa, and Stephanie Dennison. *Brazilian National Cinema.* National Cinemas. London: Routledge, 2007.

Shiel, Mark. "Cinema and the City in History and Theory." In *Cinema and the City: Film and Urban Societies in a Global Context,* edited by Mark Shiel and Tony Fitzmaurice, 1–18. Oxford: Blackwell, 2001.

Shohat, Ella, and Robert Stam. *Unthinking Eurocentrism: Multiculturalism and the Media.* New York: Routledge, 1994.

Silva Nobre, Francisco. *A margem do cinema brasileiro.* Rio de Janeiro: Pingetti, 1963.

———. *Pequena história do cinema brasileiro.* Rio de Janeiro: Associação Atlética Branco do Brasil, 1955.

Simmel, Georg. "The Metropolis and Mental Life." In *On Individuality and Social Forms: Selected Writings.* Chicago: University of Chicago Press, 1971.

Singer, Ben. *Melodrama and Modernity: Early Sensational Cinema and Its Contexts.* New York: Columbia University Press, 2001.

Skidmore, Thomas E. *Politics in Brazil, 1930–1964: An Experiment in Democracy.* New York: Oxford University Press.

Sommer, Doris. *Foundational Fictions: The National Romances of Latin America.* Berkeley: University of California Press, 1991.

Souza, Carlos Roberto de, ed. *Catálogo: Filmes produzidos pelo INCE.* Rio de Janeiro: Fundação do Cinema Brasileiro, 1990.

———. *A fascinante aventura brasileira.* São Paulo: Cinemateca Brasileira, 1981.

———. "Os pioneiros do cinema Brasileiro." *Alceu* 8, no. 15 (2007): 20–37.

———. "Resgate do cinema silencioso." Liner notes. *Resgate do cinema silencioso.* DVD. São Paulo: Cinemateca Brasileira, 2008.

Souza, José Inácio de Melo. *Imagens do passado: São Paulo e o Rio de Janeiro nos primórdios do cinema.* São Paulo: SENAC, 2003.

———. "As imperfeições do crime da mala." *Revista USP* 45 (2000): 106–12.

———. *Salas de cinema e história urbana de São Paulo (1895–1930): O cinema dos engenheiros.* São Paulo: SENAC, 2016.

Staiger, Janet. *Bad Women: Regulating Sexuality in Early American Cinema.* Minneapolis: University of Minnesota Press, 1995.

Stam, Robert. "On the Margins: Brazilian Avant-Garde Cinema." In Johnson and Stam, *Brazilian Cinema,* 306–27.

———. *Tropical Multiculturalism: A Comparative History of Race in Brazilian Cinema and Culture.* Durham, NC: Duke University Press, 1997.

Stamp, Shelley. *Movie-Struck Girls: Women and Motion Picture Culture after the Nickelodeon*. Princeton, NJ: Princeton University Press, 2000.

Staples, Amy. "The Last of the Great (Foot-Slogging) Explorers: Lewis Cotlow and the Ethnographic Imaginary in Popular Travel Film." In Ruoff, *Virtual Voyages*, 195–217.

Stepan, Nancy. *Picturing Tropical Nature*. Ithaca, NY: Cornell University Press, 2001.

Stickel, Erico J. Siriuba. *Uma pequena biblioteca particular: Subsídios para o estudo da iconografia no Brasil*. São Paulo: EDUSP, 2004.

Studlar, Gaylyn. "The Perils of Pleasure? Fan Magazine Discourse as Women's Commodified Culture in the 1920s." *Wide Angle* 13, no. 1 (1991): 6–33.

Suárez, José I., and Jack E. Tomlins. "Early Modernist Poetics and Early Poetry." In *Mário de Andrade: The Creative Works*, edited by José Suárez and Jack E. Tomlins, 31–69. Lewisburg, PA: Bucknell University Press, 2000.

Süssekind, Flora. *Cinematograph of Words: Literature, Technique, and Modernization in Brazil*. Translated by Paulo Henrique Britto. Stanford, CA: Stanford University Press, 1997.

———. *As revistas de ano e a invenção do Rio de Janeiro*. Rio de Janeiro: Editora Nova Fronteira, 1986.

Tacca, Fernando de. *A imagética da Comissão Rondon: Etnografias fílmicas estratégicas*. Campinas: Papirus, 2001.

Thompson, Kristin. *Exporting Entertainment: America in the World Film Market, 1907–1934*. BFI: London, 1985.

Trotter, David. *Cinema and Modernism*. Malden, MA: Blackwell, 2007.

Turazzi, Maria Inez. *Poses e trejeitos: A fotografia e as exposições na era do espetáculo, 1839/1889*. Rio de Janeiro: Rocco, 1995.

———. *Victor Meirelles: Novas leituras*. São Paulo: Museu Victor Meirelles, 2009.

Turvey, Malcolm. *The Filming of Modern Life: European Avant-Garde Film of the 1920s*. October Books. Cambridge, MA: MIT Press, 2011.

Unruh, Vicky. *Latin American Vanguards: The Art of Contentious Encounters*. Latin American Literature and Culture. Berkeley: University of California Press, 1994.

———. *Performing Women and Modern Literary Culture in Latin America*. Austin: University of Texas Press, 2006.

Vasudevan, Ravi, and Nehru Memorial Museum and Library. Centre for Contemporary Studies. *Film Studies, the New Cultural History and the Experience of Modernity*. New Delhi: Centre for Contemporary Studies, 1995.

Ventura, Zuenir. *Cidade partida*. São Paulo: Companhia das Letras, 1994.

Vertov, Dziga. *Kino-Eye: The Writings of Dziga Vertov*. Edited by Annette Michelson. Translated by Kevin O'Brien. Berkeley: University of California Press, 1984.

Viany, Alex. *Introdução ao cinema brasileiro*. Rio de Janeiro: Ministério da Educação e Cultura, 1956.

Vieira, João Luiz. "O marketing do desejo." In Buarque de Hollanda, *Quase Catálogo 3*, 34–42.

Vieira, João Luiz, and Margareth Pereira. "Cinemas cariocas: Da Ouvidor à Cinelândia." *Filme Cultura* 47 (1986): 25–34.

Wall-Romana, Christophe. *Cinepoetry: Imaginary Cinemas in French Poetry*. Verbal Arts: Studies in Poetics. New York: Fordham University Press, 2013.

———. *Jean Epstein: Corporal Cinema and Film Philosophy*. Oxford: Oxford University Press, 2013.

Welge, Jobst. *Genealogical Fictions: Cultural Periphery and Historical Change in the Modern Novel.* Baltimore: John Hopkins University Press, 2014.

Wild, Jennifer. *The Parisian Avant-Garde in the Age of Cinema, 1900–1923.* Berkeley: University of California Press, 2015.

Williams, Bruce. "The Lie That Told the Truth: (Self) Publicity Strategies and the Myth of Mário Peixoto's *Limite.*" *Film History* 17 (2005): 392–403.

Williams, Daryle. *Culture Wars in Brazil: The First Vargas Regime, 1930–1945.* Durham, NC: Duke University Press, 2001.

Williams, Tami. *Germaine Dulac: A Cinema of Sensations.* Champaign: University of Illinois Press, 2014.

Wollen, Peter. *Raiding the Icebox: Reflections on Twentieth-Century Culture.* Bloomington: Indiana University Press, 1993.

Wood, Marcus. *Black Milk: Imagining Slavery in the Visual Cultures of Brazil and America.* Oxford: Oxford University Press, 2013.

Xavier, Ismail. *Allegories of Underdevelopment: Aesthetics and Politics in Modern Brazilian Cinema.* Minneapolis: University of Minnesota Press, 1997.

———. "The Modern and the Contemporary: Two Representations of the Metropolis in Film." *Review: Literature of the Arts of the Americas* 39 (2006): 188–97.

———. "Progresso, disciplina fabril e desconstração operária: Retóricas do documentário brasileiro silencioso." *ArtCultura* 11 (2009): 9–24.

———. *Sétima arte: Um culto moderno. O idealismo estético e o cinema.* São Paulo: Perspectiva, 1978.

Yogerst, Chris. *From the Headlines to Hollywood: The Birth and Boom of Warner Bros.* New York: Rowman and Littlefield, 2016.

Zhen, Zhang. *An Amorous History of the Silver Screen: Shanghai Cinema, 1896–1937.* Chicago: University of Chicago Press, 2005.

Abel, Richard, 29, 31, 185,
Allen, Jeanne, 87
Almeida, Guilherme de, 183, 240
Anderson, Benedict, 8, 31, 140, 237
Andrade, Mário de: *Amar, verbo intransitive* (Love, Intransitive Verb), 184; A *escrava que não é Isaura,* 193; "Crônicas de Malazarte," 191; and Epstein, 193; and *L'Esprit Nouveau,* 186, 192; and film criticism, 183, 189–191; *Paulicéia desvairada* (Hallucinated City), 184, 191–194, 205; and photography, 189, 269n53; Simultaneism, 192–195
Andrade, Oswald de: *Os condenados* (The Condemned), 184, 194–195; film activities, 183, 186; "Manifesto Antropófago" (Cannibalist Manifesto), 187, 199; "Manifesto Pau Brasil" (Brazilwood Manifesto), 182, 198; *Memórias sentimentais de João Miramar* (Sentimental Memoirs of João Miramar), 184, 195–197, 198; *Serafim Ponte Grande* (Seraphim Grosse Pointe) 184, 195, 196–197, 198
Anthropology: and visual culture, 145–146
Appollinaire, Guilhaume, 185
Araújo, Luciana Corrêa, 121
Assis, Machado de 117, 197
Auerbach, Jonathan, 30
Azevedo, Aluísio, 78
Azevedo, Artur, 68

Barbero, Jesús Martin, 4, 243
Barreto, Lima, 34, 59
Barthes, Roland, 61, 139, 167–168
Bazin, André, 142
Bean, Jennifer M. and Diane Negra, 11, 29–30
Benjamin, Walter: 36, 49–50; 78–79, 93, 142, 191, 197, 237; on arcades, 42; optical unconscious, 185
Bernardet, Jean-Claude, 113–114, 118, 122–123, 126–127, 240–241. *See also* Classical film historiography in Brazil
Besse, Susan, 95, 98
Bhabha, Homi K., 139
Bicalho, Maria Fernanda, 98, 102, 107
Bilac, Olavo, 46, 183, 201
Bororo, 166, 169
Botelho de Magalhães, Amílcar Armando, 140, 146, 157, 166, 173, 176. *See also* Rondon Commission
Bourdieu, Pierre, 22, 25
Brito, Mário da Silva, 194, 207.
Broca, Brito, 4, 41, 50, 207,
Bruno, Giuliana, 22, 35, 70
Burch, Noël, 79
Butler, Alison, 11

Caldeira, Teresa, 73
Calil, Carlos, 209, 217
Campos, Candido Malta, 227